TIME AND THE BAHÁ'Í ERA

A Study of the Badí' Calendar

ABOUT THE AUTHOR

Gerald Keil was born in 1943 in San Francisco, California, USA and studied Linguistics at California State University at San Francisco. In 1967 he took up residence in England to continue his research in Computer Linguistics at the University of Leeds. From 1970 to 1973 he was a Research Fellow at the University of York, from 1974 to 1975 Postdoctoral Research Assistant at the University of Salford, from 1975 to 1980 lecturer at the Centre for Computational Linguistics, University of Manchester Institute of Science and Technology. In 1981 he assumed directorship of a research and development project at the University of the Saarland, Germany, in the area of computer translation. He has been active as an IT professional since 1986, initially self-employed and from 1992 until his retirement in 2007 as head of the computer department of a company producing cast steel components for industrial use.

Gerald Keil has been a Bahá'í since 1980.

TIME AND THE BAHÁ'Í ERA

A Study of the Badí' Calendar

Revised and updated

by
Gerald Keil

GEORGE RONALD
OXFORD

George Ronald Ltd, *Publisher*
Oxford
www.grbooks.com

© Gerald Keil 2008
All Rights Reserved
This revised and updated edition © Gerald Keil 2023

The German original appeared in 2005 CE (162 BE)
as a special publication of the Association for Bahá'í Studies
for German-speaking Europe

Die Zeit im Bahá'í Zeitalter: Eine Studie über den Badí'-Kalender
(Hofheim-Langenhain: Bahá'í-Verlag, ISBN 3-87037-425x; title no. 453-081)

*A catalogue record for this book is available
from the British Library*

ISBN 978-0-85398-665-2

Cover design: Steiner Graphics

Contents

Preface	ix
Acknowledgements	xiii
Concerning the Transcription of Arabic expressions	xvi
Foreword to the 2008 edition, by Udo Schaefer	xx

PART I   PREHISTORY

1 The Prehistoric Concept of Time	3
Natural time intervals	4
The lunar cycle	7
The path of the sun	12
The stars	17
Solutions to the phase synchronization problem	23
Growing demands on time calibration	28
2 The Calendar in History	35
Indo-Iranian calendar systems	36
The Zoroastrian calendar	37
The Zoroastrian calendar: A summary	42
The Iranian national calendar	44
Graeco-Roman calendar systems	46
Semitic calendar systems	53
The Jewish calendar	55
The Islamic calendar	59
3 The Time of Day	64

PART II   THE BADÍʿ CALENDAR

4 An Overview   73
    A brief history   75
    Baháʾí commemorations   78
       The Festival of the Twin Birthdays   80

5 Symbolic Implications   84
    The symbolism of the heavenly bodies   85
    The start of the year   92
    Unity in diversity: The numbers nine and nineteen   102
    Ayyám-i-Há – intercalary days   110
    The week   118
    The start of the day   121

PART III   THE FUTURE ROLE OF THE BADÍʿ CALENDAR

6 Determining the Day of Naw-Rúz   133
    Astronomical data   133
    Written sources   137
    Determining the day of Naw-Rúz using a reference spot   145
    The reference-spot method: Doctrine or alternative?   153
    The cyclic-progressive method for fixing the day of Naw-Rúz   171
    The two methods in comparison   178
    The relationship between the annual threshold and the
       date line   206

7 The Badíʿ Calendar and the Time of Day   185
    The meridional calendar   188
    Occidental time   190
    The change of day in the polar regions   198
    The occidental day and the calendar date   204
    Annual commemoration   208
       A concrete example   210
    Badíʿ time   212

8 The Rhythm of Life 216
  The status of the week and the day of rest 217
  The central role of the Nineteen Day Feast 224
  The work-free feast day 231
    Seven into nineteen 234
  The nineteen-day life rhythm 236

Conclusion 242

Appendices
  A The *Abjad* Number System 245
  B Badí' and Jalálí Leap Years in Comparison 247
  C Date Expressions between 3rd Yawm-i-Há and 1'Alá' 250
  D Annual Thresholds and Leap Years for the Badí'
    Years 1–250 254
  E Conversion between Time Modes 270

Bibliography 293
Notes and References 301
Index 327

Preface

In 1997 the Bahá'í community of Neunkirchen in the Saarland, Germany, kindly asked me to give a short talk during the festival of Naw-Rúz 154 (21 March) about the significance of the Bahá'í New Year's Day. Since the organizers had approached me a good two months in advance, I had ample time to accumulate material and to structure some thoughts I had been harbouring for years. In the end, however, most of what I had prepared had to be left out for the sake of brevity, and so I decided to commit the results of my labours to paper for subsequent circulation among the Bahá'ís of the region.

As the mass and scope of material continued to expand during the course of writing, it became increasingly clear that the topic encompassed a number of important and to the best of my knowledge hitherto largely unexplored aspects, the investigation of which would be of interest to a wider public. The resulting extension of the original concept and purpose led ultimately to the present study, published in 2005 under the auspices of the German-speaking Association for Bahá'í Studies.

When I resolved to translate the text of this study into English, I was confident that the task would prove relatively easy. The conditions were, after all, optimal: I would be translating into my own native language from a manuscript which I, being its author, knew forwards and backwards; for similar reasons I was adequately acquainted with all the technical and special knowledge areas touched upon in the text; being privy to the thought processes which lay behind the entire discourse, I was generally aware of what the author's choice of words was intended to convey; and most important, I found comfort in the assurance of the author's tacit agreement, full support and occasional forbearance for my translation strategy throughout the project.

Needless to say, despite these advantages the task was anything but straightforward. It was not simply a matter of translating words and sentences: whole stretches of text had to be reformulated from the 'German way' of saying things into the 'English way' of expressing the same ideas. For any Teutonisms which still remain I must now beg the same patience and forgiveness which I solicited from the original German-speaking readership for stubbornly persistent Anglicisms.

The decision jointly reached by George Ronald Publishers and the author to produce a second English-language edition provided the opportunity to incorporate material which had not been available for the 2008 edition, including not only the adjustments to calendar practice which took effect on 21 March 2015, but also additional and in some cases more accurate technical information which had not previously been available on the internet.

Of the copious footnotes in the original, those which constituted source references have been converted into endnotes in compliance with academic practice in English-speaking countries, whereas explanatory or supplementary footnotes have as far as possible been worked into the main body of text and thus spared the oblivion of the back pages. I have tried to compensate for the accompanying loss of two-level discourse by introducing textual clues, so that a reader who is momentarily not interested in, say, precise details of astronomical calculation or author attribution will be able to navigate around such passages. The (relatively) few remaining textual footnotes which could not be comfortably integrated into the text flow have been consigned to the endnotes, their reference numbers in the text being prefixed with an arrow to alert the interested reader.

Despite the formal and stylistic amendments necessitated by the publication of this translation, and although a considerable number of details which have accumulated since the appearance of the previous editions have been worked into the text, the ideas, opinions and conclusions presented by this edition have remained essentially the same. Nevertheless, subsequent research has provided some interesting ancillary information, additional useful references, and one or two new insights, so that this edition will be of interest even to those who are acquainted with the earlier versions.

The work is divided into three parts. The first part explores the prehistory of the Bahá'í calendar, in both senses of the word:

- prehistory in the sense of prehistoric times, i.e. an analysis of the evolution of the basic elements of the measurement and calibration of time; and

- prehistory in the sense of what came before, i.e. an examination of the various calendars used by the communities of earlier revealed religions.

The second part is concerned solely with the Bahá'í or *Badí'* calendar, the calendar of the Bahá'í Era. In addition to detailing the structure of the calendar, it explores the relationship between the symbolism inherent in this structure and the teachings of the Báb and Bahá'u'lláh.

The third part discusses points of detail still in need of clarification and legislation and introduces related topics which will need to be considered before the Badí' calendar can assume its rightful place as a world calendar, and before its symbolism can be fully appreciated. The discussion includes a number of novel approaches involving unaccustomed and at times complex concepts.

Note that the term 'calendar' is used here primarily in the sense of 'calendar system': the printed calendar is not the concern of the present study.

This study is intended in the first instance for readers acquainted with the basic tenets of Bahá'í belief. By virtue of its copious additional commentary, the text should nevertheless be intelligible to readers without such foreknowledge but who are nonetheless interested in an in-depth study of the Badí' calendar. One should bear in mind that there exist more suitable books for an initial introduction to the Bahá'í Faith; a selection of these is included in the bibliography or can be found on the home pages of the Bahá'í World Centre and the various national communities.

Technical (especially astronomical) details which are necessary for a thorough coverage of the topics introduced, not however for their basic understanding, are wherever possible enclosed in boxes or relegated to endnotes and appendices which may be skipped over by readers who do not wish to delve that deeply into the material. Specialist knowledge in the field of astronomy is not assumed.

Acknowledgements

Dr Udo Schaefer read an early, unfinished manuscript and offered many valuable suggestions. He recognized the significance of this study in spite of its then provisional state and encouraged me to carry the project through.

Equally encouraging was Dr Badi Panahi, who offered continuous moral support during the long and arduous procedure leading to publication. He also provided me with photocopies of numerous original-language texts, e.g. from the Persian Bayán and the Lawḥ-i Ittiḥád.

Dr-Ing Burghard Richter of the German Geodetic Research Institute, Munich, on several occasions provided me with extensive, informative and useful answers to my questions concerning the determination of the equinox, the calculation of the length of the tropical year and related themes.

The Research Department of the Bahá'í World Centre in Haifa, Israel kindly gave me insightful answers to two enquiries with regard to the abolition of priesthood and with regard to the mystical meanings of the Arabic letter *há'*, respectively, and complied with my request for the Persian-language original of a text passage from *Nabíl's Narrative* as well as to a follow-up request for clarification concerning the authorship of its translation in *The Bahá'í World*. Prior to publication of the first English-language edition it provided additional help in locating documents relating to an exchange of correspondence between the National Spiritual Assembly of the United States and Canada and the Bahá'í World Centre in 1940 regarding the timing of Naw-Rúz. In preparation for the second English-language edition it provided me at my request with additional, unpublished technical data with regard to the calendar changes which took effect in 2015.

I am indebted to the secretariat of the National Spiritual Assembly of the Bahá'ís of Germany for making available to me all correspondence which had accumulated in their office over the two decades prior to the publication of the German-language edition with regard to the Bahá'í calendar.

Roland Philipp completed an extensive and detailed critical analysis of the entire manuscript and contributed in innumerable ways to the improvement of the material and its presentation.

Farideh Lawaldt was always prepared to assist me in the translation of Persian-language texts.

The task of purging the (original German-language) text of Anglicisms and mistakes in diction which I still perpetrated after twenty years' residence in Germany fell to Christine Mazurkiewicz, Heinz-Dieter Maas, Ludwig Lawaldt, Paul Rudolf Zeyer, Heinz Hampel-Waffenthal and Dr Armin Eschraghi.

Dr Michael Sturm-Berger read an advanced version of the manuscript several times, offering valuable suggestions regarding language usage; in addition he drew my attention to useful additional reference material with regard to the late paleolithic period.

Prof. Dr Maria G. Firneis of the Institute for Astronomy of the University of Vienna scrutinized my coverage of astronomical themes and helped improve the presentation of several concepts.

Nicole Halenke helped me with the preparation of the illustrations on the computer, especially in the search for and preparation of appropriate templates, and Bernd Staudenraus converted my conception of the cover for the German-language edition into a camera-ready PDF file.

I am indebted to the able and tireless efforts of May Hofman of George Ronald during the preparation of both English-language editions. It was generally she who managed to find the English-language equivalents for quotations not readily available in English-language standard literature, not infrequently offering equally or even better fitting alternatives. Her valuable suggestions induced me to re-organize and thus greatly improve the presentation of several important sections of the work, and many improvements in detail bear her signature.

ACKNOWLEDGEMENTS

Without such copious support this study would never have reached publication. For this reason I wish not only to express my deepest thanks, but also to acknowledge the time and effort which many others have devoted to this project.

I should especially like to thank my wife, Melitta, who bore with equanimity the countless hours of mental and physical absence which this project demanded of me.

Concerning the Transcription of Arabic and Persian Expressions

The method of transcription of Arabic expressions used in this study conforms for the most part with the usual practice in Bahá'í literature. The few exceptions result from a desire to reproduce the written rather than the spoken form of the Arabic or Persian original as closely as possible and thus to maintain the relationship between individual terms and phrases and their *abjad* numeric equivalents (see Appendix A); in addition, they ensure a more parallel relationship between the original and its transcription, i.e. as often as possible a given unique element in the source (e.g. a letter) is accompanied by a correspondingly unique transcriptional convention. It is not intended here to achieve an isomorphic rendering of Arabic spelling (i.e. a transliteration in the narrow sense of the word), but rather a transcription which enables the unambiguous reconstruction of the original. In particular:

- The feminine singular ending – the so-called ***tá' marbúṭaτ*** – is consistently rendered as *–aτ*. This solution (a personal convention) faithfully mimics the Arabic script, in which the feminine singular ending is a unique letter, and it allows a uniform and unambiguous rendition in place of the usual (and in all cases ambiguous) conventions *-a*, *-ah* and occasionally *-at*. Thus for example *'Izzaτ, Qudraτ, hijraτ, madínaτ*. This τ is silent at the end of a phrase or in the case of isolated words, but pronounced when following a long vowel, e.g. *ṣaláτ* (Pers. *ṣalát*), 'obligatory prayer', or in medial position in word combinations (e.g. *ḥaẓíraτ* (not pronounced) vs. *ḥaẓíraτu'l-quds* (pronounced)). In the case of the plural ending and in combination with personal suffixes,

-τ mutates to -*t* in accordance with Arabic written practice (and is then always pronounced): *kalimaτ – kalimát, 'ibádaτ – 'ibádatika*. The ending *–a* always represents *faṭḥaτ* (short *a* vowel) (e.g. *bada'a*).

- The apostrophe (') used to represent non-initial **hamzaτ** (the glottal stop) is explicitly included also in cases where it is lost in Persian pronunciation, e.g. *Bahá', Asmá'*, with the single exception of the proper name 'Abdu'l-Bahá, which in deference to nearly universal Bahá'í praxis is transcribed in the present study without the final *hamzaτ*. Also in conformity with general practice, the glottal stop at the beginning of a word is not explicitly written, but implied instead by the occurrence of a vowel in initial position. Long *a* before a terminal *hamzaτ* represents *alif*, whereas terminal long *a* generally represents *yá'*: thus *bahá'* (Arab. *bá' há' alif hamzaτ*, numeric value 9), compared with *abhá* (Arab. *hamzaτ bá' há' yá'*, numeric value 18). Exception: the *á* of *'Akká* (a place name) stands for *alif*. The apostrophe is also used to indicate liaison, just as in English 'he's', 'we'll' and so on. Liaison in Arabic occurs in the majority of cases in combination with the article *al* and signifies the *omission* of a glottal stop – actually the exact opposite of the *hamzaτ* apostrophe; and although this may be confusing to the non-speaker of Arabic, it represents the usual practice both in Bahá'í and in non-Bahá'í literature.

- The Arabic letter **wáw** is always represented as *w* when used as a non-syllabic vowel (e.g. *yawm*) or as a consonant (e.g. *wáḥid*) (in Bahá'í literature these are usually written as *w* and *v*, respectively). Exception: Riḍván, a frequently occurring Bahá'í term. It is largely a matter of personal choice whether the reader wishes to treat consonantal *w* as in English or in German, reflecting the Arabic and the Persian pronunciation, respectively. *Wáw* as a syllabic vowel is transcribed as usual with *ú* (e.g. *Núr*).

- In conformity with general practice, nouns are always presented in the nominative case, with or without an article in accordance with English language usage, e.g. 'the Ma<u>sh</u>riqu'l-A<u>dh</u>kár', 'of the Ma<u>sh</u>riqu'l-A<u>dh</u>kár' (and not 'Ma<u>sh</u>riqi'l-A<u>dh</u>kár'). According to an alternative, equally widespread method of transcription which comes somewhat closer to transliteration, this would be written *ma<u>sh</u>riq al-<u>a</u>dhkár*, that is, the pronunciation (both the liaison and the correct inflection) is left to the reader. This method was deemed inappropriate for the present study for two reasons:

- it is better suited for works which can assume some knowledge of the Arabic language, and

- it requires either a mixing of conventions or the representation of accustomed Bahá'í terms in an unfamiliar manner (e.g. 'Abd al-Bahá).

- *Ezafe* is appended to the first element of a Persian-language *ezafe* construction rather than being written as a connector (so that it stands in conformity with Persian orthographic practice in the rare instances where *ezafe* is made explicit), e.g. Ayyám-i Há' and not Ayyám-i-Há'. Furthermore, the glide in the pronunciation of *ezafe* following a long vowel is depicted as part of the *ezafe* itself in order to ensure a faithful transcription of the first element, e.g. Súrih-yi Mulúk and not Súriy-i-Mulúk

In compliance with accepted Bahá'í usage, vowel length is indicated by the acute accent (á, í, ú, etc.) rather than the macron (ā, ī, ū, etc).

These conventions do not apply to citations, book titles, and so on, which are as far as possible reproduced in their original form.

Further conventions

My own translations from Arabic into German were accomplished with the aid of Hans Wehr's *Arabische Wörterbuch für die Schriftsprache der Gegenwart*, my subsequent retranslations into English with occasional support from standard English-language dictionaries (Chambers, *Oxford Unabridged* and – more recently – the online LEO German-English and English-German dictionary).

Bible quotations in English are based on the Authorized King James Version.

When not otherwise stated, quotations from the Qur'án are taken from the Arberry translation.

Astronomical data, whether presented as is or used as the basis for my own calculations, are taken from Joachim Hermann's *Wörterbuch zur Astronomie*.

Foreword to the 2008 Edition
Time is a strange thing.[1]

In resolving to make 'time' and the 'Badí' calendar' the subject of a thoroughgoing investigation – a topic which has until now by and large escaped scrutiny and whose significance is as yet little appreciated – my friend Gerald Keil has ventured into difficult territory. Bahá'ís are generally aware of the basic structure of the new calendar and can appreciate its contribution to the consolidation of their Bahá'í identity, for it provides the temporal framework for their daily prayers, their monthly gatherings, their days of commemoration, the period of fasting and the New Year festival (Naw-Rúz). Its inherent symbolism, however, has until now remained largely unexplored, so that the systematic investigation presented by this wide-ranging, impressive study is no doubt the first of its kind.

The passage of time is measurable. Rigidly periodic processes such as the rotation of the Earth on its axis, its orbit around the sun, the succession of the moon phases, or the pulsations of a pendulum, quartz crystal or atom provide *objective* forms of periodicity by means of which the passage of time can be quantified. This natural concept of time is closely linked with astronomy and theoretical physics.

Subjective time, the experience of objectively measurable periods of time in human conscience, is an altogether different matter. The same span of time can, as everyone knows, be experienced in widely varying ways. We experience as slow and burdensome time which simply passes without anything happening in particular, such as when standing in a queue or waiting for a bus or train; but when we are diverted or entertained the same physical span of time flies by quickly, and the rare moments in which we experience real happiness are fleeting in the extreme, as Goethe puts it:

FOREWORD TO THE 2008 EDITION

Werd' ich zum Augenblicke sagen,
Verweile doch! Du bist so schön!

I will beseech the moment's time,
Abide a while! Thou art sublime![2]

That which has already transpired and which we collectively consider noteworthy or important becomes history, and the question whether world history makes any sense at all – the endless historical episodes, the rise and fall of systems of political rule, the origin and demise of great cultures – is the subject of the philosophy of history.[3] History is an empirical science; but since human reason is capable of judging very little concerning the meaning and goal of history, the interpretation of world history lies beyond the reach of empirical knowledge. Without appeal to religion and theology, history remains uninterpreted.[4]

According to Bahá'í teaching, God is the Lord of history. He manifests Himself to mankind through His successive prophets and messengers, leading mankind progressively to salvation. World history is *salvation history*. It proceeds in universal cycles, within which the founders of the world's great religions leave behind historical caesurae, each of which invariably gives rise to a new chronology. The Adamic[5] cycle entered its final phase with the coming of Muḥammad, the last prophet in this series and accordingly called the 'Seal of the Prophets' in the Qur'án,[6] who foretells the great upheaval at the end of days, the 'Day of Decision'.[7]

With the coming of the Báb a new universal era began and the 'prophetic cycle' attained fulfilment: The 'Day of Resurrection'[8] was the advent of the new Revelation. The consummation of mankind will take place during the new cycle which began with the Báb. The fulfilment of the prophetic promises of the unity of mankind and of the messianic kingdom of peace will follow in the wake of an upheaval of apocalyptic proportions. The Badí' calendar, revealed by the Báb in his Persian Bayán[9] and taken over in slightly modified form by Bahá'u'lláh in the Kitáb-i Aqdas,[10] signalizes both: the incursion of transcendence through God's self-revelation and the upheaval announced to mankind, in which the 'present-day order [will] be rolled up, and a new one spread out in its stead.'[11]

The Báb, as his adopted title implies, had at first raised his claim within the traditional Shí'ite paradigm of expectation, in conformity with the concept of the Bábu'l-Imám (Gate to the Hidden Imám). He withheld from revealing his true spiritual identity for a considerable period of time and, like the Jesus of the Gospel of St Mark, kept his 'messianic secret'[12] concealed. Only gradually did he announce his prophetic claim to be a Manifestation of God, a claim which transcended the horizon of expectation of the orthodox Shí'a. At the Conference of Badásht in 1848 some of the prominent members of his community announced the abolition of Islamic religious law.

Yet the true claim of the Báb was discernible in his writings from the very beginning.[13] The abrogation of the Islamic *sharí'a* is impossible to overlook, especially in the Persian Bayán, which he composed during his imprisonment in Máh-Kú. The change which he undertook in the *basmala*[14] alone clearly demonstrates the break with the past. In this work, the Báb not only announced his teachings, rejuvenating all aspects of religious life, he also introduced a new religious law,[15] thus making clear that his mission was far more than an Islamic reform movement: he endowed mankind with an independent revealed religion, with its own 'Book', its own teachings, its own legal system and its own ritual. He thereby accomplished what no Islamic reformer had ever managed: a complete severing with the past. And nothing makes this severance more explicit than a new basis of time calculation and a new calendar.[16]

One might wonder what the purpose of the Bayánic law was, many of the details of which appear strange and severe to the uninitiated Western reader and which was ultimately to be superceded by the legislation of the Kitáb-i Aqdas less than two decades later.[17] Shoghi Effendi provides an answer to this question:

> ... the Bábí Dispensation was essentially in the nature of a religious and indeed social revolution, and its duration had therefore to be short, but full of tragic events, of sweeping and drastic reforms. Those drastic measures

enforced by the Báb and His followers were taken with the view of undermining the very foundations of Shí'ih orthodoxy, and thus paving the way for the coming of Bahá'u'lláh.[18]

Designedly severe in the rules and regulations it imposed, revolutionizing in the principles it instilled, calculated to awaken from their age-long torpor the clergy and the people, and to administer a sudden and fatal blow to obsolete and corrupt institutions, it proclaimed, through its drastic provisions, the advent of the anticipated Day . . .[19]

The Badí' calendar promulgated in the Persian Bayán is to be numbered among the revolutionary innovations which convulsed the bastions of Islamic orthodoxy; it heralded the end of the Islamic era with unsurpassable clarity, to the chagrin of the Islamic authorities. Even recently, in a Sunnite fatwa from the 1990s, the fact that the Badí' year consists of nineteen months, when of course everyone knows that there are only twelve, was noted with particular indignation.

Gerald Keil has not restricted his investigations to the historical background, the theological implications and symbolic significance of the new calendar; nearly half of his study is devoted to the problems surrounding its practical introduction. A glance at the table of contents for Part III already intimates how difficult it will one day be for the Universal House of Justice officially to implement this new calendar so that it may serve Bahá'ís the world over as their sole time system. The problems to be solved are highly complex; they range from the clarification of the written sources, through the multifaceted astronomical considerations, the various possibilities for resolving the issue of the reference point for determining the day of Naw-Rúz, up to new possibilities and challenges such as 'Badí' time' and the nineteen-day life rhythm.

It is obvious that the official, formal introduction of the Badí' calendar is not the most pressing issue facing us today. The Bahá'í community must progress much further before this matter becomes topical. We cannot predict when the critical point will be reached – we might continue to approach it slowly and steadily, or we might get there spontaneously, suddenly spurred on by unexpected events. But an appreciable span of time will undoubtedly lapse before the calendar project can be taken up in earnest.

It is therefore legitimate to ask what the point is of such a detailed introduction into the problems associated with the introduction of a new form of reckoning time. After all, the task will fall to the Universal House of Justice, which, when the time is ripe, will enact the necessary supplementary legislation. In the light of the exclusive competency of the House of Justice in this question, can it be at all legitimate and sensible to discuss the abundance of matters that will eventually need to be resolved? Wouldn't it be better simply to place one's complete trust in the wisdom and infallible leadership of the Supreme Body, which, when the appropriate time has come, will do what is right and necessary? Isn't the production of a study such as this in fact tantamount to meddling in the affairs of the Universal House of Justice?

Such objections overlook several important considerations.

As I have pointed out elsewhere,[20] the decisions of the Universal House of Justice are not revelational in character. The Universal House of Justice is not a mere recipient, transformer and mouthpiece of the Holy Spirit. Its decisions do not come about through quasi-prophetic inspiration (*'quasi per inspirationem'*, *'Divino afflante Spiritu'*),[21] but instead they are arrived at in the course of a rational discursive process in which, subsequent to the establishment of the facts and the clarification of the normative guidelines set out in the Writings, a formal process of consultation leads to a consensus, and finally to a decision reached by majority vote or by the achievement of unanimity.

As the Universal House of Justice has expressly stated, it is not omniscient.[22] Like any other decision-making body, the Universal House of Justice is dependent on information. The divine, unerring guidance which is vouchsafed to the Universal House of Justice does not hover over it like a *deus ex machina*. Instead, it manifests itself through the conduct of consultation which precedes the decision stage and in this manner enables infallible decisions through the assistance of the Holy Spirit.

Legislation is a highly complex process and impossible without expert knowledge. Among the necessary foundations are legal dogmatics and legal techniques, but every act of legislation also requires that the legislator have at his disposal all-encompassing knowledge of the relevant material. The introduction of calendar legislation presupposes that all astronomical and technical information pertaining to the calendar be considered and befittingly taken into account in the legislation. No lawgiver in the world could draft such legislation without the support of competent experts.

The procedure of clarifying all relevant questions cannot begin early enough, since the 'shining spark of truth' will first come forth after all the various differing points of view have undergone the ordeal of a public scientific discourse, so that those positions which do not stand up against critical examination need no longer be taken into consideration. Such discourse conducted world-wide can, in the first instance, relieve the wheat of much chaff. Profiting from the collective reasoning of the community at large, open discourse over the Badí' calendar would enable a preliminary scrutiny of all legal, technical and historical questions. Its fruits would represent a valuable source of information for the commission of experts which will one day be convened for the purpose of preparing the ground for the calendar legislation. This commission would not have to begin at square one, so to speak, but instead would profit from the results of informed discourse.

Any open discourse, any exchange of arguments, must be carried out in the spirit of mutual respect and forbearance, oriented on the cardinal virtues of moderation and wisdom. Open dialogue over specific questions is the 'trial by ordeal' for diverse points of view. It leads closer to the truth, even if it does not necessarily result in consensus. Such a discourse can be likened to scientific procedure, in which hypotheses are continuously being tested against the evidence of reality and, if found wanting, rejected in favour of new hypotheses in a never-ending process of inching forward towards the truth. We, too, must reflect upon our Faith in this fashion, since the Bahá'í Faith is, as Shoghi Effendi explained, 'scientific in its method'.[23]

'Abdu'l-Bahá has explained how rational dialogue is to be conducted:

Every subject presented to a thoughtful audience must be supported by rational proofs and logical arguments.²⁴

In other words, he who expounds a thesis is obliged to provide proofs in support of his position. He must present rational, logical arguments. But that also implies that his fellow participants in dialogue must address the arguments presented. They must come to terms with them and in the end explain not only what they find acceptable or otherwise, but why.

Man is a thinking being, one who strives to understand and one who poses questions in order to improve his comprehension. A Bahá'í is not content simply with believing in holy scripture, he also wants to *understand* it. God speaks to mankind in human language, and language is dependent on analysis, on interpretation. In this respect, every contact with the Writings is an act of analysis and interpretation. Even during the most casual perusal of a text the reader is at pains to understand it, i.e. he interprets *in pectore* while reading. Everything we say about the Word of God is based on personal interpretation of the Writings, whether we speak in private circles, in public, or indeed at any time while engaged in teaching and proclamation. Our understanding may be correct, or it may be in error – in any event we cannot claim any authority with respect to it.

The yearning to reach an *understanding* of the Faith is incidentally not merely the predilection of the thinking individual; it is, as Shoghi Effendi stressed, the duty of every believer. The Guardian enjoined the believers time and again to 'strive to obtain a more adequate understanding of the significance of Bahá'u'lláh's stupendous Revelation', to acquire 'a clearer apprehension of the truths it enshrines and the principles on which it is based'.²⁵

In his effort to achieve a proper understanding of scripture, the individual makes use of his ability to reason. According to the scripture, God has given a unique rank to the rational faculty, to *'aql* (reason, mind, intellect):

> First and foremost among these favours, which the Almighty hath conferred upon man, is the gift of understanding [*'aql*]. His purpose in conferring such

a gift is none other except to enable His creature to know and recognize the one true God – exalted be His glory. This gift giveth man the power to discern the truth in all things, leadeth him to that which is right, and helpeth him to discover the secrets of creation.[26]

However, reason is easily influenced by vested interests. If the individual is not purged of his attachment to his own preferences and preconceptions and to his partiality, reason will be hindered from working through to the truth. Bahá'u'lláh's call to independent search for truth, such that the searcher see with his own eyes and hear with his own ears and know with his own knowledge,[27] is well the most revolutionary innovation in His entire revelation and a leitmotif which pervades His writings. Independence of judgement is a condition of justice (*inṣáf*) and has been called 'the essence of all that We have revealed for thee',[28] and the purpose of justice is 'for man to free himself from idle fancy and imitation [*taqlíd*], discern with the eyes of oneness His glorious handiwork, and look unto all things with a searching eye.[29] Bahá'u'lláh writes, 'scrutinize the writings with thine own eyes'[30] . . . scatter the idols of vain imitation [*taqlíd*].[31]

The endeavour 'to arrive at the truth of things',[32] the search for a hermeneutic comprehension of texts, is *ijtihád*, the right and the duty of every believer. The Bahá'í community possesses no clergy, no *'ulamá'* with vested authority, no *mujtahids*, and the Bahá'í Faith knows no *taqlíd*, i.e. there exists no circle of authoritative and influential mentors whom one is obliged to follow and imitate unquestioningly. Shoghi Effendi made patently clear that every believer has the right to his own understanding of scripture and that he is entitled to express his opinion:

> Shoghi Effendi believes that we should not restrict the liberty of the individual to express his own views so long as he makes it clear that these views are his own. In fact, such explanations are often helpful and are conducive to a better understanding of the teachings. God has given man a rational power to be used and not killed.[33]

Gerald Keil has made use of this prerogative – to the benefit of the friends, who as a result will gain valuable insights into a body of material with which few are acquainted. If this study achieves nothing more than to provoke discussion – and it should, because it places a number of long-standing assumptions in question and suggests possible future developments which present genuine challenges to the community – then it will have fulfilled Gerald's own primary objective.

Hirschberg near Heidelberg, Germany
Jalál 165 – May 2008
Udo Schaefer

PART I

PREHISTORY

Temporality as such cannot be directly experienced. We sense time principally through memory: what once was – even if it lies only a split second in the past – is available to us only as reminiscence; and what is yet to be depends on the anticipation of our imagination, which in turn is based on memory. Thus our natural sense of time is purely idiosyncratic and only as good as our individual recall, which is unfortunately subject to numerous distortions. Our sense of time at any one moment is dependent on our current mood and our sense of well-being: as everyone knows, time always seems to fly by when we are busy or amused, just when we wish that the clock would stand still, and it creeps along slowly when we are tired or bored or obliged to kill time. Time seems to act in accordance with the laws of supply and demand: the more we need it, the less of it is apparently available.

With increasing age we become aware of additional distortions in our temporal perception. All of us can remember having contemplated, as children, the sheer unimaginable expanse of time which lay ahead of us before reaching maturity. But our own children, and especially our grandchildren, develop at a distressingly fast pace – during the same period of time which advances as slowly for them as that of our own childhood did for us. In addition to this sensed acceleration of time there is also an apparent deceleration. Events which lie further in the past appear to have transpired more quickly than those closer to us in time, as if time would decrease in speed. We cannot even depend on a fixed axis of time: our memory switches the order of past events nearly at will.

But there are also other forms of temporality. The existence of time as an objective and directed continuum – that is, time in its own right – was first demonstrated conclusively in the twentieth century by virtue of the irreversibility of certain quantum-mechanical processes and identified as a factor in the general theory of relativity. A third form of time, independent of the first two, is also discernible: intersubjective time, that form of time which manifests itself in our collective environment. To the degree to which our environment is a matter of common experience, so too is time measured against the backdrop of this environment mutually perceivable and as such free of the variability which accompanies the idiosyncratic, purely personal sensation of time.

The history of the calendar is to a large extent the history of the exploitation of this intersubjective sense of time for social purposes.

1
The Prehistoric Concept of Time

Man has always had cause to ponder over the course of time. As nomadic hunter and gatherer some ten to fifty thousand years ago, Stone Age man knew he had to plan his wanderings in rhythm with the wanderings of the animal herds. These movements were determined primarily by changes in vegetation, which were in turn conditioned by cyclically recurring variations in temperature, humidity and other factors. But it was the beast, and not man, which depended upon an inborn and reliable sense of time: man needed merely to follow the trail of his prey. Of course it was of considerable advantage to be able to predict the animal movements beforehand, and we may assume that someone who lived during the Late Old Stone Age had a relatively precise idea of the relationship between the periodic variations in climate and the nomadic behaviour of grazing animals. Yet his radius of decision was, in the last analysis, dictated by the animals themselves.

At the beginning of animal husbandry about ten thousand years ago there evolved a characteristic pastoral rhythm of life. This rhythm was similar to that of the hunter, except that it required that the nomad stipulate the cattle migration according to his own perception of the passing of the seasons. His thoughts about the seasons were nevertheless dominated by the one vital question, whether or not to wander – a decision which was normally at issue only twice a year. With the advent of the New Stone Age (the Neolithic period) about six thousand years ago, man, now a settled farmer, was in several respects in need of a more precise method of reckoning time. He had to plan his agricultural production carefully: to clear land of trees and thickets, to plough and fertilize, to sow seed, to loosen and perhaps irrigate the soil, to reap, dry and thresh the crop, to mow and gather hay, to manage production (crop and field rotation). These tasks extended over the greater part of the year, in some cases indeed over several years. At the very latest as tiller of the soil, man needed more than a vague notion of the seasons: he needed a calendar.

That doesn't necessarily mean that the first calendars were written down. Rather, it was important to discern order in the passage of time through the instrument of clearly observable, naturally occurring and essentially predictable events. We possess no records of the details of prehistoric man's progressively advancing ability to recognize and deal with time. However, we have two good reasons for supposing we can reconstruct how this development must have taken place:

- first, with regard to the basic elements involved in the measurement of time, the earth has not changed appreciably in the intervening six to ten thousand years; and

- second – as we shall see in the following – clear traces of prehistoric units of time are present in the numerous calendar systems still existing today.

Natural time intervals

Time as an intersubjective norm presupposes the existence of an objective 'timekeeper': some phenomenon which repeats itself regularly and unceasingly and which is discernible to all parties involved. The basic rhythm of every form of time measurement is and has always been the day, that is, the expanse of time defined by the rhythmic succession of daylight and darkness. The human being is predestined by nature to daytime activity and nocturnal rest. The human eye is, in comparison with that of most animals, relatively deficient by night: with oncoming darkness many animals can rely on their sense of sight long after humans can see nothing more – not only nocturnal creatures but for example dogs (whose sight by day is inferior to that of the human), who can still see in near-darkness enough to avoid obstructions and chase after smaller animals. By contrast, the human eye is relatively well equipped for recognizing colour – a capacity which relies on sufficient light. The olfactory sense (which of course is unaffected by light) is so poorly developed in humans that it isn't even sufficient to detect food decay with enough certainty to vouchsafe personal survival. In short, active man is by nature dependent on daylight.

The regular alternation between brightness and darkness corresponds roughly to the innate biological rhythm of the body, the 'inner clock' which coerces the organism to fluctuate between periods of activity and rest. The biological rhythm of sleeping and waking is controlled by two mutually coordinating components. The first of these consists of a vegetative regulation centre, the suprachiasmic nucleus (SCN), situated in the hypothalamus immediately above the optical nerve bundle and thus in direct connection with light receptors in the retina. In the presence of light, especially sunlight, the SCN inhibits the production of the hormone melatonin in the pineal organ. The second component consists of a pair of genes, the so-called 'period genes 1 and 2', which are present in every cell in the body and which are responsible for the activation and restriction of the metabolism under the influence of melatonin.[1] In spite of the uncertainty inherent in the purely subjective sensation of time, one is instinctively and without recourse to external criteria aware of this rhythmic alteration: it is the basic constant of the perceptibility of time, and one which man shares with most animals.

Primitive man certainly wouldn't have failed to notice the association between this rhythm of light and dark and the movement of the sun. When the sun shines, the warmth on the skin which one senses comes most intensely from the direction of the sun. When one looks skyward, the light blinds increasingly the nearer one's gaze approaches the position of the sun. When one observes the horizon by sunrise or sunset, one recognizes that there is an immediate temporal relationship between the presence of the sun and the brightness of the surrounding sky. Similarly, the angle of the shadows cast by objects corresponds to the sun's location. What is important to recognize here is that the perception of these causal relationships is in no way innate, but is rather the product of a cognitive process (however obvious or trivial this mental act might seem) and therefore qualitatively different from the unreflected, biologically conditioned adaptation to the rhythm of lightness and darkness: it is a rational, and therefore quintessentially human, achievement. But since the causal relationship between the sun and the dark–light rhythm – once grasped – is so self-evident, the axiomatic regularity of the biological rhythm is simply transferred onto the behaviour of the sun, thus fulfilling the first step in the perception of temporal flow: from this point on, the sun is not only the giver of light and warmth, but also the keeper of time. Once accomplished, this conscious transfer of function from the effect to the cause, i.e. from daylight to the sun, established the basis for all subsequent systems for the measurement of time.

In binding his perception of time with the movement of the sun, man also gained a deeper understanding of his own reality: 'The object [of the external world, here the sun] appears as the receptacle of an exterior force that differentiates it from its milieu and gives it meaning and value.'[2] The association of the passage of time with sidereal reality represents an awareness of transcendence. Time is regarded as sacred, and likewise man, who lives in time.

In the subtropical regions – that is, in those regions of the earth where the first great agrarian civilizations arose – the fluctuation of the seasons was, in addition to the succession of the days, the most important rhythmic component of agricultural activity. The sun, or rather its apparent orbit around the earth, is of course the source of both of these rhythms: the rhythm of the day by virtue of its repetition and the rhythm of the year by virtue of its orbital variations. But although Stone Age man most certainly recognized in the sun the primary cause of the rhythm of day and night, he almost equally certainly derived his knowledge of the seasons not directly from the sun, but indirectly – as the animals had done – through its observable effect on nature. During the New Stone Age this method was subjected to improvements, as we shall see.

The lunar cycle

The second important celestial timekeeper is the moon. Late Old Stone Age man was doubtless acquainted with the periodic changes in the appearance of the moon – that is, with its four phases, the rhythm of which would have aided him in scheduling middle-term community events. Several archaeological findings suggest the existence of a rudimentary system for counting objects (AMS, 'artificial memory systems') as early as the Late Paleolithic period. In particular, a bone found in Gough's Cave, Somerset, England is marked in a manner which many archaeologists interpret as evidence for the observation of moon cycles.[3]

The social fabric of Stone Age man was perhaps dominated by the pursuit of basic requirements for survival, but certainly not reduced to those alone. From the biological viewpoint there is no difference between humans then and today, and, disregarding the obvious differences in life's circumstances, chores such as the grounding of family units, the raising and training of children, perhaps also the care of the old and ill, along with normal, daily social interaction, have remained essentially the same. The moon makes it possible to keep track of recurrent events such as menstruation, to monitor the progress of pregnancy and to coordinate ceremonial occasions: rites of passage (consecration of the newborn child, attainment of the age of maturity, betrothal, marriage, etc.) and other cultural acts within the social group as a whole. However, there was no compelling reason for Stone Age man to integrate the course of the lunar phases into the general rhythm of his nomadic life. One can well imagine that the two methods of noting the passing of time – the one based on the seasons, the other on the moon – were employed quite independently of one another.

On a different plane, the moon accentuates the cyclic nature of time and of human life in time. Of all the heavenly bodies, the moon is the only one which visibly recedes to nothing and then reappears out of oblivion. To be sure, the sun sets each evening, but in doing so it merely 'hides'. The stars and planets might be veiled by clouds or blended out by daylight, but it is in each case the foreign influence, not the heavenly body itself, which is responsible for its invisibility. The moon is in this respect unique among all heavenly bodies. After a few days' duration, the full moon begins to diminish in volume, at first slowly, then with increasing speed, until towards the end it dies a slow death. Then, after three days of total annihilation, it is born again as a thin, gleaming band of light, as a 'new moon': 'The moon', as Mircea Eliade puts it, 'is the first of creatures to die, but also the first to live again ... If the moon's phases – long before the solar year and far more concretely – reveal a unit of time (the month), the moon at the same time reveals the 'eternal return' ... In the 'lunar perspective', the death of the individual and the periodic death of humanity are necessary, even as the three days of darkness preceeding the 'rebirth' of the moon are necessary. The death of the individual and the death of humanity are alike necessary for their regeneration.'[4]

With the introduction of agrarian culture and its accompanying need to fit the rhythm of life more precisely into the cycles of the seasons, the moon acquired an additional function, one which was of central importance for the development of the calendar. It is hard to imagine how, in the absence of an abstract system of counting (such as the decimal system), early Neolithic man could have coped with the cycle of over 365 days with the accuracy necessary for agriculture, had he not also had the lunar rhythm at his disposal. The names of the 'digital' numbers (= 'finger numbers') 1 to 10 are similar in all Indo-European languages: Stone Age man could certainly count at least to ten. The word 'hundred' is also Indo-European: the two basic forms of this word ('centum' and 'satem') in fact characterize the two main branches of Indo-European languages (cf. Latin and Persian). The word might originally have meant a large but not precisely quantified number (e.g. of cattle), later (usually) ten tens (i.e. five score).→[5] By contrast, the word for 'thousand' has no common Indo-European root: precise quantification on this scale apparently first developed during the period of westward and southward migrations from the Eurasian steppes.

With the lunar cycle as intermediate interval, the solar year→[6] – and therewith the seasonal cycle – is neatly divided into twelve portions of 29 or 30 days each, three such portions being roughly equivalent to the length of a season. In addition, within each complete moon cycle, or *lunation*, four easily identifiable phases – new moon (or to be more accurate, the disappearance and/or reappearance of the crescent before and after the 'dark moon': see 'Semitic calendar systems' in Chapter 2 and 'Bahá'í commemorations' in Chapter 4), ascending half moon, full moon and descending half moon – divide these portions once again into groups of roughly seven days each. The ancient Arabs, Indians and Chinese divided the moon phases into 'houses of the moon' (Arab. *dárát*) – measured on the changing position of the zodiacal constellations – in order to achieve an even more precise scale of measurement. A hierarchic system of time intervals thus evolves, of which the number of units in each successive scale is small enough to note and record using hand signals, knotted cords and so on, while at the same time the intervals in their successive orders of magnitude are large enough to facilitate the conduct of communal affairs the entire year through. What is more, these units of time can be followed simply by observing the moon with the naked eye. It would not be an exaggeration to claim that settled agrarian cultures owe their very ability to survive to the presence of the moon.

This system of temporal units is still in daily use all over the world in lightly altered form as weeks and months. It is important to differentiate between the lunar week and the solar week. The lunar week is derived from the (unequal) subdivision of the natural moon phases into four periods of $7 + 7 + 7 + 8$ or $7 + 7 + 8 + 8$ days in alternation. By contrast, the solar week[7] arises ultimately from the division of the year into quarters or seasons (see 'Semitic calendar systems' in Chapter 2). Given their approximate agreement in length, these two units of measurement doubtless reinforced one another. The quartering of the near-year of 364 days into 91-day seasons, each of these in turn into thirteen equal portions of seven days, assumes an adequate method of counting, and so we can safely assume that the lunar week is the older of the two. The fact that the sidereal month (stellar month, i.e. the period of revolution of the moon around the earth relative to the fixed stars) is only 27.3216608 days long instead of the 29.5305891 days of the synodic month suggests the theoretical possibility of a prehistoric lunar month variation of $7 + 7 + 7 + 6$ and $7 + 7 + 7 + 7$ days on the basis of houses of the moon.

The word 'month' is in all Indo-European languages similar (German *Monat*, French *mois*, Welsh *mis*, Spanish *mes*, Latin *mensis*, Greek *men*, Persian *mah*). In most cases the word for 'moon' is either the same or related: compare German *Mond-Monat*, English *moon-month*, Old English *mona-monað* (Latin and its derivatives are here the exception: *luna* is related to *luceo*, 'shine'). The close relationship of the word forms for moon and month in these languages points unambiguously to a common root from Proto-Indo-European, i.e. from the language of the peoples of the Eurasian steppes during the Late Stone Age. The reconstructed Indo-European root is **menot-*, which means 'moon, moon phase, month', derived from **me(d)-*, 'to wander, mark out, measure' (cf. 'metre', 'measure'); the Latin word for 'surveyor', *mensor*, is probably related to *mensis*. There is also a possible connection between the Indo-European *med* and the Hebrew *mâdad* and Accadian *madëdu*, both with the meaning 'measure',[8] and the Arabic *muddaτ* ('period of time', from *madda*, 'to stretch, strain, expand'). Etymologically, the characteristic property of the moon is its function as a measuring instrument. The word 'week' is related historically to the German word '*Wechsel*' (change, transition). The reference is possibly to state-changes of the moon, but there is no conclusive proof for this assumption.

Admittedly, this form of measuring time based on the moon is somewhat imprecise by modern standards. The synodic month – that is, the time the moon takes to circle the earth relative to the sun-earth axis – amounts to 29.5305891 days. This is equivalent to a mean lunar week of 7.3826472 days and a mean lunar year of 354.3670692 days, whereas the solar year currently consists of 365.242192 days (calculated mean value for 2008: see Appendix D). As long as the timespan to be measured remains small, the discrepancies between the different temporal intervals are acceptable. For the purpose of budgeting time it is sufficient to know that a certain crop is to be harvested six lunations after sowing; the precise day is determined by other factors, in particular weather conditions and the observed ripeness of the crop.

For the longer-term measuring of time it is necessary to perfom a *phase realignment* (Arab. *mu'áyaraτ*) with the beginning of the year. (Note: the term for 'phase realignment' in the original German edition of the present study is *Eichung*, a term which conveys the sense of compliance with a norm typically defined and/or sanctioned by an authoritative organization such as a bureau of standards.) The discrepancy between the lunar-based time intervals and the solar-based seasons increases with the passing of the year. Without an annual 'day one', this discrepancy would carry over from one year into the next and increase perpetually. For the purposes of phase realignment the advent of spring is best suited for two reasons:

- First, the discrepancy which accumulates during the year would be gravest in the period before springtime, a time when the fields remain untilled.

- Second, the beginning of the so-called *phenological spring* is relatively easy to determine by observation. Many smaller creatures, herbs, flowers and early blossoming trees and bushes spring to life with astonishing regularity precisely at the advent of spring – one need only think of moles, worms, dandelions and daffodils, of the blossoming of the willow, the poplar and the wild cherry trees.→9

Moreover, an agrarian culture which is dependent on the seasons of the year quickly discovers that solar years are roughly identical in length, i.e. twelve lunar months plus one lunar week plus three to six days. It would be sufficient for the whole community to agree on the first day of the year on a year-to-year basis; observance of nature then serves as a safeguard against a long-term shift in the solar cycle relative to the advent of spring.

This error-tolerant technique of measuring time satisfies the requirements of small, self-sufficient communities, but it quickly reveals deficits when the social units become larger or interdependent through culture and trade. Little by little the calendar takes on the character of a governing standard. In particular, the determination of the start of the year evolves into an official act, the details of which must somehow be made known to an entire cultural region. The evolution of increasingly larger social and political units brings with it an administrative superstructure which requires more precise dating than is necessary for sowing and harvesting. Gatherings, for which the participants are often subjected to lengthy journeys, have to be planned long-term and accurate to the day. The calendar must become more universal, more exact, if it is to satisfy the demands placed upon it.

The basis of this refinement and generalization lies not in the moon, but in the sun and the stars. We shall now take a closer look at both.

The path of the sun

For an observer on earth somewhere between the Tropic of Cancer and the northern polar circle, the daily passage of the sun westwards across the heavens displays a characteristic pattern of movement, the sun rising and setting in summer relatively further north and ascending higher over the horizon than it does in winter. Of course nowadays we understand that the apparent movement of the sun is the result of the rotation of the earth around its own axis and around the sun, together with the fact that the ecliptic (the plane of the earth's rotation around the sun) is biased relative to the celestial equator (the imaginary extension of the earth's equator into space). This modern insight is, however, irrelevant to the investigation of the relation between the apparent course of the sun and the seasons of the year. Stone Age man will certainly have recognized the connection between the observable behaviour of the sun and the course of the seasons, and he was doubtless aware very early on of the importance of following the sun's movements with utmost accuracy.

It is possible to follow the apparent movement of the sun, in particular its fluctuation over the course of the year, by charting its projection. To this end man has since prehistoric times made use of a vertically positioned pillar, called a *gnomon*, or more precisely, the shadow cast by such a pillar. This construction must be massive and stable, since observations need be carried out over a long period of time. Its use was therefore impracticable for the nomadic hunter and gatherer but predestined for the stationary tiller of the soil. Such constructions are just as expedient today as they were six thousand years ago.

The gnomon should be as lofty as possible and ideally fashioned at the top to a pointed cone. It should be firmly anchored in the middle of a flat area of ground. At short intervals of time during the course of a day, pebbles are laid on the ground, each time exactly on the spot where the tip of the gnomon's shadow falls. At the end of the day the individual pebbles are connected (for example with a length of string), whereby the polygon described by the pebbles is smoothed into a curve. This curve charts the path of the sun's projection throughout the day. A few pebbles would suffice for the initial measurements: two or three laid soon after the sun is high enough for the shadow cast by the tip of the gnomon to fall within the flat area, and a few more toward evening, when the altitude of the sun reaches the same angle in the west.

The next step is to select a point near one end of this curve, measure its distance from the tip of the gnomon, and then locate that point on the opposite side of the gnomon which is equidistant from the tip. The straight line connecting these two points yields the east-west axis of the earth. The line joining the mid-point of this line and the point directly under the tip of the gnomon lies at right angles to the first line, that is, it indicates the north-south axis. Once one knows the exact north (or in the southern hemisphere the exact south) direction, one also knows the height of the midday sun, i.e. through the projection of the sun's culmination. An alternative but analogous method is the so-called *Indian circle*, being a circle drawn on the area around the gnomon with the gnomon's tip as its fulcrum. The two points of contact between this circle and the tip of the shadow cast by the gnomon are equivalent to the two points described above. This procedure could theoretically be carried out at any time of the year, but it is more accurate during a solstice (that is, on the first day of summer or winter), since at this time the apparent path of the sun is effectively invariant.

The tip of the shadow cast by the gnomon must be recorded each successive day for an entire year, for example by means of scratches or notches in a horizontal stave securely fixed along the gnomon's north-south axis. The outermost notches in the stave indicate respectively the angles of the highest and lowest *altitude* (height above the horizon) of the midday sun, not only for the year in question but for all time.→10 In the future, one need merely await the day when the tip of the shadow once again reaches the most northerly or southerly notch in order to know approximately when the first day of winter or summer has arrived.

In order to determine the equinox, the gnomon must be furnished with a perfectly flat surface of durable material (such as a slab of split slate) directly beneath the stave and sloped in such a manner that the marks for the two solstices – determined with the aid of the notches on the stave, which has therewith fulfilled its purpose – define the base of an isosceles triangle whose apex is the tip of the gnomon. That point which lies exactly in the middle between these two marks indicates the average altitude of the sun during the vernal and autumnal equinox. The angle of slope is incidentally equivalent to the earth latitude of the spot on which the gnomon is situated.

This gnomon, together with its markings, constitutes a type of *calendrical observatory* (German: *Visurenkalender*) which fulfils the purpose of periodically realigning the measurement of time – in particular the start of the year – according to a continuously recurring phenomenon, in this case the altitude of the midday sun, which is in its turn conditioned by the age of the year. This construction must be extremely large, especially if the first day of summer and winter are to be measured with any accuracy. Whereas the marks are spread relatively far apart in the middle area – in the neighbourhood of the two equinoxes – near the ends they are packed tightly together: the positions of the marks for the individual days in the immediate proximity of the solstices are hardly discernible from one another. (This is one more reason why the equinox is better suited to herald the birth of the year.)

Note that the greatest possible difference between the maximum altitude of the sun on two successive days amounts to 24'11"63 (i.e. 24 minutes and 11.63 seconds of arc). The fact that the mean apparent diameter of the sun (31'59") lies in excess of this difference imposes a natural limit on the accuracy of the gnomon in its primitive form. In order to ensure that the markings for the days in the immediate vicinity of the equinox lie approximately 1 cm apart, the distance between the tip of the gnomon and the marked surface must amount to roughly 1.42 m, the surface itself being about 1.24 m in length.

The gnomon, especially its summit, is by its very nature extremely exposed and subject to the influence of weather; and the unprotected components of the vitally important calendar are liable to disturbance from grazing cattle, romping children, enemy attack and so on. It was certainly not long before Neolithic man constructed his calendar in a more stable, durable and easily protectable manner, for example by incorporating it into a monumental structure. Such a construction offers better protection against weathering, and it is not negatively influenced by, say, ice or snowfall. The remains of such megalithic buildings are widely distributed over the entire earth, of which Stonehenge in the south of England is probably the best known and most thoroughly researched example. Archeo-astronomical measurements have revealed that the stone pillars and border stones of this imposing edifice permit solar and astronomical calculations far beyond the functions here described (although it cannot be shown conclusively that this particular megalithic structure possesses an equinoctial reference – it appears instead to be oriented toward the solstices).

As it happens, the accuracy of the astronomical data gleaned from such a structure is subject to progressive decay in the course of the millennia (megalithic structures are extremely long-lived). We know nowadays (actually since ca. 120 BCE) that the earth slowly 'wobbles' and that the celestial pole is not constant, but instead circles around the pole of the ecliptic. This phenomenon is called *precession* and occurs as a result of the combined attraction of the sun and the moon on the rotating earth. As a result, the vernal point (see 'Astronomical data' in Chapter 6) recedes 50.3878 arc seconds per annum on the average, and a complete circumambulation of the ecliptic takes about 25,850 years (= one *Platonic year* or *world year*).

A further phenomenon must also be mentioned for the sake of completion: nutation. Nutation causes a shift of maximally 17.24 arc seconds in the position of the vernal point. This shift occurs in conjunction with the dragon points (lunar orbit nodes) around the mean lunar orbit and describes a cycle of 18.61 tropical years, in the course of which the effects of nutation cancel one another out. Unlike precession, therefore, nutation is not cumulative and would not have adversely affected the use of the megalithic monuments.

One certainly discovered quite early on – perhaps indirectly with the aid of the calendrical observatory, of which the east-west axis is a constituent part – that the sun rises exactly in the east and sets exactly in the west during the equinox. This method of determining the equinox is more accurate than the method using the shadow of the gnomon, always assuming that there is a reliable horizon to the east and the west and that the weather conditions are favourable: one must bear in mind that, at the moment of the transition between day and night, the sun's rays enter the earth's atmosphere at an extreme angle and take the longest possible route through it, in contrast to the radiation of the midday sun, which takes the shortest possible route. However, the liability of unfavourable weather conditions is balanced by the fact that the point of the rising and setting of the sun can be plotted over a longer period of time.

This method gives rise to a useful definition: the equinox has taken place as soon as the angle defined by the point of sunrise, the observer and the point of sunset has attained or surpassed 180°. Strictly speaking, this definition holds for the moment at which the sun passes through the meridian of the true horizon: because of horizontal refraction, this moment occurs not during sunrise or sunset, but rather at the moment in which the middle of the sun's disc is seen to stand at 50‘ above the horizon (assuming ideal atmospheric conditions). Calculations based on the moments of visual sunrise and sunset will result in a premature vernal equinox and a tardy autumnal equinox. At 30° latitude, for example, the mean error is $1^d 13^h 30^m 31^s$, at 60° it is $4^d 16^h 31^m 34^s$. This anomaly would probably have first become apparent to Neolithic man after he was in a position to compare the results of this method of measurement with those derived from an analysis of the celestial sphere. But the efficacy of such intersubjective measurement is less a question of precision (as understood from a modern perspective) than of reliability of observation.

It should also be noted that this definition is valid only for the spot at which the measurement takes place, and it determines the *day* of the equinox for that spot: modern methods determine the precise *moment* of the equinox, valid for the entire planet.

The stars

The night sky offered primitive cultural man an additional medium for the measurement of time. Since the stars can be observed without a cumbersome apparatus it is probable that prehistoric man was acquainted with the measurement of time on the basis of the firmament, at least in its general form, earlier than with solar-based measurement.

To an observer in the northern hemisphere facing northward, it appears as if the celestial sphere slowly rotates counter-clockwise on its own axis during the course of a night, as if it were a gigantic Ferris wheel. One star, the so-called Pole Star – the brightest star of the constellation *Ursa Minor*, called Alrukaba (Arab. *ar-rukbaτ*, 'the knee') – deviates from the hub of this wheel only by about three degrees→[11] – little enough so that for all practical purposes it may be taken to indicate the northerly direction. The true axis of rotation – in other words, the exact northerly direction – could be determined in the absence of an ideal North Star simply by charting the positions of the stars at several points of time throughout the night.

In the course of a full day the celestial sphere completes one revolution (plus a tiny bit extra: more about that presently), a phenomenon which of course can be observed only during the night.

Particularly weakly illuminated stars first become visible, or become once again invisible, as the relatively quickly changing quality of light during the changeover between night and day attains a certain degree of darkness or luminescence: a star in the eastern heavens which appears with a given light quality at dusk will disappear again as soon as the identical light quality is reached at dawn. This phenomenon can be utilized to ascertain two nocturnal moments which are temporally symmetric in relation to the meridian of solar transit.

Suitable stars are to be found everywhere in the sky, so that there are enough candidates present at every season; but no star shines exactly like another, and applying this procedure demands considerable experience. Clouds and atmospheric conditions (temperature, humidity, dust concentration and air turbulence) as well as light from the moon and from the vicinity of the observer influence the permeability of the scintillescent starlight, so that a certain margin of error must be tolerated with every individual measurement. The adaptation of the eye, which requires approximately 40 minutes to complete, also plays a minor role in the observation of a weakly illuminated star during dawn and dusk. Due to the constancy of the rotation of the stars, however, these individual errors cancel one another out in the long run.

Charting the respective position of such a star relative to the Pole Star (that is, relative to the axis of rotation of the circumpolar sky) precisely at the moment of its initial and again its final sighting results in two lines which stand at a specific angle to one another. Precisely one-half of this angle – whether it be greater (in winter) or lesser (in summer) – yields the position of the reference star at midnight of this day. Thus, as the 'sun of the night', the firmament discloses the progress of nocturnal time, just as the sun marks the temporal passage during daylight.

If one should carry out these measurements regularly for the duration of a complete year, one would discover that the celestial sphere also possesses a second rotational rhythm: in the course of the year it rotates exactly once more than the number of days in the year, the additional revolution being distributed equally over the individual days of the year.

The reason for this extra rotation is easy to explain: if one could observe the earth and the sun from a fixed point in space somewhere between the earth and the northern Pole Star, one would see that the earth rotates counter-clockwise on its own axis. At the same time the earth orbits around the sun, also counter-clockwise. The additional apparent rotation of the circumpolar stars occurs because, in the course of one year, the orbit around the sun 'swallows' one of the rotations of the earth, i.e. the earth completes 360 additional degrees of rotation without gaining an extra day, rotating on the average 360.985644 degrees per diem relative to the fixed stars. A more scientific way of explaining this phenomenon is to distinguish between a solar day (one complete rotation of the earth on its own axis relative to the earth's orientation to the sun, i.e. the time span between two successive passages of the sun through the meridian) and a stellar day (one complete rotation of the earth on its own axis relative to the fixed stars), and then to observe that the earth completes just over 365 solar days and just over 366 stellar days during the course of a solar year.

This effect is easier to observe in conjunction with the circumpolar firmament, i.e. the stars and constellations arranged around the axis of the celestial sphere, in the vicinity of the Pole Star: Ursa Major, Ursa Minor, Camelopardalis, Cepheus, Cassiopeia, Draconis, Perseus, Canes Venatici, Lacerta, Lynx.→12 Once grasped in principle, however, it is easier to measure using the zodiac. The zodiac consists of stars in the vicinity of the ecliptic (that is, roughly in line with the plane defined by the rotation of the earth around the sun) divided subjectively into twelve (actually thirteen) groups, the so-called *zodiacal constellations*: Pisces, Aries, Taurus, Gemini, Cancer, Leo, Virgo, Libra, Scorpio, Ophiuchus, Sagittarius, Capricorn, Aquarius. Were one to observe the stars each evening shortly after sunset, one would notice that the constellations, which gradually become visible as the sky darkens, advance by just under 1° per evening – on the average, 59'8"33. Zodiacal stars form, as it were, a huge chain of pearls which descends pearl for pearl under the western horizon, more or less at the point at which the sun has disappeared earlier that same evening. The effect is comparable to that of the circumpolar stars, but it offers two marked advantages for measuring the orientation of the heavens:

- First, the positions of the more deeply sunken stars can be determined more accurately on account of their proximity to the horizon: a task which can be carried out with relatively simple instruments, or even by eye, and which would also have been practicable for nomadic Old Stone Age man.

- Second, the further a given star is situated away from the fulcrum of the celestial sphere, the greater is the observed angle delineated by its shift of celestial position at two successive midnights. Thus the measurement of the evening position of a zodiacal star using primitive means is in any case more reliable than that of a circumpolar star.

Another consideration is the fact that there are many more stars involved in the zodiacal measurement that in the circumpolar. The uncountable stars of the zodiac stand in contrast to the relatively few stars in the immediate proximity of the Pole Star.

To make the distribution more even, the zodiacal *signs* – that is, idealizations of the actually occuring constellations – divide the zodiac into twelve geometrically identical portions.→13 The fact that this division into twelfths is a nearly universal practice is clearly due to the normative influence of the moon, whose rhythm of lunation divides the year into roughly twelve portions. The constellations thus serve to position the signs, which in turn serve to calibrate the year.

The passage of the sun through the zodiacal signs during the course of the year provides the most reliable means of monitoring the second rotational rhythm of the celestial sphere. But there is of course no direct way of observing the passage of the sun through the constellations. The solution to this problem lay in the (incidentally correct) assumption that the heliacal setting of a star is the precise mirror image of its heliacal rising. One observed that a star setting for the last time on the western horizon before being blotted out by the sun appears again for the first time on the eastern horizon shortly before dawn about two to three weeks later (more or less, depending on its luminescence), where it remains visible for a short time before disappearing again as the daylight intensifies. In this fashion it was possible to calculate the moment at which this star would appear exactly behind the sun: one half of the time lapse between its disappearance in the west and its reappearance in the east yields the approximate position of the midday sun in the unseen constellation. There remained merely the task of noting the position of the sun in the zodiac on the first day of spring (as derived from the gnomon or from the direction of the sun during sunrise and sunset). Thereafter, it would be possible to utilize the entry of the sun in a particular sign as a cornerstone for the calculation of the age, and especially the birth, of the year. Needless to say, the observed phenomena and their relationships remain the same regardless of the world view into which they are integrated: Stone Age man most probably understood the astronomical phenomena in a fashion which would seem fully strange to us today.

Bearing the above in mind, it is of course conceivable that the association between the beginning of spring and the 180° angle between sunrise and sunset had already been discovered in the Old Stone Age period. In that case, the refinements described in the following passages may well have occurred even earlier in human history than here suggested.

Once one has established the position of a certain point in the sky behind the midday sun on the first day of spring, one will quickly recognize that this same point lies to the south at midnight on the first day of autumn. The point marking the birth of the year can thus be seen after all, albeit with a delay of half a year and with a certain margin of error: there is a difference of up to one week between the geometric and calculatory half-year on account of the elliptical orbit of the earth, so that the position of the star may deviate by up to ±7 arc degrees from true south.

Because of the earth's precession, of course, this positional relationship between the sun and the stars relative to the earth's seasons is not constant for all time: for Neolithic man the zodiacal herald of spring was not Aries, but Gemini or Cancer (or however these signs were designated). During the Late Old Stone Age period it was Leo or Virgo, and Aries didn't become the sign of spring until classical antiquity. Since then, Aries has remained the recognized zodiacal sign for the commencement of spring, whereas as a constellation it has long since been replaced by Pisces, which in turn is now being superseded by Aquarius.

Once these measurements are complete, one knows the positions of the stars at midnight for every single day. That means that one has a second scale for determining the age of the year in addition to the position of the sun. How important this fact was for the exact calculation of the divisions of the solar year will become evident when we once again study the midday marks on our calendrical observatory.

We have already seen that the marks in the middle are spread apart, whereas those at both ends are squeezed together. In fact, these marks represent points of a circle which is (so to speak) viewed from the side – much like a coin held between two fingers in such a way that the observer sees only a horizontal bar. A mark on the edge of the coin and at its extreme left will, when the coin is rotated clockwise at a constant speed, at first appear not to move at all, but then slowly gain speed, achieving its highest velocity upon reaching the middle of the bar. Thereafter the process is the exact converse, the mark decelerating until it again becomes apparently stationary at the rightmost 'edge' of the bar. The two lines from the fulcrum of the coin respectively to the mark and to the eye of the observer describe an angle whose value we would like to know. It is clear that this angle can be estimated at only three points with any certainty – namely, exactly in the middle of the 'bar' (null degrees) and at its two extremities (90 degrees) – whereby the two right-angle estimates will necessarily be very imprecise.

The celestial sphere is comparable to the same coin – only this time held so that it appears as a disc. Observed from this angle, the marked point on the edge of the rotating disc moves in perfect constancy, and the measurement of the angle between the radius through this point and a vertical line through the centre of the disc is unproblematic and equally accurate for every degree of rotation. Thus there exists a sort of cooperation between the signals of the sun and those of the night sky: the sun yields the first day of spring as cornerstone – the null-degree position of the bar, or the twelve o'clock position of the disc – and the celestial sphere allows any conceivable subdivision of the solar year.

The moon, which had fulfilled an invaluable function at the beginning of the history of the measurement of time, no longer had a place in the astronomical calendar, but its legacy is still present today in the form of the week and in the almost universal division of the year into twelve portions. This attests to the continuing importance of the moon in two respects:

- First, the moon long continued to serve as a handy timekeeper for 'home use' – not everyone in prehistoric times enjoyed unlimited access to the results of the astronomical calculations or possessed the skill to interpret them. There is also an intimate connection between the moon phases and the tides, a dominant phenomenon in coastal areas and of central importance to seafaring, fishing and so on.

- Second, as a sign of immediate divine intervention in the affairs of man, the rhythm of the moon had in the meantime become an indelible part of the collective consciousness.

In Chapter 2 we shall witness the persistence with which the moon continued to assume its place in the calibration of time, long after its usefulness had been superseded by other bases of calculation.

Solutions to the phase synchronization problem

All calendars are faced with the problem of phase synchronization. Each of the primary astronomical periods which result from the movement of the earth and the moon (i.e. the solar day, the lunar month and the solar year) follows its own rhythm, independently of the others. The convenience of these rhythms for calibrating time is diminished by the fact that the individual rhythms don't actually fit together very well. A whole number of days, however many or few, will never cover exactly the same time period of a given whole number of lunar months or solar years. The same applies to the months, whether synodic or sidereal.→14 These circumstances also result in ambiguous secondary periods. The moon phase, or lunar week, can be either a quarter of a lunar cycle (i.e. a visible condition of the moon) or a specific number of days, but not both at the same time; and similarly, the season is either a quarter of the solar year, a specific number of lunar months or weeks, or a whole number of days. In other words, weeks and seasons can potentially orient themselves either upwards or downwards in the hierarchy, but not in both directions simultaneously. This situation inevitably results in discontinuities in the transition from one temporal level to the next: the at best approximate correspondence between the natural units of any two respective scales of calibration always results in a progressive increase in phase difference between them. This out-of-phase condition very quickly reaches a point at which the relationship between the two levels in question is no longer obvious. In terms of the calendar this observation has two implications:

- the cycles of the various natural orders of magnitude (day, lunar week, lunar month, solar year) must be realigned with one another at relatively frequent intervals; or

- the rhythms of the respective levels must be adjusted to fit together better.

The first strategy is with certainty the older of the two. Days are counted only within individual weeks, weeks only within individual months, months in turn only within individual years. With each transition from a smaller to a larger order of calibration, the time reckoned thus far is rounded up or down: discontinuities are simply ignored. This solution presupposes that all members of a calendar community comply with the same 'game rules' and perform this rounding in the same fashion. This procedure ensures that the phase gains and losses cancel one another out, and for relatively simple life situations this technique for calibrating time is quite practicable.

The second strategy is somewhat more problematic. Since the smallest countable unit of calibration is the complete day, a fine-tuning along the lines of the well-tempered musical scale – in which the half interval is defined in such a manner that exactly twelve such half intervals constitute an octave – would, in terms of the calendar, be equivalent to changing the length of the day so that a whole number of days might fit into a lunar month or solar year: clearly an impracticable solution. Things must instead be arranged so that the *average* length of a unit of calibration (in particular the month) is a fraction, each month nevertheless consisting of a whole number of days. At the same time, the month must fit comfortably in the solar year. Similar requirements may apply to the week as well. Various techniques for satisfying these conditions (phasal realignment conventions, intercalation and 'blind' periods) will be described in Chapter 2.

With the second strategy it can also come to pass that the relationship between solar year and calendar year is lost for a shorter or longer period of time. This situation can be compared with a piano on which the tone progression becomes progressively sharper or flatter with each successive octave.

The problem of the synchronization of phases did not arise as a consequence of later attempts to refine the calendar; rather, the problem is an inherent characteristic, one which only then became a problem when higher demands were placed on the system. We will look more closely at these demands and at their consequences for the structure of the calendar. First, however, we ought to take a closer look at the kind of time reckoning with which Neolithic man was probably familiar. Through the following example we shall be able to gain a better idea of how the natural calendar worked in practice.

Let us assume that a certain event is to take place in the not-too-near future, for example, a wedding. To make the calculation more interesting, we will further assume that the time which must elapse until this important social event is to take place is not simply a round number of time units: let's assume three (solar) years plus five (lunar) months plus three (lunar) weeks plus four days.

The first task for the individual scheduling this event is to work out what day it is today relative to the first day of the current year. To do so, this individual must first know how many complete moon cycles have taken place since the last New Year's Day: let's say, nine. Then he must take account of the current 'age' of the moon and compare it with the moon's age on the first day of the year: let us assume that at New Year we had the first day of the full moon (that is, it was one day after the full moon), and now we are in the sixth day of the descending half moon. That leaves altogether one moon phase plus $6 - 1 = 5$ days, so that nine months, one week and five days have transpired since New Year. He probably doesn't have to work this out especially for the occasion; presumably he is already aware of it, just as nowadays we tend to know the current calendar date.

By adding the months, weeks and days since the beginning of the year to the set time period, he comes up with three years plus $5 + 9 = 14$ months plus $3 + 1 = 4$ weeks plus $4 + 5 = 9$ days, or more simply: four years plus three months plus one week plus two days. This converts the time period into a closing date which is then disclosed to the invited guests, namely the total time since the last New Year's Day which must elapse before the festivities begin.

The roundings in this example consistently assume a *nominal* scaling of 7 days to a lunar week, 4 week units to a lunar month, 12 month units to a solar year. Of course other models could be conceived; it is only important that the members of a calendar community agree on a convention.

From this point onward, each participant merely needs to wait until four further New Year's Days have elapsed. (They're hard to overlook, since there is always a big celebration in the village on that day.) On the last of these festive days he must take note of the condition of the moon. Let's say that on this day we have the fourth day of the descending half moon. The four days are ignored for now, but they must be noted for later. He must subsequently wait a further three 'months' (thrice again descending half moon), then, following an additional 'week' (i.e. the start of the next moon phase, in this case the new moon) four additional days, to compensate for the four days 'rounded off' at the beginning of the current year. Two days later is the wedding day.

Of course, no-one in his right mind would have set the date for a wedding in the manner described in this example. The purpose of this exercise, however, is not to propose the most likely or convenient method of marrying off one's daughter, but rather to present an extreme case which demonstrates the capacity and flexibility of the natural lunar calendar.

The wedding guest wouldn't have needed to hold all the details in his head. A simple string with a few knots would suffice to document the closing date, the knots being arranged in groups representing the years, months, weeks and days, respectively, with a short gap between the groups to keep them apart: in our example: five, four, two and three knots (one extra knot in each group, to avoid the occurrence of groups of zero knots). A single year-knot would be removed at the end of each complete year (at the commencement of spring) until only one remained. The same procedure would be repeated for the month-knots with respect to the moon cycles, then the week-knots with respect to the moon phases and finally the day-knots (whose number would have been augmented in the meantime by the age of the current moon phase at the last New Year, in the present example by four days).

This form of calibrating time seems complicated to us because we are unfamiliar with it. Our reaction is comparable with the mixture of admiration and astonishment which non-Sterling countries reserved for the British during the time when the nation's currency consisted in twelve pence to the shilling, twenty shillings to the pound – not to mention the ha'penny, the half-crown (worth two shillings and sixpence) and the guinea at twenty-one shillings. For the British themselves, the perceived difficulty was exactly the reverse. I can report from personal experience: in the early 1970s worry and anxiety broke out throughout the realm as the British were obliged to give up their accustomed system of coinage. The point is that the erstwhile British currency was in no wise less 'natural' than the decimal currency which replaced it – in fact, for head calculation it was considerably simpler (even though the reader may find this claim hard to accept). The reckoning system which formed the basis of the Neolithic method of calibrating time was, like the British currency of its time, in daily use and for the people at that time completely 'natural'.

But ease of handling is not really the point at issue. Let us take a closer look at what is actually taking place. At first, the starting-point of all time reckoning is the beginning of the year, regardless of when in the first year the waiting period begins. This is necessarily so, because the first day of spring is the one day of the year when a realignment takes place between the solar and lunar rhythms, effective for the entire cultural region. During the four complete years of waiting the moon plays no role at all in the calculation. Only after the very last springtime has commenced is the moon phase once again relevant. It doesn't matter which phase is actually in play (or perhaps in which 'house' the moon is standing), one need merely take note of it. Similarly, the total number of days which elapse during a lunar week, whether it be seven or perhaps eight, is simply ignored; what counts is the moon phase, and only the moon phase. Individual days prior to the wedding are counted only after the very last complete moon phase has lapsed.

This method of calibrating time is comparable to the natural musical scale, which is acoustically pleasing only so long as the harmony is kept simple and the tunes are restricted to very few key signatures. The annual realignment on the first day of spring is the manner in which the intervening dissonances of the natural phase elements are cancelled out. The tonic note of the Neolithic calendar, that is, the pivot point of the calendar, is always the first day of spring: this day literally sets the tone. The units of time *measurement* and of time *calibration* remain essentially identical.

Whereas this method makes it possible for people to keep track of time spans of arbitrary length, it is not capable of indicating how many days are involved: the actual number of days in every unit of time calibration has to be rounded up or down relative to a nominal ideal value, since the phase units based on the movements of heavenly bodies do not fit together exactly. The week has mostly seven but often eight days, the month either twenty-nine or thirty, and the solar year mostly 365 but frequently 366, depending on the adopted standard. It requires modern techniques of measurement and the necessary technical knowledge to determine in advance exactly how many days a given natural time expression actually represents.

Growing demands on time calibration

For the hunters and gatherers of the Old Stone Age, life was presumably rather monotonous by our standards, social units being fairly homogeneous and relatively limited in complexity. Scheduling of events, as far as it occurred at all, was undertaken by people who were essentially subject to one and the same life rhythm. In the course of the New Stone Age a differentiation in working habits gradually evolved, distinguishing field workers from stonemasons on the one hand (Stonehenge comes to mind) and labourers from clerics on the other (the latter being responsible among other things for architectural specifications and for calculating the seasons, holy days and so on). In short, areas of enterprise with mutually independent rhythms of activity developed within the community. Whereas the time of harvest will have dictated the term for the completion of, say, a new granary, the technical and logistic aspects of the project itself will have governed the carpenters' and stonemasons' planning schedule for the actual construction work.

The supposition that all the various activities will have been carried out by the same labour force, at least at the beginning of this phase of differentiation, alters nothing in principle: an individual who normally tilled the field was, in his capacity as part-time stonemason, responsible for coordinating his activities with others on the basis of the timetable for the building project. More to the point: one and the same person had to lead his life in two or more different rhythms.

With the outbreak of the Bronze Age about five thousand years ago,→15 differentiation of labour progressed still further. The exploitation of zinc, tin and copper is a complicated and labour-intensive enterprise which cannot simply be carried out on the side by farmers. It requires special knowledge and skills of the trade, for the mining of ore as well as the extraction and refinement of metal and for the manufacture of end products (ploughs, sickles, knives, household utensils, objects of art, adornment and cult). In order to reach the necessary smelting temperature of 1200° centigrade, wood must first be reduced to charcoal – itself a specialist activity. Trees will soon become scarce in the immediate vicinity of the smelting ovens, and so combustible material must be transported over steadily increasing distances, giving rise to yet another special trade. Because lode areas are irregularly distributed, there evolve whole social groups dependent on barter and trade with neighbours: mining communities which need to exchange raw materials and products for outwardly produced requisites for living such as food and clothing. The refinement of the production of tools and artefacts leads ultimately to additional specialization amongst artisans, to a further fractionalization of the total range of community activity. Autonomous activities in the areas of commerce and management, again with their own internal rhythms of activity, evolve as a result of the increasingly complex coordination among these divers branches. And finally, we must think of the more regrettable social developments: increasingly divergent life styles and unequal distribution of resources and possessions foment de-solidarization of society, with the result that conflicts of interest, envy, ill-will, greed and enmity ensue. The war of spoils – which in the form of livestock and bride thievery was probably already known among Stone Age cattle breeders – reaches new dimensions: the neighbourhood skirmish gives way to the militarily organized campaign. There evolves a warrior class, whose campaigns demand exact logistic time management.

The natural lunar calendar is no longer adequate to meet the demands of a gradually industrializing society. The coordination of schedules within and between individual occupational groups must be accurate to the day, independent of natural events. At the same time, the rhythm of the seasons and with it the natural lunar calendar continue to be characteristic for these early cultures, which despite technological innovation remain essentially agricultural.

Let us assume that the earlier example of the time between the announcement and the wedding amounted to a total of 1,559 days, derived for purposes of illustration as follows: $4 \times 365.2421898 + 3.25 \times 29.5305891 + 2 = 1558.943174$, rounded up to 1,559. This figure will suffice for our purposes, although it should be noted that, because of the intermediate roundings with the natural cycles, the actual time period in a given instance could well vary from this result by several days either way.

We must not forget that we are still dealing with prehistoric times, that is, with the period before the development of writing systems. One may nonetheless imagine how it might have been possible for Neolithic or Bronze Age man to monitor the passing of the days. We know that Stone Age man was capable of dealing with quantities. Small artefacts made of fired clay, nowadays called *tokens*, have been found in archaeological digging sites scattered throughout the entire Near and Middle East. The oldest of these tokens are about ten thousand years old. One finding (of somewhat later date) is of a clay vessel with a cuneiform inscription which describes 49 domestic animals of various sorts; inside the vessel there are exactly 49 tokens.[16] Counting with the aid of surrogates was thus already known at the beginning of the Neolithic period. The evidence suggests, however, that the tokens were employed only for relatively small quantities. For the sake of the example we will ignore the question of how prehistoric man might have dealt with a quantity running into the thousands, let alone calculated the true number of days to elapse, and simply concentrate on how he might have coped with this expanse of time once it had been decided upon.

The individual responsible for timing the social event could perhaps have handed over an earthen jar containing 1,559 clay tokens to each potential guest with the instructions that one token be extracted every day, and that the guest should show up on the day the tokens run out. Of course he would keep a jar with 1,559 tokens for himself so that he could keep track of his own deadline. About three hundred invitations must go out, so he would have to prepare a fair number of jars. And these would all have to be delivered on the same day, otherwise their token count would no longer all be correct. (By comparison: with the knotted-string method based on lunar phases the knots representing the date of the event remain the same throughout the current year.) For this task he would need a complete caravan of pack animals, since hundreds of jars, each containing over one and a half thousand tokens, make up an appreciable weight.

Like everyone else he would have a large number of jars lying about at home, each with a different number of tokens, depending on the timetable being monitored. He must extract one single token each day from each jar. Woe betide him should he overlook this chore for even a single day, due to absence, illness, overwork, catastrophe or forgetfulness, since he would then lose track of all his appointments – or he would have no other recourse than to seek out someone else with at least one identical jar of tokens, compare their respective contents and then apply the discovered difference to his complete collection of jars – and to hope that his neighbour hadn't also suffered a similar lapse at one time or another.

Even assuming Neolithic society could have succeeded in

maintaining such a day-counting system in spite of all the practical difficulties involved, there would still remain the fundamental irreconcilability between the two systems. For any given appointment it would have been possible to stipulate either an exact number of days or an end date determined by the moon phases – but not both at the same time.

Put another way: a comparison of the two methods demonstrates the supremacy of the knotted string over the jar of tokens in just about every aspect, with two exceptions:

– its inability to indicate an exact day count; and

– its inalienable orientation on the first day of the year.

The token method, on the other hand, is free from precisely these two disadvantages. What was really needed was a calendar which combined the advantages of both these methods in one single system: a compromise solution in which the discrepancies between the two methods of calculation were reconciled not annually but continuously throughout the year. Society demanded a regulated calendar with preordained, unambiguous dimensions for each unit of calibration. Only then would it be possible to transform an expression of temporal calculation (i.e. a given number of days) directly into an expression of temporal calibration (i.e. a given calendar date) without involving continuous interaction with natural events.

On top of that, such a system for calibrating time must ultimately come to terms with an additional factor not yet mentioned: chronology. With its growing self-assessment as an organic whole – welded together not least through hardships such as hunger, catastrophe and war – a culture sooner or later feels the need to record events of its past in the form of stories, at first as oral tradition, later as folk legend with partly mythological character, reaching back to a presumed time of origin. In any case, the need arises to fix events over many years' time to a normative time of reference. This point in time might be characterized by a traumatic event (flood, war of conquest, etc.), or it might relate to the biography of an exceptional personality (king, folk hero), or it might be mythological (when the gods created people – that is, our tribe or community); the borders between these various times of origin can be unclear, or they can merge in the course of time. In the absence of an open-ended numbering system, the indicated number of years would have to remain relatively small, or it would need to be expressed with a simile, such as a number of human generations or human lives, or as many years as there are stars in a constellation or days in the year. This last-mentioned option invites comparison with the well-known 'prophetic day', whereby every day represents the course of a year:[17]

> After the number of the days in which ye searched the land, even forty days, each day for a year, shall ye bear your iniquities, even forty years, and ye shall know my breach of promise.[18]

> Lie thou also upon thy left side, and lay the iniquity of the house of Israel upon it: according to the number of the days that thou shalt lie upon it thou shalt bear their iniquity. For I have laid upon thee the years of their iniquity, according to the number of the days, three hundred and ninety days: so shalt thou bear the iniquity of the house of Israel. And when thou hast accomplished them, lie again on thy right side, and thou shalt bear the iniquity of the house of Judah forty days: I have appointed thee each day for a year.[19]

A further possibility consists in marking the flow of time by a temporal succession of events. A well-known version of this method is the throne succession or dynasty, of which examples can be found throughout recorded history, right down to the present day: records of the British Parliament, for example, are still chronicled according to the year of the reign of the contemporary monarch. In such a system individual years are numbered consecutively, beginning with the referential event, i.e. the coronation ceremony of the royal personage, and periods which lie further in the past can be identified uniquely with reference to the royal lineage. A variation of this method is the establishment of a 'year one' in conjunction with the coming of a major religious prophet.

Whatever the basis for the calculation of time may be, the need to calibrate longer periods of time reveals a further problem: the definition of the time-unit 'year'. The Neolithic solar year with its strictly defined starting day at the beginning of spring is unambiguous, but the introduction of a regulated calendar demands certain compromises – and one of these is frequently the length of the year. Moreover, should an existing calendar for some reason be adjusted, the continuity in the length of the year is almost invariably disturbed, regardless of whether this adjustment involves a new basis of calculation or the insertion or deletion of individual units of calibration (usually days or months).

2

The Calendar in History

Long before the transition from prehistory to history – in other words, the point at which calendars or references to calendars and their time units were first documented in written form – the basic units of the human perception and measurement of time were already firmly established. The differences among the historically documented calendar systems lie less in the basic units which they employ and more in the different methods of compensating for the discrepancies between the solar and lunar rhythms.

All historical calendars are in some manner regulated ('historical', that is, in the sense of historicity *sui generi*: in numerous autochthonous tribes and nations in the western hemisphere, for example, 'prehistoric' lunar calendars existed well into the 19th century). It is no longer possible to determine whether the fact of writing predicated the introduction of regulated calendars, or whether this form of calendar is also prehistoric. Staff and notch calendars represent intermediate forms, existing side by side with written or printed calendars throughout the centuries. The fact that these calendars need to be carved and should therefore ideally be reusable suggests a certain normalization in the division into lunar cycles. It is obvious, however, that commitment to paper or other recording medium presupposes the exact forward projection of the details of the calendar, a requirement which would not have been satisfied by the natural calendar in view of the then current possibilities of calculation.

With a regulated calendar it is possible to work out the designation of an arbitrary day in the future or past, ideally over an arbitrarily long span of time. Either the values of the units of each successive order of magnitude (typically days, weeks, months and years) are constant, or they can be predicted using some formula. The fact of regulation changes the former units of *rhythm* called week, month, etc., into units of *time* – however much the latter may be wanting in consistency. Discontinuities (usually extra days or months, but sometimes arbitrary adjustments) typically generate special problems. Adequate leap year rulings often cannot be utilized: either the calculatory accuracy necessary to formulate a leap year ruling valid for thousands of years is not yet known, or a calendar cannot be altered because of existing dependencies (such as a liturgy adapted precisely to the properties of the calendar as it stands). The improved measurement techniques of the late mediaeval period, for example, didn't find application in this respect until the Gregorian calendar reform in 1582.

At this point we will be examining historical calendar systems from three cultural areas: the Indo-Iranian, the Graeco-Roman and the Semitic. These cultures include most of the great revealed religions which preceded the Bábí and Bahá'í Faiths: Zoroastrianism, Hinduism/Buddhism, Judaism, Christianity and Islam.

Indo-Iranian calendar systems

The Indo-Iranians were a branch of the Indo-European group, dwelling originally in the steppes of Central Asia. In the course of their wanderings toward the South, the Indians and the Iranians separated some time in the late Neolithic period. Both cultures possessed an orally handed-down religious tradition – the Avesta of the Iranians and the Vedas of the Indians – which show significant linguistic and contextual parallels. From these facts it can be assumed that the time references of both peoples also possessed affinities.

In the case of the Indians we know that the calendars of today (there are many) are based on approximate lunar cycles. The year is typically divided into twelve months of thirty days each, and the calendar year wanders through the seasons.[1] This form of calendar is presumably a regulated version of an original natural lunar calendar. In addition, the religious rites of the Hindus and Buddhists are oriented partly in line with the lunar phases – the *Puja*, for example, is celebrated during full moon – and partly according to the natural seasons. This could either mean that the original calendar lost its binding on the natural season upon becoming regulated, or that two systems of time calibration – based respectively on the lunar and the solar rhythm – existed side by side. It is more probable, however, that the liturgical practice had simply become fixed to the seasonal changes before the calendar was regulated.

The Hindu calendar was taken over by Buddhism and enjoyed a considerable dispersion in the course of the expansion of this religion to the north and east of its original home in India. Thus it came into contact with differently structured and in part highly developed calendar systems, especially in China. A discussion of the further development of the calibration of time in these regions would lead far beyond the framework of the present study.

We will examine the development of the calendar among the early Iranian people more closely. On the one hand, this development took place in the immediate cultural environment of the birthplace of the Bahá'í Faith and is for that reason alone of interest to us. On the other hand, the history of the calendar of the Zoroastrians contains examples of nearly everything which can conceivably go wrong, and that, too, makes it particularly worthy of scrutiny.

The Zoroastrian calendar

We know from the Avesta that the religious practices of the original Zoroastrians were oriented on the natural seasons. The founder-prophet Zoroaster was probably born in the west but lived in the north-east of today's Iran, where he exerted his influence following his emigration, probably some 2,750 to 3,000 years ago. This estimate of Zoroaster's age is based on an exhaustive analysis of statements from 'Abdu'l-Bahá and Shoghi Effendi.[2] Other estimates diverge widely, currently varying between the 14th and the 6th centuries BCE. The *Bahman Yasht* mentions a cosmic tree with seven branches respectively of gold, bronze, silver, copper, tin, steel and an 'iron mixture',[3] thus lending support to a post-

Neolithic dating. On the other hand, neither metals nor smelting techniques were unknown in the 'Stone' Age (see 'Growing demands on time calibration' in Chapter 1). The internal evidence is thus inconclusive.

In addition to the five daily prayers and worship – at sunrise, mid-morning, midday, sunset and midnight – Zoroaster dedicated seven high festivals respectively to Ahura Mazda (the one, uncreated God) and the Amesha Spentas (the holy immortals). The six Spenta or 'Gahambar' festivals were spread throughout the year and characterized the natural high points of pastoral and agricultural life: 'Midspring', 'Midsummer', 'Grain Harvest', 'Gathering of the Cattle', 'Midwinter' and finally 'Festival of the Fravashi' (the souls of the dead) immediately before the vernal equinox. The seventh high festival was *Naw-Rúz*, 'New Day', celebrated on the day of the vernal equinox.[4]

The earliest textual references indicate a calendar similar to the Mesopotamian one, to which it was presumably related, existing during the late Achaemenid period some 2,500 years ago. Iran was ruled at that time by the Medeans, later the Persians (from Pars in south-west Iran), population groups which had had centuries of contact with the great cultures to their west – Babylon, Elam and Assyria – long before the new religion from the east gained hold on them as well. The 'Zoroastrian' calendar was therefore apparently of Babylonian or west Persian origin and first became associated with Zoroastrianism following the latter's establishment as the state religion. Later in this chapter we shall witness a similar, geographically almost parallel development with the 'Christian' calendar (see 'Graeco-Roman calendar systems' below).

Like its Mesopotamian precursor, this calendar had twelve thirty-day months, which results in a calendar year of 360 days. The Zoroastrians divided the month into four phases, the first day of each of which (that is, the first, eighth, fifteenth and twenty-third day of each month) was dedicated to Ahura Mazda;[5] the 'weeks' consisted of twice seven and twice eight days. The fact that every day and every month possessed a dedication led to the adoption of additional 'name day' festivals, which of course further increased the ritual activity of an already rich liturgy.

The 360-day year is called a *round year*, the twelve 30-day months *round months*. This form of calendar, with somewhat overlong months and an underdimensioned year, is a compromise solution which is found all over the globe. The resemblance of the Mesopotamian round year to those of India is therefore not evidence *per se* of a common origin. Because the total number of days in the round year falls short of the solar year by five-plus days, an additional month must be interjected into the calendar following each series of roughly six years if the calendar is to remain in any way in accord with the seasons.

Zoroastrianism was raised to the status of state religion under Ardashir (224–241 CE),[6] the founder of the Sasanid dynasty, at which time the Zoroastrian priests implemented a calendar reform: based on the model of the Egyptian calendar (see 'The Jewish calendar' below) they added five days to the end of the calendar year, the so-called 'Gatha' days (named after the Gathas, the oral-traditional hymns of Zoroaster). Whereas the Fravashi festival had until then carried over without break into the Naw-Rúz celebrations, the two were now separated from from one another through five additional, 'non-calendar' days, and the festivities could no longer be held in the accustomed manner. Partly for this reason the new calendar met with mixed approval, and at first the festival of Naw-Rúz was not uniformly celebrated. Two years later, however, the celebration of Naw-Rúz strictly according to the new calendar was made obligatory by virtue of a royal edict. This meant that the old 360-day calendar (which was still being used by most people) had to be adjusted by ten additional days in order to bring it into line with the revised timing for Naw-Rúz.[7] In order to maintain synchrony between the two calendars a compromise solution evolved by which the Fravashi festival lasted ten days: the five Gatha days plus the five surplus days. This arrangement was the cause of much uncertainty among the people. Equally as confusing was the fact that New Year's Day now took place on the first day of autumn: the reformers had simply aligned the calendar with whatever equinox happened to be closest at hand.[8]

About three hundred years later, still in the Sasanid era, a further calendar reform took place. Since no further adjustments to the course of the days had been undertaken since the introduction of the 365-day calendar, the Naw-Rúz festival had gradually slipped from the first day of autumn back to about the middle of summer. Given an actual solar year of 365.2422 days, the calendar would by then have fallen about 73 days short of its erstwhile seasonal position. This gap amounts to two days less than two-and-a-half round months – just about in the middle between the two equinoxes. The elders decided to leave the months as they were but to shift the Naw-Rúz festival forward to its original position on the first day of spring and to adjust the six remaining Gahambar festivals and the ten Fravashi days accordingly. It was further decreed that once every 120 years an additional 30-day month should be inserted into the calendar year. In this manner, Naw-Rúz and the Fravashi and Gahambar celebrations, including the day of the ascension of the Prophet, would more or less maintain their relationship to the first day of spring and to one another, whereas the other festivals would not be influenced by this intercalary month, and with the passing of future millennia they would gradually recede backwards though the seasons.[9]

As is so often the case with good intentions, untimely circumstances (to put it mildly) disrupted the implementation of this decree. The Muslim conquest of Iran in the 7th century CE signalled the end of Zoroastrianism as the state religion and hampered the administration of internal religious matters. It wasn't until the beginning of the 11th century – almost exactly 500 years after the second Sasanid reform – that the Zoroastrians once again concerned themselves with calendar issues. By this time the Naw-Rúz festival had as usual slid backwards through the seasons, this time by roughly a third of a year, and was being celebrated in winter. By a lucky coincidence, in 1006 CE the first day of the original first calendar month (*Farvardín*) once again coincided with the first day of spring: after more than 1,500 years of meandering through the seasons, exactly one solar year had been lost relative to the original start position. (Calculation: 0.2422 (annual day shift) x 1,508 passing years = 365.2376, or in other words nearly exactly the 365.2422 days of the solar year.) The necessary reform thus suggested itself: Naw-Rúz was moved back onto the first day of Farvardín with the Gatha days immediately preceding it, and the Gahambar and Fravashi festivals were reinstated into their original positions in the calendar.[10]

This was the last reform which was to be valid for the whole community, that is, for the Zoroastrians in Iran as well as for the Parsi in the Indian province of Gujarat, north of the city of Bombay. The Parsi, who had emigrated to India mostly between the 8th and the 10th century CE following Muslim repressions, maintained whenever possible close contact with the Iranian mother community. In contrast to the Iranian community, which was subject to a continuous decrease in size, the Parsi community flourished and became increasingly independent from the mother community, and in the 12th century CE the Parsi decided to introduce an intercalary month. Despite the fact that this was the extra month which was due following 120 common years and which should have been binding for the whole Zoroastrian community,[11] the Iranian community did not follow suit. Since that time, the calendars of the two communities continue out of phase with one another: neither in Iran nor in India has a similar measure been undertaken to this day, and so the long-standing weakness of the calendar – the slow backwards shift of the months through the seasons – continues to hold sway.

In the 18th century CE (in 1746) a movement began in India with the view to bringing the two communities back together. This party, the *Kadmí*, preferred the calendar of the mother country and declared the intercalated month of the Indian calendar null and void. The opposition party, the *Sháhensháhí* ('royal'), stuck to the Parsi reform.[12] Rational arguments are hard to find on either side of the debate. In the 740 years which had elapsed since the last common calendar reform, the seasonal skew was again so far advanced (by about 179 days) that Naw-Rúz was once again being celebrated in the autumn: in this respect, neither calendar was satisfactory. The end result of this controversy was that, from that time onward, both calendars continued to exist side by side in Gujarat, creating an artificial schism within the Parsi community.

An additional well-intentioned attempt to reform the calendar in the year 1906 merely served to aggravate the situation. Motivated by the conviction that the placing of the Naw-Rúz festival exactly on the first day of spring was a central pillar of the teachings of Zoroaster, many were of the opinion that these teachings could only be upheld through the adoption of a calendar on the model of the Gregorian calendar: a year with 365 days with roughly every fourth year a leap year in accordance with the calculation of the vernal equinox.[13] This so-called *Faslí* movement enjoyed only moderate support in the Indian community, but the new calendar, which was propagated under the effective trade name *Bastání* ('ancient') calendar,[14] was introduced in 1939 in Iran. Part of the community, the Yazdí in the south of Iran, abandoned this calendar shortly thereafter, reverting back to their customary *Qadímí* (i.e. 'old-fashioned') calendar. This perfected the confusion which persists to the present day: within the Iranian community, which had by this time shrunk drastically in size – not least because of multitudinous conversions to the Bahá'í Faith[15] – was thus split into two even smaller groups: the urban-progressive Teheran community used the new calendar (which was called 'ancient'), while the rural-conservative Yazdí community used the multiply-reformed old version. In the Parsi community in India there were in fact three calendars: in addition to the above-mentioned forms, the calendar of the *Sháhensháhí.*→[16]

The Zoroastrian calendar: A summary

The first question which comes to mind when we consider the Bastání calendar is: why wasn't a similar solution available right at the beginning? The Bastání supporters asked themselves precisely this same question and came to the conclusion that the original, pre-Achaemenid calendar must of necessity have been oriented on the first day of spring. Considering the evidence regarding the Neolithic capacity to measure time, this position seems quite realistic. However, we should temper our judgement over the various rulings in light of the prevailing circumstances.

The calendar at the time of Zoroaster was most probably a natural lunar calendar of the Neolithic variety, realigned annually with the first day of spring. In Achaemenid times a secular calendar was introduced which only incidentally fulfilled a religious function. This 360-day lunar calendar presented a thoroughly reasonable form of calendar regulation: the advantage of a division of the year into months of constant size compensates for the disadvantage of the discrepancy of roughly half a day between calendar month and lunation, and the simplicity of counting in twelves, which is well suited for head reckoning, makes up for the disadvantage of a continuously receding New Year. In other words, this calendar had all the advantages of 'token-jar' scheduling and none of its disadvantages, since the Mesopotamian civilizations – in contrast to the semi-nomadic peoples of north-eastern Iran at that time – possessed systems for writing and counting (a fact which is attested conclusively by the many cuneiform fragments, some of which date back 4,500 years, consisting for the most part of inventories). But the loss of orientation on the beginning of spring – a loss which the instigators of the calendar had been quite willing to accept – turned out to be disastrous for the subsequently adopted Zoroastrian liturgy.

The Achaemenids – or perhaps the Medeans and Persians before them, who had not yet become Zoroastrian – had taken over the regulated calendar of their Assyrian and Babylonian neighbours: the priests had no other choice but to make the best of the situation. It was only in later years that the priests could bring their meanwhile enhanced influence to bear on the further fashioning of the calendar. Until then, however, much symbolic content had already become inalienably associated with the calendar in its then current form. Each and every day of the thirty-day month had its inviolable dedication, so that the expansion of individual months was unthinkable. It should be remembered that the introduction of the Gatha days resulted in much distress and confusion in the community at the time, one which represented a dangerous destabilization of the Fravashi rites. To be sure, the extension of the calendar from 360 to 365 days slowed down the seasonal shift, but as history has proved, it could not prevent it altogether. The inclusion of yet another Gatha day in roughly every fourth year would certainly have been impracticable. The decision to include an intercalated month once every 120 years was perhaps made more palatable by the fact that the measure would perforce be carried out by persons other than the decision-makers. (Priests are, after all, only human.) History has shown that this expectation was unrealistic: the first deadline was already overstepped well before the Muslim invasion.

More tragic than the effects of the earlier reforms was the atomization of the community through latter-day and in part piecemeal improvements, none of which succeeded in gaining acceptance by the entire community. The result was that there were no longer any common dates for the celebration of the various festivals and rituals.

The Iranian national calendar

In addition to the Zoroastrian calendar, three additional calendars are in use in Iran today. Two of these are used for special purposes: the Gregorian calendar in business, especially in international trade, and the Islamic calendar for the scheduling of religious festivals. Both of these calendars are treated later in this chapter. In general, however, the Iranian national calendar, or *Jalálí* calendar, is used. It has the following twelve months:

1	*Farvardín*	7	*Mehr*
2	*Ordí behesht*	8	*Ábán*
3	*Khordád*	9	*Ázar*
4	*Tír*	10	*Déi*
5	*Mordád*	11	*Bahman*
6	*Shahrívar*	12	*Esfand*

The final month, *Esfand*, has 29 days in common years and 30 days in leap years. Of the remaining months, the first six always have 31 days and the rest 30. This distribution results in a relatively close agreement between the four groups of three months and the four seasons of the year: because of the elliptical orbit of the earth and its concomitant variation of roughly 11 per cent between the *perihelion* (point of least distance from the sun, currently 2 January) and the *aphelion* (point of greatest distance, currently ca. 3 July), the 'quarters' of the year are of unequal length, the (north hemispheric) winter half-year being currently 7.58 days shorter than the summer half-year. As a result of precession, of course, these relationships will have reversed themselves in about twelve thousand years.

The Jalálí calendar also recognizes the seven-day week:

Saturday	S<u>h</u>anbeh (pronounced '<u>sh</u>ambeh')
Sunday	Yek<u>sh</u>anbeh
Monday	Do<u>sh</u>anbeh
Tuesday	Seh<u>sh</u>anbeh
Wednesday	C<u>h</u>ahar<u>sh</u>anbeh
Thursday	Panj<u>sh</u>anbeh
Friday	Jom'eh

With the exception of Friday, whose name is borrowed from the Islamic calendar and means 'the day of assembly', the names of the days of the week have no symbolic or functional significance: following 'S<u>h</u>anbeh', which means 'Saturday', the remaining days are simply numbered from one to five.

Also in common with the Islamic calendar, the years are counted starting with the year of the *hijraτ* (the Emigration of Muhammad), but in this case in solar years instead of the lunar years of the Islamic calendar. For that reason this calendar is commonly called *taqvím-e hijrí-ye <u>sh</u>amsí*, (or simply *taqvím-e <u>sh</u>amsí*) in Iran, that is, the solar (*hijrí*) calendar, to distinguish it from *taqvím-e [hijrí-ye] qamarí*, the lunar (*hijrí*) (=Islamic) calendar. The start of year one was set equal to the vernal equinox preceding the *hijraτ*, i.e. about 6 months before the Emigration took place in 622 CE.

In every cycle of 33 years there occur regularly eight leap years, in the years 1, 5, 9, 13, 17, 22, 26 and 30 of the cycle, which results in a year length of $365^{8/33}$ or 365.2424242 days. To adjust for the fact that this is slightly more than the tropical year of 365.2421892 days (in 2008), at irregular intervals one cycle is increased by a so-called 'gap year' to a total of 34 years. For example, a gap year following a series of 32 cycles would result in an average year length over the total period of 1,057 years of $365^{256/1057}$ or 365.2421949 days, which represents a better adjustment relative to the length of the tropical year. Exactly when a gap year is to occur is determined on the basis of the measurement of the precise moment of the vernal equinox. Should this event transpire before midday, then the current day is the day of Naw-Rúz, otherwise the following day. The gap years are distributed so as to guarantee the integrity of this relationship.

The calendar day begins at midnight. This, in conjunction with the midday boundary criterion, ensures that the year always begins with that midnight which stands in closest temporal proximity to the vernal equinox. Naw-Rúz, a festival derived from the Zoroastrian tradition, is in the Jalálí calendar thus redefined: what is celebrated is first and foremost the astronomical moment of the start of the new year, regardless of which moment of the day or night this may occur, and regardless of whether this moment falls on 29 Esfand, 30 Esfand or 1 Farvardín.

The Jalálí calendar was named after Jalálu'd-Din Malek-Sháh-i Saljuqí and was developed in the late 5th century AH (12th century CE) in the form which is still valid today, by a committee which included the poet and mathematician Omar Khayyam.[17] In 1930 it was elevated by Reza Shah Pahlavi to the status of the national calendar of Iran. The Jalálí calendar is used today not only in Iran but also in neighbouring, mainly Shí'ite areas in Afghanistan, in Iraq and in several Central Asian republics.

Graeco-Roman calendar systems

In earlier times, the Greeks possessed a lunar calendar with intercalary months to adjust for the length of the solar year,[18] structurally similar to the Semitic (see below). In 432 BCE it was noted that 235 synodic moon cycles correspond almost exactly to nineteen solar years. This relationship, which is named the Metonic Cycle after its presumed discoverer, formed the basis of a calendar consisting of a series of twelve years with twelve synodic months each, followed by a series of seven years with thirteen synodic months each.[19] This sequence resulted in an average of 12.368421 genuine lunar months per year. Managing this lunisolar calendar was undoubtedly difficult. First of all, there was a discrepancy of approximately 0.00125 per cent or one day every 219 years between the two macro-phases. Moreover, since the individual months had to be aligned very carefully in accordance with the lunar cycle, the relationship of the calendar year to the solar year was complicated in practice.

In the course of their self-Hellenization the Romans formally adopted the lunisolar calendar of the Greeks, in practice however retaining their traditional *Romulus calendar* (hence the Latin expression *ad calendas graecas*, 'postponed indefinitely'). This latter calendar consisted of 38 eight-day market cycles (*nundina*), equivalent to ten synodic months, starting at the vernal equinox, followed by a 'gap' of somewhat over two lunations. The first four months had meaningful names. One (*Aprilis mensis*) was called the 'opening' month since it fell in the middle of spring, and three were dedicated to gods (*Maius mensis*, Jupiter; *Iunius mensis*, Juno; *Martius mensis*, Mars, the god of war: the beginning of the year was also the time for breaking camp in preparation for new military campaigns). The six remaining months were simply numbered successively from five to ten (*Quinctilis mensis, Sextilis mensis, September mensis, October mensis, November mensis, December mensis*). The *calendae* (from *calare*, 'to call') were the days in which the first sighting of the new moon was proclaimed ('called out') in the Roman forum by the high priests, marking in each case the initial day of each month (see 'Semitic calendar systems' below): the months were thus originally aligned with the lunation. However, their lengths were eventually regulated in the series 31-30-31-30-31-30-30-31-30-30.

In the 7th pre-Christian century two additional months were added on to the end of the existing ones, *Ianuarius mensis* with 29 days (named after the god Ianus, who had two faces staring in opposite directions) and *Februarius mensis* with 28 days, named after *Februum*, the (religious) festival of purification. At the same time the 30-day months were reduced in length to 29, resulting in a calendar with 355 days. Since the Romans considered even numbers to be unlucky, only the final month, dedicated to the minor gods, was permitted to be divisible by two. Alignment with the solar year was achieved through an intercalary month, *Intercalaris mensis*, which was inserted into the year following Februarius mensis at irregular intervals and which ensured that the year always began at or around the vernal equinox.[20]

The *Republican calendar* (ca. 70 BCE) was characterized by a new intercalation rhythm: in every second year, Februarius mensis was reduced to 23 days and an additional month, *Mercedonius mensis* ('wages month') intercalated immediately thereafter. This month consisted of alternately 27 and 28 days, and the calendar year thus had a mean length of 366.25 days. This is the first calendar in recorded history with a regular and automatic intercalation ruling, but unfortunately the inaccurate estimation of the length of the solar year generated a surplus which was carried over from year to year.

With the Julian reform in the year 46 BCE every fourth year was a leap year, resulting in a calendar with 365.25 days – an improved (but still inaccurate) estimation of the length of the solar year. The days were reoriented with relation to the seasons through a once-only intercalary month of 90 days – effectively three intercalary months at once. The shifting of the beginning of the year to Ianuarius mensis and the consequent loss of the relationship between the 'numbered' months and their ordinal place in the lunar series is presumably due to Etruscan influence.

The following year (45 BCE) witnessed the establishment of the calendar scheme which has, with minor adjustments, continued in use in the Western world and its sphere of influence to the present day. Two of these adjustments have to do with the names of the months. In the aftermath of the calendar reform (in 44 BCE) the 'fifth' month was renamed in honour of Julius Caesar, during whose reign the reform had been carried out. Later – around the year 8 BCE – the 'sixth' month was likewise renamed, this time in honour of Augustus (the honorific title of Octavian, meaning 'the exalted').

The renaming of Sextilis mensis to *Augustus mensis* may well have been accompanied by a further adjustment to the calendar. Some historians surmise that the number of days for the calendar months Sextilis mensis through December mensis originally (that is, immediately following the Julian reform) represented the sequence 30-31-30-31-30, whereby Februarius mensis had 29 days in a common year and 30 in a leap year. This sequence would have resulted in a calendar with an unbroken sequence of alternating 31 and 30 days, at least in every leap year, which would have been consistent with the Roman predilection for symmetry. According to this theory, the sequence of the months Sextilis (Augustus) mensis through December mensis were simply reversed to

31-30-31-30-31 to ensure that the month named in honour of Octavian contained as many days as that named after Julius, and in compensation Februarius mensis was shortened by one day. This theory can neither be proved nor rejected on the basis of historical sources, but it does offer a plausible explanation for the curious arrangement with which we are obliged to cope to the present day.

Just in time for inclusion in the Julian reform, Roman historians worked out that the age of the City of Rome was 708 years. This year of the grounding of the City (*ab urbe condita*) became the year one of the calendar.[21]

The Christians, whose priests living within the Roman empire had during the reign of Constantine become Roman civil servants, faithfully adopted the Julian calendar. They thus found themselves in a situation similar to that of the Zoroastrian priests in the late Achaemenid period, who had to make do with the Mesopotamian calendar. Ironically, this meant for the Christians the adoption of a pagan symbol system, of a calendar one of whose months was named in honour of Octavian (Augustus). Gaius Octavius, Julius Caesar's grandnephew and adopted son, reigned at the time of Jesus' birth.[22]

During the first 500 years of the Christian Era the passage of the years continued to be marked by the reigning years of the various Roman caesars and regents, in line with established practice. Some time in the 6th century CE the Julian, or Spanish, era appeared, whose year one was fixed retrospectively to the year of the Julian reform. The era (the word is West Gothic for 'year' [dative *jēra*, cf. Dan./Swed. *år*] and is not related to the word 'era' [from late Lat. *aera*], meaning 'period or epoch') was in use most notably in Spain but at different times in large areas of Western Europe and North Africa at least into the 15th century. From the 11th/12th century on, the *Anno Domini* convention, i.e. the measurement of time from the birth of Jesus, gradually became established in the Church and through it in the entire European cultural area.[23] In the year 321 and still during the reign of Constantine, the Semitic week (see 'Semitic calendar systems' below) was introduced.[24] The Semitic order of the days of the week was retained, but the first day (Sunday) was declared the 'day of the

Lord' after the day of the Resurrection, thus replacing Saturday as the sabbath.[25]

In 1582 a further adjustment to the calendar system was ordained by Pope Gregory XIII, resulting in the so-called *Gregorian calendar*. This adjustment consisted in two correctives. The first corrective was the refinement of the calculation of leap year: a round century (a year divisible by 100) was henceforth only then counted as a leap year if it was also divisible by 400.[26] The result was a mean calendar year length of 365.2425 days.

The leap-year ruling could of course be refined one step further: if every year which is divisible by 4,000 counted as a common year, then the calendar year would have an average length of 365.24225 days. The discrepancy would be further reduced, but since the length of the tropical year is not constant (see Appendix D) it can never disappear entirely, not even with the most ideal leap-year formula. The proposed quadrimillennial amendment is not yet part of the official standard, but there is no urgency, since there still remain nearly two millennia to consider the matter.

The greatest advantage of this form of determining which years are leap years lies in its objective determinability: the leap years are identified over an arbitrarily long period of time and the length of the year is well defined, eliminating the need for an annually convening, norm-imposing authority. It should be noted, however, that a formula for defining the leap-year sequence is not the same as calendar alignment:

– First, with every formula there remains a discrepancy – be it ever so small – between the solar year and the calendar year: in the case of the Gregorian calendar the discrepancy amounts to one day every 3,333 years or so.

– Second, the adjustment to the length of each given year occurs in accordance with the formula and not with the (in principle calculable) alignment theoretically required; the lengths of the successive years are non-linear, a fact which leads to inaccuracies which can only be ironed out over a period of many years.

- Third – the opposite side of the coin – a direct association with natural phenomena is notably absent, and a solemn consecration of the year in accordance with the signs of the firmament is therefore not given.

The second corrective of the Gregorian reform involved the realignment of the months relative to the seasons. The Julian calendar year had had a mean length of 365.25 days, since every fourth year was a leap year: in comparison with the solar year, the calendar year was on the average 0.0078 days too long. To compensate among other things for this error, a total of ten days – from 5 to 14 October – were summarily cancelled for that single year 1582.

Why exactly ten days should have been deleted is a mystery which has puzzled specialists over the centuries. On the basis of the relative lengths of the solar and the Julian year it is obvious that during the 1,628 years which had expired between the time of the Julian reform and that of the Gregorian, the calendar had accumulated a surplus of not ten, but 12.6984 days.

To make matters worse, during the years between 44 BCE and 8 CE intercalation was carried out mistakenly every three years instead of every four: the expression 'every fourth year' was ambiguous in antique times, since it could be understood either inclusively or exclusively. This misunderstanding resulted in a surplus of five intercalations – which in turn would seem to imply that the Gregorian readjustment was short not by three, but indeed by eight days: thus the contradiction should accordingly be much greater. On the other hand, we may assume that the Romans would have made the necessary five-day adjustment already in 8 CE or shortly afterwards: it would be odd if they had noticed the mistake but failed to do anything about it.

Various attempts have been made to explain (or explain away) the remaining three days. The Vatican explanation is that the adjustment had been calculated starting from the time of the Council of Nicaea (325 CE). Although this explanation works arithmetically, and although it might even be an historically accurate description of the conscious intention at the time of the reform, it does not resolve the contradiction but instead simply relocates it to the time before Nicaea. Another explanation is that during antique Roman times the first point of Aries was not yet fixed to any particular day in the calendar, or alternatively, that it was fixed at 18 March. Both these theories are disproved by the fact that Augustus (Octavian) was, by his own account, born on the day of the autumnal equinox, that is, on 23 September. A more adventurous explanation assumes that, in the course of the Dark Ages, Europe somehow gained a book-entry of nearly three surplus centuries, and that in fact we are now living in the opening years of the 18th century.[27]

As was perhaps to be expected, the Gregorian reform came into effect at first only in the predominantly Roman Catholic countries of Europe, i.e. in France, Italy, Luxembourg, Portugal and Spain; within the next two years in Belgium, the Catholic areas of the Low Countries and the Catholic mini-states of Germany; and finally three years later in Hungary. The Protestant countries resisted for over a century: Denmark (including Norway and the North Atlantic possessions), the remainder of the Low Countries and the rest of the German mini-states adopted the reform toward the beginning of the 18th century, followed by Great Britain and its colonies (including the later United States) in 1752, Sweden a year later, Japan in 1873 and Egypt in 1875. Switzerland required no less than 230 years (1582–1812) to complete the changeover. The Eastern Orthodox countries couldn't bring themselves to accept the new calendar until well into the 20th century: Albania, Bulgaria, Romania, the Baltic countries, the USSR and Greece joined between 1912 and 1923, along with China and Turkey.

The Gregorian calendar has evolved from an original lunar calendar with a compromise solution for the discrepancy between the solar and lunar cycles, different in detail but similar in principle to the 360-day round year with its twelve 30-day round months. In the case of the Julian/Gregorian calendar, eleven or twelve *epagomenae* (complementary days) dispersed as equally as possible throughout the year serve to extend the 354 days of the twelve regulated moon cycles just enough so that the total year length is as nearly as possible equal to the length of the solar year. In comparison with the round year, the improved correspondence of this calendar with the solar year compensates for the somewhat more complicated handling involved in including months with alternating numbers of days.

Semitic calendar systems

The calendars in the Semitic cultural area are derived from two systems of scaling, both of which are mentioned in the Bible: one based on solar and lunar scales,[28] the other based on the regulated (seven-day) week. Both of these have co-existed side by side, unreconciled, over thousands of years.

It may be assumed that both systems extend back into pre-biblical (i.e. prehistoric) time. The measure of the moon was derived from the *interlunium* (new moon)→[29] and resulted in months with alternately 29 and 30 days and thus a calendar with a total of 354 days. Given a lunar calendar in this form, two sorts of adjustment are necessary if it is to stay even moderately in line with the natural phases of the sun and the moon. Since the synodic month with its 29.5305891 days is somewhat longer than the average 29.5 days of the calendar months, one calendar month should be augmented by one day after a lapse of at most 33 months; and every second or third year would require the intrusion of an intercalary month in order to prevent the calendar year from slipping backwards through the seasons. (Since the course of the month follows the lunation as closely as possible, it is not feasible to align the new year on a preordained day such as the first day of spring.) The differences between the various Semitic calendars still used today are largely to be found in their respective methods for dealing with these two requirements.

The measure of the week results from the division of the year into four seasons of 91 days each, each of which can then be further divided either by seven or by thirteen. There are thus two theoretical possibilities for further subdividing the season, and both in fact occur in history:

– The Egyptians, for example, utilized in addition to the round year a system whereby the quarter-year was divided into seven units of thirteen days each,[30] plus supplementary days for the purpose of alignment with the solar year.

- In the semitic world the subdivision was just the reverse: every season consisted of thirteen weeks of seven days each.

In contrast to lunar-based scales, the biblical symbolism of Creation and the Mosaic laws rule out the possibility of a synchronization of the scale of the week with the solar year: the rhythm of the week simply continues perpetually, and every year (however defined) typically begins on a different day of the week. The 'immunity' of this septadian rhythm is unambiguously confirmed in the Decalogue:

> Remember the sabbath day, to keep it holy. Six days shalt thou labour, and do all thy work: But the seventh day is the sabbath of the Lord thy God: in it thou shalt not do any work, thou, nor thy son, nor thy daughter, thy manservant, nor thy maidservant, nor thy cattle, nor thy stranger that is within thy gates: For in six days the Lord made heaven and earth, the sea, and all that in them is, and rested the seventh day: wherefore the Lord blessed the sabbath day, and hallowed it.[31]

It is fruitless to speculate in what fashion or to what degree the pre-biblical rhythm of the week stands in relation to the holiness of the number seven. It is true that this number occurs time and again in conjuction with the Creation in all known revealed religions: the Zoroastrian world consists of seven stone circles, the Islamic Heaven is sevenfold[32] and the Creation took place in seven ages (*ayyám*).→[33] Joseph's dream springs to mind, with its seven well-nurtured and seven lean cows, representing two cycles of seven years;[34] or the response of Eliphaz to Job's lamentation: 'He shall deliver thee in six troubles: yea, in seven there shall no evil touch thee;'[35] or of the promise of Isaiah: 'Moreover the light of the moon shall be as the light of the sun, and the light of the sun shall be sevenfold, as the light of seven days, in the day that the Lord bindeth up the breach of his people, and healeth the stroke of their wound.'[36] A literal interpretation of these biblical passages would require either the denial of a direct connection or an understanding of the week as an allegorical divine token. An allegorical interpretation leaves the question open – without compromising personal belief – with regard to how far the notion of the prehistoric solar week as a 'complete unit (of time)' has been integrated into traditional Abrahamic symbolism.

The Jewish calendar

The twelve months of the Jewish calendar are:[37]

1	Tishrei	7	Nisan
2	Cheshvan	8	Iyyar
3	Kislev	9	Sivan
4	Tebeth	10	Tammuz
5	Shebat	11	Av
6	Adar (I)	12	Elul

The months alternate for the most part between 30 and 29 days, starting with 30; the Jewish calendar is in its structure a regulated lunar calendar. The second and third months (*Cheshvan* and *Kislev*) vary in length, consisting of 29+29, 29+30 or 30+30 days, depending on circumstances, thus resulting in a common year of 353, 354 or 355 days and an approximate agreement between the month and the lunation. An intercalary month, *Adar II* (immediately following Adar I) is responsible for maintaining parity between the calendar and the solar year, so that the start of the year on 1 Tishrei always remains within proximity of the first day of autumn. Adar II always has 29 days, and whenever it occurs Adar I has 30 days instead of the usual 29. This arrangement results in a leap year with 383, 384 or 385 days. The frequency of the leap year is determined on the basis of the Metonic Cycle: in every series of 19 years there occur seven intercalary months, namely in the years 3, 6, 8, 11, 14, 17 and 19.[38] Although it is possible to suspect late Hellenistic influence in this ruling, it more probably has a Mesopotamian origin.→[39]

In light of the above, one can no more speak of a true annual calendar realignment with regard to the Jewish calendar than one can with regard to the Gregorian: the adjustment of the year follows a strict formula which, because of the inexactitude of the Metonic cycle, results in either a slowly increasing *epact* (alteration in the moon's phasal age at the start of the new year) or in a gradual slipping of the beginning of the 19-year cycle away from the equinox. Also, the modern Jewish calendar realigns its months with the lunar cycle only once a year, which of course implies that the careful orientation of each individual month on the new moon has in the meantime been abandoned. In addition, alignment has the primary function of determining the day of the week on which the year begins: the number of days in the months of Cheshvan and Kislev are worked out according to a complicated series of rules devised to guarantee that a holy day never occurs on a Sunday.[40] As late as post-biblical antiquity, each month began on the day of the new moon, the occurrence of which was determined on the basis of reliable witness accounts, and celebrated with special ritual observances (sacrifice, abstention from work).[41] The regulated day-count was introduced subsequently, but the liturgical significance of the new moon has been retained to this day.[42]

The fact that the intercalary month always occurs in the vicinity of the vernal equinox lends support to the supposition that the Semitic year began in spring at some period in the past. There exists a biblical reference to the festival of *Pesach* in the first month.[43] Pesach – a springtime celebration from which the Christian Easter evolved – occurs in the month of Nisan; this passage of the Bible appears to suggest that 1 Nisan instead of 1 Tishri once counted as the beginning of the year, a reading which is confirmed by another biblical passage which characterizes the month Shebat as the eleventh month.[44] But there is also a biblical reference to the 'feast of ingathering, which is in the end of the year'[45] – in other words, in the vicinity of the autumnal equinox. The Babylonian name of the first autumn month, *Tashritu*, is derived from s̲h̲urri, 'to begin'[46] (cf. Arab. s̲h̲ara'a). This fact appears to indicate that the Babylonian new year also occurred in autumn. At different times in biblical history the start of the year was associated with either spring or autumn. The scholars discuss this matter in the Talmud, without however offering a definitive conclusion. The autumnal beginning first gained the upper hand in the period of the Mishnah (3rd century CE).[47]

The definition of the year, too, has fundamental religious meaning in Judaism. In addition to the concept of a sabbath *day* there exists the sabbath *year*,[48] also called *sabbath of the land*:

> When ye come into the land which I give you, then shall the land keep a sabbath unto the Lord. Six years thou shalt sow thy field, and six years thou shalt prune thy vineyard, and gather in the fruit thereof; but in the seventh year shall be a sabbath of rest unto the land, a sabbath for the Lord: . . .[49]

Additionally, there exist the concepts of the *sabbath of years* and the *year of jubilee*:

> And thou shalt number seven sabbaths of years unto thee, seven times seven years; and the space of the seven sabbaths of years shall be unto thee forty and nine years . . . A jubilee shall that fiftieth year→[50] be unto you: ye shall not sow, neither reap that which groweth of itself in it, nor gather the grapes in it of thy vine undressed . . . In the year of this jubilee ye shall return every man unto his possession.[51]

From these and earlier quotations it is evident that the Jewish year is oriented on the seasons. The lunar month prevents an annual realignment which is exact to the day, but the discrepancy between 1 Tishri and the autumnal equinox is never more than half a month in length.

Jewish chronology begins with the Creation, which according to Jewish biblical exegesis took place 5,000 years before the year 1240 CE, i.e. in 3761 BCE; for example, the year 2000 according to the Gregorian calendar is equivalent to most of the Jewish year 5760 plus the beginning of 5761 (1 Tishri 5761 – New Year – is equivalent to 30 September 2000).

Note that the method of date conversion described here facilitates the conversion between Jewish and Julian/Gregorian dates CE (here: $2000 - 1240 = 760 + 5000 = 5760$).

The Jewish day begins at sunset. This practice, too, derives its authority from the Bible:

> And God said, let there be light: and there was light. And God saw the light, that it was good: and God divided the light from the darkness. And God called the light Day, and the darkness he called Night. And the evening and the morning were the first day.[52]

> [with reference to the day of atonement] . . . in the ninth day of the month at even, from even unto even, shall ye celebrate your sabbath.[53]

The days of the week don't have names; following the Book of Genesis, i.e. with reference to the seven days of Creation, they are simply numbered consecutively, beginning with Sunday. Saturday, the final day of the week, is also called '(the day of) the Sabbath':

Sunday	*Yom Rishon*
Monday	*Yom Sheni*
Tuesday	*Yom Shlishi*
Wednesday	*Yom Revi'i*
Thursday	*Yom Chamishi*
Friday	*Yom Shishi*
Saturday	*Yom Shevi'i* or *(Yom ha)Shabbat*

From time to time there existed differences of opinion regarding the liturgical significance of the rhythm of the week. Originally, the Jews had recognized only the seven-day week, alongside the natural solar year. The solar calendar was brought into the homeland for the first time in 538 BCE by Jews who had fled to Egypt about 50 years earlier following the destruction of Jerusalem by Nebuchadnezzar and who now felt it safe to return. The Egyptian calendar consisted of twelve months of 30 days each plus five intercalary days, a total of 365 days per calendar year. The Jews discarded the intercalary days and introduced in their place an additional day into every third month; in this fashion a calendar emerged which had four seasons of 91 days or thirteen weeks each. Both calendars – the lunar calendar and this 364-day solar calendar – probably existed side-by-side for centuries, the solar calendar being used to administer temple worship and general religious matters, whereas the lunar calendar was used in trade and politics and, at least partly, for everyday affairs. It was not until 167 BCE that the solar calendar gave way to the lunar calendar for temple worship,[54] an incident which polarized the Jewish community and thus contributed to the founding of the Essene Union around 150 BCE.[55] The Essenes rejected the lunar calendar, preferring the pure week-based calendar devoid of supplementary or intercalary days. Although it is true that this calendar wandered backwards slowly through the seasons, for the Essenes it was more important that every holiday fell on the same day of the week each year and never on a Sunday – a simple and self-regulating system, free of dependency on Temple clerics responsible for carrying out the complicated leap-year calculations for the lunar calendar.

The use of multiple calendar systems within the Jewish community during the late biblical period did not arise out of disagreement over the implementation of calendar reforms, as was the case in the Christian and Zoroastrian communities. Instead, the two calendar systems, both of which had long flourished in parallel, were inexorably bound with one or the other of two rival points of view regarding the correct – that is, the legal – observance of temple worship.

The Islamic calendar

The wide-ranging parallels between the Jewish and the Islamic lunar calendars make it possible to compare the two calendars directly and thereby to highlight their differences all the more clearly. First the similarities:

- The calendar possesses twelve lunar months, the numbers of whose days alternate between 30 and 29, beginning with 30.
- The month begins with the interlunium.
- The seven-day rhythm of the week is perpetually constant.
- The day begins at sunset.

The twelve Islamic months are:

	Name of month	Meaning
1	Muḥarram	holy, sanctified
2	Ṣafar	yellow, pale
3	Rabí'u'l-Awwál (Rabí' I)	first Spring
4	Rabí'u th-Thání (Rabí' II)	second Spring
5	Jumádá'l-Úlá (Jumádá I)	start of the torpidity
6	Jumádá'l-Ákhirat (Jumádá II)	end of the torpidity
7	Rajab	avoidance, shunning
8	Sha'bán	ingathering, collection
9	Ramaḍán	scorched (earth)
10	Shawwál	becoming scarce
11	Dhu'l-Qa'dat→[56]	possessor of the seat
12	Dhu'l-Ḥijjat	possessor of the pilgrimage

For the Muslim, the twelve-month cycle represents a unit of time ordained by God; as a result, the Islamic calendar has no intercalary month, and the months thus roam through the seasons. An Islamic year has a mean length of 354.3670692 days (the 354 days plus gain through realignment, see below), or 10.8751308 days less than a solar year: 1 Muḥarram thus completes a backward cycle through the seasons on the average once every 33.585 years.

By contrast, the calendar of the *jáhiliyyat* ('time of ignorance/ paganism', that is, the pre-Islamic period on the Arabian peninsula) was adjusted to accord with the seasons through the intercalation of a complete month every two to three years; it resembled in this respect the Jewish calendar, a fact which suggests a common Babylonian origin. The names of the months still bear reference to the seasons in which they originally occurred: Rabí' I and Rabí' II in spring; Ramaḍán, when the earth is plagued by aridity and heat. Other months suggest stations in the semi-nomadic life of the cattle-drivers: Sha'bán, the time when the herds are gathered together; Shawwál, the month of the feeding of cattle with dry fodder, etc. Aside from the new liturgical significance ascribed to certain of the months – especially the time of fasting during Ramaḍán and the *ḥajj* (pilgrimage) during the month of D̲h̲u'l-Ḥijjaτ – one can at best speak of an Islamic calendar reform. The sacrosanctity of the months of Muḥarram, Ramaḍán, D̲h̲u'l-Qaʻdaτ and D̲h̲u'l-Ḥijjaτ also has its origins in pre-Islamic times;[57] these were the months during which war, feud and blood revenge were forbidden, allowing the Arabs to pursue their business, to visit the market-place and to go on pilgrimage to the *Kaʻba*τ in relative security.[58] Since the details were known to everyone, there was no need to spell them out in the Qur'án.→[59] In short, the 'reform' consisted solely in the discontinuation of the practice of intercalation, in accordance with a Qur'ánic verse:

> The number of months, with God, is twelve in the Book of God, the day that He created the heavens and the earth; four of them are sacred.[60]

The Arabic word for 'month' (*s̲h̲ahr*) also means 'new moon', which would appear to suggest that the months are to be kept painstakingly in alignment with the moon. Nevertheless, the method for ascertaining the advent of the new moon – or rather the crescent following the new moon – is not uniformly laid down. Muslims in some countries rely solely on astronomical calculations, in other countries they require confirmation of sighting by reliable witnesses in good standing, analogous to the ancient Jewish practice.[61] Whatever the method employed, the day of the first appearance of the new moon crescent is then the first day of the month. During the lifetime of Muhammad, the beginning of each and every month was determined strictly according to observation, in compliance with the Qur'ánic verse:

> It is He Who made the sun a radiance, and the moon a light, and determined it by stations, that you might know the number of the years and the reckoning (*ḥisáb*).[62]

The more practical and convenient regulated months replaced the natural months some time shortly after the death of Muhammad, but the sighting method has been retained in order to avoid an epact at the beginning of the year: should the new moon not be verified during the course of the day following 29 Dhu'l-Ḥijjaʇ, then this month is prolonged for one additional day and 1 Muḥarram is postponed accordingly. Nowadays the alignment is carried out with reference to astronomical calculation (a practice which in no way contradicts the Qur'án); the entire Islamic world has agreed on Cairo as the place of reference and the renowned Al-Azhar University as the deciding authority for the determination of New Year's Day.[63]

With regard to the determination of the period of fasting, custom appears to vary strongly from one country to another. The possibilities for the timing of the fasting period range from the traditional sighting method, through the use of astronomical conventions, to the acceptance of the – regulated – month boundaries. In both of the first two instances, the month of Ramaḍán begins and ends with the observed or calculated new lunar crescent, and the two neighbouring months are lengthened or shortened as necessary. Since this observation or calculation is based on local circumstances, the start and the end of Ramaḍán will vary from place to place. Different Islamic groups in one and the same country (especially in the diaspora) – even in the same neighbourhood or place of work – might orient themselves according to different criteria or authorities and thus fast on different days.

The names of the days of the week are:

Yawmu'l-Aḥad	Sunday
Yawmu'l-Ithnayn	Monday
Yawmu'th-Thaláthá'	Tuesday
Yawmu'l-Arbi'á'	Wednesday
Yawmu'l-Khamís	Thursday
Yawmu'l-Jum'aʇ	Friday
Yawmu's-Sabt	Saturday

Yawmu'l-Jum'aʇ (the sixth day of the week) means 'the day of assembly', by which the common Friday prayer is implied. In all other cases the

Arabic denotations mean in effect 'the first, second . . . seventh day'; furthermore, the numeric component of the word for Sunday is grammatically singular, that for Monday is dual, and for Tuesday and Wednesday they are plural. Thus Sunday is, etymologically speaking, the initial day of the week, in agreement with the Jewish and Gregorian calendars. To the Muslim, however, Friday is the 'natural' first day of the week; it is the day of prayer and commemoration, the day of the *hijraτ*, Muhammad's emigration from Mecca to Yathrib, later called Medina (*al-madínaτ*, 'the city [of the Prophet]'). The *hijraτ* also constitutes the starting point for Muslim chronology. For this reason the Islamic calendar is also called the *hijrí calendar*. This description is ambiguous, however, since the Iranian national calendar is also called a *hijrí* calendar on the strength of the same criterion.

3

The Time of Day

A study of the development of the measurement of time would be incomplete without a consideration of techniques for the measurement and calibration of subdivisions of the day. In addition, the development of these techniques exhibits noteworthy interfaces with the evolution of the calendar.

The basis for the subdiurnal measurement of time is, once again, the sun and the celestial sphere. Daytime and night-time are respectively divided first into halves (marking off the period before or after midday or midnight), then quartered; finally, the division of the remaining quarter-portions into thirds yields temporal units called 'hours'. There is incidentally an interesting parallelism between this conscious partition of the day into twelfths and the derivation of the 48 points of the compass, whose names exactly reflect their subdivision: the arc between two cardinal points is first divided in two (e.g. northeast lies half-way between north and east), the halves are once again halved (e.g. north-northeast lies half-way between north and northeast), and finally the quarters are divided into thirds (e.g. north-northeast by north and north by east subdivide the field between north and north-northeast). This suggests a general-purpose technique of stepwise refinement by which any expanse can be quickly apportioned by eye into twelve parts.

In addition to that, the four spread-out fingers of one hand encompass a span which, with the arm held straight, is equivalent to one twelfth of the length of the arc from horizon to horizon; this circumstance gives rise to the so-called 'cock-strutting' method by which the hourly passage of the sun, the moon, the polar stars and the zodiacal constellations can be gauged without the aid of instruments. The German word *Stunde* is related to the word *Stand* and refers to the position of the sun or the stars. (The Latin word *hora* [Eng. 'hour', Fr. *heure*] comes from the Greek and simply means 'a twelfth part of a day or night'.)

It is not possible to determine whether or not there is a causal relationship between the division of the year into twelve portions and the similar division of the day or the night. The number twelve was in any case a mystic number for the Babylonians, consistent with the division of the day into 2×12 hours, the hour into 5×12 minutes and the minute into 5×12 seconds.[1]

During the hours of sunlight two initial quantities are necessary to determine the current nominal hour: the midday position of the sun (as revealed for example by the gnomon or adapted from the most recent actual measurement) and the horizontal plane, determined perhaps using a water level. The current position of the sun relative to these two coordinates reveals the time of day. This is in principle exactly how a sundial works: differences are to be found primarily in the manner in which different sundials account for the seasonally conditioned alteration in the path of the sun. Things are even simpler at night: once one knows which orientation of the stars is valid for midnight for the current day, one need merely note its deviation from the current orientation.

Note that the daylight hour was originally a 'natural' unit of time (the so-called *temporal hour*); its duration depended on the season of the year. The period of time between sunrise and sunset was invariably divided into twelve equal portions, each of whose absolute duration was greater in summer than in winter. By contrast, the night hour tended to be more constant, since the apparent rotation of the celestial sphere is not influenced by the season (discounting of course the slight variation caused by the elliptical orbit of the earth around the sun), which implies that there were nominally more night hours in winter than in summer.→[2] The sum of the daytime and night-time hours amounted to exactly 24 hours in the modern sense on only two days of the year. The result was a discrepancy in the absolute length of the hour during the transition between daytime and night-time. This discrepancy was in earlier times not easily measurable, since a 'blind period' occurs between the observable night sky and the moment of the rising or the setting of the sun. But that is a problem only if the time of day is perceived as a calibrated continuum, a concept which did not exist at the time.

In Europe, the time of day didn't become regulated until the development of the mechanical clock during the late mediaeval period, as a result of which the solar day became apportioned equally into twenty-four so-called *equinoctial hours*. The advantage of mechanical clockwork over hour-glasses and water clocks, which had existed for centuries, was to be found primarily in its long interval of uninterrupted performance. A weight which provides the necessary energy input to drive the mechanism will continue to function perfectly constantly until it reaches an obstruction (such as the floor). Building a clockwork for example into a high tower not only enhances its visibility, it also provides for continuous operation over days and weeks on end before requiring attention. A mechanical failure tolerance of several minutes a day would be perfectly tolerable, since the clocks could be adjusted on a daily basis in accordance with the position of the midday sun. The result was that every city, every village maintained its own time, midday being signalled to everyone in hearing distance for example through bell-ringing or cannon fire. From then on, as dictated by the new circumstances, the day was no longer divided primarily into two typically unequal portions called daytime and night-time, but instead into the two halves of the day between the two meridians (from the Latin *meridies* or *(tempus) meridianum*, 'midday'), since in accordance with the requirements of the mechanical timekeeper the period between midday and midnight always makes out precisely one half of the length of the day, regardless of the season of the year.

This development proved convenient for those calendars which were (or could become) meridional, but much less so for *occidental* calendars (from the Latin *occidens, (sol) occidentis*, 'setting', therefore 'the setting sun': the word as used in the present study refers exclusively to the axis sunrise/sunset and has nothing to do with the Occident, i.e. the West). In particular, the meridional reorientation of the time axis presented no ideational problems for communities in the West, whose calendar is virtually devoid of non-pagan symbolism, nor for the Persians, whose national calendar was introduced subsequently to this reorientation and for which meridionality is an inalienable feature (see 'The Iranian national calendar' in Chapter 2). By contrast, the occidental orientation of both the Jewish and the Islamic calendar is scripturally prescribed (see 'Semitic calendar systems' in Chapter 2) and therefore immutable. As a result, the concept of 'day' in these calendars is incompatible with definition of the day as the time interval between two midnights. The practical difficulties which this circumstance presents will be discussed in detail in Chapter 7.

In the Ottoman Empire, the introduction of the mechanical clock in the fifteenth century at first resulted merely in the transition from temporal to equinoctial hours,[3] the traditional occidental (*ghurûbî*, Turk. *gurubi*) timekeeping involving little more than setting the clock to 12:00 at sunset instead of at midday. Needless to say, the fact that sunrise and sunset were almost never exactly twelve equinoctial hours apart made nonsense of the division of the day into two twelve-hour portions, but the incidental retention of this design element of clocks initially imported from Europe facilitated the later introduction and spread of meridional (*zawâlî*, Turk. *zevali*) timekeeping, which from the middle of the nineteenth century onward increasingly took root in conjunction with the 'international' (i.e. Julian, later Gregorian) calendar, so that by the end of the century both systems were being used side by side,[4] personal (and institutional) preference being as much a matter of circumstance as it was of religious identity – just one facet of the *alaturka/alafranga* (Turkish vs. European) lifestyle controversy which raged throughout the period of the Tanzimat and beyond.[5] The fact that occidental timekeeping necessitated daily adjustment of clocks and watches on account of the shifting time of sunset was of no decisive disadvantage vis-à-vis meridional timekeeping, considering that the efficacy of affordable clocks and watches was in either case conditional on regular synchronization with, for example, a tower clock in the near vicinity. Neither system was of any particular use for liturgical purposes, the call to prayer (*adhân*) traditionally being scheduled on the basis of experiential criteria (position of the sun, degree of darkness, shadow length), later by a professional timekeeper (*muwaqqit*, Turk. *muvakit*),[6] who calculated local prayer times in advance with the aid of astronomical tables. This state of affairs continued until early in 1926, when the Gregorian calendar and mean time (see below) became the official standard throughout the Turkish republic[7] and *ghurúbí* time-keeping was no longer publicly supported.

The Jewish community continues to this day for liturgical purposes to employ the ancient temporal hours (*zmanim*) in conjunction with the Jewish calendar,[8] maintaining strict disjunction between halachic and civil timekeeping.

For the global-scale seafaring which blossomed in the 17th and 18th centuries it became increasingly necessary for navigators to be able to determine the longitudinal position of their ships (latitudinal calculation had never been a problem). The process is basically simple: one compares the time at one's current location with the local time at some point of reference whose longitude is known; the time difference can in turn be re-expressed as the longitudinal difference between the two locations. This method presupposes instruments capable of keeping precise time. Stationary clocks had long existed which were correct to one or two seconds in the month, and by the final third of the 18th century maritime chronometers maintained a failure tolerance of less than 8 seconds per day, even in the most extreme environments. But precise measurement is not enough: the process also requires a method of calibrating time which can get along without constant readjustment. Solar time is not practical for this purpose, since the absolute duration of the day varies slightly from one day to the next, primarily because of the elliptical orbit of the earth around the sun. The solution lay in the introduction of *mean time*, by which the duration of the tropical year is divided by the average number of days in the year (i.e. by taking leap years into account) to yield a mean day length, whose subsequent sub-division by 24 results in a constant hour length. The reconciliation of the discrepancy between mean time and solar time, called the *equation of time* (see also 'Occidental time' in Chapter 7) was then made available in tabular form to permit the transformation of the solar time calculated on board on the basis of the heavenly bodies into its mean time equivalent, which in turn could be compared with the reference time shown on the ship's chronometer (which was synchronized with the 'mother' chronometer at home port).

Note that, in addition to the equation of time, a potential difference of up to one second can occur between the calculated and actually occurring hour angle of the sun on account of the irregular rotation of the earth. This difference is made up of:

- variation in the rate of thaw in the polar regions. A fluctuation of ± 0.3 arc seconds (± 0.02 temporal seconds) remains after taking into account the mean annual periodical variation of + 0.9 arc seconds in July and − 0.75 arc seconds in November; and

- the nutation constant of ± 9.21 arc seconds (0.614 temporal seconds) divided over the entire period of nutation. This constant could, however, be completely accommodated in an appropriately enhanced equation of time.

Shifts in the liquid earth mass, which currently can be neither calculated in advance nor quantified on the basis of precedence (in contrast, for example, to the characteristics of global thaw), are not included in the calculation. However, the resulting deviations, which can amount to several temporal minutes, accumulate only very slowly over a period of many years.

Up until the 19th century, mean time remained primarily a maritime technique; otherwise natural solar time prevailed, as it 'always' had. With the development of the railway, however, the pressure for an equivalent standardization of time on land became ever more acute. In face of the not inconsiderable distances sometimes involved, in particular for east-west routes, railway companies adopted mean time for their timetabling, thus propagating the novel timescale first among the travelling public, then gradually in society in general.

Toward the middle of the century, normal (mean) time was introduced in England as the legal system of time calibration,[9] but it wasn't until the Standard Meridian Convention in 1884 that standard mean time, together with the twenty-four time zones, the prime meridian (0°) through Greenwich, and the 180th meridian as the basis for the international date line, became the international standard. In addition, the convention of dividing the day into two twelve-hour portions was abandoned, the full hours being numbered henceforth from 00:00 to 24:00: a sensible step, since mean time bears no direct relationship to the meridian of solar transit. It is an irony of history that, to this day, the English-speaking peoples, who had been the staunchest proponents of the introduction of an international convention based on mean time, retain for their own civil timekeeping the semidiurnal method of indicating the hours.

PART II
THE BADÍ' CALENDAR

4

An Overview

The calendar which the Báb revealed and named the *Badí' calendar* is nowadays popularly referred to as the *Bahá'í calendar*. *Badí'*, an Arabic word with multifaceted meaning and complex religious connotations, cannot be translated with a single word.→¹ The stem form *bada'a* means 'to create anew', 'to bring about', 'to do for the first time'. *Badí'* is an active participle and thus means 'creating anew', 'bringing about for the first time', also in a religious sense, as well as 'wondrous', 'unique'; *Al-Badí'* occurs frequently in the Qur'án as an epithet for God.

The choice of the word *badí'* for the new calendar instead of any other of the numerous paraphrases for God has symbolic significance: the Badí' calendar stands at the beginning of a new Creation, that is, a new Era, and is closely associated with the Revelation of the Báb (see the Súratu'l-Mulk, the first Súrah of the Qayyúmu'l-Asmá'): *al-amru'l-badí'*, translated as 'wondrous Revelation' in *Selections of the Writings of the Báb*[2] and as 'revolutionary/new Cause' in the provisional translation by Stephen Lambden.[3] *Badí' calendar* can thus be understood as 'unique calendar', 'calendar of God', 'creative calendar', or better, all three together.[4] The uniqueness of the Badí' calendar is most easily appreciated by examining its properties. That it is from God is for Bahá'ís clear from the fact that it is derived directly from the revealed writings of both the Báb and Bahá'u'lláh. That the calendar is also creative is one of the main themes of this present study: creative in the sense that, through its symbolic association with different aspects of the Bahá'í religion, it can serve to represent and illustrate many of the central tenets of the Bahá'í Faith.

The Badí' calendar is not simply revealed, it is itself revelation: it is instructions for use and divine message at the same time. Symbol and object converge in the Badí' calendar in a manner which is unique in the entire revelation: the central principles of the Faith can be found in allegorical form in its structure, and its content is highly metaphorical with regard both to the omnipresent theme of the heavenly bodies and to the number symbolism which pervades it.

The full effect the Badí' calendar will have on society is hardly predictable at present or in the near future. Just as the actual unfolding of the World Order of Bahá'u'lláh will reveal to future generations aspects of practical and spiritual life which we cannot even imagine today, so too will the world-wide application of the Badí' calendar exert an influence on the physical and spiritual rhythm of life in a fashion and to a degree which we cannot yet appreciate. The Badí' calendar is *evolving revelation*: its meaning will first become fully evident to those privileged to live in the pulse of this future World Order.

Seen from this perspective, this present attempt to characterize the symbolic content of the Badí' calendar must be considered provisional and highly speculative – not least because it represents the largely personal deliberations of an individual who himself is living in, and trying to make sense of, the 'pre-Badí'' phase of the Formative Age of the Faith of Bahá'u'lláh.

The physical properties of the Badí' calendar are quickly described. The year is divided into nineteen months of nineteen days each, the day beginning at the moment of sunset. In addition, four or five intercalary days – in Arabic *Ayyámu'l-Há',*→[5] among Bahá'ís normally (and in this study henceforth) in the hybrid Persian-Arabic form *Ayyám-i Há'* – occurring immediately before the final month of the year bridge the difference between the 361 month-days and the 365 or 366 days of the solar year, which commences on the first day of spring in Teheran. The years are numbered consecutively, beginning with the year in which the Báb announced His mission on 24 May 1844, being the eighth day of the fourth month in year one of the Bahá'í Era (BE). In addition, the seven-day rhythm of the week as it is found in the Jewish, Christian and Islamic calendars as well as in the Iranian national calendar has been retained.

All Bahá'ís are familiar with these basic features, since they govern the rhythm of the private and community life of the believers. The daily prayers, the monthly gatherings (Nineteen Day Feasts), the social period (during the intercalary days), the period of fasting (subsuming the nineteenth month) and the annual New Year celebration (Naw-Rúz) occur strictly in accordance with the temporal divisions arising from this calendar. For this reason alone, the Badí' calendar is indispensable for the Bahá'í world.

At the same time, the Gregorian calendar is regularly employed by Bahá'ís at the international level and at least throughout the regions of Western Christian cultural influence, among other things for the purpose of announcing forthcoming Bahá'í activities. This practice stands in no way in contradiction to the importance of the community's own calendar; it simply reflects the predominant status of the Gregorian calendar in the contemporary world. For the practical co-ordination between the religious and secular activities of the believers and for the integration of befriended non-Bahá'ís into Bahá'í events, this practice is indispensable at the present time. It is to be expected that, to the extent to which the Bahá'í rhythm of life establishes itself both within the Bahá'í community and in the world at large, the use of the Badí' calendar will increase naturally and inevitably.

A brief history

The Báb, forerunner of Bahá'u'lláh and Himself the founder of an independent revealed religion, ordained the introduction of this novel calendar, certain details of which were later clarified and instigated by Bahá'u'lláh. Information concerning the Badí' calendar was first written down in the Persian Bayán, the 'Mother Book of the Bábí Revelation':

> ... God hath fixed the number of all years from [the time of] the Manifestation of the Bayán according to the 'Names of All Things' (= 361) and hath fixed each year at 19 months, and each month at 19 days, in order that all may behold the Letters of the Unity in 19 degrees from the Point of the entry of the Sun into the Sign of Aries until its final arrival in the Sign of Pisces.

And the first month is to be called *Bahá*, and the last *'Alá* . . . And in the first three months is the Fire of God; and in the four subsequent months, the Air of Eternity without Beginning (*Azal*); and in the six subsequent months the Water of Unification . . . ; and the subsequent six months are connected with the earth . . . And the first month is the Month of the Point, round which the (18) months of the Living revolve; its similitude amongst the months is as the Sun, while the rest of the months are like Mirrors, and it is named by God the month of *Bahá*, seeing that the splendour (*Bahá*) of all the months is included in it. For God hath set it apart for Him whom God shall manifest; and to each day thereof He hath given an affinity with one of the Letters of the Unity. And the First Day [of this first month], which is the New Year's Day (*Naw-rúz*), is the day of 'there is no god but God'.[6]

Concerning the Fast: commemorate God during 19 days of each year, at the end thereof, whilst ye are fasting.[7]

The sequence 3, 4, 6, 6 occurs numerous times in the Bayán and represents the series of letters in the individual word groups of the expression *bismi'lláhi'l-amna'i'l-aqdas* ('in the name of God, the unattainable, the most holy'),[8] transliterated BSM ALLH AL'MN' AL'QDS. Nabíl-i A'ẓam reported that the details which he had collated regarding the calendar were derived from the Báb's Kitáb-i Asmá'.[9] We know from Nabíl's explication that the Báb also specified names (*asmá'*) for the remaining seventeen months as well as for the days of the month, the days of the week and the individual years within each series of nineteen years (= 1 *wáḥid*). Moreover, the Báb gave the name *Ayyám-i Há'* (days of *há'*) to the days making up the difference between the sum of the days of the months and those of the solar year, but without explicitly defining the relationship between the Ayyám-i Há' and the rest of the calendar year. He further ordained that the day begin at sunset.

In the Kitáb-i Aqdas, Bahá'u'lláh confirmed the validity of the Badí' calendar, clarified the status of the final month of the year as the month of fasting and the first day of the first month as day of festivity at the close of the fasting period, established the chronological start of the calendar as the year of the announcement of the mission of His blessed precursor and determined the point in the calendar where the intercalary days were to occur. Ever since then, the Badíʻ calendar has been in use the world over exactly in the form specified by Baháʼuʼlláh – with but few exceptions, of which the most important had until 172 BE (21 March 2015) been the question of the determination of the first day of the year. Pending a final decision by the Universal House of Justice, the interim practice introduced during the time of ʻAbduʼl-Bahá→10 and subseqently confirmed by Shoghi Effendi→11 continued to remain in force, according to which the calendar year began for the Baháʼís in the West on 21 March according to the Gregorian calendar, regardless of the astronomical commencement of spring.→12 Although this practice implied that the fifth intercalary day was effectively a device for maintaining parity with the Gregorian calendar rather than for guaranteeing the alignment of New Yearʼs Day with the advent of spring, it did result in an equivalence between the two calendars which was constant year after year and consistent for every day of the year.

In face of this extremely convenient state of affairs it is hardly surprising that this ruling remained in force as long as it did. Moreover, although it would have been perfectly feasible to give up this one-for-one correspondence at any time without incurring any noteworthy disadvantages, the emancipation of the Badíʻ calendar from the dictates of the Gregorian calendar in fact involves far more than mere abandonment of the Gregorian leap year formula, as we shall see in Part III. In any case, the Universal House of Justice has ruled that, starting in the year 172 BE (i.e. from 21 March 2015 onwards), the first day of the Baháʼí year is to be determined for the entire world community in the manner which has hitherto been valid only for the Baháʼís in the Orient, i.e. on the first day of spring in Teheran (see details in ʻDetermining the day of Naw-Rúz using a reference spotʼ in Chapter 6; see also Appendix B and ʻThe Iranian national calendarʼ in Chapter 2).

Regarding the nature of the calendar, Esslemont explains that, ʻas in the Gregorian Calendar, the lunar month is abandoned and the solar year is adoptedʼ.[13] In the context of the Islamic culture out of whose midst the Bábí Faith arose, the Badíʻ calendar indeed represents a radical break with the strict lunar rhythm ordained in the Qur'án. The abrogation of the Islamic calendar is in itself an indication that the Báb regarded his Mission as an independent, post-Islamic movement right from the beginning. The similarity between the words *badí'at* and *bid'at* – both are derived from the same root BD'– was certainly not overlooked by the Muslims and in particular by the Shí'ites: the latter is a key concept in the controversy between 'Uthmán (the third *khalífat*) and 'Alí (the fourth *khalífat* and the first *imám*), and therefore of the schism between the Sunnites and the Shí'ites. *Bid'at* means 'innovation' in the sense of 'deviation from the pure teachings of the Qur'án', even 'heresy'. Since the Islamic lunar calendar is an integral part of the Qur'ánic teachings, from the Muslim viewpoint the Badí' calendar is truly *bid'at*. Furthermore, the name of the calendar has its parallel in the Persian expression *dawreh-ye badí'*, 'new cycle', i.e. the beginning of the first and most revolutionary of a series of divine revelations. This expression occurs in the Báb's Dalá'il-i Sab'ih (Seven Proofs).[14] This terminology appears to suggest that the Badí' calendar is to hold over the entire Bahá'í cycle, i.e. beyond the period of validity of the Dispensation of Bahá'u'lláh.

In a different sense, Esslemont's statement is not completely accurate, since the Gregorian calendar (as we have seen) is not a natural-born solar calendar, but rather a lunar calendar which has in its own way been adjusted to comply with the solar year, as had so many other historical (and prehistoric) lunar calendars as well. The Badí' calendar, structured exclusively according to solar criteria, is without historical precedence.

Bahá'í commemorations

The following solemn occasions are celebrated during the Bahá'í year, here listed in historical-chronological order:

- *Birth of Bahá'u'lláh*: at the hour of dawn[15] on 12 November 1817 or 2 Muḥarram 1233 in Teheran.

- *Birth of the Báb*: on 20 October 1819 or 1 Muḥarram 1235 in Shiraz.

- *Declaration of the Báb* (i.e. the announcement of His mission): on 8 'Aẓamaт, two hours and eleven minutes after sunset (i.e. 24 May) of the year 1 BE (1844 CE) in Shiraz (celebrated on 7 Aẓamaт prior to 172 BE). The festival of the Declaration of the Báb also commemorates the fulfilment of the Greater Covenant of Muḥammad:

> His Holiness the Prophet Muḥammad made a covenant concerning His Holiness the Báb and the Báb was the One promised by Muḥammad, for Muḥammad gave the tidings of His coming.[16]

- *Martyrdom of the Báb*: at midday of 17 Raḥmaт in the year 7 BE (10 July 1850) in Tabríz (celebrated on 16 Raḥmaт prior to 172 BE).

- *Riḍván*: the days between 13 Jalál and 5 Jamál in the year 20 BE (21 April–2 May 1863). During this time, as He was residing in a garden→[17] outside Baghdad awaiting His further banishment to Istanbul, Bahá'u'lláh announced His Mission.→[18] Riḍván, the 'Most Great Festival' (*'Ídu'l-A'ẓam*), is the holiest festival of the Bahá'í community. The festival of Riḍván also commemorates the fulfilment of the Greater Covenant of the Báb:

> The Báb made a Covenant concerning the Blessed Beauty of Bahá'u'lláh and gave the glad-tidings of His coming, for the Blessed Beauty was the One promised by His Holiness the Báb.[19]

Of the twelve days of the Riḍván period, the first, ninth and twelfth (13 Jalál, 2 Jamál and 5 Jamál) are days of rest.

- *Ascension of Bahá'u'lláh*: about three o'clock in the morning of 13 'Aẓamaт in the year 49 BE (29 May 1892) in Bahjí.→[20]

- *Day of the Covenant* (a day of remembrance): on 4 Qawl, in commemoration of the designation of 'Abdu'l-Bahá as the Centre of the Covenant. The historical reference of the Day of the Covenant cannot be assigned to a particular year: 'Abdu'l-Bahá was named by Bahá'u'lláh as His successor in the Kitáb-i 'Ahd and the Kitáb-i Aqdas, and the day to commemorate this fact was introduced during 'Abdu'l-Bahá's lifetime. The commemoration was fixed by 'Abdu'l-Bahá at 4 Qawl; this day occurs 181 days after the day of the Ascension of Bahá'u'lláh, that is, a date nearly as far away as possible from that highly solemn occasion. The Day of the Covenant was celebrated for the first time in Chicago, USA in 1901 CE.[21]

- *Ascension of 'Abdu'l-Bahá* (a day of remembrance): at 1:30 in the morning of 6 Qawl in the year 78 BE (28 November 1921) in Haifa.

With the exception of the two days of remembrance, all holy days are days of rest.

The Festival of the Twin Birthdays

The Festival of the Twin Birthdays (Persian: *'eid-e moulúd*, 'the festival of birth': note the singular) takes place on two successive calendar days, albeit from year to year at varying times within a fixed period of the year, in a manner which will be explained below.

Prior to 172 BE, the birthdays of the Báb and Bahá'u'lláh were celebrated on the calendar dates of their historical occurrence, in the Orient in accordance with the Islamic calendar, otherwise in accordance with the Gregorian calendar. As a result, the birthdays were celebrated in the West 23 days apart, on fixed days according to the Badí' calendar (5 'Ilm and 9 Qudraṭ), whereas in the Orient the celebrations always fell on two successive days, but these wandered backwards through the calendar and could occur at any time during the Badí' calendar year, frequently clashing with other commemorations and with the Fast. These phenomena result from the different year rhythms of the various calendar systems:

- The *lunar year* consists of twelve lunations (synodic lunar cycles), amounting to 354 days in a common year and 355 days in a leap year.

- The *solar year* is the time span between two vernal equinoxes, or 365 days in a common year and 366 days in a leap year.

The method adopted in 2014 for the commemoration of the births of Bahá'u'lláh and the Báb from then on retains the advantages of both methods whilst avoiding their inherent disadvantages: a rare occurrence of a compromise solution which outperforms both starting positions.

Before going into details, we must hold on to the fact that the birth of Bahá'u'lláh and the birth of the Báb took place historically 707 days apart – irrespective of calendar. What this means in terms of annual recurrence depends on which year length is assumed:

From the *lunar* perspective, Bahá'u'lláh was born on 2 Muḥarram 1233, the Báb on 1 Muḥarram 1235. That is equivalent to one day less than two complete lunar years:

$$((1235 - 1233 = 2) \times 354 = 708) - 1 = 707.$$

From the *solar* perspective, Bahá'u'lláh was born on 12 November 1817, the Báb on 20 October 1819. Since 20 October and the following 12 November are separated by 23 days, i.e.

$$(31 \ \{\text{days in October}\} - 20 = 11) + 12 = 23,$$

it follows that the two birthdays are separated by 23 days less than two complete solar years:

$$((1819 - 1817 = 2) \times 365 = 730) - 23 = 707.$$

As it happens, leap days occurred in none of the calendars involved during the historical period with which we are concerned, so we may simply ignore them here.

It is incontestable that celebrating the Twin Birthdays on two consecutive days more closely reflects the spirit of Bahá'u'lláh's remark that 'these two days are accounted as one in the sight of God'[22] than does their celebration as temporally disjoint events. Retention of this desirable characteristic presupposes the inclusion of a *lunar factor* in the calculation of the annual recurrence of these two days.

On the other hand, in a letter written on behalf of Shoghi Effendi it was stated that 'in the Future, no doubt all of the Holy Days will follow the Solar calendar, and provisions [will] be made as to how the Twin Festivals will be celebrated universally.'[23] In other words, the same calculation must also include a *solar factor*, i.e. it must relate to the start of the year according to the Badí' calendar.

The solution adopted by the Universal House of Justice was to schedule the celebration of the Twin Birthdays as the first two days following the occurrence of the eighth new moon after the day of Naw-Rúz in Teheran.→[24] This solution may seem perplexing at first, but once the principle is grasped, its historic and its symbolic associations become poignantly clear:

The vernal equinox which preceded the birth of Bahá'u'lláh occurred on 3 Jumádá'l-Úlá 1232, that preceding the birth of the Báb on 25 Jumádá'l-Úlá 1234 d.H. – in both cases in Jumádá'l-Úlá, which is the fifth Islamic month of the Islamic calendar and the eighth month preceding the start of the Islamic year on 1 Muḥarram. Thus the Báb and Bahá'u'lláh were born respectively on the first and second day after the eighth new moon following the day of a vernal equinox. By virtue of the new ruling, this historical fact is replicated each year anew.

Since in a given year maximally one complete lunar cycle (i.e. somewhere between 0,00...001 and 29.5305892 days) may lapse between Naw-Rúz and the next-occurring new moon,→[25] there is a span of at least 207 and at most 237 complete days between the end of the day of Naw-Rúz and the beginning of the two-day commemoration, which accordingly occurs some time between 18 Ma<u>sh</u>iyyat and 10 Qudrat. A welcome side effect is that the festival will never collide with other commemorative events or overlap with the period of the Fast.

The timing of the introduction of this method of scheduling the Festival of the Twin Birthdays was propitious. First of all, 1 Bahá' 172 coincided with the close of the ninth cycle of nineteen years of the first period of the Bahá'í Era (i.e. the ninth *wáḥid* of the first *kull-i shay'*: see 'Unity in diversity: The numbers nine and nineteen' in Chapter 5). Whatever symbolic significance this moment in history might be held to convey, it is in any case easy to note and remember. In addition, the celebration of the Twin Birthdays commenced in that year on 10 Qudrat, just one day later than Bahá'u'lláh's birthday would otherwise have been celebrated in the West, had the new ruling not been introduced. And finally, Naw-Rúz fell on 21 March in that year, as it had been doing all along in the West. These circumstances doubtless eased the introduction of the new ruling, at least in the West.

By 'new moon' is meant not the first light of the new moon crescent, as is the case with the Islamic calendar, but rather the lunar conjunction,[26] i.e. the moment when the sun and the moon share the same ecliptic longitude. This so-called 'dark moon' can occur up to 36 hours before the appearance of the corresponding new moon crescent, so that reckoning from the day following the lunar conjunction produces results which approximate those of the Islamic practice of counting the day during which the new moon crescent occurs. Thus the timing of the Festival of the Twin Birthdays is methodically comparable to but independent from the provisions and practice of the Islamic calendar. And since 1 Bahá' is now universally determined on the basis of the astronomic calculation of the first point of Aries, parity with – and therefore dependence on – the Gregorian calendar has likewise been abandoned. On 1 Bahá' 172 the Badí' calendar came of age.

5
Symbolic Implications

People think in symbols. Indeed, human thinking would be impossible without symbolism, a fact which is most immediately evident in language, which is in any case hardly separable from human thought. Only through symbolic implication is it possible for even the simplest of words – for example, 'tree' or 'cat' – to be associated with the entirety of the individual objects which they imply. It allows us to comprehend the sentence 'The cat was sitting in the tree,' for example, without necessarily knowing which specific cat or which particular tree is being referred to. If we consider that this scene might be observed in a modern suburb or alternatively in the African Savannah, then it becomes clear that the symbolism involved is multivariate and adaptable in a complex fashion, that symbols are coordinated with one another within systems of references, that symbols can represent symbols. Even when we are personally acquainted with the seated quadruped in question, it is only thanks to symbolism that we are able to recognize it as a cat in the first place: through our idealized, i.e. symbolic, concept of 'cat', which is modelled on all the cats we have ever experienced. Most of us will have had some initial classification problems with our very first lion, but having once successfully expanded our cat-symbol, the job becomes much easier subsequently with leopards, cheetahs and tigers.

Likewise, our ability to think abstractly is for the most part the ability to process symbols. Concepts such as 'democracy', 'surface', 'increase', 'relation', say, or 'sing', 'experiment', 'admire', 'sixteen', 'yesterday', 'respectively' or 'not', assume the ability to derive categories from a myriad of experienced scenes, actions, conditions and circumstances and to associate them with representative symbols. In particular, we are totally dependent on symbols for the description of religious experience, which in any case transcends the realm of direct sense perception or intellectual processing. The divine Word is necessarily and specifically symbolic: we are able to gain entry to its conceptual realms only through the symbols which allude to them. Precisely here lies the greatest danger with any exegesis of the revealed Word: extracted from its context, a symbolically laden expression can be interpreted almost at will.

It would be surprising if, out of the entire range of topics covered by the Bábí and Bahá'í religions, of all things the calendar were *not* symbolic – where history teaches us that the various religious communities of the past treated their calendars, particularly with respect to semiotics, with utmost care (if not always with the desired practical results). It is therefore legitimate to investigate the symbolic content of the Badí' calender as well. This does not imply that this symbolism can be interpreted independently from the context of the Writings of the Báb and Bahá'u'lláh: one must be wary of treating the calendar in any manner as either a replacement for or an extension to the revealed Word. However well the calendar may serve to represent the core teachings of Bahá'u'lláh, the justification for any particular understanding must rest on the explicitly revealed Word. The question posed here is not: 'What do the religious founders, the Báb and Bahá'u'lláh, mean by such and such?' – that would be impudent, and any attempt to answer such a question would be both speculative and insufficient. Instead, we will content ourselves with a more modest question: 'What parallels can we discover between the semiotics of the calendar and the tenets of the Bahá'í Faith?' Every answer to this question lies within the acceptable bounds of individual interpretation. In this fashion the symbolism of the calendar can become part of one's personal repertoire of learning and teaching aids, useful and legitimate to the extent that it faithfully reflects the revealed text.

The symbolism of the heavenly bodies

The Báb and Bahá'u'lláh made clear that all the Manifestations of God reveal the unadulterated divine Word and proclaim the same eternal

Truth, and that in this respect there are no differences among them:

> In the time of the First Manifestation the Primal Will appeared in Adam; in the day of Noah It became known in Noah; in the day of Abraham in Him; and so in the day of Moses; the day of Jesus; the day of Muḥammad, the Apostle of God; the day of the 'Point of the Bayán'; the day of Him Whom God shall make manifest; and the day of the One Who will appear after Him Whom God shall make manifest.[1]

> ... all the Prophets are the Temples of the Cause of God, Who have appeared clothed in divers attire. If thou wilt observe with discriminating eyes, thou wilt behold Them all abiding in the same tabernacle, soaring in the same heaven, seated upon the same throne, uttering the same speech, and proclaiming the same Faith. Such is the unity of those Essences of Being, those Luminaries of infinite and immeasurable splendour! Wherefore, should one of these Manifestations of Holiness proclaim saying: 'I am the return of all the Prophets,' He, verily, speaketh the truth. In like manner, in every subsequent Revelation, the return of the former Revelation is a fact, the truth of which is firmly established...[2]

> Beware, O believers in the Unity of God, lest ye be tempted to make any distinction between any of the Manifestations of His Cause ... Whoso maketh the slightest possible difference between their persons, their words, their messages, their acts and manners, hath indeed disbelieved in God, hath repudiated His signs, and betrayed the Cause of His Messengers.[3]

> They all have but one purpose; their secret is the same secret. To prefer one in honour to another, to exalt certain ones above the rest, is in no wise to be permitted. Every true Prophet hath regarded His Message as fundamentally the same as the Revelation of every other Prophet gone before him.[4]

What are perceived as differences between the Prophets in word and action are in fact the consequence of their having appeared at different moments in human history and accordingly having adjusted their message to the particular problems and the capacity of understanding of the people alive during the time of their respective Dispensations:

> Little wonder, then, if the treatment prescribed by the physician in this day should not be found to be identical with that which he prescribed before. How could it be otherwise when the ills affecting the sufferer necessitate at every stage of his sickness a special remedy? In like manner, every time the Prophets of God have illumined the world with the resplendent radiance of the Day Star of Divine knowledge, they have invariably summoned its peoples to embrace the light of God through such means as best befitted the exigencies of the age in which they appeared.[5]

> Know of a certainty that in every Dispensation the light of Divine Revelation hath been vouchsafed unto men in direct proportion to their spiritual capacity.[6]

Nevertheless, in the advent of Bahá'u'lláh the Bahá'ís recognize more than simply the most recent of the historical series of divine messengers. Bahá'ís believe that Muḥammad, the 'Seal of the Prophets',→[7] was the last prophet of the age which, according both to Biblical tradition and to Qur'ánic and Bahá'í teachings, began with Adam, the first of the known prophets. The nature of the message of all prophets prior to the Báb was eschatological: prophetic utterances concerning a coming end time for which mankind should prepare itself occur with astounding regularity not only in the revealed religions but also in mythologies (such as the Greek and Nordic) and in natural religions. The Báb's Message left no doubt that his Coming represents the fulfilment of the 'last day' prophesied by all divine Messengers of the past:

> When God sent forth His Prophet Muḥammad, on that day the termination of the prophetic cycle was foreordained in the knowledge of God. Yea, that promise hath indeed come true and the decree of God hath been accomplished as He hath ordained. Assuredly we are today living in the Days of God. These are the glorious days on the like of which the sun hath never risen

in the past. These are the days which the people in bygone times eagerly expected . . . These are the days wherein God hath caused the Day-Star of Truth to shine resplendent . . . These are the appointed days which ye have been yearningly awaiting in the past – the days of the advent of divine justice. Render ye thanks unto God, O ye concourse of believers.[8]

The Báb was the Herald of a new Era, a new cycle of revelation which would begin with the coming of *Man yuẓhiruhu'lláh*, 'Him Whom God shall make manifest':

> I swear by the most holy Essence of God – exalted and glorified be He – that in the Day of the appearance of Him Whom God shall make manifest a thousand perusals of the Bayán cannot equal the perusal of a single verse to be revealed by Him Whom God shall make manifest.[9]

> Indeed those who will bear allegiance unto Him Whom God shall make manifest are the ones who have grasped the meaning of that which hath been revealed in the Bayán; they are indeed the sincere ones, while those who turn away from Him at the time of His appearance will have utterly failed to comprehend a single letter of the Bayán, even though they profess belief and assurance in whatever is revealed in it or observe its precepts.[10]

'He Whom God shall make manifest' is Bahá'u'lláh, and the new Era is the era of the fulfilment of the promises of all prophets, the 'day of resurrection'. Through that infusion of divine grace and power whose source lies in the Mission of Bahá'u'lláh, mankind will overcome the hardships of dispersion and merge to an organic whole. Just as families merged to clans, clans to tribes, tribes to peoples and peoples to nations, at each stage of which process a measure of autonomy was transferred to the next higher social level, the nations will finally overcome the 'fetish of national sovereignty'[11] and grow together into a world-embracing community which no longer has room for hate, war, exploitation and the dominance of one political, social, racial or ethnic group over another. An all-encompassing social and spiritual paradigm shift[12] is in the air, such as the world has never experienced since the beginning of human society.

It is only appropriate that such a transition in human history should be accompanied by the introduction of a new calendar, one which is, as Esslemont so aptly puts it, 'free from the objections and associations which make each of the older calendars unacceptable to large sections of the world's population.'[13] But the Badí' calendar is more than expediency, more than simply an accompanying circumstance of the unfolding of a new era; it is itself an expression and a symbol of this all-encompassing change.

The calendars of previous revealed religions reflected the characteristics of the moon and the stars. By contrast, the Badí' calendar reflects the characteristics of the sun. The word 'sun' has many possible symbolic interpretations in the holy writings of all religions, not the least in Bábí and Bahá'í writings. It is sometimes a metaphor for God:

> O my Brother! A pure heart is as a mirror; cleanse it with the burnish of love and severance from all save God, that the true sun may shine within it and the eternal morning dawn.[14]

> Then, ere the nightingale of the mystic paradise repair to the garden of God, and the rays of the heavenly morning return to the Sun of Truth – make thou an effort . . .[15]

Alternatively, 'sun' often means the unity of God's Self-Revelation, since there is and will always be only one sun for the earth:

> He [the Báb] is none other but the Apostle of God Himself, inasmuch as the Revelation of God may be likened to the sun. No matter how innumerable its risings, there is only one sun, and upon it depends the life of all things.[16]

> In this city, even the veils of light are split asunder and vanish away. 'His beauty hath no veiling save light, His face no covering save revelation' (Ḥadíth). How strange that while the Beloved is visible as the sun, yet the heedless still hunt after tinsel and base metal. Yea, the intensity of His

revelation hath covered Him, and the fullness of His shining forth hath hidden Him.[17]

Similarly, the sun is a metaphor for the reality of prophethood, whose manifestation in the phenomenal world is contingent upon time but in the realm of God is timeless and unbounded:

> For God the end is the same thing as the beginning. So the reckoning of days, weeks, months and years, of yesterday and today, is connected with the terrestrial globe; but in the sun there is no such thing – there is neither yesterday, today nor tomorrow, neither months nor years: all are equal. In the same way the Word of God is purified from all these conditions and is exempt from the boundaries, the laws and the limits of the world of contingency. Therefore, the reality of prophethood, which is the Word of God and the perfect state of manifestation, did not have any beginning and will not have any end; its rising is different from all others and is like that of the sun.[18]

The Manifestations themselves are often alluded to with the words 'sun', 'Sun of Truth', 'mirror of the sun', since they are the perfect representation of God's Primal Will and in this respect indivisible from one another and from God:

> Hence the inner meaning of the words uttered by the Apostle of God, 'I am all the Prophets', inasmuch as what shineth resplendent in each one of Them hath been and will ever remain the one and the same sun.[19]

The moon does not shine in its own right, it simply reflects the light of the sun. Nonetheless the image it projects is that of itself. In addition, the luminosity of the moon and of the stars is very weak in comparison with that of the sun, and these heavenly bodies first become prominent after the sun has altogether disappeared beneath the horizon. For that reason, the words 'moon' and 'stars' often represent the spiritual leaders of past religions whose interpretations of the Messages of the Envoys of God were deemed binding for the lay believers:

> The acts of Him Whom God shall make manifest are like unto the sun, while the works of men, provided they conform to the good-pleasure of God, resemble the stars or the moon . . .[20]

However well-meaning the intentions underlying it, exegesis will always remain a human product which, according to Bahá'í understanding, may never be regarded as the inerrant interpretation of the Will of God. The custodians of all earlier revealed religions have held it necessary to interpose themselves between the lay community and the Message of God – because the revelation was only imperfectly preserved, because additional salvific rites and procedures were deemed indispensable, or because there had evolved a demand for philosophical and theological addenda with respect to topics which the revelation did not cover explicitly or which it left in some way unresolved. Especially in times of widespread illiteracy, a priestly class often represented the only feasible and effective means of propagating the divine Word. Bahá'u'lláh acknowledges the accomplishments of sincere and well-meaning clerics:

> Those divines who are truly adorned with the ornament of knowledge and of a goodly character are, verily, as a head to the body of the world, and as eyes to the nations . . . The divine whose conduct is upright, and the sage who is just, are as the spirit unto the body of the world . . . Great is the blessedness of that divine that hath not allowed knowledge to become a veil between him and the One Who is the Object of all knowledge . . .[21]

Nonetheless, the motivation of the priestly class was not always purely altruistic. The traditional corpus of belief was often expanded intentionally to cement the influence and protect the privileges of its rulers. In the course of time such amendments often distorted the original religious content beyond recognition, dimming the light of the Sun of Truth and veiling the divine Will:

> Leaders of religion, in every age, have hindered their people from attaining the shores of eternal salvation, inasmuch as they held the reins of authority

in their mighty grasp. Some for the lust of leadership, others through want of knowledge and understanding, have been the cause of the deprivation of the people.[22]

The solar symbolism of the Badí' calendar underscores the most emphatic commandment to the followers of Bahá'u'lláh: that they orient themselves directly and exclusively on the revealed Word of God. Investiture or the granting of authority to a priesthood in any form whatsoever is strictly forbidden in the Bahá'í Faith: every Bahá'í has both the privilege and the duty to find his own way through the extensive Writings of Bahá'u'lláh, the authenticity of which has been testified by Bahá'u'lláh Himself and vouchsafed with His own seal.

Just as the moon and stars had served an indispensable function in the evolution of the techniques of measuring time, so too have the priests and the learned of earlier divine Missions fulfilled an important role, so long as the general populace had a genuine need for them. The refinement of the techniques for measuring astronomical phenomena has in the meantime rendered the retention of the moon phases and zodiacal signs superfluous, if not indeed burdensome – much like the function of the priesthood in the Age of Bahá. Man no longer needs a moon or stars between himself and the Sun of Truth.

The start of the year

Just as the sun is a metaphor for the Word of God, so is the course of the solar year a metaphor for the period of validity of a divine Dispensation:

> The spiritual cycles of the Sun of Reality are like the cycles of the material sun: they are always revolving and being renewed.[23]

The advent of spring has always been imbued with special significance. In prehistoric times it played a key role in registering time, as we have seen; and for the Iranian, Kurdish and Turkish peoples of Central Asia, the first day of spring has always been a time of celebration and continues to be so today. Since the Bábí and Bahá'í religions originated in this region of the earth, the fact that the first day of spring marks the start of the Bahá'í year could easily lead to the conclusion that this is simply the adoption of an immediate cultural precedent. Later, however ('Determining the day of Naw-Rúz' in Chapter 6), we shall see that the various divine decrees with respect to the timing of New Year are coordinated with one another in such a way that the change of year at the moment of the equinox is in fact a technical necessity. But we will restrict our attention at this point to the symbolic meaning of this feature of the calendar.→[24]

The advent of spring, acknowledged in all cultures as the time of renewal and serving as the standard point of departure for the scientific definition of the year, assumes a new dimension in light of the Bahá'í teachings on progressive revelation. With each waning of the powers of the previous divine Dispensation and the dilution of its original teachings through the hand of man, there follows a time of darkness, accompanied by a moral and ethical vacuum and leading to materialism and egotism, to the loss of spiritual values, to disorientation and meaninglessness. This spiritual winter is followed by a springtime in which, with increasing impetus, darkness gives way to the growing power of the sun of renewed divine effulgence. With the coming of spring there begins symbolically a new divine cycle, a revitalization of God's Will transmitted through a new Messenger: the time of light begins anew.

> It is the same with the spiritual cycles of the Prophets [as it is with the cycle and revolution of the material world] – that is to say, the day of the appearance of the Holy Manifestations is the spiritual springtime; it is the divine splendour; it is the heavenly bounty, the breeze of life, the rising of the Sun of Reality . . .[25]

> O My servants! It behoveth you to refresh and revive your souls through the gracious favours which, in this Divine, this soul-stirring Springtime, are being showered upon you. The Day Star of His great glory hath shed its radiance upon you, and the clouds of His limitless grace have overshadowed you . . .[26]

Winter's chill has not yet been completely overcome, but the signs of its approaching end are manifest. The new revelation must overcome resistance, oppression and indolence of the heart, as well as defence of the personal interests of personages whose status and privileges are anchored in the old cycle. At the beginning there are few who turn to the new springtime, but the ultimate victory is God's Will and therefore inevitable. He who has eyes and spiritual understanding, he who recognizes the new Messenger of God and dedicates his life to Him, sees in the first signs of spring the impending time of bloom.

> When the victory arriveth, every man shall profess himself as believer and shall hasten to the shelter of God's Faith. Happy are they who in the days of world-encompassing trials have stood fast in the Cause and refused to swerve from its truth.[27]

In another sense, spring has a particular affinity with the human condition at the threshold of a new historical phase, of a decisive turning-point in the development of mankind, which has been heralded in by the Bábí and Bahá'í Revelations:

> Centuries, nay ages, must pass away, ere the Day-Star of Truth shineth again in its mid-summer splendour, or appeareth once more in its vernal glory . . . How thankful must we be for having been made in this Day the recipients of so overwhelming a favour![28]

> The turmoil now convulsing human affairs is unprecedented, and many of its consequences enormously destructive. Dangers unimagined in all history gather around a distracted humanity . . . A world is passing away and a new one is struggling to be born. The habits, attitudes, and institutions that have accumulated over the centuries are being subjected to tests that are as necessary to human development as they are inescapable. What is required of the peoples of the world is a measure of faith and resolve to match the enormous energies with which the Creator of all things has endowed this spiritual springtime of the race.[29]

This 'spiritual springtime of the race' is the transition from the period of childhood, the phase of experimenting, of learning through error, of the slow and painful acquisition of those insights which are indispensable for subsequent progress. The condition of human development at the time of the coming of Bahá'u'lláh is often compared to the advent of adolescence, the threshold of adulthood: a dangerous time, one in which the fate of mankind hangs in the balance.[30]

> The long ages of infancy and childhood, through which the human race had to pass, have receded into the background. Humanity is now experiencing the commotions invariably associated with the most turbulent stage of its evolution, the stage of adolescence, when the impetuosity of youth and its vehemence reach their climax, and must gradually be superseded by the calmness, the wisdom, and the maturity that characterize the stage of manhood. Then will the human race reach that stature of ripeness which will enable it to acquire all the powers and capacities upon which its ultimate development must depend.[31]

> The Bahá'í Faith regards the current world confusion and calamitous condition in human affairs as a natural phase in the organic process leading ultimately and irresistibly to the unification of the human race in a single social order whose boundaries are those of the planet. The human race, as a distinct, organic unit, has passed through evolutionary stages analogous to the stages of infancy and childhood in the lives of its individual members, and is now in the culminating period of its turbulent adolescence approaching its long-awaited coming of age.[32]

In this biological stage of life, the emotional level is still that of the child, whereas the physical development has already reached adult proportions. Where damage caused by youthful excesses is bound by the limited physical and material resources available to the child and thus relatively harmless, that of the adolescent can assume disastrous proportions: that is what makes the stage of adolescence so precarious. The same applies in principle to the whole of human society: still imprisoned in the habits of its past, it has meanwhile acquired the material capacity to threaten its own continued existence in numerous ways. Mankind has the choice: it can insist on perpetuating its immaturity, its superficiality and self-centredness; it can persist in maintaining its prejudices, injustices and enmities, hindering its own transition into the phase of maturity or perhaps even destroying itself in the process – or it can perhaps come to its senses in time, place its mental and material resources in the service of justice, unanimity and peace, make the way free for a new spirituality, a new orientation on divine values. It can learn to appreciate its own organic unity, learn that the prosperity of the individual depends on the prosperity of the entire human race.

> 'The days are approaching their end, and yet the peoples of the earth are seen sunk in grievous heedlessness, and lost in manifest error.' 'Great, great is the Cause! The hour is approaching when the most great convulsion will have appeared. I swear by Him Who is the Truth! It shall cause separation to afflict everyone, even those who circle around Me.' 'Say: O concourse of the heedless! I swear by God! The promised day is come, the day when tormenting trials will have surged above your heads, and beneath your feet, saying: "Taste ye what your hands have wrought!"' . . .'The day is approaching when its [civilization's] flame will devour the cities, when the Tongue of Grandeur will proclaim: "The Kingdom is God's, the Almighty, the All-Praised!"' 'O ye that are bereft of understanding! A severe trial pursueth you, and will suddenly overtake you. Bestir yourselves, that haply it may pass and inflict no harm upon you.'[33]

The events which haven taken place since the second half of the 19th century – when Bahá'u'lláh pronounced these words – have demonstrated the degree of devastation which modern humankind is prepared to endure; and yet the disasters which have so far taken place are merely a hint of its destructive capability. This destructiveness is evident not only in the perfection of waging war, but also in the ruthless exploitation of natural resources, the contamination of the earth, the sea and the atmosphere, prolific consumption by the very few in the face of the relentless onward march of hunger and misery, the globalization of ethically neutral and self-dynamic economic mechanisms,[34] the eradication of every conceivable ethic and moral orientation.[35]

The Bahá'ís understand these threatening developments as the accompanying circumstances of the '*Sturm-und-Drang*' phase of a humankind approaching maturity. Bahá'ís are oblivious neither to the marvellous scientific and technological advances of contemporary society nor to the latent spiritual potential which is destined at some unspecified time in the future to usher in the Most Great Peace prophesied by Bahá'u'lláh. Bahá'ís recognize in Bahá'u'lláh's teachings the key to the maturation of mankind, and they perceive their own greatest responsibility in making this key accessible to others. Through proclaiming the divine Message, through personal example – individually as well as collectively – and through active participation in existing organizations and institutions, Bahá'ís endeavour to give expression to Bahá'í ideals and, where possible, to redirect divisive and occasionally destructive energy into constructive and conciliatory thought and action. Bahá'ís do their best to live up to the high expectations Bahá'u'lláh has placed in them:

> 'O friends! Be not careless of the virtues with which ye have been endowed, neither be neglectful of your high destiny . . . Ye are the stars of the heaven of understanding, the breeze that stirreth at the break of day, the soft-flowing waters upon which must depend the very life of all men, the letters inscribed upon His sacred scroll.' 'O people of Bahá! Ye are the breezes of spring that are wafted over the world. Through you We have adorned the world of being with the ornament of the knowledge of the Most Merciful. Through you the countenance of the world hath been wreathed in smiles, and the brightness of His light shone forth.'[36]

The advent of spring thus symbolizes on the one hand the present condition of the whole of mankind, which stands on the threshold of its adulthood and organic unity; and on the other hand the formative role which the followers of Bahá'u'lláh are destined to assume in this process of maturation.

Naw-Rúz, the first day of spring, is inalienably bound with the characteristics of the calendar, in contrast with the remaining holy days, all of which fall on those days of the calendar year on which the events they commemorate historically occurred (see 'Bahá'í commemorations' in Chapter 4). Naw-Rúz is the Day of God:

> God has related one day in the year to Himself, and called it the Day of God ... This day is the day whereon the Sun passes from Pisces into Aries at the moment of its passing, whether it be night or day ... And that day is the day of the *Nuqta*, the 18 days following being the days of the Letters, more noble than the days of the 18 other months, each one of which is related to the decrees of all things [*kull-i shay'*].[37]

The moment of the start of the new year – i.e. at sunset at the end of the final calendar day of the old Bahá'í year – also terminates the period of fasting; that is, it is the moment at which the last of the nineteen successive daily periods of physical abstinence comes to an end. Details for celebrating the day of Naw-Rúz are not prescribed, but it is the predominant practice that Bahá'ís and friends experience this moment together in the course of an appropriately festive ceremony. Immediately preceding the commencement of the new year there is typically a programme of worship and perhaps one or more speakers, followed by the breaking of the fast with a banquet and subsequent programme of entertainment and good cheer. Thus it is usual to view Naw-Rúz principally as the ending of the fast and to mark the occasion with all due exuberance. Neither with this association nor with the joyful celebration can there be any objection: a prayer revealed by Bahá'u'lláh for the occasion of the celebration of Naw-Rúz begins:

> Praised be Thou, O my God, that Thou hast ordained Naw-Rúz as a festival unto those who have observed the fast for love of Thee and abstained from all that is abhorrent unto Thee.[38]

Naw-Rúz should nevertheless be first and foremost an occasion to contemplate the glorious Plan of God. The celebration is an ideal occasion to reflect upon the existentially important responsibility which the Bahá'í community faces in this historic phase of the coming of age of mankind. At the same time, the festival commemorates the divine assistance which has accompanied man throughout history and will continue to accompany him for all time in the future.

The perennial return of spring is – like the rainbow for the children of Noah[39] and circumcision for the children of Abraham[40] – a symbol for the renewal of the Eternal Covenant[41] between God and man, a sign of His promise to guide the destiny of human progress for all eternity, so long as mankind recognizes His Messengers and abides by their laws:

> God leaves not His children comfortless, but, when the darkness of winter overshadows them, then again He sends His Messengers, the Prophets, with a renewal of the blessed spring.[42]

> The Divine Springtime is come, O Most Exalted Pen, for the Festival of the All-Merciful is fast approaching.[43]

Just as God has made his covenant with mankind, so too does each prophet of God make his Greater Covenant with his own blessed Successor:

> The Lord of the universe hath never raised up a prophet nor hath He sent down a Book unless He hath established His covenant with all men, calling for their acceptance of the next Revelation and of the next Book; inasmuch as the outpourings of His bounty are ceaseless and without limit.[44]

As a festival, Naw-Rúz is not focused solely on the Bahá'í Dispensation, but rather addresses the entirety of the single religion of God – religion in the sense of *religio*, reverence for the one, true, unchanging God, regardless of the form which this reverence assumes and regardless of which conception of God it entails. An analogy to this perception can be found in the *Mashriqu'l-Adhkár*, the House of Worship – a place for the remembrance and the praise of God and for the mention of His names, erected by the Bahá'ís but intended for use by people of every faith. Texts and prayers from the holy scriptures of all revealed religions are chanted or recited in the House of Worship. The nine portals which encircle and enclose the central dome symbolize the equal validity of all forms of religious observance.

It is therefore only consistent that the Bahá'ís should welcome non-Bahá'ís to their Naw-Rúz festivities. It goes without saying that non-Bahá'ís are heartily welcome to other Bahá'í commemorations as well. However, the 'technical' nature of the scheduling of the festival of Naw-Rúz, which has its obvious parallel in the New Year celebrations of society in general, along with the typical accompaniment of banquet, musical presentations and other forms of entertainment, offers a more perceptible approach to Bahá'í celebrations for individuals with varying degrees of acquaintance with the spiritual content of the Bahá'í Faith than the relatively more inwardly oriented worship characteristic of the other commemorative occasions. Springtime is nature's offer to all persons regardless of their individual attitudes towards life, just as the Eternal Covenant is God's offer to all persons regardless of their religious adherence. Both are offers of growth. The outward signs of the season must be observed and the fields tended and sown, if benefit is to be derived from the potential of growth inherent in the physical springtime. In the same fashion, acceptance of the prophets of God and adherence to their divine guidance is necessary to transform the growth potential of each divine springtime into human progress.

For the present era, this means achieving the global unity of mankind and the ultimate attainment of the *Most Great Peace*, a condition which implies far more than merely political accord and the cessation of war, a time of the spiritual maturity of mankind, the ultimate fruit of the reign of divine law on earth.[45]

> If you arise in the Cause of God with divine power, heavenly grace, the sincerity of the Kingdom, a merciful heart and decisive intention, it is certain that the world of humanity will be entirely illumined, the moralities of mankind will become merciful, the foundations of the Most Great Peace will be

laid, and the oneness of the kingdom of man will become a reality. This is the great bounty I desire for you, and I pray and supplicate the divine threshold, imploring in your behalf.[46]

The association of the period of fasting with the festival of Naw-Rúz which terminates it reflects the fact that the fulfilment of the promise of God depends on our readiness to accept the holy statutes and to set our full trust in God and in Bahá'u'lláh, God's Messenger for our time. The festival of Naw-Rúz is thus not (or at least not merely) a festival of joy and pleasure, the banquet is in no way a 'reimbursement' for the abstinence endured over the preceding nineteen days. On the contrary, the celebration is a solemn symbolic act. The immediate association of obedience to God's commandment – in this case fasting – with the showering of divine grace, represented by the banquet, reflects the interrelationship between God and man, the reciprocal obligation which is expressed in the Eternal Covenant.

The vernal equinox is therefore more than a mere criterion for the definition of the year; rather, it is a sign of the absolute authority of God, a symbolic representation of the 'unerring Balance'[47] with which we are to test our *Weltanschauung* and to judge our actions. It is patently clear that a leap year formula of whatever form or complexity for the long-term synchronization of the calendar year with the seasons is insufficient to do justice to this symbolism – just as it is not enough to follow the will of God 'more or less' or to recognize the Revelation of Bahá'u'lláh 'by and large'. It is appropriate that the Bahá'í community approach the question of the scheduling of the day of Naw-Rúz with scrupulous care (see 'Determining the day of Naw-Rúz' in Chapter 6).

> The rising of the sun at the equinox is the symbol of life, and likewise it is the symbol of the Divine Manifestation of God, for the rising of the Sun of Truth in the heaven of Divine Bounty established the signal of Life for the world. The human reality begins to live, our thoughts are transformed and our intelligence is quickened. The Sun of Truth bestows eternal Life, just as the solar sun is the cause of terrestrial life.[48]

Unity in diversity: The numbers nine and nineteen

In addition to dividing the year into nineteen months of nineteen days each, the Báb ordained that nineteen years should comprise a cycle (called *wáḥid*), and that nineteen such cycles (*wuḥdán*) should comprise a period, Arabic *kullu shay'* (in Persian, *kull-i shay'*). There thus ensues a uniform and heirarchically ordered numeric system for measuring time in days, months, years and cycles within the period with the same factor for each degree of magnitude: nineteen.

Interestingly, one *wáḥid* comprises almost exactly a *Metonic cycle*, or *moon circle*; in this respect the *wáḥid* is reminiscent of the lunisolar year of Greek antiquity, albeit with an altogether different consistency (see 'Graeco-Roman calendar systems' in Chapter 2). The moon would thus be reconciled in a certain sense with the sun after all, were it not for the fact that the moon circle includes a cumulative error over longer stretches of time (roughly 1 day in 11.5 cycles).

The subdivision of the Bahá'í year into nineteen nineteen-day months can readily be explained mathematically: nineteen is that natural number whose square (361) is nearest to the number of days in the solar year (365/366). If the sole significance of the number nineteen were to be found in the convenient value of its square, however, one would have to consider that this represents but one of many possible schemes for the subdivision of the year: in comparison for example with $3 \times 11 \times 11$ (= 363), $4 \times 13 \times 7$ (= 364) or 73×5 (= 365), this choice would not even represent the closest arithmetic approximation. The continuation of this ratio in the superstructural units *wáḥid* and *kullu shay'* would then be nothing more than the construction of an artificial symmetry, however appealing this scheme might appear.

Quite apart from whatever the relationship between the number nineteen and the properties of planetary motion may or may not imply, the fact remains that for the Bahá'ís this number is laden with significance.

First, the number nineteen carries symbolic meaning. According to the *abjad* number system (see Appendix A), nineteen is the value of the word *wáḥid* (unity, one) and thus a symbolic expression of the principle of unity so central to Bahá'í belief: the unity of God, the unity of the Manifestations of God, the unity of religion, the unity of mankind.

> In every Dispensation . . . the light of Divine Guidance has been focused upon one central theme . . . In this wondrous Revelation, this glorious century, the foundation of the Faith of God and the distinguishing feature of His Law is the consciousness of the Oneness of Mankind.[49]

The *abjad* value of the word *wujúd*, 'existence', 'being', and especially 'the absolute existence of God', is likewise nineteen.

In addition, nineteen is a prime number – that is, an integer which is divisible only in a tautological sense (that is, divisible by itself or by one) – and moreover the ninth of the series of prime numbers→[50] (the number nine also has wide-ranging mystic and symbolic significance in the Bahá'í Faith).→[51] As a prime number, nineteen is therefore unitary (being indivisible) and at the same time diverse (being a multiple value) and thereby a symbolic representation of unity in diversity, the recognition of the basic individual right to cultural and social uniqueness within the framework of the fundamental unity of the human race:

> If you beheld a garden in which all the plants were the same as to form, colour and perfume, it would not seem beautiful to you at all, but, rather, monotonous and dull. The garden which is pleasing to the eye and which makes the heart glad is the garden in which are growing side by side flowers of every hue, form and perfume, and the joyous contrast of colour is what makes for charm and beauty . . . Thus should it be among the children of men! The diversity in the human family should be the cause of love and harmony . . .[52]

> O well-beloved ones! The tabernacle of unity hath been raised; regard ye not one another as strangers. Ye are the fruits of one tree, and the leaves of one branch.[53]

The square of a prime number (from the Latin *primus*, 'the first/beginning/choicest') is integrally divisible by no natural number other than its own square root (aside from the tautological cases); thus the number 361, being the square of the number nineteen, can be divided by only one natural number: nineteen. There is thus an organic mathematical relationship between the numbers nineteen and 361. And since the number nineteen represents the *abjad* value of the word 'one' (*wáḥid*), the year is also a unity: 19 x 19 = 361, 1 x 1 = 1.→54

In addition, the number 361 is the *abjad* value of the expression *kullu shay'*. This expression occurs in the Qur'án as well as in the Bábí and Bahá'í writings in the sense of a universal whole:

> To him belongs the Kingdom of the heavens and the earth; He gives life, and He makes to die, and He is powerful over everything (*'alá kulli shay'in*).
> He is the First and the Last, the Outward and the Inward; He has knowledge of everything (*bikulli shay'in*) . . .55

> This [the valley of true poverty and absolute nothingness] is the plane whereon the vestiges of all things (*kull-i shay'*) are destroyed in the traveller, and on the horizon of eternity the Divine Face riseth out of the darkness, and the meaning of 'All on the earth shall pass away, but the face of thy Lord . . .' is made manifest.56

> . . . and He, in truth, hath power over all things (. . . *wa kána'lláhu 'alá kulli shay' qadíran*).57

The number nineteen also has mystical associations. The Persian Bayán, the most important work from the pen of the Báb – is apportioned into nine *wuḥdán* with nineteen chapters each.58 In the introduction to the Bayán the Báb writes: 'God hath ordained the Creation of all things according to the "Number of All Things", and accordingly the Chapters of the Religion of the Bayán have been arranged according to the Number of All Things'.59 Since the Persian Bayán consists of only nine *wuḥdán*, it is not clear whether this statement applies to the immediate text or to the entirety of the writings of the Báb, which He also referred to collectively as the Bayán ('exposition'). The final *wáḥid* of the Bayán possesses but ten chapters – in other words, the final nine chapters of the ninth *wáḥid* are missing. The numeric value of the word *bahá'* is nine; this fact could imply a veiled reference to the coming of *Man yuẓhiruhu'lláh*, who shall be called *Bahá'* (= 9), in consideration of which the Mission of the Báb is to be understood to be 'uncompleted'. The Báb enjoined His followers to read a particular verse contained in this work once every nineteen days; the verse has to do with the recognition and acceptance of *Man yuẓhiruhu'lláh*.[60] 'Nineteen days' also means 'nineteen years' in the language of the prophets (see 'Growing demands on time calibration' in Chapter 1) and is an allusion to the space of time within which *Man yuẓhiruhu'lláh* is to appear. The public proclamation of Bahá'u'lláh's mission in fact took place in the nineteenth year following that of the Báb – as the Báb had prophesied:

> And concerning the manifestation of Him whom God shall manifest, God knows in what limit of years He will manifest him; but watch from the beginning of the Manifestation until the number of the *Wáḥid* (19) for in each year Faith in one of the letters will appear.[61]

The use of the word *wáḥid* here is more than a couched allusion: it refers not only to the *abjad* value of the word, but also concretely to the cycle of nineteen years.

The first piece of writing from the pen of Bahá'u'lláh following his mystical experience in the Síyáh-Chál is Qaṣídiy-i Rashḥ-i 'Amá' ('Poem on the Sprinkling of the [Divine] Cloud'),→[62] consisting of nineteen verses.[63]

Each of six verses of the Bahá'í Prayer for the Dead is repeated nineteen times, and the *dhikr* consists of five times nineteen repetitions of the phrase "God is the most glorious" in Arabic.→[64] A portion of *Ḥuqúqu'lláh* (a form of capital levy),→[65] calculated as nineteen per cent of the increase in wealth (after open debts have been settled and living and business expenses deducted), is complete as soon as this increase attains the value of nineteen mithqáls (Arab. *mathaqíl*) (69.192g) of gold,[66] whereby a Bahá'í mithqál consists of nineteen instead of the usual 24 nakhuds.[67]

The dowry given by a bridegroom to his bride can comprise up to five units of nineteen mi<u>th</u>qáls of gold or silver, depending on circumstances. And the twin revelations of the Báb and Bahá'u'lláh took place in the 19th century subsequent to the coming of Jesus Christ.

Nineteen is also the sum of the values twelve and seven. These are respectively the mystic number of the Mesopotamian and the holy number of the Semitic cultural area, and furthermore the numbers underlying the subdivision of the earlier calendar and time measurement systems. Coincidence or not, this fact reminds us of a substantial aspect of the Bahá'í principle of progressive revelation, i.e. that every new Dispensation builds on the foundation of the revelation preceding it and confirms its validity, while at the same time bringing something completely new.

Additionally, the number nineteen, together with the words *wáḥid* and *kull-i <u>sh</u>ay'*, preserves a direct historical connection to the mission of the Báb. The number nineteen is a central feature of the very first instruction issued by the Báb following the announcement of His mission. Having revealed the Qayyúmu'l-Asmá' (the commentary to Súratu Yúsuf), the Báb said to Mullá Ḥusayn-i Bu<u>sh</u>rú'í:

> O thou who art the first to believe in Me! Verily I say, I am the Báb, the Gate of God, and thou art the Bábu'l-Báb, the gate of that Gate. Eighteen souls must, in the beginning, spontaneously and of their own accord, accept Me and recognize the truth of My Revelation. Unwarned and uninvited, each of these must seek independently to find Me.[68]

Later, as the Báb was about to send his first supporters into the various provinces of Iran,

> ... He instructed them, each and all, to record separately the name of every believer who embraced the Faith and identified himself with its teachings. The list of these believers He bade them enclose in sealed letters, and address them to His maternal uncle ... who would in turn deliver them to Him. 'I shall classify these lists', He told them, 'into eighteen sets of nineteen names each.

Each set will constitute one váḥid. All these names, in these eighteen sets, will, together with the first váḥid, consisting of My own name and those of the eighteen Letters of the Living, constitute the number of Kull-i-Shay'...⁶⁹

At the same time, this instruction contains a reference to the revelation of *Man yuẓhiruhu'lláh*. The Báb's discourse continues:

> Of all these believers I shall make mention in the Tablet of God, so that upon each one of them the Beloved of our hearts may, in the Day when He shall have ascended the throne of glory, confer His inestimable blessings, and declare them the dwellers of His Paradise.

When one reflects that the structural principle underlying the Badí' calendar can be satisfied by no other natural number than nineteen, it appears that this number functions as a leitmotif in the Bábí Dispensation: on the one hand by virtue of the multifarious mystical and prophetic implications of the number nineteen, and on the other hand by the fact that the calendar is arranged on the basis of this same number. In other words, the structure of the calendar was already immanent in the first hour of the new revelation.

The names which the Báb gave to the months and the days of the months represent divine attributes:→⁷⁰

1	*Bahá'*		Splendour, glory
2	*Jalál*		Glory, eminence
3	*Jamál*		Beauty
4	*'Aẓamaτ*		Grandeur, greatness, majesty
5	*Núr*		Light, enlightenment
6	*Raḥmaτ*		Mercy, compassion, grace
7	*Kalimát*		Words
8	*Kamál*		Perfection
9	*Asmá'*		Names
10	*'Izzaτ*		Might, dignity, self-respect
11	*Mashiyyaτ*		Will, wish

12	*'Ilm*	Knowledge, recognition, science
13	*Qudraṭ*	Power, omnipotence
14	*Qawl*	Speech, logos
15	*Masá'il*	Questions
16	<u>Sh</u>*araf*	Honour, nobility, fame
17	*Sulṭán*	Sovereignty
18	*Mulk*	Dominion, kingdom
19	*'Alá'*	Loftiness, nobility

The first-mentioned English translation is in each case the usual rendering in Bahá'í literature and in printed calendars.

The choice of prayers revealed by the Báb, Bahá'u'lláh and 'Abdu'l-Bahá to be recited during communal worship at the start of the monthly Bahá'í gathering (the so-called Nineteen Day Feast) often reflects the theme implied by the name of the month. The extensive revealed texts which can be employed for this purpose offer endless possibilities to illuminate the divine attribute from every conceivable perspective. The didactic component, which is perforce present in every reading or recitation of holy scripture, is understandably reinforced by adherence to an underlying theme. But the texts speak for themselves, there being no additional commentary whatsoever, so that communal worship retains its character and does not run danger of degenerating into a tutorial or even a sermon.

The nineteen years of the *wáḥid* also bear names:

1	*Alif*	(A)
2	*Bá'*	(B)
3	*Ab*	Father
4	*Dál*	(D)
5	*Báb*	Gate
6	*Wáw*	(W)
7	*Abad*	Eternity
8	*Jád*	Generosity

SYMBOLIC IMPLICATIONS

9	*Bahá'*	Splendour
10	*Ḥubb*	Love
11	*Bahháj*	Delightful
12	*Jawáb*	Answer
13	*Aḥad*	Single, the one God
14	*Wahháb*	Bountiful
15	*Widád*	Affection
16	*Badí'*	Beginning, uniqueness
17	*Bahí*	Luminous, splendid
18	*Abhá*	Most glorious
19	*Wáḥid*	Unity, the number one

The names of the individual years within a *wáḥid* possess the *abjad* values of their ordinal positions: four of them – *Alif, Bá', Dál* and *Wáw* – are the names of Arabic letters, the others indicate divine attributes. It is striking how often the word *bahá'* occurs in the names introduced by the Báb: as the first day, as the first month, as the ninth and – in transmuted form – the seventeenth→[71] and eighteenth year of the *wáḥid*. In light of the particular importance of the numbers one and nine (in addition to nineteen), this fact highlights the primacy which this word occupied in the semiotics of the Báb.

It might be suspected that the names of the years comprising a *wáḥid* should at the same time represent the names of the *wuḥdán* within a *kullu shay'*, just as the names of the days and those of the months are identical. There is, however, no textual evidence known to me to support this supposition.

Mihrshahi's study,[72] which contains detailed descriptions of both the lexical and the symbolic meanings of the names of the days, months and years as well as an analysis of their occurrence in Islamic, Bábí and Bahá'í sacred writings, is an important contribution to an area which heretofore was only partially satisfied in Western literature by Walbridge's valuable but somewhat cursory explanations of the Arabic terms employed in the Badí' calendar.[73]

Ayyám-i Há' – intercalary days

The intercalary days, of which there are four in common years and five in leap years, occur in the Badí' calendar between the months of Mulk and 'Alá'. They are considered special days and are to be celebrated accordingly. Bahá'u'lláh writes:

> It behoveth the people of Bahá, throughout these days, to provide good cheer for themselves, their kindred and, beyond them, the poor and needy, and with joy and exultation to hail and glorify their Lord, to sing His praise and magnify His Name; and when they end – these days of giving that precede the season of restraint – let them enter upon the Fast.[74]

In other words, these days are dedicated to two aspects of love:

- love of one's neighbour, and

- love of God.

Neighbourly or brotherly love is expressed in the social activities associated with these days: together with relatives (*dhawí'l-qurbá*, literally 'the near ones'), the believers are to gather together for communal meals (*yaṭa'mú*), at the same time seeing to the feeding of the poor (*fuqará'*) and of those in need (*misákín*). These days of giving (*a'ṭá'*) stand in contrast to the days of abstinence (*imsák*) which are to follow. The word used to describe the time of fasting (*imsák*) is from the same root as the word for the needy (*misákín*). In this fashion, Bahá'u'lláh reminds us of a fundamental principle of social solidarity: personal abstinence during the pending time of fasting is also intended to impart a feeling for the plight of the needy. In another sense, through fasting we become more aware of our own neediness before God and dependency on His bounty, as expressed for example in the second sentence of the short obligatory prayer:

I testify at this moment to my powerlessness and to Thy might, to my poverty and to Thy wealth.

and in the prayer which ends:

All are but poor and needy, and Thou, verily, art the All-Possessing, the All-Subduing, the All-Powerful.[75]

Love of God is expressed by the praising of the Lord, which is to assume a prominent role in the gatherings. The passage from the Kitáb-i Aqdas (para. 16, quoted above) translated into English as 'to hail and glorify their Lord, to sing His praise and magnify His Name' represents expressions which, in the Arabic original, stem directly from Islamic tradition:

- *yuhallilanna*, 'he [the believer] should indeed give praise unto God', implies the formula *lá iláha illá'lláh* ('there is no god other than God');

- *yukabbiranna*, 'he should indeed honour God', refers to the formula *Alláhu akbar* ('God is great', or better: 'God is greater [than everything else]');

- *yusabbiḥanna*, 'he should indeed sing God's praise', represents the formula *Subḥána'lláh* ('Praise of (to) God');

- *yumajjidanna* means 'he should indeed extol God'.

The injunction to praise God also offers a partial answer to the question why these days are called Ayyám-i Há' (days of *há'*). The letter *há'* is a symbol for the essential reality, the divine essence (*adh-dhátu'l-iláhí*) of God, both in Islamic and in Bahá'í writings.[76] It is the first letter of the pronoun *huwa*, 'he' (or 'he is'), which in Arabic also carries the meaning 'God'; as a suffix (i.e. 'him/his') it is in fact written with this single letter. *Há'* is also the final letter of *Alláh*. The assertion *huwa'lláh* means 'He is God', at the same time, 'God is God', in full accordance with the *shahádaτ*, the Islamic declaration of belief: *lá iláha illá'lláh*, 'There is no god other than God', also in the form *lá iláha illá huwa*. The Arabic word *huwiyyaτ* ('he-ness, being he') means 'divine self-identity', also 'divine essence' – see for example Bahá'u'lláh's Hidden Words, Arabic 66, which in Shoghi Effendi's translation begins: 'O Children of the divine and invisible essence (*yá-bná'al-huwiyyaτ fí'l-ghayb*)'; and the term *Háhút*, 'sphere of the divine Ipseity', is a word form coined originally by Sufi mystics and signifying the ontological sphere consisting of the selfness of God, modelled on the names of the lower ontological realms of creation (*Láhút, Jabarút, Malakút, Násút*[77]) in conjunction with the letter *há'*.[78]

Another possible answer to the question why these days are named after the letter *há'* can be found in Tafsír-i Hú (Commentary on the phrase 'he is': *hú* is the Persian pronunciation of Arabic *huwa*, both transliterated HW), where Bahá'u'lláh writes: 'God made His name "He is" (*huwa*) the greatest of the divine designations, for it is a Mirror of all the divine Names and Attributes.'[79] Projected onto the calendar, this would suggest that the names of the months and of the days of the months, being attributes of God, are mirrored in the greatest of the designated days, the Ayyám-i Há'.

The *abjad* value of the letter *há'* is 5, which is also the *abjad* value of the word *báb*.[80] The Days of Há' immediately precede the month of 'Alá', which is the month associated with the Báb;[81] taken together, these constitute an allusion to the fact that the Báb paved the way for his successor (*Man yuẓhiruhu'lláh*), with whom the succeeding month is associated: Bahá', the first month of the year to follow, thereby terminating the 6,000-year Prophetic Era which began with Adam and initiating the Era of Fulfilment, which will endure at least 500 millennia.[82]

The basis for the calibration of time is thus represented by a steady and unvarying block of 361 days. By contrast, the Ayyám-i Há' may vary in length from year to year, thus permitting the synchronization of the calendar with the tropical year. There exists thereby a reciprocal relationship between the portion of the year consisting of month-days and that consisting of intercalary days. On the one hand, the strict constancy of the months is only possible because the Ayyám-i Há' exist; and on the other hand, it is only in the context of the constitution of the months in the Badí' calendar and the properties of the tropical year that the Ayyám-i Há' acquire their coherence and justification.

The mutual dependency between two things of different form and function which are nevertheless equivalent with respect to their higher-order unity is a frequently recurring theme in the Bahá'í writings, particularly in expositions of 'Abdu'l-Bahá:

- the relationship between man and woman;

- the agreement between science and religion;

- the balance between reason and belief;

- the role of an international auxiliary language and that of the individual national, regional and cultural languages;

- the unity and at the same time the diversity of individuals, races and cultures.

'Abdu'l-Bahá often uses the simile of the two wings of a bird to emphasize the equal value of the diverse elements and the necessity of their mutual cooperation. This principle of equivalence is also present in the concept of justice as it is understood in the Bahá'í Faith. The word 'justice' in the translations of the holy texts is used for two different words in the original language: *'adl* and *inṣáf*, which also frequently occur together: *al-'adl wa'l-inṣáf*.[83] Insofar as they express consummate divine justice, these two concepts are inseparable. In the world of creation, however, *'adl* and *inṣáf* represent two complementary facets of justice.

'Adl is the principle underlying all action of the world community of Bahá'ís. It concerns that facet of the law which governs the relationship between the community and the individual, subsuming two different concepts of justice: *iustitia distributiva* (equitable justice) and *iustitia legalis* (legal justice), that is, on the one hand the responsibilities of

the community with respect to the individual, and on the other hand the obligations of the individual to the community. This system of justice begins with the Universal House of Justice, in whose name (*Baytu'l-'Adl*) this principle is anchored, and ends with the individual believer. The law is universal, binding, and applicable without consideration of persons affected or circumstances involved:

> Know verily that the essence of justice and the source thereof are both embodied in the ordinances prescribed by Him who is the Manifestation of the Self of God amongst men, if ye be of them that recognize this truth. He doth verily incarnate the highest, the infallible standard of justice unto all creation. Were His law to be such as to strike terror into the hearts of all that are in heaven and on earth, that law is naught but manifest justice.[84]

> Beware lest, through compassion, ye neglect to carry out the statutes of the religion of God; . . .[85]

At first glance this admonition from Bahá'u'lláh appears stringent and inflexible; but without strict observance of the revealed statutes it would be impossible to preserve a notion of justice which is free from arbitrariness and protected from the dangers of manipulation, nepotism and favouritism. Bahá'u'lláh assures us that the divine law is for the well-being of mankind:

> Say: True liberty consisteth in man's submission unto My commandments, little as ye know it . . . Say: The liberty that profiteth you is to be found nowhere except in complete servitude unto God, the Eternal Truth.[86]

Moreover, *'adl* is only one half of the story: *'adl* without *inṣáf* is like a bird with only one wing.

Inṣáf, 'compensatory justice' (*iustitia communativa*, just demeanour),[87] is the translation of inner, subjective, non-quantifiable qualities of the spirit into action: love of one's fellow man, mercy, commitment to peace and freedom from prejudice, moderation in all things.

It expresses itself not only through practised restraint from engaging in backbiting and slander, but also from every inner impulse to do so. It expresses itself in the fundamental acceptance of the equal validity and the inviolability of the dignity of every human being. Inṣáf is the sum of all those principles of personal conduct which should be the hallmark of every Bahá'í in society – with respect to himself as well as to all others.

> O Son of Spirit! The best beloved of all things in My sight is Justice [*inṣáf*]; turn not away therefrom if thou desirest Me, and neglect it not that I may confide in thee . . . Ponder this in thy heart; how it behooveth thee to be. Verily justice is My gift to thee and the sign of My loving-kindness. Set it then before thine eyes.[88]

The understanding of justice which characterizes the Bahá'í Faith lends a social, indeed a political quality (in the Aristotelian sense) to the personal conduct of life, in the history of religion unique in its clarity. As complements, *'adl* and *inṣáf* are the forces which support the new World Order of Bahá'u'lláh. It would perhaps be sufficient to guarantee the *Lesser Peace* announced by Bahá'u'lláh if the principles of social order implicit in *'adl* were to prevail.[89] But the promised goal of mankind, the *Most Great Peace*, will be obtained only after the social maturity and the spiritualization of mankind has taken place – in other words, when *inṣáf* has finally made its way into the hearts, the thoughts and the actions of individuals across the planet.

This conception of justice is also reflected in the first sentence of the short obligatory prayer:

> I bear witness, O my God, that thou hast created me to know Thee and to worship Thee.

This same sentence in Arabic is:

> a<u>sh</u>hadu yá iláhí bi-annaka <u>kh</u>alaqtaní li-'irfánika wa 'ibádatika.

The central concepts in this sentence are *'irfán* und *'ibádat*. God has granted us existence for the very purpose of attaining these two qualities.

'Irfán means 'mystic recognition'. This word is used in Sufi Islam in the sense of merging with God. In the Bahá'í Faith, for which the transcendence of God is absolute, it represents first and foremost the recognition of God through His Messengers, and indirectly through the perception of His multifarious attributes in the world of creation:

> The knowledge of the Reality of the Divinity is impossible and unattainable, but the knowledge of the Manifestations of God is the knowledge of God, for the bounties, splendours and divine attributes are apparent in Them. Therefore, if man attains to the knowledge of the Manifestations of God, he will attain to the knowledge of God; and if he be neglectful of the knowledge of the Holy Manifestations, he will be bereft of the knowledge of God.[90]

For him who attains 'irfán '[h]is inner eyes will open'; he is 'content with the decree of God', he 'findeth in death the secrets of everlasting life ... With inward and outward eyes he witnesseth the mysteries of resurrection in the realms of creation and the souls of men,' and he 'beholdeth justice in injustice, and in justice, grace'.[91] *'Irfán* is the spiritual state of being which *inṣáf* presupposes.

> There are innumerable states for the Fire [i.e. Hell-Fire], but the Essence thereof is lack of wisdom (*'irfán*).[92]

'Ibádat means 'worship' in the sense of 'to bear witness by virtue of embracing God's commandments'. The root of this word is *'abada*, 'to serve'. Willingness to serve God with all one's being, to accept His Covenant and to obey His explicit laws expresses itself in action as *'adl*.

This mutual conditioning of *'irfán* and *'ibádat* is also reflected in the opening paragraph of the Kitáb-i Aqdas:

> The first duty prescribed by God for His servants is the recognition of Him Who is the Dayspring of His Revelation and the Fountain of His

laws, Who representeth the Godhead in both the Kingdom of His Cause and the world of creation.[93]

The Arabic text is:

anna awwal má kataba'lláhu 'alá-l-'ibádi 'irfánu mashriqi waḥíhi wa-maṭla'i amrihi alladhí kána maqámu nafsihi fí 'álami'l-amri wa'l-khalq.

'Servants' is the translation of the word *'ibád*, the plural form of *'abd*, and *'irfán* is their first duty. Both the opening sentence of the Kitáb-i Aqdas and the short obligatory prayer make clear that attaining recognition of God is not merely a possibility, it is in fact the first and most important goal of every believer. *'Ibádat* without *'irfán* would be equivalent to submission and self-effacement in face of God's omnipotence. To know God means to love God and to place one's entire trust in Him, to recognize in Him the source of all justice and to orient oneself accordingly. Under these circumstances, holding to the Laws ordained by God is equivalent to being true to the insights and convictions which lie at the core of one's own self.

The Arabic word for equinox – the starting point of the Bahá'í year – is *i'tidál*, from the same root as the word *'adl. I'tidál* also means 'the cardinal virtue of equity'.

The Ayyám-i Há' do not yet enjoy the prominence which they deserve, at least not in the West. This has partly to do with the fact that these days are intended as a family occasion and that outside of Iran the still relatively young and expanding community consists predominantly of believers of the first few generations: we shall have to wait several more generations before highly networked Bahá'í community structures become established in these parts of the world as well. In the meantime it is not always easy, especially for young Bahá'í parents, to replace the firmly established Christmas festivity with the Ayyám-i Há' in the face of resistance or expectations from relatives and in light of the forces of the playground or school yard: normative pressure is always greatest where the sensibilities and priorities of non-Bahá'ís are involved.

The association of the Ayyám-i Há' festivities with the family circle expresses in a vivid manner the inner dynamism of *'adl wa inṣáf*: the goal of world culture is causally linked with the smallest and most intimate level of social adhesion. Freedom on earth is not a pious wish, it is a methodically pursued goal; and the family is the germ cell of world peace.

The week

The Báb also assigned names to the seven days of the week, which in conformity with Islamic practice are generally ranged from Saturday to Friday in Bahá'í literature:

1	*Jalál*	Glory, fame, pomp	Saturday
2	*Jamál*	Beauty	Sunday
3	*Kamál*	Perfection	Monday
4	*Fiḍál*	Grace→94	Tuesday
5	*'Idál*	Justice→95	Wednesday
6	*Istijlál*	Majesty, eminence, loftiness	Thursday
7	*Istiqlál*	Independence	Friday

The fact that the days of the week bear names is proof enough that the traditional Semitic solar week has not been abandoned. However, the week has no liturgical significance in the Bahá'í Faith. In particular, the Guardian has made it clear that the justification for its inclusion is not based on the biblical Creation myth as presented in Genesis 1:1–2:3. In a letter written on behalf of Shoghi Effendi is stated:

> We Bahá'ís do not believe in Genesis literally. We know this world was not created in seven days, or six, or eight, but evolved gradually over a period of millions of years, as science has proved. As to where the idea of a seven-day week originated, it is certainly very ancient and you should refer to scholars for an answer.[96]

From these remarks it is clear that the concept of the week does not figure among the eternal truths which are confirmed and revitalized by every new Dispensation (such as the transcendental nature of God, the Covenant between God and man, progressive revelation, God's love for mankind, the commandment to love one's neighbour, the institution of marriage),→97 but instead is one of the temporally conditioned teachings which can be altered or rescinded with every new Divine Mission, such as dietary habits, stipulations concerning clothing and hygiene, liturgical practices. The question is therefore justified as to what role the week is to play in the Bahá'í Era.

A simple and at the same time plausible explanation would be that the rhythm of the week is, after all, an established and widespread phenomenon and that its retention simply reflects the path of least resistance, one which guarantees a certain continuity in accustomed life patterns. The week dictates the rhythm of labour in the greater part of the world, and Bahá'ís must necessarily co-exist with the traditional flow of life for some time to come. If this were the only explanation for retaining the week, one might predict that it should diminish in importance over time to the degree that the importance of the Bahá'í nineteen-day rhythm increases; and one would understandably ask oneself why the Báb should have gone to the trouble of assigning names in the first place.

This approach is inadequate, however, since it overlooks a vital principle of the Bahá'í Faith: it is not the seven-day rhythm which seems to me to be at issue, but the sabbath – and not with respect to Bahá'í teachings (which do not include the concept of the sabbath), but rather in consideration of the other revealed religions. The *shabbat* (that is, Saturday) is holy for the Jews because God rested on this day and, through the medium of Moses, of 'Him Who spoke with God', forbade the Jews every form of toil, slaughter or use of fire. For Christians Sunday is holy because, according to their traditions, the Resurrection of Jesus, 'the Spirit of God', occurred on this day. And *Yawmu'l-Jum'aτ* is for the Muslims the day of remembrance of the emigration (*al-hijraτ*) of Muhammad, which took place on a Friday. It is true that Bahá'ís spare no effort in making the Message of God available to all mankind and are convinced that the world-wide acceptance of Bahá'í principles and insights offers the only chance of overcoming the problems which threaten human society and of establishing an enduring world peace. However, Bahá'ís are also aware that the decision to accept the Message of Bahá'u'lláh is the sovereign prerogative of every individual. The Bahá'í Faith does not stand in competition with other world religions, it stands in loving fraternity with them and respects their tenets and priorities. The inclusion of the concept of the week in the Badí' calendar emphasizes this aspired relationship with other religious communities and serves as a guarantee that the respective sabbath of each of the other religions which observe it will continue to be respected throughout the Era of Fulfilment.

Concerning the practical application of the seven- or nineteen-day rhythm, we should remember that we live in a pluralistic society in which the boundaries between cultures are increasingly becoming blurred. In a world in which we were all citizens with equal rights everywhere, where individuals could live and pursue their affairs wherever they found it most appropriate, conditions which recognize and honour the cultural sensitivities of every individual would have to prevail. A more flexible structuring of working conditions would vouchsafe to everyone a life rhythm which is best in conformity with his personal world view. Side by side with Bahá'ís, whose days of rest would perhaps be oriented on a nineteen-day cycle – so that, among other things, the start of each month would remain free for attending the Nineteen Day Feast (see Chapter 8) – Muslim, Jewish and Christian colleagues would live and work, for whom the normal days of rest would fall on their respective week-end. Honest work is, after all, considered by Bahá'ís to be a form of worship:

> It is enjoined upon every one of you to engage in some form of occupation, such as crafts, trades and the like. We have graciously exalted your engagement in such work to the rank of worship unto God, the True One.[98]

It is all the more appropriate that, in a world strongly influenced by Bahá'í ideals, secular and religious aspects of life should proceed hand in hand and free of conflict. The calendar for such a world is not complete without the seven-day week.

Mihrshahi attributes numerous mystical and symbolic references to the number seven over and above the Biblical and Qur'ánic associations presented here: the seven central figures of the prophetic cycle begun by Adam and completed by the Báb;[99] the seven stages of coming into being, i.e. the descending arc of the ontological circle of Shí'ite tradition, as described by Shaykh Aḥmad-i Ahsá'í, elaborated by the Báb and discussed by Bahá'u'lláh;[100] the seven verses of the *fátiḥat* (the 'opening', i.e. initial Súrah of the Qur'án).[101] Mihrshahi observes that the number seven is featured prominently in the Báb's earlier texts, especially those which were penned prior to His declaration, whereas in His later writings the symbolism of the number nineteen came to assume the central role.[102] This shift in focus is consistent with the suggestion that the practical significance of the Bahá'í week is to be found primarily in its social function as bridge or interface to the religious communities of past revelations.

This theme will be taken up again in Chapter 8, where the future role of the week will be discussed in the context of relevant text passages – so far as such discussion is at all possible in anticipation of an authoritative clarification from the Universal House of Justice.

The start of the day

The rotation of the earth on its own axis is continual and offers no obvious moment for establishing the start of the day. Every calendar system must therefore settle on a convention for the regular transition from one calendar day into the next. The four naturally occurring 'cornerstones' – sunrise, midday, sunset and midnight – are particularly attractive as candidates in this respect because they are objectively discernible to the interested observer.

It might seem at first sight that midnight is the best choice because people are generally asleep by this time; incrementing the calendar date at midnight would therefore guarantee that the entire waking period would normally fit into the same nominal day. However, there are other considerations which speak against this view. It will be assumed at this point that the change of day in a religiously inspired calendar is more than simply a formality, that it has something to do with our religious consciousness and that it should for that reason alone be experienced during waking hours. We will return to this theme shortly; but before that we must return to our opening proposition and examine these four cornerstones with respect to their verifiability.

It is not sufficient simply to look at the sun to know if it is midday or not. The two defining characteristics of a celestial body – here the sun – as seen from the Earth at any given moment are its altitude and the compass direction of its position (i.e. its azimuth). Since the altitude of the sun varies with the time of both the day and the year, the point of the upper culmination of the sun – that is, the moment of midday – is only then apparent to the eye after the altitude of the sun has again begun to decline. All that one can directly experience is the fact that midday is already past. Reference to the cardinal direction presupposes knowledge of the north-south axis. Of course in the northern hemisphere one might simply consult a compass to determine when the sun's azimuth is 0° (due south) – assuming that we know the magnetic declination for the point of observation and thus the discrepancy between the compass point and geographic north – but the determination of the precise moment of midday is then reduced to a purely intellectual abstraction. It would be far easier simply to use a clock or watch – whereby the position of the sun is reduced to a fact of subordinate importance. Moreover, the clock ticks according to mean time, which can be translated into true solar time only by taking the equation of time into account (an example is contained in the calculation of the true time of the Ascension of 'Abdu'l-Bahá in Appendix E). Furthermore, given that the meridional change of day is itself linked to zone time, the relationship between the upper culmination of the sun and the moment of midday is absent in any event.

The moment of midnight can be ascertained by observation only with reference to the celestial sphere – assuming that one knows which day of the year it is, and further assuming the availability of the necessary apparatus: first to reveal the precalculated orientation of the heavens for the current midnight, and second to measure their present orientation. When the two findings agree, it is midnight. This procedure is similar in principle to reading the time of day from a clock, though considerably more complicated. It likewise has little to do with immediate sense perception.

Not so with sunrise and sunset. He who sojourns in flat countryside or on the eastern shore of a sea or large lake can directly experience the moment when the sun fully disappears beneath the horizon: this is the moment of sunset (*mutatis mutandis* for sunrise). But it is not necessary to observe the sun directly. The beginning of dusk is accompanied by a rapidly altering light quality. At the moment of sunset the colours lose their discrimination: trees which moments before had had brown furrowed stems and lush green leaves become half-silhouettes with washed-out colours before the background of a pastel blue-grey sky – regardless of the season and relatively independent of prevailing weather conditions. The Qur'án capitalizes on this phenomenon for determining the time of fasting. With reference to the commencement of fasting it states:

> ... and eat and drink, until the white thread shows clearly to you from the black thread at the dawn; ... .[103]

Repeated attempts on my part to carry out this instruction resulted in the following observation: in middle European climes (and thus with a mean twilight duration) one must wait approximately forty minutes following sunset before a white thread can no longer be differentiated from a black thread. A glance at the original text (*wa kulú wa shrabú hattá yatabayyana lakumu'l-khaytu'l-abyadu mina'l-khayti'l-aswadi mina'l-fajr*) resolves the issue: *yatabayyana* means 'may be clearly distinguished', a fact which is incidentally more evident in the Arberry translation than in the German translations at my disposal at the time of writing the original version of this book. Here Muhammad is not describing an exact measuring device, but rather an aid for training one's own receptivity. He is implying that everyone is capable of developing the necessary sensitivity to recognize the moment of changeover with sufficient accuracy to satisfy the requirements of fasting.

In summary: a concept of day which is oriented on the midday-midnight axis (i.e. meridional) can be delimited only through technical means. This axis serves well for the objective determination of the change of day, but it does not allow an immediate sensory perception of this change. A concept of day which is oriented on the sunrise-sunset axis (i.e. occidental) also fulfils the requirement of objectivity – not, however, without consequences which will be discussed later (see 'Occidental time' in Chapter 7). The great advantage lies in the perceptibility of the change of day.

Everything said so far applies equally as well to sunrise as it does to sunset as the potential juncture between successive days. Since the Badí' calendar does not make use of the interlunium, →104 there is no practical purpose for the sighting of the new moon crescent and therefore no longer a compelling rational justification for preferring sunset over sunrise. The reason must be sought elsewhere – or rather, in another manner. It will help to remind ourselves that the calendar is of divine origin. If the language of revelation is symbolic, then the commencement of the day at sunset is also a symbolic statement which has to do with our human, or more specifically with our spiritual condition. As soon as we look at the message of the new day in this light, we are rewarded with a rich harvest.

The occidental day is subdivided into two natural phases, the phase of light and the phase of darkness. As we saw right at the beginning of the present study, this steady oscillation between light and darkness corresponds to the natural biological rhythm of the body, which from earliest times has served both as the basis for man's perception of time and as the basic rhythm for his patterns of behaviour. The daylight phase is for most people the time for enterprise and achievement. For children it is the time for school and learning, for adults the time for securing the means of material survival and well-being and for carrying out domestic chores. In all cases it is the public time, the time for action and for external accomplishment: it is the time for doing. In contrast, the phase of darkness is private time, time for oneself and others, especially within the circle of family and friends. It is the time for sleeping, the time for reflection and entertainment, the time for internal growth and accomplishment: it is the time for being.

This differentiation is of course simplistic and polarized: perish the thought that the period of daytime activity be devoid of leisure and contemplation or that the work-free period should be filled exclusively with introspection. One's relations with colleagues at work can – and should – be characterized by the same love and devotion as those with family and within one's circle of friends, and leisure activities can under circumstances be just as hectic and stressing as a heavy work load. But the dichotomy as presented is tendentially accurate and in harmony with the predisposition of the biological 'inner clock' (see 'Natural time intervals' in Chapter 1).

People are in the habit of regarding the so-called 'free time' as a form of resuscitation, time to be used to recover from the wear and tear of the day. After a long working day full of stress and overburdening, the evening can be exploited to regenerate the inner powers sufficient to face a new tomorrow – a vicious circle which continues day after day. This attitude would be in accord with a day which commences at sunrise.

The Bahá'í day, which begins at sunset, instead places the time for being *before* the time for doing. It reinterprets private time as a time of *preparation* rather than of reparation: a period of time during which, through prayer and meditation and through sustained study of the holy scriptures, a Bahá'í may gain an ever-increasing understanding of his own role in God's Plan. The insights which he thereby earns alter, among other things, his attitude towards labour and achievement. A Bahá'í considers work a form of worship, quality and conscientiousness first and foremost an obligation to God and to one's own inner self.

This subdivision of the day makes its presence felt most markedly during the month of fasting. Sunset terminates both the day and the period of physical abstinence. Each new day begins with inner, spiritual fasting: during this period the heart is more receptive, concentration higher, the intellect quickened: this is for example the very best time to come to terms in particular with the mystical writings. The second half of the day is the time of outward, physical fasting: abstinence from every form of food, drink or other consumable commodity (such as tobacco; alcohol and drugs are prohibited absolutely). Physical fasting takes place during the normal daytime routine; it is neither feasible at present nor foreseen for the future that the period of fasting should be regarded as a work-free month: Bahá'u'lláh specified the circumstances under which physical fasting should not be undertaken, among other things during strenuous physical toil.[105] It is the goal of every individual Bahá'í to project the spiritual state which he achieves during inner fasting – and which may well be more intense than at any other time of the year – into the daily period of external fasting. The purely physical act of abstinence is almost of secondary importance.

In another sense, the day which begins in darkness and unfolds in the light is reminiscent of the condition of human life, which begins in the darkness of the womb and is born into the light of earthly existence. The innate talents and abilities of the child begin their development not at birth, but rather during the months in darkness: only with difficulty, if at all, can the post-natal individual compensate for that which it has forsaken during the pre-natal stage of preparation. This simile also describes the relationship between life in the material world and life after physical death: our life on earth is a preparation for the time in which we cast down the dark veils of our material existence and immerse ourselves in the divine light of eternal life:

> O Son of the Supreme! I have made death a messenger of joy to thee. Wherefore dost thou grieve? I made the light to shed on thee its splendour. Why dost thou veil thyself therefrom?[106]

> O Son of Spirit! With the joyful tidings of light I hail thee: rejoice! To the court of holiness I summon thee; abide therein that thou mayest live in peace forevermore.[107]

In a manner similar to that of the embryo in the womb, we have here and now a unique opportunity to acquire spiritual qualities which we shall need in the life to come:

> The world beyond is as different from this world as this world is different

from that of the child while still in the womb of its mother. When the soul attaineth the Presence of God, it will assume the form that best befitteth its immortality and is worthy of its celestial habitation.[108]

In the alternation of night and day, and what God has created in the heavens and the earth – surely there are signs for a godfearing people.[109]

With the nominal start of the day at sunset, the moment of sunrise gains a complementary significance: as 'second birth' of the day it symbolizes the spiritual rebirth of the individual, the promise of eternal life:

> Except a man be born again, he cannot see the kingdom of God . . . That which is born of the flesh is flesh; and that which is born of the Spirit is spirit.[110]

> By the terms 'life' and 'death', spoken of in the scriptures, is intended the life of faith and the death of unbelief.[111]

In comparison with the condition following the birth in spirit, mere physical existence is equivalent to death:

> And he [Jesus] said unto another, Follow me. But he said, Lord, suffer me first to go and bury my father. Jesus said unto him, Let the dead bury their dead: but go thou and preach the kingdom of God.[112]

> Not equal are the blind and the seeing man,
> the shadows and the light,
> the shade and the torrid heat;
> not equal are the living and the dead.
> God makes to hear whomsoever He will;
> thou canst not make those in their tombs to hear . . .[113]

> Why, is he who was dead, and We gave him life, and appointed for him a light to walk by among the people as one whose likeness is in the shadows, and comes not forth from them?[114]

> Arise, and lift up your voices, that haply they that are fast asleep may be awakened. Say: O ye who are as dead! The Hand of Divine bounty proffereth unto you the Water of Life. Hasten and drink your fill. Whoso hath been re-born in this Day, shall never die; whoso remaineth dead, shall never live.[115]

In order to be born in spirit, one must free oneself from the darkness of egocentricity, covetousness and dependency on the indulgences of material life and with pure and humble heart open oneself to the effulgence of God's love:

> Only when the lamp of search, of earnest striving, of longing desire, of passionate devotion, of fervid love, of rapture, and ecstasy, is kindled within the seeker's heart, and the breeze of His loving-kindness is wafted upon his soul, will the darkness of error be dispelled, the mists of doubts and misgivings be dissipated, and the lights of knowledge and certitude envelop his being.[116]

It is the responsibility of every individual to experience his own personal sunrise, to discover the dwelling-place of God in himself and for himself, of his own free choice to enter the state of certitude, a step which God in his immeasurable love fervently awaits:

> O Son of Being! Thy heart is My home; sanctify it for My descent. Thy spirit is My place of revelation; cleanse it for My manifestation.[117]

> O Son of Love! Thou art but one step away from the glorious heights above and from the celestial tree of love. Take thou one pace and with the next advance into the immortal realm and enter the pavilion of eternity. Give ear to that which hath been revealed by the Pen of Glory.[118]

No-one, not even God, can take up this offer on one's behalf:

> O Son of Being! Love Me, that I may love thee. If thou lovest Me not, My love can in no wise reach thee. Know this, O servant.[119]

O Bond Slave of the World! Many a dawn hath the breeze of My loving-kindness wafted over thee and found thee upon the bed of heedlessness fast asleep. Bewailing then thy plight it returned whence it came.[120]

Spiritual birth alters one's self-conception fundamentally and radically. He who is born of flesh considers himself essentially a biological, intellectual or rational being who has – perhaps – been 'equipped' with a soul. He who has experienced his second birth recognizes in himself first and foremost a spiritual being, eternally and intimately bound to God; he knows that his association with his body is temporary, and that physical death is the promise of freedom from mortality:

Death proffereth unto every confident believer the cup that is life indeed. It bestoweth joy, and is the bearer of gladness. It conferreth the gift of everlasting life.[121]

But if he [man] possesses the knowledge of God, becomes ignited through the fire of the love of God, witnesses the great and mighty signs of the Kingdom, becomes the cause of love among mankind and lives in the utmost state of sanctity and holiness, he shall surely attain to second birth, be baptized by the Holy Spirit and enjoy everlasting existence.[122]

The moment of sunset varies according to the season: in summer the sun ascends early and tarries long, whereas in winter it makes only a short appearance before it disappears once again into the long night. It is the same with people: some experience their second birth early in life, whereas others first realize late how much time they have already wasted.

O Son of Man! Many a day hath passed over thee whilst thou hast busied thyself with thy fancies and idle imaginings. How long art thou to slumber on thy bed? Lift up thy head from slumber, for the Sun hath risen to the zenith, haply it my shine upon thee with the light of beauty.[123]

No-one can stipulate the time of his birth – neither the first nor the second.

And no-one can claim with certainty that he has been completely re-born in spirit – perhaps he has merely felt the first pangs of birth, or he has possibly assumed an attitude of expectation or wishful thinking. And finally, spiritual birth is not automatic – it presupposes an act of free will and could be reversed through exercise of that self-same freedom:

> The incomparable Creator hath created all men from one same substance, and hath exalted their reality above the rest of His creatures. Success or failure, gain or loss, must, therefore, depend upon man's own exertions. The more he striveth, the greater will be his progress.[124]

> Unto each one hath been prescribed a pre-ordained measure, as decreed in God's mighty and guarded Tablets. All that which ye potentially possess can, however, be manifested only as a result of your own volition.[125]

To be re-born in spirit is not a condition: it is a process which must continue without abatement until the final separation of the soul from the body.

> How often hath a sinner, at the hour of death, attained to the essence of faith, and, quaffing the immortal draught, hath taken his flight unto the celestial Concourse. And how often hath a devout believer, at the hour of his soul's ascension, been so changed as to fall into the nethermost fire.[126]

The moments of sunrise and sunset offer the Bahá'í daily opportunities to pause and reflect over the actual purpose and meaning of his life and over the daunting obligations which he has taken upon himself out of love for Bahá'u'lláh, for God and for His Creation. It is certainly more than a mere formality that these two moments are narrowly entwined with the commandments regarding fasting and daily prayer.

> Reflect, O people, on the grace and blessings of your Lord, and yield Him thanks at eventide and dawn.[127]

PART III

THE FUTURE ROLE OF THE BADÍʻ CALENDAR

In the remainder of this study, a number of topics will be discussed in the expectation that the Badíʻ calendar is destined in the future to serve the community as an independent and self-sufficient system. The spectrum of topics reaches from

- open questions with regard to the operation of the calendar, through

- consideration of other areas which will be directly effected by the widespread adoption of the calendar, to

- challenges arising from the use of the new calendar.

The list of topics covered is far from exhaustive, and the treatment is in some places perforce incomplete. The detailed exposition of some of the themes involved should ideally be left in the hands of those with the necessary specialist knowledge. For example, legal issues are mentioned but not elaborated, and I will occasionally remind the reader that the astronomical calculations are at best interim approximations.

To the best of my knowledge, a good deal of the subject matter in this part has never been systematically examined prior to the publication of this study. For that reason, everything which follows by way of explanation reflects first of all my own personal understanding, and it goes without saying that the views expressed here do not automatically reflect those of any other individual or institution, and that virtually everything is subject to confirmation (or rejection or revision) in light of future decisions of the Universal House of Justice. In what follows, the reader will be repeatedly apprised of the non-committal quality of the content.

Most especially, I wish to provoke discussion. It is my earnest hope that the present study will one day give rise to a whole series of treatises on the Badí' calendar in which numerous points of view from various disciplines will be aired.

6

Determining the Day of Naw-Rúz

The question of the determination of the beginning of the year is of central and decisive importance for the definition of the Bahá'í year – both with regard to the specification of the calendar itself and in consideration of the scheduling of the days of commemoration and celebration. Since the concept of the annual cycle is both a natural phenomenon and the subject of divine decree, its precise definition and practical implementation requires a careful consideration of

- the relevant astronomical facts, alongside

- the binding standard of the holy writings.

In order to establish an unambiguous terminology for a number of concepts which will occur repeatedly in the text to follow, we will first turn our attention to the natural phenomena involved.

Astronomical data

At any given moment, roughly one half of the surface of the earth is bathed in sunlight. Since the diameter of the sun is many times greater than that of the earth (roughly 109 to 1), the illuminated portion amounts to somewhat more than half the total surface area. However, due to the great distance of the sun from the earth – on average 1.4959787×10^8 km, = 1 *astronomical unit* – half the mean apparent angular diameter of the sun amounts to only 15'59"5. For the purpose of establishing the peripheral angle of incidence of sunlight, 8"79 of this total must be deducted on account of the horizontal (solar) parallax.

Horizontal refraction plays an even greater role than the above two factors taken together. Because of the thermal layering of the earth's atmosphere, sunlight is broken in such a way as to cause the extremely low-lying sun to be 'lifted' by approximately 34 arc minutes, resulting in a discrepancy between the geometric and the apparent sunrise and sunset.

Taking the various factors together, the official moment of sunset is fixed at 90°50' relative to the zenith distance of the centre of the solar disc. Smaller, incalculable refraction anomalies due to variation in air pressure and temperature cannot be taken into account. Also necessarily missing from this calculation is the dip of the horizon, that is, the angular distance between the apparent and the true horizon (this depends on the height of the observer above sea level), as well as the topography in the vicinity of the point of observation. Additional factors relevant for the perception but not for the determination of the moment of sunset include (1) the half-shaded area of the earth which is still illuminated by a part of the sun, i.e. when the sun has only partially disappeared beneath the horizon: this area counts as part of the illuminated hemisphere; and (2) the area of the earth in which the sun lies below the horizon, but its light is being refracted from the still illuminated upper regions of the atmosphere, i.e. the gloaming: this area counts as part of the non-illuminated hemisphere.

The boundary between the illuminated and the non-illuminated hemisphere, called the *terminator*, is the threshold between daytime and night-time with respect both to sunrise and to sunset. Here we are interested only in that half of the boundary demarcating sunset. Since it is simultaneously the threshold between two successive Bahá'í days, this line of demarcation will be designated the *diurnal threshold* in the present study. The diurnal threshold advances westwards along the equator at a constant speed of nearly 1,670 kilometres per hour and circumambulates the earth on average once every 24 hours: see exposition in 'Occidental time' in Chapter 7. At the moment of the *vernal* (or *spring*) *equinox*, the position of the earth in its orbit around the sun is called the *vernal point*. Strictly speaking, the etymology of the term equinox ('equal [day and] night') is misleading, since at the time of either equinox daytime everywhere lasts at least 13^m20^s longer than night-time. The line between the centre of the sun and the geometric centre of the earth intersects with the earth's equator at the moment of an equinox, so that the light-dark ratio is equivalent in both halves of the globe. Note further that the term 'vernal' is understood in this study to mean 'vernal with respect to the northern hemisphere' unless otherwise specified. Since the vernal point is crucial to the determination of the Bahá'í New Year's Day (an assertion which will be vindicated below in 'Written sources'), the diurnal threshold at the moment of the vernal equinox will henceforth be called the *annual threshold*.

The vernal point is also traditionally called the *first point of Aries*. Note that this is a reference to the sign, not the constellation: at the vernal point the sun is nowadays in fact no longer in (astronomical) Aries, but in Aquarius (see 'The stars' in Chapter 1).

It is worth noting that the diurnal threshold always runs parallel to and east of a great circle whose plane passes through the centre of the sun at right angles to the celestial equator, at a distance of 92.7662 km (= 0°50' at the equator) from this circle. For this reason, on a Mercator projection of the world (that is, where longitudinal divisions are depicted as parallel lines) the annual threshold appears as a curve in the shape of an extremely drawn-out opening round bracket. We will henceforth call any such curve an *equinoctial terminator path*. The equinoctial terminator path for any given longitude (i.e. its reference longitude) is the line of demarcation which the diurnal threshold would assume if it were to overlay this longitude at the equator precisely at the moment of the vernal equinox (see Illustration 1 on page 149). Technical details are presented here in a text box for those interested:

> *The actual longitude of the annual threshold T at latitude L is calculated by incrementing the reference longitude (if east of the prime meridian) or decrementing it (if west) by the so-called terminator offset $(1 / \cos L - 1) \times 0°50'$.*[1] *Thus $T = T_L$ for $L = 0°$, i.e. the reference longitude is equal to the geographic longitude at the equator. In all other cases the reference longitude T_L lies to the west of the equinoctial terminator path T to a greater or lesser degree. For example: at 23°26'21"45 (at the tropics) the terminator offset amounts to merely 4'29"82, at 50° (roughly Frankfurt/Main) still only 27'47"17 and at 66°33'38"55 (at the polar circles) 1°15'43"72. From here on, the cosine starts to make a larger impact: at 80° the offset is already 3°57'56"31, at 88°, 23°2'41", and at 89°, 46°54'56".*[2] *(Note: these calculations assume a spherical earth. Since the actual shape of the earth, called geoid, is more or less ellipsoid, tiny fluctuations exist in the distance between the terminator and the great circle, fluctuations which however are ignored in the present study.)*

Since the tropical year does not comprise an exact number of days, the position of each and every annual threshold is unique. At the beginning of each year the annual threshold lies roughly 87.192 degrees west of its position at the start of the previous year, equivalent to a duration of 5 hours, 48 minutes and approximately 46 seconds. That amounts to just under a quarter of the total circumference of the earth, so that in the course of four years the annual threshold wanders nearly once around the earth. After five thousand years it will have wandered 1,211 times around the earth, and the equinoctial terminator paths with which it will have coincided during this time are distributed around the globe at an average of once every 0.297274979 degrees (17'50"19, equivalent to a duration of one minute and 11.35 seconds). Moreover, the annual threshold never returns exactly to its point of departure, but misses it by a few millimetres. This pattern of migration, which is characteristic of the movement of the annual threshold, will be designated *cyclic progression*. Accordingly, a movement of this nature will henceforth be called *cyclic-progressive*.

The above description assumes a tropical year length of 365.2422 days, which represents almost exactly the situation in 1832 CE. On account of the gradual deceleration of the earth's rotation on its own axis (caused mainly by the friction of the tides), the absolute duration of a day increases in the course of time, so that the span of time between two successive vernal equinoxes decreases on the average of about 0.6×10^{-7} days per year (roughly half a second per century). In 2000 CE the tropical year comprised merely 365.2421925617370561667 days. Furthermore, we have here to do with mean values: the actual length of a given year can deviate up to several minutes from the calculated mean (see Appendix D).

Written sources

The beginning of the year, binding for all Bahá'ís, is to be determined in accordance with the law laid down by Bahá'u'lláh:

> The Festival of Naw-Rúz falleth on the day that the sun entereth the sign of Aries, even should this occur no more than one minute before sunset.[3]

This passage is the only place in the Most Holy Book – indeed, as far as I have been able to ascertain, in the whole of Bahá'u'lláh's writings – in which the criterion for determining the border between successive calendar years is mentioned. The possibility of comparing different texts with possibly varying formulations is therefore not given. It is thus all the more important to consider this statement with the utmost scrutiny. In particular, it is incumbent to consider the original Persian text, which reads:

> har rúz keh shams taḥvíl beḥamal shavad hamán yawm 'eid ast agar cheh yek daqíqeh beh ghorúb mándeh báshad.

An English-language paraphrase which follows the wording of the original as closely as possible might read:

That day [*har rúz*] on which the sun [*keh shams*] receives a shift (in)to the ram (i.e. Aries) [*taḥvíl beḥamal shavad*], that same day [*hamán yawm*] is the festival [*'eid ast*], even if [*agar cheh*] one minute [*yek daqíqeh*] until sunset [*beh ghorúb*] may remain [*mándeh báshad*].

Note that this representation has at best the quality of a computer rendition and is not a translation in the true sense. Since Persian – an Indo-European language – is quite close in structure to English, such a rendition can nevertheless be helpful for gaining an understanding of the original text (in contrast to Arabic, for which at most a gloss might prove productive).

The Persian language original uses two words for 'day': one is the (ambiguous) Persian word *rúz* [= either 'complete day' or 'period of daylight'] and the other is the (unambiguous) Arabic word *yawm*. The latter always indicates a period of 24 hours; the phase of daylight is in Arabic *nahár* (in contrast to *laylaτ*, 'night'). The demonstrative adjective *án* ('that') in the emphatic form *hamán* indicates identity: *hamán yawm* = 'that very day', 'the self-same day'. The alternation of *rúz* and *yawm* serves stylistically to soften the syntactically imposed repetition of the concept 'day'. Thus the subject of the sentence (*har rúz*) is brought into the spacial proximity of the predicate (*'eid*) through its re-introduction in varied form (*hamán yawm*) following the embedded relative clause. This type of cleft construction is unusual for the English language, but a virtually word-for-word translation from Persian produces a stylistically well-formed sentence for example in French: *Le jour pendant lequel le soleil entre dans le signe du bélier, cette journée là est jour de fête . . .* (my translation). Since the words *rúz* and *yawm* reference the same entity, it is the natural day – the period of time between two successive sunsets – which is indicated in both cases.

This understanding is further supported by a comparison with the description of this same criterion from the pen of the Báb, as translated by E. G. Browne:

> This day is the day whereon the Sun passes from Pisces into Aries at the moment of its passing, whether it be night or day.[4]

The similarity in style and content between these two passages, the one from Bahá'u'lláh and the other from the Báb, is obvious. This similarity is even more striking when one compares the original Persian-language texts, since the text of the English-language edition of the Kitáb-i Aqdas has been subjected to several stylistic adjustments which will be discussed in the following paragraphs.

This sentence from the Bayán reads in Persian:

va án yawm ast keh shams montaqel mígardad az borj-e ḥúb beḥamal dar ḥín-e taḥvíl cheh leyl váqi' shavad va cheh nahár.

A word-for-word paraphrase which follows the original as closely as possible might look like the following:

And this is the day [*wa án yawm ast*] on which the sun traverses [*keh shams montaqel mígardad*] from the sign of the fish [*az borj-e ḥúb*] (in)to the ram [*beḥamal*] at the moment of the shift [*dar ḥín-e taḥvíl*], whether this should occur in the night [*cheh leyl váqi' shavad*] and (here meaning 'or') whether day [*va cheh nahár*].

Because of the use of the word *yawm* and because of the statement that this event can take place any time during the night (*leyl*) or the day (*nahár*), we may assume with reasonable certainty that the period of time which is indicated here is that of the 24-hour day.

It should be mentioned that the exposition of the Báb is being cited here only as an aid to understanding Bahá'u'lláh's own legislation. The Dispensation of Bahá'u'lláh is an independent divine revelation with its own laws, of which some are identical to the laws laid down by the Báb, whereas others differ:

The Báb states that His laws are provisional and depend upon the acceptance of the future Manifestation. This is why in the Book of Aqdas Bahá'u'lláh sanctions some of the laws found in the Bayán, modifies others and sets aside many.[5]

The significance of this sentence from the Bayán lies in the close similarity in both revelations with respect to the presentation of the criteria for determining the day of Naw-Rúz. We may safely assume that Bahá'u'lláh had detailed knowledge of the Bayán (by whatever means):→[6] in numerous places in the Kitáb-i Aqdas the Persian Bayán is referred to directly (paras. 179, 180), or it is paraphrased (paras. 77, 126, 131, 142), or even cited word for word (para. 139). We may justifiably assume that the agreement between Bahá'u'lláh's provisions and those of the Báb was intentional.

Ḥamal is an Arabic word meaning 'sign of Aries'. The translators of the Kitáb-i Aqdas have confirmed this in a footnote to the text, in which it is further clarified that it signifies the vernal equinox (i.e. the vernal point) in the northern hemisphere. This interpretation is substantiated by a talk given by 'Abdu'l-Bahá in Paris on 21 March 1913, i.e. on Naw-Rúz of the year 70 be, in which he explained the significance of the vernal point with regard to the day of Naw-Rúz :

> At this moment the sun appears at the meridian and the day and night are equal. Until today the north pole has been in darkness. This sacred day when the sun illumines equally the whole earth is called the equinox . . .[7]

Furthermore, it is clear that this criterion has to do with the *moment* of the equinox rather than with the day on which the equinox occurs. This fact is made explicit in the passage quoted from the Bayán: 'at the moment of its passing'. In Bahá'u'lláh's wording it is only implicit, but nonetheless equally clear: only a moment – not a whole day – can occur one minute (or less) before sunset.

The Persian word *'eid* is identical to the Arabic *'íd* (the difference in written form exists only in transcription, not in the original). In the Bahá'í literature available in Western languages, *'íd* (or *'eid*) is translated sometimes as 'day' (of Naw-Rúz), sometimes as 'festival' (of Naw-Rúz). In fact, in Persian and Arabic, the languages of revelation for the Bábí and Bahá'í religions, this term is always understood exactly as it is understood everywhere in the Islamic cultural world: as a sacred period of one or more days. Thus the Islamic *'Ídu'l-Fiṭr* (the festival of the breaking of the fast) is three days long, whereas *'Ídu'l-Aḍḥá* (the festival of offering) lasts a full four days,[8] which of course doesn't mean that people celebrate uninterruptedly for three or four days, respectively. The 'Most Great Festival' of the Bahá'í Faith (*'Ídu'l-A'ẓam*, known as *Riḍván*: see 'Bahá'í commemorations' in Chapter 4) lasts twelve days, of which only the first, the ninth and the final day count as days of rest (i.e. 'holidays' in the stricter sense).[9] That which is normally called a 'festival' in English is in Arabic *iḥtifál* ('festivity', from *ḥafala*, 'to gather', VIII. stem = 'celebrate'). It is perhaps unfortunate that these concepts are not translated less ambiguously, e.g. *'íd* (*'eid*) where possible as 'festival day(s)' or 'festival period', and *iḥtifál* – if it should occur at all in the Writings – as 'festivity', thereby avoiding the undifferentiated word 'festival', which has in the West become thoroughly secularized, but this would no doubt be stylistically unsustainable. Moreover, this translation is not exactly wrong, it is merely imprecise, since the Arabic *'íd* also includes the aspect of (solemn or joyful) celebration, but under the basic assumption that this act of celebration occurs within the more general context '(religious) festival day or succession of festival days'.

In the English-language translation of the Kitáb-i Aqdas, this criterion – that is, the moment of the equinox – refers to the *day* on which the festival of Naw-Rúz 'falls'; it is not mentioned exactly when during this day this 'festival' is to take place. In light of the confusion which exists between the concepts of 'festival day' and 'festivity', this formulation invokes the impression that Naw-Rúz and the 'day on which the vernal equinox takes place' are two different events – one liturgical and social, the other geodetic and astronomical – whose time periods partially coincide per definition. However, the passage quoted from the *Bayán* makes it clear that these two time periods are equivalent to one another. Bahá'u'lláh is even clearer: with regard to the day on which the equinox takes place, *that very same day* [hamán yawm] *is the festival*. The two periods of time are identical.

In Bahá'u'lláh's formulation, the Persian word *rúz* occurs in combination with the astronomical circumstance of the equinox (*ḥamal*), whereas the word *yawm* – a word taken over from the Islamic conceptual world – stands in close syntactic and spatial relationship with the religious festival (*'eid*). These two terms for 'day' thus describe circumstances in two worlds: the one in the (physical) world of creation and the other in the (spiritual) world of revelation. This dichotomy inspires the charming idea that, with this brief text, Bahá'u'lláh managed not only to provide a precise instruction concerning the fixing of the calendar New Year, but also to make subtle reference to the agreement between these two worlds of God, between *'álamu'l-khalq* and *'álamu'l-amr* – in short, between science and religion.

So far as I have be able to ascertain, an explicit revealed statement concerning the scheduling of the *festivity* is nowhere to be found, neither in the Kitáb-i Aqdas nor elsewhere in the holy scripture. A festival is of course meant to be celebrated, but there appears to be nothing laid down concerning the format or timetable in which this celebration is to take place. It is customary for Bahá'ís to time the Naw-Rúz festivity in such a manner that the moment of the termination of the Fast, which is likewise the first moment of 1 Bahá', is included in the festive programme. With regard to the formal determination of the start of the year, however, the details and the timing of the actual celebration are irrelevant.

The expression *yek daqíqeh* ('one minute') has in my opinion three theoretically possible but mutually exclusive meanings in this context:

a. a short duration whose precise value is not significant,
b. a maximum duration (up to 60 seconds), or
c. an exact duration (a total of 60.0 seconds).

In the case of possibility (a) one would assume that Bahá'u'lláh wished to draw attention to the sunset (*ghorúb*) and not to the time lapse as such. Accordingly, Bahá'u'lláh might just as well have said 'one second' or 'a single instant'. Only the proximity to the end of the day would be important: the actual span of time mentioned would imply, say, a degree of accuracy or margin of error.

Possibility (b) suggests that the indicated minute is a borderline value, that is, the application of the criterion would be obligatory as long as more than one minute remained before sunset. Just what this would mean for the case when only one minute or less remained is not explicitly stated.

Possibility (c) would mean that Bahá'u'lláh had introduced a concept of 'day' whose duration extended from exactly one minute before sunset to exactly one minute before the subsequent sunset. This reading implies the co-existence of two concepts of day with an overlap of over 99.93 per cent and can, in the absence of a plausible explanation for this near-identity, be ruled out on grounds of non-productivity.

The transposition of this text passage into English exemplifies a classic translation dilemma. Since time expressions in languages which are highly influenced by technology and science such as Modern English tend to be understood as precise specification, a literal translation of the expression *yek daqíqeh* would have accentuated possibility (c). In order to exclude this reading, the target text must be rendered unambiguous – a process which has the side effect of also eliminating one or the other of the two remaining possibilities. The solution chosen for the English translation, i.e. the addition of the words 'no more than', suggests possibility (b), an upper limit. Interestingly, the German translation employs the expression *nur eine Minute* (only one minute), which instead tends more to emphasize possibility (a). To make matters even more confusing, this passage is once again paraphrased in Note 26 to the Kitáb-i Aqdas, but this time without 'no more than': '. . . even if this should occur one minute before sunset'. In light of the ambiguity of the authorized translations I would prefer to leave this issue open for the time being and to reconsider it in connection with possible methods for implementing the calendar legislation, to be discussed later.

The fact that the day of Naw-Rúz is at the same time the beginning of the calendar year is made clear by another passage of the Kitáb-i Aqdas:

> Happy the one who entereth upon the first day [*yawm*] of the month of Bahá, the day which God hath consecrated to this Great Name . . . Say: This day,

verily, is the crown of all the months and the source thereof, the day on which the breath of life is wafted over all created things.[10]

The whole of the first day of Bahá' is at the same time (literally) the source or origin of the months, i.e. the first day of the first month of the year. Another passage in the text makes it clear that this day is identical with the *'eid* of the introductory quotation:

> We have enjoined upon you fasting [*aṣ-ṣiyám*] during a brief period, and at its close have designated for you Naw-Rúz as a feast [*'íd*, therefore 'festival day'] . . . Let the days in excess of the months be placed before the month of fasting [*qabla shahri'ṣ-ṣiyám*] . . .[11]

The expression 'at its close' in the above text is in Arabic *ba'd akmálihá*, 'after its close': the 'after' of the original becomes 'at' in translation, i.e. 'immediately after'. This is in no way an alteration of the meaning of the orginal text, but simply a further compensation for the transcultural semantic shift of the concept of 'festival'. Since the fasting period terminates precisely at the moment of sunset of the last day of the month which comprises it, and since the calendar day of the festival commences at that same moment, in the Oriental cultural context this immediacy is sufficiently implied by the original wording.

The question remains open as to *whose* sunset is meant, or in other words, from which perspective the sunset is to be observed. There appear to be only two possible answers to this question:

1. from the perspective of a single spot on the earth, often called the *reference spot*. The moment of sunset at this spot would accordingly be the basis for the world-wide definition of the day for the purpose of applying this criterion.
2. from each and every spot on the earth. Every individual experiences his own sunset, the exact time of which is dependent on where on the surface of the earth he momentarily happens to be. He will experience sunset earlier than those to the west of him and later than those to the

east: the sidereal slice of time for one and the same calendar day is in each case different. (Sunsets in the extreme northern and southern latitudes represent a special case: see 'The change of day in the polar regions' in Chapter 7.)

Except for these two possibilities of interpretation, it seems to me that the scripturally revealed criteria for determining the start of the year are clear and unambiguous. In addition, however, the implementation of these criteria in the form of practical legislation requires a methodology which yields an unambiguous result for every single case, and moreover, one which is in accordance with the divine law. Just what this methodology entails depends closely on which of the above options for defining sunset is assumed. We shall see that the identical astronomical facts result in two radically different scenarios, depending on which of these two possibilities underlies the calculation of the beginning of the Badí' year.

Determining the day of Naw-Rúz using a reference spot

According to this method, the day of Naw-Rúz is to be determined for a single place on earth specially chosen for this purpose: the so-called place of reference, or more exactly, a specific spot within this place, the reference spot. In my understanding of the significance of the reference spot, the procedure has nothing to do with the technical determination of the vernal point as such. This calculation is carried out nowadays by qualified specialists with the aid of high-performance computers, based on a considerable quantity of geodetic and astronomical data collected in many parts of the world. The precise instant of the vernal equinox is precalculated years in advance with an error tolerance in the order of milliseconds (see Appendix D). Without such a precalculation it would be impossible to meet the demands of our modern society. Simply announcing the *calendae* in the Forum as the Romans did, so that everyone in shouting distance is informed which day it is, is no longer adequate – even if this 'announcement' should take place using electronic communication. Today's world demands a legally binding time scale which permits reckoning in periods of time well into the future with an arbitrarily precise degree of accuracy. At the very least, the day of Naw-Rúz must be predictable at least 20 days in advance of the advent of the equinox in order to determine whether or not a fifth *Yawm-i Há'* is to occur in the current year. As I see it, the reference-spot method has nothing to do with astronomical measurement, but rather with the integration of the moment of the equinox (which is known from other sources) into a universally applicable date convention.

Moreover, even assuming it were a viable technical alternative, the use of a reference spot literally as the measuring point for the equinox would have disturbing side-effects. The idea of building an astronomical observatory precisely on the designated spot considerably reduces the number of suitable places of reference; and the costs of such an undertaking stand in no relation to the derived benefits – especially when one considers that the necessary information is available essentially free of charge, for example in the annually published *Astronomical Almanac* or from multiple sources on the internet.

One might think that it would be perfectly adequate to determine the *day* of the equinox, that is, without direct reference to the *moment* of the equinox, using a simple but effective measuring technique known at least since Neolithic times (see 'The path of the sun' in Chapter 1), for which a massive edifice is unnecessary. However, this *modus operandi* is not a real alternative, since a more exact measurement would still be necessary in border situations, i.e. whenever the vernal equinox occurs very near to the moment of sunset at the reference spot. Furthermore, in my opinion this procedure would not reflect the spirit of the divine law, which associates the threshold criterion unequivocably with the moment, not the day of the equinox.

In my understanding, the reference spot instead serves to contextualize the concept of 'sunset' in terms of the revealed law. The 'canonical' day is a natural day, i.e. it encompasses the sidereal duration between two successive sunsets occurring exactly on the reference spot. The day of Naw-Rúz is accordingly that canonical day during which the moment of the beginning of spring occurs, and it carries the calendar name 1 Bahá'.

Fixing the day of Naw-Rúz at the reference spot, however, represents only one part of the procedure. A decisive aspect is still missing: the synchronization of the canonical calendar day with the actually occurring calendar day on every spot on earth. Without an unambiguous date equivalence, it would be impossible to know for certain on which natural day 1 Bahá' occurs elsewhere than at the reference spot itself. This equivalence is currently made possible by the international date line (IDL) in conjunction with the annual threshold. The IDL assumes of course that the day starts at midnight, that is, it is oriented on the *meridional* concept of day and is thus based on a great circle rather than an equinoctial terminator path. This orientation is less problematic, however, than the fact that the convention is static. A cyclic-progressive annual threshold and a static date line means that the positional relationship between threshold and date line varies from year to year. Sometimes the two lie at a considerable distance from one another and divide the globe into two typically different-sized zones; and sometimes they lie so near one another that they cross over several times. As a result, at the moment of the vernal equinox there are always at least two calendar days in currency – in the last-mentioned case, three. This complicated state of affairs is a consequence of the different nature of the two time boundaries (great circle vs. equinoctial terminator path) along with the fact that the international date line diverges considerably from the 180th longitude in two instances: once to pass through the Bering Strait and once to circumvent some current and former British island dependencies in the South Pacific.

For a concrete example we shall take a closer look at the year 154 of the Bahá'í Era (1997 according to the Gregorian calendar). The annual threshold at the start of this year runs approximately along the border between Iran and Pakistan. Our objective is to form a picture of the world-wide distribution of calendar days at the moment of the first point of Aries, when the paths of the annual and diurnal thresholds are identical. The diurnal threshold is by definition the border between two successive occidental days. As a consequence, during the time in which the people in Iran are experiencing late afternoon on one calendar day (day A), the people in Pakistan are experiencing early evening on the following day (day B). *Whenever we mentally cross the diurnal threshold in the eastward direction we must add one to our day count.*

Calendar day B extends at this moment across Pakistan and the rest of Asia right up to the international date line, whereas on the other side of this line, calendar day A is again in effect. *Whenever we mentally cross the date line in the eastward direction we must subtract one from our day count.* The IDL fulfils the indispensable global function of compensating for the day shift which occurs in conjunction with the diurnal threshold (see Illustration 2).

Whenever the annual threshold and the date line happen to overlap, as is the case for example in 2004, 2008, 2037 and 2041 (see Appendix D), there occur two spatially constricted zones, each consisting of several smaller, disjoint areas with deviating dates – either one day earlier or one day later than the calendar day in the zone which is current for the predominantly greater part of the globe: the former where the date line lies slightly to the west of the annual threshold, the latter where it lies slightly to the east (see Illustration 3). For a detailed description of this phenomenon see 'The occidental day and the calendar date' in Chapter 7.

Since only one of the days current at the moment of the vernal equinox can count as 1 Bahá', fixing the day of Naw-Rúz effectively means deciding in which of the two (or in the extreme case, three) zones of the earth the calendar date is to have the honour of coinciding with the equinox: namely, that zone in which the reference spot is situated. Let us assume for the sake of argument that the reference spot is the Shrine of Bahá'u'lláh in Bahjí (rather than somewhere in Teheran, to underline the hypothetical nature of the example). That would mean that, by definition, at the moment of the vernal equinox it is always 1 Bahá' at this spot in Bahjí. Should the vernal equinox occur in a given year shortly before sunset in Bahjí (so that the annual threshold lies slightly to the east of Bahjí), Naw-Rúz would occur on the first day of spring in Polynesia, on the American continents and in the greater part of Europe and Africa, that is, in all regions which lie in the same date zone as the Shrine of Bahá'u'lláh. The remaining parts of the earth (that is, in Asia, Australia

DETERMINING THE DAY OF NAW-RÚZ

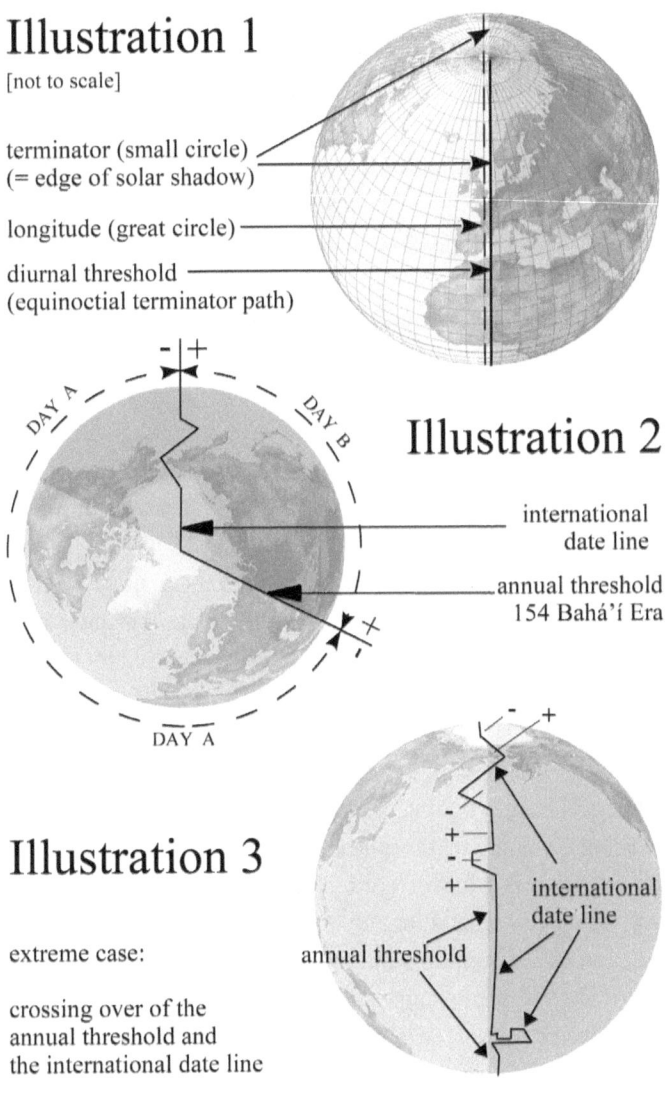

Illustration 1
[not to scale]

terminator (small circle)
(= edge of solar shadow)

longitude (great circle)

diurnal threshold
(equinoctial terminator path)

Illustration 2

international date line

annual threshold
154 Bahá'í Era

DAY A

Illustration 3

extreme case:

crossing over of the annual threshold and the international date line

annual threshold

international date line

and New Zealand, in Indo-, Micro- and Melanesia) lie in the zone of 2 Bahá, so that Naw-Rúz will already have occurred there on the calendar day *preceding* the first day of spring. If the equinox were instead to occur only a few seconds *after* sunset in Bahjí, the situation would be the reverse: the annual threshold would lie slightly west of Bahjí. As a result, the people in the first-mentioned part of the earth (America, etc.) would celebrate Naw-Rúz on the day *following* the astronomical first day of spring, since at the moment of the equinox they are situated in the zone of 19 'Alá', whereas those in the last-mentioned part (Asia etc.) together with Bahjí are situated in the zone of 1 Bahá', so that for them Naw-Rúz occurs on the 'correct' day.

Conversely, the precise day to be nominated as the day of Naw-Rúz can shift by up to one calendar day in one direction or the other depending on the geographic location of the chosen reference spot. To illustrate this effect, let us assume two (hypothetical) reference candidates: Bahjí and Golestan Palace in Teheran. The former lies at 35°5'30" East, the latter at 51°25'13" East: the arc difference of 16°19'43" represents a true time difference of $1^h5^m19^s$. Let us further assume that 20^m59^s of daylight still remain in Bahjí when the vernal equinox occurs – a situation which will in fact obtain in the year 2055. Since it is over an hour later in Teheran according to true solar time, sunset has already occurred there 43 minutes and 36 seconds ago in this sidereally identical moment: today's date is therefore one day later in Teheran than it is in Bahjí. (Aside: the missing 44 seconds have to do with the fact that Teheran is further away from the equator than is Bahjí). In other words, the day of Naw-Rúz which is determined using Teheran as the place of reference would be a complete formal day earlier that that determined using Bahjí. It is easy to appreciate that shifting the reference spot only a few metres (indeed, even a few millimetres) can decisively influence the determination of the reference day.

As the double name suggests, the reference spot (or place of reference) is expected to fulfil two requirements at once: in addition to its role as criterion of distinction between two possible days for Naw-Rúz (in other words, its role as reference spot), it is generally expected (in its function as place of reference) to be imbued with special historical or symbolic significance for the Bahá'í Faith. As far as I know, this expectation is nowhere to be found in writing, but it mirrors my own subjective but often repeated observation of the expectations of my fellow believers. It appears impossible at one and the same time to satisfy both requirements completely. From a purely technical standpoint, the optimal reference spot would be the intersection of the prime meridian with the equator. This choice would guarantee that, of the two (or three) possible candidate zones of the earth, that candidate with the greatest surface area would invariably be privileged. As a result, nowhere on earth would the moment of the vernal equinox ever occur more than about thirteen hours before the start or after the finish of the day of Naw-Rúz. Assuming that the position of the annual threshold is determined using a methodology which does not rely on sighting, for practical purposes it is irrelevant that this spot lies in the open sea, since no-one will ever have to visit it to take measurements. Nonetheless, this spot is problematic in that it has no particular symbolic association with the Bahá'í Faith.

That place on earth which best fulfils both requirements is London, the symbolic spot being the resting-place of Shoghi Effendi in the north of the city. This spot lies a mere twelve kilometres or so west of the prime meridian. To be sure, there would be a measurable variation in the precise sidereal moment of sunset from one year to the next on account of this location's relatively great distance from the equator, but this variation would never amount to more than a few minutes. By contrast, the preference for a place of reference with a symbolic connection with the Báb or Bahá'u'lláh, the founders of the Bábí and Bahá'í religions, respectively, implies a compromise. One must either

- tolerate the unequal division of the globe and the ensuing consequence that in some years the smaller part of the earth would dictate the choice of the day of Naw-Rúz, or

- decide on a new date line 180° away from the longitude of the reference spot and thus deviate from the internationally accepted convention.→[12]

Past statements by the Universal House of Justice seem to emphasize the practical side of this issue over the symbolic, treating the reference spot primarily as a technical prerequisite for implementing the divine law:

> Until the Universal House of Justice decides upon the spot on which the calculations for establishing the date of Naw-Rúz each year are to be based it is not possible to state exactly the correspondence between Bahá'í dates and Gregorian dates for any year . . . The Universal House of Justice feels that this is not a matter of urgency and, in the meantime, is having research conducted into such questions.[13]

In its wisdom, the Universal House of Justice has made the final ruling on calendar matters dependent on the prior examination of all relevant texts, historical documents and astronomical data.[14] The view that the selection of a particular spot on earth is necessary must therefore also be considered to be provisional, since the factors on which this view is based likewise belong to the data which, according to the Universal House of Justice, first have to be examined and studied.

The reference-spot method for the determination of New Year is closely reminiscent of that of the Iranian national calendar (see 'Indo-Iranian calendar systems' in Chapter 2), the two differing from one another in three respects:

- First, the Jalálí method serves to identify the calendar day which *begins* at the moment nearest to the moment of the vernal equinox. In contrast, the Badí' method serves to identify the day *in the course of which* the vernal point is reached.

- Second, the Jalálí calendar was conceived for a cultural area whose geographic extension to the east and west incorporated a time difference of a few hours at the very most. At the time of its conception, the question of the relation between the demarcation of the day and something like a date line was simply not given. In contrast, the Badí' calendar was, right from its inception, deliberately intended to serve as a world calendar. As a result, the role of the date line in connection with the annual threshold is for the Badí' calendar at least as crucial for determining the start of the year as is the reference spot.

- Third, for the Badí' calendar the delineation between two calendar days is the moment of sunset, and not midnight, as is the case with the Jalálí calendar. In this connection, the expression *yek daqíqeh* ('one minute') can be seen to serve a contrastive function, i.e. to emphasize the difference between the old (Jalálí) and the new (Badí') calendar. This view stands in agreement with the reading (a) discussed above, which was disadvantaged by the English-language translation but favoured by the German.

The reference-spot method: Doctrine or alternative?

It has always been considered beyond dispute that the future New Year ruling would be formulated on the basis of a reference spot, whatever its ultimate location. Two arguments in particular have generally been cited to support this conclusion:

- A reference spot is technically indispensable; and

- Shoghi Effendi explicitly stipulated the use of a reference spot.

The first argument will be dealt with below in 'The cyclic-progressive method for fixing the day of Naw-Rúz', where it will be amply demonstrated that strict observance of the divine law is feasible and practicable without the aid of a reference spot. Therefore, the notion of the indispensability of the reference spot *in principle* rests solely on the second argument.

In a note accompanying the text of the English translation of the Kitáb-i Aqdas, the editors observe:

> The Guardian has stated that the implementation, worldwide, of the law

concerning the timing of Naw-Rúz will require the choice of a particular spot on earth which will serve as the standard for the fixing of the time of the spring equinox. He also indicated that the choice of this spot has been left to the decision of the Universal House of Justice.[15]

This text reflects the consensus opinion that the reference spot is an inalienable component of the calendar ruling, stressing that this view has been confirmed by the Guardian himself. In face of such a clear and unambiguous summary of Shoghi Effendi's position and in light of his unchallengeable authority, it might well be asked if it is legitimate to discuss alternative methods at all.

Total reliance on a paraphrase, whatever its source, is an inappropriate strategy for coping with an issue of such vital importance to the correct understanding of a passage from one of the central figures of the Bahá'í Faith; we should instead insist on examining Shoghi Effendi's own words. The editors did not provide a source reference, but there does exist a letter to the National Spiritual Assembly of the United States written on 15 May 1940 on behalf of Shoghi Effendi containing a passage which reads:

> Regarding Naw-Ruz: if the vernal equinox falls on the 21st of March before sunset it is celebrated on that day. If at any time after sunset, Naw-Rúz will then, as stated by Baha'u'llah, fall on the 22nd. *As to which spot should be regarded as the standard, this is a matter which the Universal House of Justice will have to decide* [my italics]. The American National Spiritual Assembly need not therefore take any action in this matter at present.[16]

One cannot fail to notice the nearly complete thematic identity between the note in the Kitáb-i Aqdas and the italicized portion of the above passage. Without wishing to exclude the possibility that additional, perhaps unpublished material may in fact exist, I suggest with all due caution that this is the statement which the note in the Kitáb-i Aqdas was intended to paraphrase. We will examine this passage in detail.→[17]

Although the letter in which the passage occurs was not written personally by Shoghi Effendi, it does have official character, being directed to a National Spiritual Assembly and addressing 'a large number of questions about different aspects of the Bahá'í Faith and the operation of its Administrative Order.'[18] We may safely assume that the gist of the individual responses in that letter stems from the Guardian himself, routine details perhaps being left for his secretary to fill in. Along with the editors of the English version of the Kitáb-i Aqdas we will assume here that, for all intents and purposes, Shoghi Effendi is the author of the letter.

It is my understanding that, whatever the passage may additionally mean, it was intended as an instruction to the National Assembly not to take any action *whatsoever* with regard to determining Naw-Rúz on the basis of the vernal equinox. Apparently not everyone shares this view. By assuming that the two occurrences of the word 'matter' refer to the same thing, i.e. that the injunction to non-action applies solely to the issue of the spot, the first part of the passage can be interpreted as an elaboration of the interim ruling currently in force. For example, in the German Bahá'í pocket calendar up to the year 157 BE (2000–2001 CE) the current ruling was explained as follows :

> The start of the year (Naw-Rúz) is celebrated on the day during which the sun reaches the first point of spring. Pending a convention regarding the reference spot for this date, this day is 21 March. Where the vernal equinox occurs after sunset on this day, the New Year celebration shall not take place until the following day, on which the numbering of the days should theoretically begin [German: *beginnen müßte* (nowadays *müsste*); my translation].

In other words, the presentation treats the passage from May 1940 as the official provisional Naw-Rúz ruling, acknowledging at the same time that this ruling is not upheld in practice. This understanding is of course highly problematic, since it implies that Shoghi Effendi had issued a directive which everyone simply ignored. Note that the word 'where' suggests that the *local* sunset is to be used as the criterion for delimiting the day, presumably unless or until such time as the Universal House of Justice should decide otherwise. This 'ruling', if actually carried out in full as it stands, would of course render the calendar useless as an instrument for coordinating the affairs of the international community.

Prompted by remarks in an early draft of the original German-language version of the present study, in which this description was critically examined, a proofreader (who is also a prominent member of the German-speaking Bahá'í community) directed an enquiry to the National Spiritual Assembly of Germany asking for clarification. The result was that, in subsequent years, the phrase 'on which the numbering of the days should theoretically begin' was replaced with 'even though the days are numbered from the 21st' – clearly in an attempt to achieve the impossible task of reconciling the 'directive' of 15 May 1940 with the ruling explained in a letter written some ten years later (see below), but in effect only manufacturing an artificial situation in which – if the 'instruction' were to be taken literally – the festival of Naw-Rúz would forfeit its relationship to the day of Naw-Rúz, with all the consequences this would have on its liturgical significance as culmination of the period of fasting.

In fact, as the note in the Kitáb-i Aqdas correctly points out, the purpose of the 1940 passage is to explain the conditions necessary for the future world-wide implementation of a final ruling. The convention Shoghi Effendi had deemed appropriate at that stage assiduously avoided the sunset and equinox criteria (and therewith the reference spot issue) and instead bound the Bahá'í calendar to an already existing system, namely to the Gregorian calendar in the West and, to a certain extent, to the Iranian national calendar in the Orient. The interim convention valid for the West was clearly summarized in a letter written on behalf of Shoghi Effendi on 5 July 1950, addressed to the National Spiritual Assembly of the United States:

> He would like to point out that if the believers gather before sundown on a certain date it does not matter if the meeting continues after sunset; it may still be considered as being held on the day they gathered. The Naw-Rúz Feast should be held [i.e. commenced – my comment] on March 21 before sunset . . . the Naw-Rúz is our New Year, a Feast of hospitality and rejoicing.[19]

Note that the words 'sundown' and 'sunset' are not being used here in conjunction with the time of the equinox; they simply designate the natural (i.e. local) sunset which marks the boundary between two Bahá'í calendar days.

In its enquiry of 18 April 1940, which prompted the response of 15 May 1940, the National Spiritual Assembly of the United States and Canada had suggested implementing a ruling based instead on the calculated time of the equinox:→[20]

> The ... Chicago Assembly suggests that the NSA determine the correct date of Naw-Rúz astronomically and notify the believers in advance, to prevent confusion. The Egyptian statement declares that Naw-Rúz begins when the sun enters the sign of Aries, and the reckoning of the beginning of spring is made by the astronomical observatories for years in advance. The NSA could obtain the information from the Naval Observatory each year. However, the question is raised whether the determination of Naw-Rúz should come from the Bahá'í World Centre.[21]

The 'Egyptian statement' referred to in this enquiry is a statement issued by the National Spiritual Assembly of Egypt and the Sudan in the early 1930s, the historic significance of which has been documented by Shoghi Effendi.[22] The Arabic original was published in *The Bahá'í World* in 1936,[23] a Persian translation subsequently in 1940.[24] The document contains only one paragraph (item 52) dealing with the calendar, and its content is essentially a paraphrase of the divine law as specified in the Kitáb-i Aqdas (para. 16, Q35).

Note that the enquiry from the American National Spiritual Assembly in no way encourages a statement or explanation from Shoghi Effendi regarding the reference spot: neither in the text of the enquiry nor in the Egyptian statement is this subject touched upon at all. It is therefore clear that Shoghi Effendi introduced the subject for some good reason of his own – and the most obvious reason might appear to be that he considered the reference spot an essential component of the New Year ruling as revealed by Bahá'u'lláh, just as the text of Note 26 of the Kitáb-i Aqdas suggests.

And yet there is another, indeed a compelling reason why Shoghi

Effendi should have chosen to mention the reference spot. We must bear in mind that, by proposing a New Year calculation based on the true moment of the vernal equinox, the American National Spiritual Assembly was in effect demanding the immediate implementation of this aspect of divine law. Shoghi Effendi didn't react to this suggestion simply with a blank refusal; instead, he carefully explained why the implementation of the Assembly's suggestion was not feasible at the time. The reasoning which informed Shoghi Effendi's response can best be illustrated by treating the response as if it were a syllogism, i.e. a formal proof comprising three propositions: two premises and a conclusion.

The first or major premise consists of a paraphrase of the Law as stipulated in the Kitáb-i Aqdas:

> Regarding Naw-Rúz: If the vernal equinox falls on the 21st of March before sunset, it is celebrated on that day. If at any time after sunset, Naw-Rúz will then, as stated by Bahá'u'lláh, fall on the 22nd.

In this paraphrase, Shoghi Effendi accomplishes two things. First, he takes up the ostensible theme of the Assembly's suggestion, that being to 'determine the correct date of Naw-Rúz'. The date of Naw-Rúz in the Badí' calender is always 1 Bahá': this date is fixed by definition and cannot be 'determined' – neither by astronomical nor by any other means. The 'correct date' can here only be a reference to the corresponding date in another calendar. It is highly probable that this was a slip on the part of the Assembly, which really meant 'the correct (i.e. astronomically accurate) *day* of Naw-Rúz', and equally probable that Shoghi Effendi recognized it as such. Nevertheless, he responded according to what was actually said, not to what might otherwise have been meant. It is noteworthy that Shoghi Effendi's paraphrase is not a formulation of the law as such, but rather a non-rigorous restatement of it in terms of the Gregorian calendar. We shall later encounter a possible explanation why the wording might have assumed just this form.

Second, he shifts the emphasis away from the question of the correct date (which is never really explained, there being no need) and concentrates instead on the effect of the occurrence of sunset in relation to the Gregorian calendar date: note the twofold occurrence of the word 'sunset' in this short passage. The gist of this paraphrase is that the determination of the day of Naw-Rúz is conditioned by the conjunction of two events: the advent of the vernal equinox and the moment of sunset. Obviously, a definition of 'day of Naw-Rúz' sufficiently well-defined to satisfy the requirements of law is not possible unless the events on which this definition is based are themselves well-defined. Whereas the meaning of the term 'vernal equinox' is undisputed, as discussed in 'Written sources' above, the definition of the term 'sunset' is still open. Reduced to its essentials, the major premise of the syllogism thus reads:

> The implementation of the divine law regarding the determination of the day of Naw-Rúz presupposes the unambiguous definition of the concept of 'sunset' for the purpose of the law.

The cogency of a well-formed syllogism depends on the demonstrable validity of its premises. The validity of the major premise is in the present case established by appeal to the revealed Word ('as stated by Bahá'u'lláh').

The second or minor premise is that very statement whose correct interpretation is of central concern to us here:

> As to which spot should be regarded as the standard, this is a matter which the Universal House of Justice will have to decide.

In other words, the precise meaning of the term 'sunset' as used in the major premise cannot be known until the Universal House of Justice has legislated with regard to the issue of the 'spot' (more below).

The logical and unavoidable conclusion (signalled by the word 'therefore') which follows from these two premises is that

> [t]he American National Spiritual Assembly need not therefore take any action in this matter at present

– whereby 'need not take any action' is, as I read it, a diplomatic way of instructing the National Spiritual Assembly to abandon the idea altogether.

Let us now examine the minor premise in more detail. Shoghi Effendi does not offer an explicit verification as he did for the major premise, but it is nevertheless relatively easy to infer. The premise is in fact itself a proposition, being the conclusion of an embedded syllogism which might look something like this:

major premise:	Matters which are not explicitly revealed in the Writings must be decided by the Universal House of Justice.
minor premise:	The reference spot is a matter which is not explicitly mentioned in the Writings.
conclusion:	The matter of the reference spot must be decided by the Universal House of Justice.

As before, the demonstration of the validity of the major premise lies in the written word – in this case specifically in the Lesser Covenant,→25 according to which Shoghi Effendi possesses the authority to interpret the revealed Word of God, whereas anything which is not explicitly mentioned in the Writings is 'a matter which the Universal House of Justice will have to decide', or as expressed in the Will and Testament of 'Abdu'l-Bahá,

> [u]nto the Most Holy Book everyone must turn and all that is not expressly recorded therein must be referred to the Universal House of Justice.[26]

Shoghi Effendi took great pains to uphold the division of authority and responsibility between the Guardianship and the House of Justice:

> [T]he Guardian of the Faith has been made the Interpreter of the Word and ... the Universal House of Justice has been invested with the function of legislating on matters not expressly revealed in the teachings. The interpretation of the Guardian, functioning within his own sphere, is as authoritative

and binding as the enactments of the International House of Justice, whose exclusive right and prerogative is to pronounce upon and deliver the final judgment on such laws and ordinances as Bahá'u'lláh has not expressly revealed. Neither can, nor will ever, infringe upon the sacred and prescribed domain of the other. Neither will seek to curtail the specific and undoubted authority with which both have been divinely invested.[27]

The Guardian could not settle the question of the reference spot himself, since to do so would in effect 'infringe upon the sacred and prescribed domain' and 'curtail the specific and undoubted authority' of the future Universal House of Justice. There are indeed numerous examples of interim rulings by Shoghi Effendi in non-scriptural matters which could not reasonably be postponed until the supreme legislative body of the Bahá'í Faith had been established – the structure of the elections for the inauguration of the Universal House of Justice, for example – but only in cases where a later revision by the House would be feasible, and always explicitly qualified in this respect. In the case of the choice of reference spot, however, an 'interim' ruling would be extremely difficult to revise subsequently (recall the fate of the Zoroastrian calendar): therefore, 'this is a matter which the Universal House of Justice will *have to* decide.'

Note that the 'sacred and prescribed domains' of the Guardian and the Universal House of Justice are mutually exclusive. As a consequence, in the 'inner syllogism' discussed above, the minor premise and the conclusion are interchangeable:

- The Lesser Covenant stipulates that a matter is to be decided by the Universal House of Justice if – and only if – it is not expressly revealed in the Writings;

- Shoghi Effendi has clarified that the matter of the reference spot is to be decided by the Universal House of Justice;

- therefore, Shoghi Effendi has clarified that the matter of the reference spot is not expressly revealed in the Writings.

In other words: far from being an indication that the reference spot is mandatory, the letter of May 1940 effectively confirms that the concept of the reference spot is non-scriptural.

Moreover, Shoghi Effendi did not write something like 'the Universal House of Justice will have to select an appropriate spot'; instead he wrote 'this is a *matter* which the Universal House of Justice will have to decide'. This choice of words clearly indicates that the *entire issue* of the reference spot, not simply its location, awaited legislation. And quite aside from this formulation, the non-scriptural nature of the notion of the reference spot in itself guarantees that the supreme legislative body was free to take whatever decision it deemed appropriate – including whether or not a reference spot is to be employed *at all*.

Judging from the economy of the expression 'which spot should be regarded as the standard,' Shoghi Effendi obviously felt safe in assuming that the American National Spiritual Assembly would already be acquainted with the notion – despite the fact that no mention of it appears to exist in the published writings of any of the central figures of the Bahá'í Faith, nor for example in Esslemont's *Bahá'u'lláh and the New Era* (the standard introductory work available at that time, some chapters of which had been read and approved by 'Abdu'l-Bahá), nor apparently in any previous letters from or on behalf of Shoghi Effendi. But although the mechanisms of oral transmission explain how this idea might be perpetuated despite the silence of the scriptures – I have been unable to locate any written explanation of the purpose of the spot formulated earlier than November 1973[28] – they fail to explain where the notion came from in the first place.

Logically there are only two possibilities: either the origin is to be attributed to putative oral teachings of the Báb and/or of Bahá'u'lláh, or it is to be sought in some source external to the Bahá'í Faith. The first hypothesis would certainly provide a satisfactory explanation for the birth of the idea, but since it is pure conjecture either way, it is of no help in determining doctrinal status – quite aside from the Bahá'í Faith's rejection in principle of teachings based on hearsay or 'pilgrims' notes':

DETERMINING THE DAY OF NAW-RÚZ

According to the Teachings of Bahá'u'lláh no authority can be attached to a mere hearsay, no matter through whom it may come. The Tablets that bear the seal or signature of Bahá'u'lláh and the Master are the only parts of the literature that have any authority and that constitute the basis of our belief. All other forms of literature may bear points of interest but they cannot be considered as authentic.[29]

As for the second hypothesis, the successful identification of an external influence would in no way prove that the notion of a reference spot stood in contradiction to Bahá'u'lláh's intentions, any more than, say, Bahá'u'lláh's teachings on ontology are invalidated by the clear evidence of their Islamic provenance. However, since we are here merely endeavouring to demonstrate that the use of the reference spot is not *necessarily* a doctrinal imperative, in the absence of written evidence to the contrary it will suffice for our purposes to present a reasonable explanation where such a belief might well have originated. Surprisingly, the opening chapter of this story is relatively well documented in a reliable, if not normative, written source from the earliest days of the Faith. As official chronicler of Bábí/Bahá'í early history, Nabíl-i A'ẓam wrote:

> *yawm-e nawrúz hamán rúz ast keh beh qá'ede-ye taqvím-e írán dar shab yá rúz án rúz shams beh borj-e ḥamal várd shavad agar cheh yek daqíqe qabl az ghorúb-e áftáb báshad bar khaláf-e qá'ede-ye sábeq-e ahl-e írán keh agar taḥvíl ba'ad az ẓohr váqe' mishad rúz-e ba'ad-ra nawrúz qorár mídádand* . . .[30]

(On the basis of the Iranian calendar, the day of Naw-Rúz is the day on which the sun enters the sign of Aries, whether at night or during the day, even if this happens one minute prior to sunset, in contrast to the earlier ruling in Iran, according to which one chose the following day as Naw-Rúz if the shift [i.e. the entering of the sun into the sign of Aries: my comment] should occur after midday . . . [my translation])

The 'earlier ruling' mentioned here was, needless to say, the general practice of the populace in Iran at that time: Nabíl clearly viewed the Jalálí calendar, for which the place of reference is an intrinsic feature, as the natural precursor of the Badí' calendar. If we remove all parts of Nabíl's explanation which are nearly identical to the aforementioned passages from the Bayán and the Kitáb-i Aqdas we are left with the following:

> On the basis of the Iranian calendar . . . (Badí' ruling) . . . in contrast to the earlier ruling in Iran, according to which one chose the following day as Naw-Rúz if the shift should occur after midday.

From these words it is clear that Nabíl considered the two respective methods for determining the start of the new year to be identical in all respects save for the latter's replacement of the midday ruling with the sunset ruling – the one feature which Bahá'u'lláh had explicitly mentioned in the passage which Nabíl was obviously paraphrasing here.[31] It would be of decisive importance to learn on whose authority Nabíl invoked the Jalálí calendar in this fashion. Had he cited a source, or if a comparable statement could be found anywhere in the writings of the Báb or Bahá'u'lláh, then this question could be settled on the basis of textual evidence. Since that is apparently not the case, however, we might consider taking Nabíl's testimony at face value and entertaining the possibility of an altogether different explanation: namely, that for everyone in the prevailing cultural context of 19th-century Iran – and that includes Nabíl, along with the rest of the Bábí community – the assumption of a close family relationship between the two calendars was simply too self-evident to be deemed worthy of special mention.

It is not hard to imagine that the Jalálí calendar served as a model for the early Bábí and Bahá'í communities in Iran. Indeed, it may well be that, at least at the beginning, the Bábís followed the leap-year rhythm of the Jalálí calendar, just as the Bahá'ís in the West followed that of the Gregorian calendar. Adopting this calendar's method for determining New Year's Day would have presented the Iranian believers of the first hour with a solution which was not only ready-made but also optimal in numerous respects:

- First, in all social classes in Iran the Jalálí calendar, not the Islamic calendar, is the calendar which was then and is still today most generally in use and which therefore enjoys the same predominance in Iran as the Gregorian calendar does in the West. Conformity with the Jalálí New Year, which guaranteed equivalence between the two calendars year after year, would therefore have been just as operationally convenient for the Bábís (and later the Bahá'ís) in the Orient as parity with the Gregorian first day of spring had been for Bahá'ís in the West prior to 172 BE / 2015 CE.

- Second, the agreement between tropical and calendar year was more exact in the Jalálí calendar than in any other predecessor to the Badí' calendar. Of all possible prototypes, the Jalálí method remains without peer (particularly when employed within the boundaries of Iran).

- Third, a deviation from the appointed date of the Iranian national holiday Naw-Rúz (resulting for example from the use of a different basis or method of calculation) would have been an unnecessary provocation in a time of vehement and brutal Shí'ite animosity against the Bábí community of believers.

Nabíl's comparison with the Jalálí calendar could be an indication that this practice had in the meantime been abandoned, resulting in a disparity between the Jalálí and the Badí' calendars in the timing of Naw-Rúz (see Appendix B), but it is equally possible that it was intended as a corrective for posterity, perhaps for Nabíl's contemporaries as well.

Furthermore, with the exception of one curious remark concerning its possible abolition,[32] the significance of the date line seems until now never to have been seriously discussed in writing, if at all. And yet, as we have seen, the date line is a key factor in the fixing of the start of the year in the Badí' calendar – not just in theory but also in practice, especially in the wake of the global expansion of the Bahá'í Faith since the early part of the 20th century.

Taking all things together, it seems to me that Bahá'u'lláh's and

'Abdu'l-Bahá's toleration of the *status quo* cannot justifiably be interpreted as a tacit decision regarding the New Year ruling; instead, it appears to indicate that the time for the final shaping of the calendar simply wasn't yet ripe – a hypothesis which appears to be borne out by the testimony of Shoghi Effendi as well as by earlier remarks from the Universal House of Justice, which saw itself called upon to deliberate upon a solution to be implemented as a comprehensive piece of legislation at some appropriate time in the future.[33]

It is plausible to assume that the whole question of the place of reference didn't became a topic of lively discussion until after the Shrine of Bahá'u'lláh in Bahjí became the Qiblih for Bahá'ís, resulting in the first serious alternative candidate to the traditional place of reference Teheran. This was also a period in which a relatively peaceful (if not exactly long-lived) co-existence between the Shí'ites and the Bahá'ís had set in, in other words, a period during which a deviation from the timetable imposed by Shí'i practice became imaginable for the first time."[34] It is even conceivable that the very idea of the 'spot' as a freely determinable factor first became established in the collective consciousness of the Bahá'í community at this time. The issue as to whether or not a place of reference is a technical necessity would hardly have played a significant role: even in the unlikely event that this issue was ever contemplated, the inseparability of the practical and symbolic functions of the reference spot *cum* place of reference would have guaranteed that it would hardly have been given any serious attention. For here were two symbolically laden places on earth competing for the honour of being crowned with the title of place of reference for the world calendar of the new Era: the one, the city of Bahá'u'lláh's birth and the cradle of the Bahá'í Faith; the other, the final resting-place of Bahá'u'lláh, to Bahá'ís the most sacred spot on earth. A controversy such as this could well have seriously threatened the inner cohesion of the young community of believers, and 'Abdu'l-Bahá would surely have been at pains to keep the entire discussion concerning the New Year regulation under quarantine. This could also possibly explain why we have no written instructions from 'Abdu'l-Bahá on this topic: a public admonition could well have fuelled the very discussion which it had been intended to curb.

Iranian Bahá'í teachers who pioneered to Europe and the United States during and after the closing years of the 19th century naturally handed on whatever they thought they knew about the Bahá'í Faith, including the idea of the reference spot, and their Western neophytes would understandably pass on whatever they had learnt to those whom they in turn brought into the Faith. Unlike the Bahá'ís in the Orient, however, Western Bahá'ís typically knew nothing about the Jalálí or Iranian national calendar. Divorced from its cultural origins, the indispensability of a reference spot inevitably mutated for them into something akin to an apodictic truth – of all forms of belief, the one most immune to scrutiny – which has been accepted without question down to the present day.

Let us once again examine the motivation behind the wording of Shoghi Effendi's 1940 statement. One might argue that the division of responsibility between the Guardianship and the House of Justice was at best a side issue, that Shoghi Effendi mentioned the reference spot primarily for the same reason that he mentioned sunset or the vernal equinox: because it is impossible to talk sensibly about the New Year ruling revealed by Bahá'u'lláh without touching on all its essential features. The corollary, of course, is that Shoghi Effendi would consider any discussion of the New Year ruling which did *not* include mention of the reference spot to be incomplete and incoherent.

In this light it is worth examining a document which is similar in content to the paragraph in the 1940 response from Shoghi Effendi. An English-language rendition of the passage concerning the New Year ruling quoted earlier from Nabíl's chronicle appeared in *The Bahá'í World* in a section entitled 'Additional Material gleaned from Nabíl's Narrative (Vol. II), Regarding the Bahá'í Calendar' for the first time in Volume III (1928–1930), in corrected form again in Volume IV (1930–1932) and thereafter without change in each and every subsequent volume until and including Volume XX (1986–1992). Shoghi Effendi was with absolute certainty intimately acquainted with this section; in fact he was very likely its author.

Since Shoghi Effendi's association with this section is pivotal to this discussion, we will take the trouble here to examine the evidence of authorship in detail. First, Shoghi Effendi's continuously active participation in the collection of material for and the layout of *The Bahá'í World* is amply documented in his letters of 27 November 1924 and 12 October 1925 concerning the then pending appearance of the first volume, known at that time as *The Bahá'í Yearbook*, as well as through numerous statements which occur in Volume XIII (1954–1963, the first volume to appear following the death of Shoghi Effendi and dedicated to his memory), especially in the introduction to the volume, in the tribute by Horace Holley in the section entitled 'In Memoriam'[35] and in the article 'The Guardian of the Bahá'í Faith' by Amatu'l-Bahá' Rúḥiyyih Khánum.[36] Second, publication of Shoghi Effendi's English-language translation of the first volume of Nabíl's chronicle under the title *The Dawn-Breakers* (1932), along with the section entitled 'Historical Data gleaned from Nabíl's Narrative (Vol. II), Regarding Bahá'u'lláh' which appeared for the first time in Volume IV (1930–1932) (note the similar title), together with a letter of 20 March 1932, in which he confirms his authorship of this section, attest to his intensive occupation with Nabíl's work just at this time. Finally, Shoghi Effendi relates in this same letter that he has personally proof-read the section on the calendar which appeared in Volume III of *The Bahá'í World*, listing some of the errors which he had discovered. The corrections which appear for the first time in the identical section in Volume IV correspond to the remarks in this letter and are dispersed throughout the section, occurring both before and after the point in the text where the statement at issue is located.

Excerpts from the letters mentioned in this examination were kindly included in a detailed memorandum from the Research Department of the Bahá'í World Centre[37] composed in answer to an enquiry from me. This memorandum closes with the understatement: 'It therefore seems quite reasonable to assume that Shoghi Effendi was aware of the content of the section in question and that he might well have been its author.'

The text is not a translation in the strict sense, since it was prepared with the intention of rendering the subject matter accessible to a wide reading public. In the above-mentioned memorandum the Research Department wrote, '... we are of the opinion that the English passage in question . . . may be described as a partial paraphrase which emphasizes the principal content and the central principle of the Persian text in order to make the Bahá'í Naw-Rúz clear to Persian and non-Persian as well as non-Bahá'í readers of the *Bahá'í World*.' For example, at one point in the text a practical example addresses the year 1930, although the original text was written in 1891. In the same spirit, the passage in question dealing with the day of Naw-Rúz is presented in relation to the Gregorian calendar instead of the Iranian national calendar, a revision which in turn necessitated a reformulation of the entire passage:

> The day of Naw-Rúz falls on the 21st of March only if the vernal Equinox precedes the setting of the sun on that day. Should the vernal Equinox take place after sunset, Naw-Rúz will have to be celebrated on the following day.

This passage describes the relationship between the vernal equinox and sunset in terms of the Gregorian calendar, bearing in mind that the passage was written for 'Persian and non-Persian as well as non-Bahá'í readers of the *Bahá'í World'*. The calendar expression '21st of March' is in my view to be treated as exemplary: since this is not a formulation of the calendar law, but merely an example of what its implementation would *look like* from the perspective of the Gregorian calendar, an exhaustive description would be more confusing than illustrative. (The vernal equinox occurred at the prime meridian on 21 March in over 84 per cent of the years between 1900 and 1931.)

It is instructive to note that this passage is nearly word for word the same as what we have described above as the major premise in the relevant passage of the letter of 15 May 1940:

> Regarding Naw-Rúz: if the vernal equinox falls on the 21st of March before sunset, it is celebrated on that day. If at any time after sunset, Naw-Rúz will then, as stated by Bahá'u'lláh, fall on the 22nd.

When filling in the details of letters to be sent on his behalf, Shoghi Effendi's secretaries habitually consulted archives and other sources in search of appropriate text passages which he had previously written or approved. There is therefore a high degree of probability that this self-same passage in *The Bahá'í World* written ten years earlier served directly or indirectly as the textual precedent for the corresponding passage in the letter of 1940. That would explain why the wording of this passage of the letter did not optimally match the original enquiry in theme, style and level of discourse.

A reference spot is mentioned nowhere in this section – a fact which is all the more striking, considering that the Jalálí place of reference is unmistakably present in spirit in the Persian original. But even if we overlook this omission in the text in the volume of *The Bahá'í World* in which it first appeared, we would expect that the renewed focus on the whole 'spot' issue occasioned by composing the 1940 letter would have induced Shoghi Effendi to arrange for a corresponding amendment to this perennial section of *The Bahá'í World*. However, in the seventeen years which elapsed between the writing of the letter and the death of Shoghi Effendi, no such amendment was ever undertaken. This state of affairs is inconsistent with the thesis that the indispensability of the reference spot is confirmed by its being mentioned in the letter of 1940.

In summary: however one views the 1940 statement, the weight of evidence which it provides is not sufficient to justify concluding categorically that Shoghi Effendi insisted on the use of a reference spot in the implementation of the New Year ruling as stipulated by Bahá'u'lláh. If anything, the evidence supports precisely the opposite – and suggests moreover that the wording in Kitáb-i Aqdas Q35 does not, as Nabíl seems to have assumed, imply the wholesale adoption of the Jalálí technique, including its use of a reference spot. That having been said, the example set by the Jalálí calendar and the presentation in this study both demonstrate that the reference-spot method is indeed a practicable solution. I would merely argue that the implementation of the reference-spot method should not be treated as having been a foregone conclusion.

The cyclic-progressive method for fixing the day of Naw-Rúz

The second method which we will investigate is based on the assumption that the day on which the vernal equinox is to take place is the *local* day, and the sunset which delineates the day is unique to each respective locality: in other words, that Bahá'u'lláh's decree applies equally to every individual believer, regardless of where he happens to be on the face of the earth. Just how the day of Naw-Rúz can be determined under these circumstances will be explained here in full detail.

As in the case of the reference-spot method, the date line is of crucial importance for satisfying the requirements of the divine law as presented here. In contrast to the reference-spot method, however, its definition does not rely on complementary ordinances or external conventions; instead, its occurrence proceeds naturally and automatically from the application of the provisions of Bahá'u'lláh. In the description to follow we will at first ignore the issue of the date line; it will come up on its own in the course of discussion.

We ought to start by gaining an exact picture of how the first point of Aries is experienced overall on Earth. For this purpose, let us observe our world with our mind's eye at a distance of some 50,000 km, the planet hovering in the centre of our field of view with the North Pole at the top. The rays of the sun shine from the left side of the field of vision and illuminate roughly half the earth: the border of the shadow, i.e. the diurnal threshold, extends in an apparently straight line from the North Pole to the South Pole nearly through the middle of that part of the surface of the earth which is visible to us, which is accordingly bright on the left side and dark on the right (see Illustration 1 on page 149). Moreover, since precisely at this moment the earth has reached that location in its orbit which is known as the vernal point, the diurnal threshold is likewise the annual threshold. We must hold the picture frozen in this state for the time being.

This is the moment at which the current day is to be regarded as the day of Naw-Rúz in accordance with this assumed reading of the divine law: it should at this very moment be 1 Bahá' everywhere in the world.

The natural day is relatively more or less advanced for a given individual, depending on where on the face of the earth this individual happens to be. In order to visualize this situation, let us imagine different people spread across the earth, say, as a human chain along a single latitude. This chain extends to the right (i.e. eastward) from the diurnal threshold up to the 'edge' of the globe, then disappears behind the visual half of the globe, appearing again on the left 'edge' of the globe and continuing until it once again reaches the middle of the picture (see Illustration 4). The position of the sun, and therefore the age of the day, will be considered in the following from the perspective of the individuals in the chain.

The person standing exactly to the right of the diurnal threshold experiences this moment both as the start of a new natural day and as the beginning of a new tropical year. For this person, the requirement that the first point of Aries must be reached at some time during this day is fulfilled in the *first possible instant* of 1 Bahá'. The same day began somewhat earlier for the persons standing further to the right (east) in the picture: every one of these persons is just now experiencing a moment of the day somewhere between sunset and midnight. Since the first moment of spring has occurred some time during the first quarter of this day, it counts as New Year's Day for these persons as well.

Those individuals who are situated in that part of the human chain visible on the left half of the picture are experiencing a moment in time toward the close of the day, somewhere between midday and sunset – likewise on 1 Bahá' (the first day of spring), that is, on the same natural day as those in the invisible half of the globe and those in the right half of the picture. For the person in the chain whose foot lies just short of the diurnal threshold, the divinely ordained condition is fulfilled in the *last possible instant* of New Year's Day.

Note that the world-wide fulfilment of the divine law is technically possible only in the very instant of the actual astronomical vernal equinox – not a moment earlier or later. Note also that, with the sole exception of those persons standing precisely on the diurnal threshold, the day of

Naw-Rúz began *prior* to the actual moment of the equinox, that is, the fulfilment of the specified condition (i.e. the occurrence of the vernal equinox) generally occurs some seconds, minutes or hours *following* the local start of the new year.

This state of affairs has two decisive consequences for the fixing of New Year's Day. The first of these is that the annual threshold also assumes the function of the date line. (This statement will be reexamined later on in this chapter in 'The relationship between the annual threshold and the date line'.) To demonstrate the truth of this assertion we need merely concentrate our gaze on the very last person in the human chain and consider the state of the same scenario a few seconds later. The annual threshold remains in position, whereas the diurnal threshold has shifted slightly westward, creating a gap between the two which becomes progressively wider as time progresses. Those persons within this gap, who a moment before had existed just *before* sunset on 1 Bahá', now exist just *after* sunset on 2 Bahá'. Their immediate neighbours to the east, who had earlier been standing right up against the diurnal threshold and for whom 1 Bahá' had just then begun, continue to write their current date as 1 Bahá'. In other words, the divine law as it is here conceived can be fulfilled only on the condition that the annual threshold and the date line are coextensive.

From a technical point of view, the following situation holds at the moment of the vernal equinox: the day which one gains by virtue of mentally crossing the diurnal threshold eastwards is simultaneously cancelled out by virtue of having also mentally crossed the date line in the same direction. The situation at the moment of the vernal equinox is therefore a perfectly regular case of the effect of the diurnal threshold and the date line on the day count: the identical date is written on both sides of this momentarily identical demarcation, as a result of which it is 1 Bahá' *everywhere in the world.*

The second consequence derives from the first – in conjunction with cyclic progression. The annual threshold, once established, is in effect only for the current year. Following the expiration of a further tropical year the first point of Aries will be reached anew, at which moment a new annual threshold will come into being just short of a quarter of the way further to the west around the globe. Since the date line is perforce cyclic-progressive – just like the annual threshold which it accompanies – the calendar date must orient itself in the following year around a new line of demarcation. How this may be accomplished will be described in the following paragraphs.

We will now need to take a second look at the earth through our mental eye: just as we did before, except that this time the angle of vision is shifted 45° further to the east, so that the longitude running through the middle of the picture represents 21:00 instead of 18:00, that is, about three hours after sunset. We can still see the same annual threshold we saw previously, but this time it appears as an oval-shaped curve. The illumination of the earth from this perspective resembles that of the moon between descending half moon and dark moon, i.e. with the 'old sickle' on the left-hand side. For the sake of example, let us say that this is the moment of the vernal equinox at the beginning of the Bahá'í year 154 (see Illustration 5). The annual threshold, in this moment coinciding with the edge of the shadow, should be marked for future reference, say, with a white chalk line, so that later on it will be more clearly visible on the shaded surface of the earth.

We must now jump one whole imaginary year forward, right up to the moment of the vernal equinox of the Bahá'í year 155 (1998 CE). From exactly the same angle of view we can now clearly make out the position of both annual thresholds on the surface of the earth: the old one (from the year 154) as a chalk line in the middle of the shaded area, and the new one (the one for the year 155) in the form of the shadow's edge (see Illustration 6). These two annual thresholds divide the visible part of the globe into three areas:

– to the right (east) of the annual threshold for the year 154,

– between the two annual thresholds, and

– to the left (west) of the annual threshold for the year 155.

DETERMINING THE DAY OF NAW-RÚZ

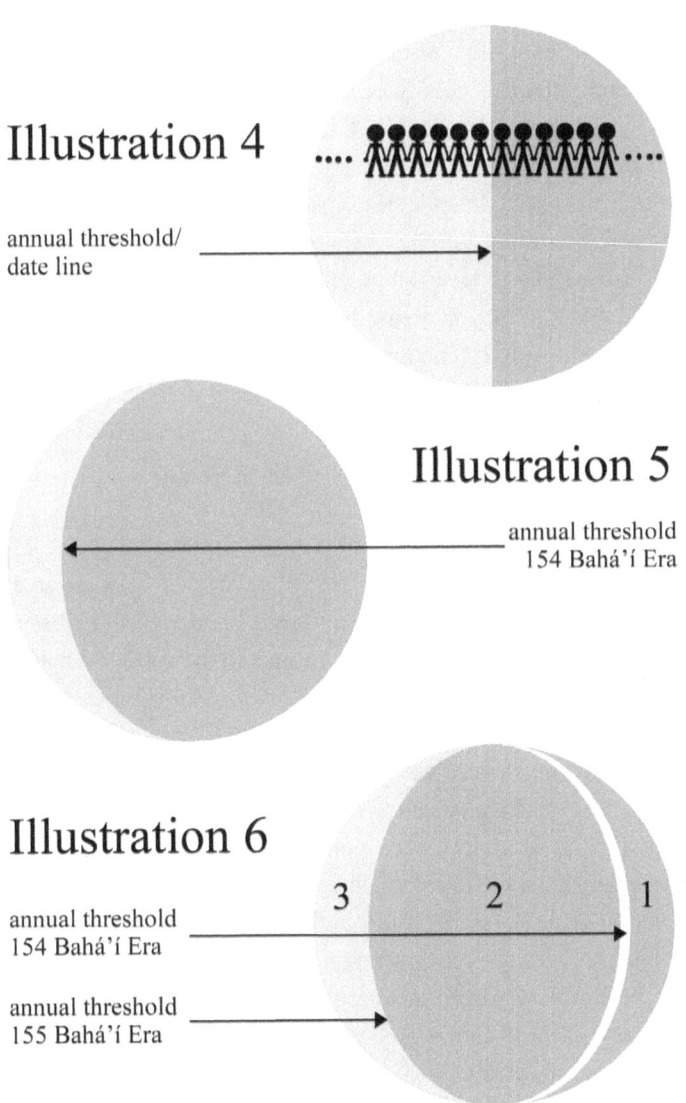

Illustration 4

annual threshold/
date line

Illustration 5

annual threshold
154 Bahá'í Era

Illustration 6

annual threshold
154 Bahá'í Era

annual threshold
155 Bahá'í Era

The annual threshold at the start of the year 154 crosses the equator at 61°17'17" East (see Appendix D) and extends from the vicinity of the North Pole through the Ural Mountains, then roughly along the border between Iran and Afghanistan/Pakistan, and lastly through the Indian Ocean, ending in the vicinity of the South Pole. At the start of the year 155 it lies on the equator at 25°54'05" West and runs along the east coast of Greenland and through Iceland slightly east of Reykjavik, then through the North and South Atlantic, just missing the coast of Brazil. Area 2 thus includes almost all of Europe, the Near and Middle East and Africa.

As the people in area 1 first began in 154 to write the current day's date as 1 Bahá', those in area 2 had been doing just that for almost the whole day and were just about to start writing the date 2 Bahá': a person located just west of the annual threshold was virtually a full day ahead of his neighbour just across the threshold. By contrast, the people in areas 2 and 3 shared a common date for the greater part of the day. This situation continued a full year through.

By the start of the year 155, the annual threshold (and with it the date line) has shifted westward, away from the boundary between areas 1 and 2 and thither to the boundary between areas 2 and 3. Nothing has changed for the people in areas 1 and 3 with respect to the calendar date: the date line lies somewhere between them in both the years in question. For the people in area 2 the situation is different: whereas in the previous year the date line had lain on their east flank, it now lies on their west flank. They must literally 'change sides'. To accomplish this transition, they – and they alone – must insert an additional day into their calendar so that the forthcoming 1 Bahá' is postponed by one day. *This extra day is the fifth intercalary day.* Since this intercalation takes place immediately before the month of fasting, it means that this year the people in Europe, in the Near and Middle East and in Africa celebrate the four normal intercalary days in calendrical conformity with the populace in North and South America; and following the delay occasioned by the fifth intercalary day, they experience the fast and its culmination in the festival of Naw-Rúz at the beginning of the year 155 in calendrical conformity with the populace in Asia.

Since the fifth intercalary day (the 'leap day') occurs exclusively within the area between two successive date lines, it might be appropriate to call this area the *leap area*. It is noteworthy that the definition of the leap area on the basis of the longitudinal coordinates which enclose it is only practicable so long as the moment of the equinox is the threshold criterion. At all other times, the diurnal threshold runs more or less diagonally across the longitudes – even if only a fraction of a day lies in between – and the description of its path is several orders of magnitude more complicated.

The dynamics of the process just described has no counterpart in our experience, and it is understandably difficult at first to discern with the mind's eye. But once the principle is clear for the example years 154 and 155, the pattern of events can easily be mentally extended a year further: the result is after all identical, except that it all takes place further west, slightly less than a quarter of the way around the globe. Then one year more, and again a year, and so forth, in the manner of a time-lapse film. In this fashion it becomes clear how, year after year, the leap area wanders progressively and continuously westwards, whereby in the course of any given period of four years it covers all of the earth's surface except for a small sliver of roughly 11.232 arc degrees, equivalent to 1248.1 kilometres in width at the equator. In the following year it then subsumes this sliver plus the greater part of the leap area from five years earlier.

This behaviour suggests a new and plausible explanation for the expression Ayyám-i Há', 'the days of the letter Há"' – which in view of the *abjad* value of *há'* also means 'five days': there are indeed in *every* year five intercalary days, and every year is a 'leap year' – though not everywhere. (In 'Occidental time' in Chapter 7 a temporal mode will be portrayed in which a fifth intercalary day actually occurs everywhere each year) In this spirit, the leap area will henceforth be called the *region of Há'*.

That it is perfectly feasible to apply the statute laid down by Bahá'u'lláh everywhere in the world in accordance with the local course of the day has been amply demonstrated. To open ourselves to this idea, however, we must part company with traditional patterns of thought and rely exclusively on the revealed Word.

Say: O leaders of religion! Weigh not the Book of God with such standards and sciences as are current amongst you, for the Book itself is the unerring Balance established amongst men. In this most perfect Balance whatsoever the peoples and kindreds of the earth possess must be weighed, while the measure of its weight should be tested according to its own standard, did ye but know it.[38]

The two methods in comparison

Inasmuch as it permits maximum retention of existing standards and conventions, the reference-spot method exacts from us relatively little mental adjustment: the static international date line continues unaltered, and the extra 'leap' day occurs on the accustomed all-or-nothing basis. The only tangible difference is that the (Gregorian) day on which 1 Bahá' begins varies slightly from year to year. The cyclic-progressive method would demand of us a comparatively greater adjustment to the way we view the world. Be that as it may, the question whether familiar conventions should be carried over into the new era where possible, or whether we should instead pour new wine into new wineskins, is a matter of principle which should not influence – or at least not dominate – consideration of the merits of each of these two methods. Here we are not concerned with the adoption of personal expectations or preferences, but solely with the observance of the pronouncement of Bahá'u'lláh:

> *har rúz keh shams taḥvíl beḥamal shavad hamán yawm 'eid ast agar cheh yek daqíqeh beh ghorúb mándeh báshad.*[39]

We have seen that the wording of this statement from Bahá'u'lláh in the Kitáb-i Aqdas appears to permit two legitimate readings, leading to two different possible implementations. By closer examination, however, the first reading presents some grave problems.

We have already observed (see 'Written sources') that the words *rúz*, *yawm* and *'eid* describe one and the same period of time. Now if *rúz* refers to the 'canonical' day at the reference spot – and this is the pivotal assumption of the reference-spot method – then the moment of sunset *at the reference spot* is also the criterion for defining the time period of *'eid* as well. But when we consider that

- the start of the day of Naw-Rúz is also the close of the month of 'Alá', the month of fasting,[40] and that

- during the fast, abstinence from eating and drinking is ordained for the time between sunrise and sunset at the place of fasting,[41]

it becomes clear that *'eid* must in this context be defined in relation to the *local* sunset for each fasting individual – which can diverge from the moment of sunset at the reference spot by well over twelve hours (depending on the details of implementation). This interpretation thus requires two separate meanings for *'eid* within the framework of the divine law: *one* meaning for the New Year regulation and *another* meaning for every other context. In the case of the cyclic-progressive method, the local day is implied in all instances without exception.

With the reference-spot method, the divine legislation deals only with the function of the vernal equinox; the two other major factors – the location of the reference spot and the position of the date line – rely on conventions and decisions which lie outside the confines of divine law."→[42] With the cyclic-progressive method, every single aspect of the New Year regulation proceeds directly, unambiguously and exclusively from the words uttered by Bahá'u'lláh.

Given the reference-spot method, the reference spot itself is the only point on earth where the astronomical equinox invariably takes place on 1 Bahá'. At every other location it can take place on the previous or the following calendar date, depending on circumstances: the further the distance from the reference spot, the greater the probability of a date shift. In contrast, the cyclic-progressive method allows a precision never before achieved in the history of the calendar. At the start of every year the calendar is aligned exactly on the first point of Aries: the length of the year is both well-defined and constant, free of the discontinuities of all calendars preceding it. The highly symbolic moment of the beginning of spring occurs without exception on 1 Bahá' for each and every person on earth.

For those who celebrate a fifth Yawm-i Há' in a given year, cyclic progression guarantees that the moment of the vernal equinox will occur within 5 hours, 48 minutes and roughly 46 seconds after the termination of the Fast and could conveniently be integrated into the festivities being held within the region of Há' and experienced communally and with due solemnity by the participants.

Each of these two methods offers its own symbolic association with the Bahá'í Faith. In the case of the reference-spot method, this association is the location of the spot itself. With the cyclic-progressive method the association is metaphorical: the region of Há' stands for the principle of progressive revelation. The perpetual synchronization of each year's region of Há' with that of the previous year stresses the continuity of God's plan: the fact that every Manifestation of God brings not only a renewal, but also a confirmation and continuation of the missions of His predecessors.

In 172 BE, when the Universal House of Justice decided that the time was ripe to synchronize calendrical practice throughout the community of believers, the Bahá'í Faith was only just beginning to emerge from obscurity on the world stage – clearly too early for the introduction of a calendar convention which abandoned internationally recognized standards. The only viable way forward was to select one of the two already existing modes of operation to the exclusion of the other. Privileging the method in use in the West would have had two unacceptable consequences: not only would it have bound the Badí' calendar even more rigidly than ever before to the Gregorian leap year formula, it would have perpetuated a hitherto interim practice which is ultimately at odds with the instructions in the Most Holy Book. Thus the only realistic option was to adopt the method already in use in Iran and at the Bahá'í World Centre in Israel, including official designation of Teheran as place of reference.

The relationship between the annual threshold and the date line

It was amply demonstrated in the foregoing that, from a technical point of view, the crucial relationship affecting the implementation of the calendar statutes, regardless of method, is that which holds between the annual threshold and the date line – however prominently the reference-spot symbolism may loom from a different perspective. For the cyclic-progressive method, it is imperative that this relationship be that of identity, since this condition alone is capable of guaranteeing the existence of only one single calendar date at the decisive moment, thus enabling the world-wide fulfilment of the divine law to the letter. In contrast with the IDL, whose entire course runs through open sea, given a long enough period of time the annual threshold will have assumed virtually every conceivable equinoctial terminator path, and so the precise agreement between annual threshold and date line will give rise to certain logistic problems from time to time, such as that illustrated by the following:

> In a given year the annual threshold runs right through the middle of the dining room of a certain wedded couple. At breakfast the woman sits to the west of the date line, her husband to the east. Everything which the man says to his wife during their morning meal reaches her tomorrow, but he hears her replies yesterday.

This example is admittedly somewhat pointed, but it does illustrate the coordination difficulties which must be anticipated if the agreement between threshold and date line are to be taken absolutely literally. It is therefore worth considering whether there might be an interpretation of the text which satisfies the understandable desire for uniformity within the geographical bounds of an administrative unit – which for Bahá'ís probably means within the area of influence and/or jurisdiction of a local Spiritual Assembly – without sacrificing this agreement. In other words, the exact course of the west flank of the region of Há' could be determined locally, taking both the revealed Word and the local cultural and geographical conditions into account. This would mean that the date line would no longer run exactly along the annual threshold, but rather along the jurisdictional boundaries more or less in its proximity. The key to such a compromise might be found in the words *agar <u>ch</u>eh yek daqíqeh beh <u>gh</u>orúb mándeh bá<u>sh</u>ad* (the 'one-minute clause'), which could be taken to imply a degree of 'give and take' in the ruling, sufficient to permit minimal adjustments to the path of the date line. However, there are two reservations which we ought to consider. First, it is questionable whether boundary alignment would really deliver the benefits expected of it. The informal cohesion in and among Bahá'í communities is in reality seldom identical to the administrative units along whose boundaries the date line would ideally be readjusted. Individual Bahá'ís residing outside the immediate jurisdiction of existing spiritual assemblies must cross such boundaries to uphold contact with Bahá'í institutions, and it is often the case that neighbouring assemblies (which could in principle find themselves on either side of the date line) hold joint events such as commemorative festivals, child and adult study classes, Bahá'í and inter-religious worship and prayer meetings, venues for teaching and proclamation – often enough across national as well as local borders: the formation of Bahá'í clusters and Regional Councils throughout the world was designed among other things to facilitate just this sort of intercommunity cooperation. In short, the problems which date-line readjustment is supposed to solve would continue to thrive to a greater or lesser degree, regardless of how this readjustment might possibly be carried out.

Second, this line of reasoning comes dangerously close to what might be called goal-directed exegesis, that is, interpretation of a text for the purpose of deriving results to solve a perceived problem. In this case, the underlying assumption that the one-minute clause is a fuzz factor is tantamount to assuming a specific *intent* on the part of Bahá'u'lláh for which there is no cogent textual proof. We are treading here on very thin exegetic ice.

In summary, an error-tolerant interpretation of Bahá'u'lláh's instructions presents new problems without really resolving existing ones.

A strict interpretation of the revealed Word would rule out all possibility of a deviation of the date line from the annual threshold."→43 But this rigid approach is not without its advantages. Formally, it is well-defined: the relationship between global and local day is unambiguous for every point on the earth, and the position of the date line can always be determined on the basis of earth coordinates alone – rendering the use of clocks and watches equipped with date display and global positioning sensors a viable proposition. It is perpetually self-correcting; it is even immune to tectonic shifts in the earth's crust which could influence the coordinates of specific localities.

Furthermore, it ought to be carefully considered whether the goal of achieving calendrical uniformity within a community couldn't be accomplished more effectively and in a manner more commensurate with Bahá'í principles, i.e. by way of consultation among those immediately effected. Where there is danger of ambiguity, a date expression within the region of Há' could be appropriately highlighted to make its status clear, for example by suffixing the date expression with 'H'. It is probably true to say that the actual problem lies less in any genuine difficulties associated with the near proximity of the date line and more in the simple fact that we are not accustomed to these circumstances.

The immediate experience of continuously shifting proximity to the date line is a fitting metaphor for the historical progress of a divine Dispensation. Those who lived during the lifetime of a Manifestation of God and who attained recognition of His station experienced the tensions and disruptions of the time, to be sure, and many laid down their lives in the process; but they also witnessed and participated in the dawning of a new era and were graced with the immediate presence of their Beloved. At the time of the preparation of the present edition, 179 years after the birth of the Bábí-Bahá'í twin Dispensations and at least 821 years before the next Dispensation can be expected to occur, it is not possible to experience such events first-hand. Instead, we observe commemorations whose primary purpose is precisely to recapture the sense of immediacy of the events which took place during the embryonic years of the most recent 'return of all the prophets'. The cyclic-progressive date line offers a powerful symbol for this remembrance: those who in a given year are privileged to live in proximity of the date line symbolically reenact those exciting, turbulent times, and their talisman is the geographical proximity of two time continuums, representing two holy Dispensations: one just coming to an end, the other in the process of being born.

7

The Badíʻ Calendar and the Time of Day

We have already noted in Chapter 3 that, in the wake of the development of the mechanical clock and the ensuing dominance of the meridional time convention, certain problems ensued for those calendars for which sunset continued to function as the day-boundary. We will now investigate this problem area somewhat more closely, since it has implications for the universal application of the Badíʻ calendar, which has up until now likewise been used in conjunction with meridional time. In the absence of a conscious decision to the contrary on the part of the Baháʼí world community, these conditions will automatically continue to hold in the future – a situation which is not without complications, as we shall see by way of example:

Let us assume that we intend to take part in a major regional event at 19:15 (7:15 p.m.) on 17 Raḥmat to commemorate the Martyrdom of the Báb: for the purpose of this example it will be assumed that 1 Baháʼ is equivalent to 21 March, i.e. that it consists of the span of time between sunset on 20 March and sunset on 21 March, which means that the equivalent Gregorian date for the commemoration is 10 July. So long as we are aware of the time zone of the place of venue, and so long as we know whether normal or summer time (or even double summer time) holds on the day in question, we have no problem coping with the time expression itself. For the sake of simplicity, the time of day in this scenario is consistently expressed in standard time.

With regard to the *date* of the event, however, we need to establish just when sunset occurs at the place of gathering. If this lies exactly on the equator we know without further deliberation that sunset takes place at around 18:00 and that the given Badíʻ date is equivalent to 10 July according to the Gregorian calendar. The further north the venue lies, the later sunset takes place on this summer day. At a certain latitude, sunset occurs exactly at 19:15. One centimetre north of this latitude the announcement implies 11 July, one centimetre south of it, 10 July.

Note that sunset is a natural phenomenon which occurs in solar time, whereas the meridional time expression 19:15 is based on mean time. In the course of the year, mean time undulates with respect to solar time: in early November the former runs ahead of the latter by over sixteen minutes, and in mid-February it runs almost fifteen minutes behind. As described in Chapter 3, the continuously shifting difference between solar and mean time is accommodated by the equation of time. On 10-11 July, mean time is approximately 5 minutes and 24 seconds ahead. We must take this difference into account.

Furthermore, we must give attention to the fact that, concomitant with mean time, the time zones are likewise in effect: we must thus know where the place of gathering is in relation to the standard meridian, i.e. the longitude at which it is actually 19:15 mean time. If the meeting takes place west of this longitude, then local mean time runs behind zone time; if east, then it runs ahead. If we could at least assume that the time zones are 'ideal' – that is, that they run exactly north-south and are centred on longitudes which are wholly divisible by 15 – then we could be assured that the difference never amounts to more than plus-minus half an hour, so that this aspect of the total problem would be restricted to a single 'dangerous' hour (bearing in mind that in some parts of the earth, for example in Iran and in several Australian territories, the zone time is staggered by half an hour or 7°30' relative to general practice). Unfortunately, the zone boundaries occur with this regularity at best in the middle of a sparsely populated ocean; everywhere else they are adjusted to conform to political boundaries. The deviation between local mean time and zone time can amount to as much as two hours, potentially in both directions: the bandwidth of this 'dangerous' period is thus expanded in principle to a good five hours. All these differences play a role in the answer to the question whether 19:15 occurs before or after sunset.

A further consideration affects the extreme north and south, where

THE BADÍ' CALENDAR AND THE TIME OF DAY

the difference in the length of daylight between summer and winter is so extreme that the actually occurring sunset must be relativized. In the context of fasting and prayer, Bahá'u'lláh explains:

> In regions where the days and nights grow long, let times of prayer be gauged by clocks and other instruments that mark the passage of the hours.[1]

This quotation shows that there are situations in which, for practical reasons, a sort of 'conceptual' sunset should assume precedence over the actually occurring sunset. (This quotation will be taken up again later in this chapter, in 'The change of day in the polar regions'.) However, the question as to how this ruling is to be applied has yet to be resolved. As long as the start of the day remains a purely personal affair serving to apportion time for the purposes of fasting and prayer, potential differences in interpretation are tolerable. But as soon as whole communities are dependent on a common and consistent date ruling – as is the case with the calendar – then a ruling must be uniformly and exhaustively specified. Whatever the method used to achieve uniformity, the procedure for the determination of the Bahá'í calendar day in conjunction with meridional time will be fraught with additional complications.

A simple but effective solution to this dilemma might consist simply in augmenting borderline time expressions with the word 'early' or 'late'. The expression '19:15 late on 17 Raḥmat' would then mean, 'where the event takes place, 19:15 occurs toward the end of 17 Raḥmat, that is, before sunset'. As a consequence, it would fall unambiguously on 10 July. The interpretation of such expressions admittedly requires some mental juggling, but that might simply be a matter of practice. The distinguishing supplement would furthermore only be necessary where a potential ambiguity exists. Unfortunately, this is the case during that very part of the day when the vast majority of events tend to be scheduled. Moreover, the task of working out the place of venue's true relation to sunset would simply devolve upon the party responsible for formulating the time expression. The responsibility for clarification would merely be shifted: the necessary calculation with all its problematic complexity would remain the same.

When all is said and done, it would appear that the only practical interface between occidental calendar and meridional time would involve defining the change of calendar day in accordance with formal criteria derived from the meridional apportionment of time rather than in accordance with astronomical conditions, as is the case for example with the Jewish calendar, for which the start of the day is formally set to 18:00 (i.e. a *pro forma* approximation of sunset) for the purpose of the calculation of the epact. And this solution is clearly at odds with the law of Bahá'u'lláh.

All aspects of this problem result from the fact that the basis of calibration for the clock is different from that for the calendar. A possible way out of the dilemma would be to put both on the same basis: either the calendar must become meridional or the time of day occidental. We will now examine these alternatives in detail.

The meridional calendar

There are two possible versions of this alternative. The first version assumes that both the meridional day and the (meridionally oriented) Gregorian calendar will continue to exercise dominant influence throughout the Bahá'í Era: the Badí' calendar would continue to exist as a sort of 'auxiliary' calendar for private use among the believers. The Badí' calendar would thus suffer the same fate as the Jewish and the Islamic calendars, both of which have been almost completely superseded by the Gregorian calendar in the globalized world. But a niche role is certainly not in conformity with the vision of Shoghi Effendi, who made it abundantly clear that the Badí' calendar is destined to *replace*, not to supplement, the Gregorian calendar. Such a reduction in status could perhaps be counterbalanced by establishing the practice of using the Gregorian calendar only when the indicated time of day comes within dangerous proximity to sunset. However, as with the 'late/early' infix, this is at best a partial solution to the problem as a whole, one which moreover presupposes that the potential ambiguity is detectable in every concrete case. The most notable achievement of this approach is to demonstrate to everyone concerned that the meridional time of day and the Badí' calendar are basically irreconcilable.

The Gregorian calendar has long since been declared an international standard by the United Nations; the 'objections and associations' which made this calendar 'unacceptable to large sections of the world's population'[2] have apparently been resolved (or ignored). The acceptance of this state of affairs for non-Christians is perhaps partially due to the fact that the reference to the supposed year of the birth of Jesus is the only genuine Christian association to be found in this calendar. Probably more decisive, however, is the fact that the Gregorian calendar, together with the prime meridian through Greenwich and the international date line at 180°, has functioned *de facto* as a world standard for some considerable time – a situation which has to do with the political, commercial and scientific predominance of Western European and in particular Anglo-Saxon culture since the 17th century – and that the official step was nothing more than open recognition of an already engrained convention. Attempts by the United Nations to agree on a calendar which deviated from the Gregorian have invariably been successfully opposed by the Western Christian churches and – whenever the seven-day week was put to question – by the Jewish community.

Both the meridional time of day and the Gregorian calendar are thus already used everywhere in the world, and the international Bahá'í community is no exception. A future world which reflects Bahá'í values will certainly continue to respect the needs of non-Bahá'ís. Of all possible solutions, the 'conservative' one – that is, simply accepting the *status quo* – represents the path of least resistance. This attitude naturally invites the objection: if we were to do everything as we have always done, then we would still be living in caves. But more important: the Badí' calendar is a component of the divine revelation, and for Bahá'ís it assumes the status of law: its ultimate unreserved introduction is a binding obligation on the Bahá'í community. To relegate the calendar once and for all time to a subsidiary position in this way is not consistent with its status as the object of a holy statute.

The second version of the meridional solution consists in treating the calendar day of the Badí' calendar as if it were meridional, i.e. 17 Raḥmat would correspond exactly to 10 July in every respect except the name.

The *calendar* day would begin at 0:00 (12:00 p.m.) according to the meridional clock, whereas the *religious* day would begin at sunset on the evening before. This impression is unintentionally encouraged by current forms of the printed Badí' calendar in which the individual days are graphically represented by rectangles, each containing two date expressions: the one according to the Gregorian calendar and the other according to the Badí' calendar. Aside from the obvious accusation of false labelling, the danger of this approach lies in its ambiguity. In the simple case one might be able to assume that a date *with* time indication would always refer to the (meridional) calendar day, whereas *without* a time expression the (occidental) religious day would be indicated; but language usage all too often presents border cases. Furthermore, it is at best a counterfeit solution: except for the avoidance of the date boundary at sunset it resolves none of the inherent ambiguities discussed above. And lastly, the objection is also valid here that the solution perpetuates an extension to the Badí' concept of day which is not explicitly sanctioned by the holy statutes.

Occidental time

In place of the midday-midnight axis, *occidental time* is delineated by sunset: at precisely this moment, clocks and watches always indicate 00:00. This method of measuring the time of the day is not the same as that form of occidental measurement which was in use well into the Middle Ages. The then current *temporal hour* was based on the equal division into twelfths of the course of the sun between sunrise and sunset, and the relationship between daytime and night-time hours changed with the seasons. We have here to do with a scheme very much like solar time, albeit beginning with sunset instead of midnight and exhibiting some significant differences, to be discussed below. In occidental time, the event described at the beginning of this discussion would not take place at 19:15 (7:15 p.m.), but instead at e.g. 23:22 or 00:38 *local time* (LT) – that is, unambiguously before or after the change of day according to sunset at the locality of the event. Integrating occidental time into the Badí' calendar would thus be just as unproblematic as was the integration of meridional time into the Gregorian calendar – or more accurately, as was the adaptation of the Gregorian concept of 'day' to the requisites of the meridional apportionment of time (see Chapter 3).

Local (occidental) time (LT) is functionally identical to *ghurúbí* time as employed in the Ottoman Empire from the Late Middle Ages until the early 20th century (see Chapter 3). Though unfamiliar to the Bahá'ís in Iran, occidental timekeeping will have been well known to the communities in Baghdad, Istanbul, Edirne, 'Akká/Haifa and Alexandria; but given the anglocentric administration of Palestine under the Mandate from 1920 onwards and the growing internationalization of Bahá'í administration under Shoghi Effendi, its adoption as the official Bahá'í timekeeping standard during that phase of history would clearly have been untimely.

Since occidental time is unfamiliar to most of us today, we would do well to examine the properties of this alternative in somewhat more detail, contrasting these with the conventions to which we are accustomed.

First: the division of the day into two equal twelve-hour periods is inappropriate for occidental time, which is oriented not on the meridian of solar transit (hence a.m. and p.m. for ante- and postmeridian), but instead on the moment of sunset; and since the moment of sunrise is only rarely symmetrically opposed to sunset, there is nothing which can sensibly be 'halved'. This state of affairs fosters the globalization of standards, impelling the alignment of Anglo-Saxon practice with the rest of the world.

Second: the customary (i.e. meridional) calibration of the time of day is based on mean time: it is constant and represents an idealized day length, projected over the entire year. By contrast, the occidental calibration of time is based on solar time, i.e. the time of day is equivalent to the genuine orientation of the earth to the sun. Only in this manner is it possible to synchronize the date transition with the actually occurring sunset.

Third: the absolute duration of the occidental day (the period of time which occurs between two successive sunsets) is not a constant period of 24 mean hours (i.e. from midnight to midnight, as is the case with the meridional day), but instead it varies continuously in accordance with the seasons (ignoring the special case of the day length at the equator). The day of the year with the longest absolute duration is the day of the vernal equinox, that with the shortest duration the day of the autumnal equinox: the further away from the equator, the greater the difference. Only twice a year is the day 24 hours long everywhere, namely during the aestival and hibernal solstices, i.e. on the first days of summer and winter, respectively. The reason for the variation in the length of the day becomes clear when we consider that each day begins at a different (meridional) moment of time: at 50° latitude (roughly the latitude of Frankfurt am Main), the difference in the duration of daytime (or night-time) between the first day of summer and the first day of winter amounts to almost exactly eight meridional hours.→3 Bahá'ís are familiar with this phenomenon, since during the fasting month of 'Alá they generally abide by the times given for sunrise and sunset in the tables at their disposal, primarily in printed calendars.

The oscillation would hardly be noticeable in the daily course of events, since the difference between the extremes is spread out over an interval of half a year. At 50° latitude, the longest occidental day of the year is just under two minutes longer than 24 mean hours, deviating from the length of the meridional day by about 0.01 per cent. The 7½-hour work shift immediately before or after the day of the vernal equinox (Naw-Rúz itself is a day of rest) thus lasts roughly 36 seconds longer than the same shift measured according to the meridional clock. In compensation, the work shift on the first day of autumn is about 36 seconds shorter. On the first day of summer and winter, the occidental and meridional clocks run just about neck and neck, with a slight deviation owing to the equation of time.

Fourth: Given a time convention oriented on the meridian, there are two reasons why it is practicable to divide the world into permanent time zones:

- At every point along a given longitude, the moments of midday and midnight – the cornerstones of meridional calibration of time – are the same during all seasons of the year; the time zones are identical in summer and winter.

- The discrepancy between solar time and zone time is relatively uncritical; it even tolerates an additional one- to two-hour distortion through summer time – not to mention zone adjustments to accommodate natural and political boundaries. The change of day is in this case simply not a matter of sense perception.

For the same two reasons, given a time convention which is in any way oriented on the sunset, a gross partitioning into time zones would no longer be possible.

- Firstly, the time zones would be subject to continual readjustment: in summer (in the northern hemisphere) they would run diagonally across the longitudes from north-east to south-west, in winter from north-west to south-east; *mutatis mutandis* for the southern hemisphere. Nowhere would they remain stationary except at the equator. (Fixed time zones would result in artificial zone boundaries between locations with otherwise identical time; boundaries would in addition constantly be shifting position relative to solar time.)

- Secondly, the ability to perceive sunset is crucial. Even if we disregard the religiously motivated considerations described earlier, the fact remains that people on the western fringe of even an ideally placed time zone would experience 'sunset' bathed in sunlight, those on the eastern fringe at an advanced stage of twilight if not in fact in total darkness. Given the actually existing time zones, adjusted as they are to conform with natural and political boundaries, the incongruencies would be even greater.

Summer time (misleadingly called 'daylight saving time' in the Unied States) would also be abandoned: its purpose – the artificial prolongation of the early evening light during the summer months – is fundamentally incompatible with the sunset orientation of occidental time.

The absence of time zones means that there are also time differences from place to place within self-contained political units. For example, the clocks in Leipzig run 11 minutes and 36 seconds ahead of those in Kassel, so that 22:30:00 in Kassel is the same sidereal instant as 22:41:46 in Leipzig. Of course, even in the meridional system we are already accustomed to the fact that longer journeys over one or more time zone boundaries involve time shifts. This situation even leads in some cases to curious anomalies: the clocks in Rennes are a whole hour ahead of those in Dover, even though the latter lies clearly to the east of Rennes. Such anomalies are even more conspicuous where the time zones run though a land mass (as in the case of Eastern Europe), following an intricate pattern of political boundaries. Occidental time of course eliminates these anomalies.

Less familiar to us is the effect on north-south journeys. The occidental clocks in Hamburg and Ulm tick almost identically on the first day of spring or autumn, since both lie approximately on the same longitude. On the first day of summer, however, the clocks in Ulm (latitude 53°33'2" north) run roughly 12½ minutes ahead of, and on the first day of winter roughly 12½ minutes behind, those in Hamburg. This circumstance arises from the fact that the diurnal threshold extends diagonally across the longitudes at an angle of 23°26'21"45 – the so-called *obliquity of the ecliptic*[→4] – at the time of a solstice, running south-westward on the first day of summer and south-eastward on the first day of winter.

With few exceptions one may assume that a journey from any one place to any other will be accompanied by a shift in the time of day, lesser or greater, depending on time of year, the distance and the compass direction. This shouldn't present any practical difficulties, however. If one travels by car, the time shift per hour of travel –a few minutes at the very most – is hardly noticeable in comparison with other incalculabilities (traffic density, weather conditions, road works, traffic signals and so on). In the case of public transport, the time differences will already be accounted for in the printed (or electronically accessible) timetables.

Nevertheless there are situations in which a constant temporal rhythm is necessary, unaffected by geographical location or season of the year: control instruments and time synchronization in electronic data communication are just two examples. Such a rhythm exists: it is called *equatorial time* (ET). The equatorial time for a given location is the occidental time of day at the intersection of the equator and the equinoctial terminator path which passes through that location. Equatorial time is devoid of the variations due to the change of seasons. It is like the accustomed meridional time in all respects except for the fact that it is based on solar time rather than mean time (that is, it is not adjusted via the equation of time), plus of course for the fact that it starts at sunset instead of midnight. For highly critical time synchronization, one would need recourse to dynamic time (as is usual in scientific circles today). Dynamic time, also called *ephemeral time*, runs according to the atomic clock and is independent of not only the equation of time but also of precession, nutation and aperiodical fluctuations in the earth's rotation.

The third indispensable mode for indicating occidental time is called *global time* (GT): this is a special case of equatorial time, namely the time of day relative to the intersection of the equator and the annual threshold. At the precise moment of the vernal equinox the time is 00:00 LT, ET and GT along the entire length of the annual threshold. A global time expression uniquely identifies a specific position of the globe on the ecliptic relative to the first point of Aries. It goes without saying that this mode of time only makes sense in combination with a cyclic-progressive date line.

Global time is in turn the primary factor for the definition of the *global day*, being the duration of time between 24:00 GT of the preceding day and the next-occurring 24:00 GT, the days being counted beginning with Naw-Rúz (1 Bahá'). With the exception of the fifth Yawm-i Há', 00:00 GT of any given day is contemporaneous with 24:00 GT of the previous day. The fifth Yawm-i Há', which as a *global* day is valid *everywhere annually*, begins instead at approx. 18:11:14 GT and lasts 5 hours, 48 minutes and roughly 46 seconds. Thus the number of global days is a constant fraction, fully in accord with Shoghi Effendi's translation of Nabíl's description:

> The Báb has regarded the solar year, of 365 days, 5 hours, and fifty odd minutes, as consisting of 19 months of 19 days each, with the addition of certain intercalary days.[5]

The concept of the global day is not identical to that of the local or equatorial day, not least because in the former case the fifth Yawm-i Há' lasts $5^h48^m46^s$ and in the latter case 24 (occidental) hours. Furthermore, the global day is valid the whole world over, without reference to a specific place: it is not 'located' at the annual threshold, but rather defined in terms of it.

The introduction of global time and the concept of the global day would permit for the first time since Neolithic times a scheme in which the units of the *measurement* of time and those of the *calibration* of time are essentially identical – with the additional advantage that, in the case of the Badí' calendar, there would be no discrepancy between the astronomical year and the calendar year. Each moment of time within a tropical year can be expressed as a point on the ecliptic at a specific and determinable arc degree relative to the first point of Aries; such a point is the mid-point in what is known as an *ecliptic longitude*. If we were to note the ecliptic longitude of each of these commemorative moments each year, it would be possible to celebrate *simultaneously* the world over, so that the believers might take part in prayer and meditation in the consciousness of global temporal communality. In addition, all of the equinoxes and solstices, and with them the astronomical commencement of all four seasons, would occur year for year at a constant ecliptic longitude (column 2 below), i.e. on the same day (column 3) and indeed always at just about the same time of day, or in the case of the vernal equinox, at the precise same moment (column 4):

vernal equinox	0°	1 Bahá'	00:00 GT
summer solstice	90°	17 Núr	18:01 GT
autumnal equinox	180°	16 'Izzaт	09:59 GT
winter solstice	270°	11 Masá'il	06:32 GT

The time expressions for the autumnal equinox and the solstices are only approximate, since the lengths of the seasons in the information source on which they are based are rounded to the nearest complete minute.[6] Note that the seasons vary in duration on account of the elliptic orbit of the earth around the sun combined with the effects of precession. At present, for example, the spring/summer period lasts about 7^d14^h longer than the autumn/winter period (in the northern hemisphere). This relationship will gradually be reversed over the next 12,925 years. As a result, the first point of autumn currently occurs every year on the average 1 minute and 41.4 seconds earlier than in the previous year, and its ecliptic longitude recedes accordingly.

Additional modes of time expression are imaginable, in each case uniform for whole nations or for sub- or multinational regions (California time, British time, EU time, etc.), in each case in two possible variations (e.g. British local time, British equatorial time), depending on the purpose for which it is intended. Time modes such as these would fulfil more or less the same pragmatic function as today's time zones. Nevertheless, only the local, equatorial and global time modes (LT, ET and GT) are formally defined. We will encounter all three of these time modes frequently in the text to follow.

It would be no problem at all in our technological age to construct timekeeping devices in such a way that they would accelerate and decelerate slightly in accordance with the seasons, so that they constantly display 00:00 precisely at sunset: at every point of the globe and on every day of the year, a glance would suffice to ascertain to the split second when it is officially sunset. Equipped with a sensor for local positioning, such a clock would be able to adjust itself continuously with every change of location according to an arbitrarily fine mesh of coordinates. Similarly, entering the geographical coordinates of a given location would suffice to find out what time it is at any point on earth, or at the press of a button to display not only the local time but also the equatorial and global times and dates, plus the zone time and the Gregorian date for good measure. The objection that we would make ourselves dependent on technology is no more or less valid than in virtually every other area of life as well: to try to ignore the existence of electronics is to fail to recognize the realities – and the possibilities – of the age we live in. This objection is in any case irrelevant: traditional methods for determining the moment of sunset have existed since the Old Stone Age – technology simply makes things more convenient. If any time measurement system is totally dependent on technology, then it is the meridional mean time which we take so much for granted today. Moreover, the use of instruments for measuring time was explicitly allowed[7] and indeed recommended[8] by Bahá'u'lláh.

The first English-language edition of this book predicted that the accuracy of global positioning sensors would increase dramatically and their unit price would plummet within very few years. At the time of the preparation of the second edition, this prediction had been radically overtaken by events, and nowadays virtually every communication device is equipped with global positioning. Enabling 'smart' watches and telephones with the capability of monitoring occidental time is now merely a matter of developing an appropriate 'app'.

The change of day in the polar regions

The differences between meridional and occidental time suggest different approaches to the question of determining the official sunset in the polar regions. With meridional time, sunrise and sunset are more or less temporally equidistant from the calendar day boundary (i.e. midnight), so that in demarcating the 'conceptual' daytime (for example for the purpose of fixing the time of fasting) one is naturally predisposed to adjust both moments in concert in order to avoid disturbing this symmetry – the establishment of which was after all the reason for having introduced meridional time in the first place (see Chapter 3). However, this scheme has the unfortunate consequence that the 'conceptual' sunset deviates considerably from the natural sunset for large portions of the earth – with, of course, negative consequences for the apperception of the change of day.

In the case of occidental time, meridional symmetry is not an issue. Wherever on earth a natural sunset takes place, it can in every season and in every situation serve as the criterion for the change of day: exceptional circumstances prevail only in the extreme northern and southern polar regions. At the moment of the equinox, this special-case area is restricted to a tiny circle at latitude 89°10' North and South; it even disappears completely for a moment in the vicinity of the vernal and autumnal equinoxes. Its greatest expansion is reached at the moment of the solstice, attaining latitude 67°23'38"55 in summer and 65°43'38"55 in winter. (The sizes of the special-case areas at the respective solstices differ because the boundary of the shadow is displaced eastward in each case by 0°50' [3 minutes and 20 seconds] on account of horizontal refraction, among other things: see 'Astronomical data' in Chapter 6.) Thus the area in which a special-case ruling for determining sunset must apply is not constant, but instead oscillates during the course of the year. An adequate definition of the official day boundary should ideally take this oscillation dynamically into account. One possibility would be the following:

> If at a given latitude and longitude a natural sunset does not occur within the course of a solar day, the moment of the change of day is identical to that which occurs at a point along the same longitude and at the nearest latitude at which a natural sunset actually does take place.

In other words, for each respective hemisphere the diurnal threshold follows the course of the terminator up to its apex (the point of greatest proximity to the pole), thence along the longitude which intersects with the terminator at this point until it reaches the pole. The practical consequence is that the change of day in the special-case areas near the earth's poles always takes place at the meridian of solar transit: at solar midnight in summer and at solar midday in winter (see Illustration 7). In this fashion the change of day is well-defined, and at the same time a deviation from the primary criterion of the natural sunset is avoided. The well-definedness of the concept of 'year' presupposes a watertight definition of the change of day at least at the moment of the vernal equinox. As we have seen, the size of the area requiring a conceptual sunset is at this moment minimal.

The change of day exerts its most pervading influence on the daily routine of the individual believer during the fasting period. Two aspects are especially significant in this regard: the length of the daily period of physical fasting, and the portion of the day during which this fasting is to be carried out. In the extreme polar regions, aberrations can occur with respect to both. Regarding the length of fasting, Bahá'u'lláh has given clear instructions:

Illustration 7

path of the diurnal threshold in the polar regions

(a) during the summer solstice

(b) ca. 2 days before spring or after autumn

(c) during the winter solstice

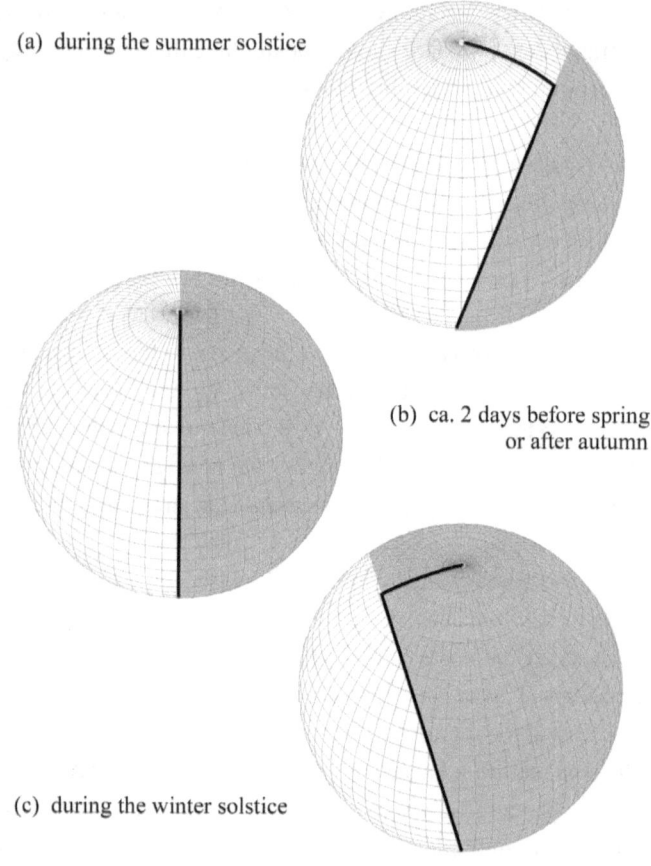

In regions where the days and nights grow long, let times of prayer be gauged by clocks and other instruments that mark the passage of the hours.[9]

In an elaboration of this statement, Bahá'u'lláh explains that this ruling is to be applied only in extreme situations:

> The intention is those territories that are remote. In these climes, however, the difference in length is but a few hours, and therefore this ruling doth not apply.[10]

It is clear from these two statements (which, it is important to note, apply both generally and specifically with respect to the period of fasting)[11] that a special-case ruling is only applicable when the difference in duration between daytime and night-time amounts to more than 'a few hours' – also in the polar regions.

The period of fasting takes place during the final nineteen days before the vernal equinox. At the earliest possible beginning of the first day of the fast (i.e. at the moment of sunrise at the intersection of the annual threshold with the equator) the angle of the diurnal threshold relative to the earth's axis is 7°31'32", thereafter diminishing until it reaches 0° at the moment of the equinox. This is the most 'inconvenient' starting point: the further west an individual is from the annual threshold, the later begins the fast for him and accordingly the smaller is the angle of the diurnal threshold. For the individual standing just east of the annual threshold (i.e. as far westwards as one can go without crossing it), the angle amounts to only 7°8'33". In any case, this angle stands in direct proportion to the length of the daylight period relative to night. The difference in duration between daytime and night-time is four times the LT-ET difference plus a total of $6^m 40^s$ on account of horizontal refraction (see the calculation of the angle of the shadow and the LT-ET time difference in *Annual commemoration* below). At 50° north (roughly the latitude of Frankfurt am Main) this difference amounts to two hours, thirty minutes and twenty-one seconds at the most, that is, comfortably within the tolerance bounds. On the polar circle of the northern hemisphere it reaches five hours, twenty six minutes and fifty seconds, which seems to exceed what can be described as 'but a few hours'. But where exactly is the cut-off point?

In order to come closer to a possible answer to this question we must first establish a reference value. Bahá'u'lláh probably spoke these words in Bahjí, and thus the words 'in these climes' refers in the first instance to this location, or more generally to its latitude. Bahjí lies at 32°56'25" North. The angle of the diurnal threshold is maximally 23°26'21"45 (i.e. on the first day of summer or winter), which means that the largest possible difference in duration between daytime and night-time, and therefore a minimal reference value for 'a few hours', amounts to four hours, forty-one minutes and thirty seconds. This is equivalent to the greatest possible day-night difference at sunrise of the first day of fasting at latitude 63°36'10" North, that is, south of Reykjavik and 5'50" (about 13.7 km) north of the southernmost point of Iceland. One could take this to mean that a special-case ruling regarding fasting is to apply in principle only north of this latitude. This understanding is in complete accord with existing decisions of the Universal House of Justice:

> It is true that Bahá'u'lláh has ordained in the Kitáb-i-Aqdas that in the high latitudes where the duration of days and nights varies considerably clocks should be relied upon rather than the rising and setting of the sun. However, we feel that Dublin is too far south for the application of this law.[12]

> In the high latitudes . . . it is permissible to observe the laws of prayer and fasting in accordance with the clock rather than with the rising and setting of the sun. As Iceland lies in such latitudes, it is for your Assembly to decide this matter.[13]

To use the vocabulary of the present study, the Universal House of Justice indicated that the special-case ruling is applicable in principle to Iceland (for which details of implementation were to be worked out at national level), but not to Ireland.

Furthermore, the difference is greatest on the first day of fasting, diminishing with each passing day until on the final day it virtually disappears. A dynamic application of the durational difference of $4^h41^m30^s$ would result in a continual decline in the size of the special-case areas in the immediate vicinity of the poles. Toward the end of the fasting period, no habitable point of earth would be affected any more by a special-case ruling.

With the exception of the continent of Antarctica and of a few uninhabitable island groups, the southern tip of the southernmost land mass (Tierra del Fuego) lies at about 57° (as far south as Aberdeen is north) – that is, well below the absolute tolerance for a special ruling. (The difference at this latitude amounts to three hours, fifty-nine minutes and two seconds.)

With respect to the second aspect – that portion of the day during which fasting is in force – a few additional observations are relevant. The further north, i.e. the greater the distance from the equator, the earlier occurs sunset and the later occurs sunrise. Wherever there is no special-case ruling regarding fasting, these two moments remain meridionally symmetrical and provide no grounds for adjusting the boundaries of this portion of the day. Within the polar circle, the moment of the change of day shifts tendentially in the direction of the meridian of solar transit. At and beyond latitude 82°30'3" North the first daily phase of abstinence begins at midday, in accordance with the guideline described above for the northward extension of the diurnal threshold. As the time of fasting progresses, this exception area shrinks to nothing (latitude 90°), expanding again during the last two days until it reaches 89°10'. For this tiny circle immediately around the north pole, the beginning of the day then occurs at midnight. In the south the situation is more straightforward: the latitude of the southern special-case area is initially 80°50'3" on the first day, decreasing to 89°10' on the final day of fasting; each day begins at midnight during this entire period of time.

We are talking here about areas with no permanent residents, where the very few who do sojourn there for a time hardly follow a 'normal' office routine. From a practical point of view, therefore, there are no impelling grounds for subjecting these areas to an exceptional ruling. The termination of that portion of the day reserved for fasting could be determined by the diurnal threshold as normal, commencement being calculated retrospectively from this moment, just as in the remainder of the special-case area.

The precise moment of the transition between day and night is also significant for determining the times for the daily obligatory prayers. For the long prayer (*aṣ-ṣalátu'l-kabír*), neither the difference in duration between day and night nor the moment of the change of day is problematic, since this prayer may be recited at any time during the day. By contrast, the short and middle prayers are to be recited during specific times defined in terms of natural phenomena, a fact which poses certain problems in implementation, since in winter both sunset and sunrise occur officially at midday. (It is assumed here that sunrise is to be handled analogously to sunset in the special-case areas.) The short obligatory prayer (*aṣ-ṣalátu'ṣ-ṣaghír*) is to be recited between midday and sunset, and so in the absence of a special ruling it would theoretically have to be recited precisely at this moment. With the medium obligatory prayer (*aṣ-ṣalátu'l-wasṭá*) this problem is present for two of the three prescribed periods: between sunrise and midday, and between midday and sunset. These 'problems' are surely not difficult to resolve, and incidentally not restricted to occidental time; it is my intention here merely to point out an area which potentially requires clarification.

The occidental day and the calendar date

So far we have addressed the question of the locally valid date only in connection with the first point of Aries. In fact, the equinox represents a special case: at this moment the change of occidental date occurs in a manner comparable to that of the familiar meridional system. We will now take another imaginary trip into space to see why this is otherwise never the case. Although the description to follow assumes a cyclic-progressive date line, it holds regardless of the method chosen for establishing which day is Naw-Rúz, i.e. it holds both for the reference-spot method familiar to us and for the cyclic-progressive method.

We are observing the earth from a distance of about 50,000

kilometres, as we were doing once before (see 'The cyclic-progressive method for fixing the day of Naw-Rúz' in Chapter 6) – except this time not at the moment of the equinox, but instead on 17 Núr, the first day of summer and thus roughly the moment of the summer solstice. The date line lies as usual just about in the middle of the picture. It is 02:00 GT on 17 Núr, and the diurnal threshold runs diagonally from north-east to south-west at an angle of 23°26'21"45, crossing the equator at a point somewhat west of the intersection of the equator and the annual threshold (i.e. the date line). Three areas are discernible in this picture (see Illustration 8):

1. in the northern hemisphere between the diurnal threshold and the date line;
2. predominantly in the southern hemisphere between the date line and the diurnal threshold;
3. the rest of the globe.

Illustration 8

diurnal threshold, date line and calendar date

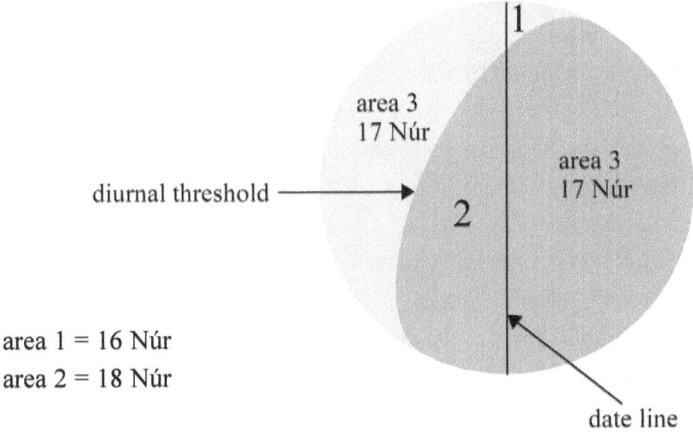

In the predominant part of the earth (in area 3) it is at this moment 17 Núr. This area is not affected by the bias of the diurnal threshold, and it behaves exactly as it did on the first day of spring. East of areas 1 and 2 the day of 17 Núr has (more or less) just begun, and west of them it is now (more or less) coming to a close. But in neither of these other two areas is it 17 Núr. In area 1 it is still 16 Núr because this area lies east of the date line and sunset has not yet taken place. In area 2 the situation is just the reverse: it lies west of the date line and sunset has already occurred. Therefore it is at this moment 18 Núr in area 2.

In the course of the day the diurnal threshold advances progressively westward, and the intersection between the diurnal threshold and the date line moves correspondingly northward. Area 2 acts like a wedge which forges its way unrelentlessly northward, area 1 retreating at the same pace. As sunset progressively overruns the annual threshold, the region of 18 Núr gains ever more territory, whilst the region of the remainder of the calendar day 16 Núr shrinks in size accordingly. Some time after the very last bit of 16 Núr has disappeared in the north, the first trace of 19 Núr can be made out in the extreme south. This process then repeats itself, but this time with the calendar dates 17, 18 and 19 Núr.

The first day of winter (11 Masá'il) behaves analogously but in the opposite direction. The intersection between diurnal threshold and date line begins in the northern polar region and spreads out towards the south, i.e. the wedge of the new date (12 Masá'il) grows from north to south and the wedge of the old date (10 Masá'il) shrinks toward the south.

On every other day of the year the slope of the diurnal threshold lies somewhere between these two extremes, and the tips of the respective wedges are accordingly more or less acute. On the day of a solstice, the tip of the new date's wedge requires a full twelve hours to advance from one polar circle to the other, whereas on the day before or after an equinox it accomplishes this journey in just over a minute, on the day of the autumnal equinox (16 'Izzaṭ) in a few seconds.

During the course of twenty-four hours there will correspondingly be a period of somewhere between twelve and twenty-four hours' duration (depending on the slope of the diurnal threshold) during which the threshold and date line are sufficiently distant from one another that they do not intersect. During this time there exist only two areas: east of the diurnal threshold and west of the annual threshold-cum-date line that of the new day, otherwise (i.e. east of the annual and west of the diurnal threshold) that of the preceding day.

The conditions surrounding the change of day/date during the fourth and fifth Yawm-i Há' are in principle the same, but their ramifications are somewhat more complicated. A complete description of this process has been relegated to Appendix C to avoid burdening the discussion at this point with excessive detail.

This phenomenon already takes place today in the vicinity of the international date line along longitude 180°. The only difference is that this date line is far away from 'us', so that we don't normally have to come to terms with the dynamics. By way of compensation, however, the inhabitants of the Aleutian Islands, New Zealand and the islands of the South Pacific cope with this situation daily. Given the cyclic-progressive method described earlier, the migrating date line would distribute this phenomenon equitably over the entire globe, thus effectively putting into practice the Bahá'í principle of the equality of all peoples, races, nations and cultures.

In the example just presented, the global date happens to be identical to the local date for the predominant part of the globe. This situation owes its existence to the fact that the tip of the advancing wedge (area 2) has already crossed the equator. Just over two hours earlier, this would not have been the case: the global date was then still 16 Núr, that is, the same date as that of the retreating wedge (area 1), a relatively small proportion of the total surface of the earth. Thus there would appear to be a discrepancy between GT and LT. However, it should be borne in mind that at the beginning of a global year, formally at 00:00 on 1 Bahá' GT, the diurnal and annual thresholds are identical. At this moment in sidereal time it is 1 Bahá' everywhere in the world, in some parts for nearly 24 hours already – in fulfilment of the law of Bahá'u'lláh as described in 'The cyclic-progressive method for fixing the day of Naw-Rúz' in Chapter 6. Thus it becomes clear why the global date frequently appears to lag behind the local date.

Annual commemoration

Annual commemoration is a virtually universal practice – one need only think of birthdays, name days, wedding and other anniversaries, and the festival days of nearly all religions, whereby the Jewish year of jubilee constitutes an exception (see 'The Jewish calendar' in Chapter 2); but even here, the year serves as the basic unit of counting. What is not evident at first glance is the immediate relationship between the 'annuality' of such festivals and each culture's respective definition of the year, as has been discussed in the historical overview in Part I.

The annual rhythm of the Zoroastrian year was just as confusing as the calendar itself, with its numerous reformations; even Naw-Rúz, the traditional festival of spring, landed at one time or another in history on well-nigh every day of the year. In India, the rhythm of the year is a (regulated) lunar one for some festivals and a solar one for others: in this cultural context the term 'annual' is ambiguous.

The Jewish calendar year has either ca. 354 or ca. 384 days, depending on whether or not the leap month (Adar II) occurs in the year in question. The Jewish calendar is the best example of the extent to which the definition of the length of the year is conditioned by the formal characteristics of the calendar used – or better, how difficult it is to distinguish between the definition and the calendar characteristics. From the astronomical point of view, the arbitrariness of this apportionment into annual units appears to outweigh its periodicity. In the case of the Gregorian, Iranian and Islamic calendars, this variation in the length of the year is restricted to a single day, but it is nonetheless still present: the fact that one year lasts 365 or 354 days and the next year 366 or 355 clearly demonstrates the degree to which the concept of 'year' must be adjusted according to an artificial (if ostensibly unavoidable) calendar dictate at the cost of astronomical reality.

The reason why the trustees of the historical calendars took such pains to keep their calendars in line with the rhythm of the sun and moon is to be sought primarily in the symbolic associations both of the natural phenomena themselves and of the calendars based on them. In a regulated calendar, in contrast to the case of the Neolithic calendar, the agricultural, liturgical or other life rhythms need no longer be derived from constant signal dates, as the Islamic calendar and the Christian Easter serve to demonstrate. It is more the case that such days, and in particular the one initiating the cycle of the year, attain metaphorical character: divine guidance, atonement, rejuvenation, rebirth, progress, transcience, temporality itself. Without reference to objectively observable natural events, this symbolism would lose vitality and conviction. The symbolic infusion of meaning enhances the significance of these natural events, but it doesn't transfigure them. Symbols cannot simply detach themselves from the world of objects – not even through centuries-old habit, as the Zoroastrian example amply demonstrates.→14

True to the Bahá'í principle of agreement between religion and science, the Badí' calendar presents a definition of the religious year – a divinely revealed definition at that – which is in complete accord with astronomical reality. Furthermore, the cyclic-progressive region of Há', as an alternative to the traditional leap year approach, offers for the first time ever the possibility of embedding this overall agreement into the very structure of the calendar itself.

The Day of the Covenant is an example of a solemn occasion which by nature lasts for a specific duration of time: in this case a complete day. However, one must bear in mind that this day – 4 Qawl – is a *nominal* day which, though always delineated by sunset, begins and ends at a different siderial moment for every locality. As people immediately east of the date line first begin to commemorate this day, the same day has already come to a close for their neighbours to the west. Thus the 'day of commemoration' lasts 48 hours – 24 hours respectively for every locality on earth. Should one wish to celebrate this day the whole world over during the *identical* 24 hours, then it would have to be understood for example as a *global* day, that is, the period of time between 00:00 and 24:00 GT. This global day would begin at every point on earth at a different time on 3, 4 or 5 Qawl and terminate on the following calendar day, be this 4, 5 or 6 Qawl; and in any given location, the local time would be different each year, and oftentimes the local calendar date as well.

Five of the commemorative festivals document events which occurred at specific and known moments in Bábí-Bahá'í history: the Birth of Bahá'u'lláh, the Declaration of the Báb, the Martyrdom of the Báb, the Ascension of Bahá'u'lláh and the Ascension of 'Abdu'l-Bahá. (Missing in this list are the moment of the birth of the Báb and the exact day and time of the first announcement of Bahá'u'lláh's mission in the Garden of Riḍván; given the current state of research, this information seems to have been lost to history.) In other words, one commemorates primarily the *moment* of the event, and secondarily, as an extension of this moment, the day of its occurrence. It is arguably a matter of fundamental significance to mark this historic moment precisely according to astronomical criteria.

This goal could be achieved on the basis of the Gregorian calendar and meridional time only with utmost difficulty. Reference to the solar age of the year is obscured by the nonlinear leap year system, whereas mean and zone time camouflage the true age of the day. The Badí' calendar together with the cyclic-progressive region of Há' is free from the first of these problems, occidental time from the second. One of the most significant features of global time is that it stands in a defined relationship both to the ecliptic longitude and to local time for every point on earth. Once the historical moments of the respective events have been calculated in terms of global time, the resulting date and time expressions represent for all time thereafter the astronomically precise annual recurrence of these moments.

A concrete example

We will now consider a concrete example – the Ascension of 'Abdu'l-Bahá – by way of demonstration. This is one of the two events for which the diurnal threshold and the date line intersect at the moment of its historical occurrence (the other is the Ascension of Bahá'u'lláh), so that we can observe the interplay between three adjoining calendar dates as described in 'The occidental day and the calendar date' earlier in this chapter. It is also historically the latest of the commemorative events under consideration, having taken place in Palestine during the time of the British mandate, so that we can be certain that mean zone time was in use. Furthermore, it so happens that the time zone of Israel/Palestine (UTC+2) has not been adjusted to correspond to political boundaries, as it has been for example in Iran. And finally, the event took place in winter, so that we do not have to cope with the uncertainties associated with summer time.

'Abdu'l-Bahá departed from this world at His home at Haparsim St. 7, Haifa at 1:30 in the morning of 6 Qawl 78 (28 November 1921). That is equivalent in occidental time to 19:28:57 GT (see Appendix E).

A global date and time expression denotes the exact span of time which has lapsed since the first point of Aries, and it is constant for all time; to be of practical use, however, it must be converted each year anew for every locality on earth into a corresponding calendar date and local time. Given the timekeeping devices described earlier we would simply depress the <LT> and <GT> buttons to convert back and forth between local and global time expressions. But since we don't have such timepieces yet, it is up to us to carry out these conversions for ourselves. For this exercise we will need some geographical data and a computer (or a scientific pocket calculator and a modicum of patience). Full details of the calculation strategy can be found in Appendix E, together with the computed results for a representative selection of locations around the globe.

What influence occidental time might exert on the fixing of the respective calendar date and time of day for the commemoration of the various festivals remains – in each case prior to a ruling by the Universal House of Justice – open to speculation. In particular, the question arises whether the scheduling of the festivities should be influenced at all by the precise historical moment being commemorated in each instance. A reader of an early draft of the German edition of this study wrote to me in this regard: 'The celebration in the appropriate moment of the year's cycle ... is however only one of many possible approaches which present themselves for such a celebration. Another possibility would be to reconstruct the original circumstances as nearly as possible. The commemoration of the Ascension of Bahá'u'lláh is a good example of what I mean: the birds begin to sing (at least in our part of the world) just about the time of the recitation of the Tablet of Visitation. If one were to schedule the celebration according to legal time [summer time] instead of normal time, then one would have to forgo this deeply emotional impression: everything remains silent and pitch dark.'[15]

For some festivals the time of day for the commemoration has already been fixed:

> As the Guardian indicated, the commemoration of the Ascension of Bahá'u'lláh should be held, if feasible, at 3 a.m. on 29 May, and that of the Ascension of 'Abdu'l-Bahá at 1 a.m. on 28 November. These times should be measured according to standard time in each area. If daylight saving time [i.e. summer time – my comment] is being used in the country, the commemorations should continue to be observed according to standard time.[16]

Fixed times are recommended for the following commemorations as well: Declaration of the Báb, two hours after sunset; Martyrdom of the Báb, at midday; 1st day of Riḍván, at 3 p.m.[17] In the event of a shift from meridional to occidental time, the task would fall to the Universal House of Justice to decide how these instructions should then be adjusted, if at all.

The possibilities arising through the existence of global time should perhaps be viewed in the first instance as an enrichment to the existing freedom of individual action. In particular, if at some location on earth the moment of the ecliptic longitude of a given event should approximate the prescribed time for the commemoration, then this moment could be conveniently included in the programme without competing with other conventions.

Badí' time

In Part I we saw that the 24-hour rhythm of the traditional system for recording the time of day, which represented a convenient basis for estimating by eye the position of the sun, had become so entrenched that it continued to exist after the introduction of the mechanical clock – just as the phases and weeks derived from the moon continued to be represented in calendars long after regulation had deprived the calendar of its immediate fixation on natural phenomena.

With its nineteen nineteen-day months, the Badí' calendar is the only existing calendar to have departed completely from this venerable but now pointless orientation on time units derived from the moon phases and cycles. A transition to occidental time would offer a unique opportunity to undertake a similar departure from the traditional rhythm of the hour (see Chapter 3) and, inspired by the structure of the Badí' calendar, to introduce a new scheme of division: the day with nineteen hours, the hour with nineteen *degrees*, the degree with nineteen minutes and the minute with nineteen seconds. The reduction from 24 to 19 hours is reminiscent of the reduction of the number of *nakhud* in a *mithqál* from 24 to 19 (see 'Unity in diversity: The numbers nine and nineteen' in Chapter 5). In light of its parallelism with the calendar structure, this scheme will be referred to here as *Badí' time*.

The following table offers an impression of the durations of the individual Badí' units of time:

Badí' unit	Erstwhile unit
1 hour	1.2632 hours ($1^h15^m47^s52$)
1 degree	3.9889 minutes (3^m59^s33)
1 minute	12.5966 seconds
1 second	0.6630 second

The synodic day (the solar day) consists of 361 temporal degrees, almost exactly equal to the number of arc degrees in a circle, greatly simplifying the estimation of east-west time differences. The clocks in Warsaw, which lies about 21° east of London, are roughly 21 temporal degrees, or one hour and two degrees, ahead of the clocks in London – whereby this quick estimate incurs a deviation of 0.277 per cent from the exact time difference, or in this case about 12.7 erstwhile seconds. The exact relationship is: degrees of arc = $n + n/360$ degrees of time. With a bit of rounding, this formula also lends itself to head reckoning. In the present example: $21^{21}/_{360}$ = approx. $21^{2}/_{36} = 21^{1}/_{18}$, or just over 21 degrees and 1 minute Badí' time, with an error of 0.1 erstwhile seconds. But this refinement is seldom necessary, since the quick estimate of the longest possible time difference (180 degrees of arc) yields an error of less than two erstwhile minutes. Interestingly, a rotation of 361 arc degrees is almost exactly equivalent to the average sidereal revolution of the earth in one day, deviating by only 0.0039767 per cent, or 1° in roughly 68.85 years.

This scheme represents a stepwise subdivision from the smallest unit of time (the second) up to the largest unit (*kullu shay'*, or 361 years) with a constant factor of nineteen, resulting in a regular pattern of size relationships among the scale of seven time divisions within the calendar year, i.e. second, minute, degree, hour, day, month, year (excluding Ayyám-i Há'), the relationship in each case being directly proportional to the distance in this scale between the two time divisions involved:

Distance	Relationship	Smallest example	Largest example
1	1:19	second:minute	month:year
2	1:361	second:degree	day:year
3	1:6 859	second:hour	hour:year
4	1:130 321	second:day	degree:year
5	1:2 476 099	second:month	minute:year
6	1:47 045 881	second:year	second:year

These relationships apply similarly to the epochal units of time, of course, commencing with the solar year:

1	1:19	year:wáḥid	wáḥid:kullu shay'
2	1:361	year: kullu shay'	year: kullu shay'

These Badí' time units would be restricted to expressions of the occidental time of day in connection with the Badí' calendar and would have no effect on other international units of measurement such as energy, speed or acceleration, or on meridional time expressions, e.g. in conjunction with the Gregorian calendar, where the traditional units would continue to be valid. This restriction is unavoidable not only because the entire scientific and technical world is so inalienably bound up with these time units; it is dictated primarily by the fact that the Badíʻ time units are not constant, but are instead synchronized with the – variable – duration of the occidental day. The use of Badíʻ units of time would in itself emphasize the fundamentally different nature of these two systems of time measurement.

That there be no misunderstanding, let me emphasize that this scheme of diurnal time calibration is in no way textually supported either by the Holy Writings or by any exposition on the part of ʻAbduʼl-Bahá or Shoghi Effendi; it is the result of my own deliberations and should be judged accordingly. On the other hand, there is to my knowledge nothing in the literature which perpetuates the traditional scheme of division by twelfths – which is probably derived from Babylonian numerology (see Chapter 3) – for all eternity.

I would further suggest that Badíʻ units of time be expressed *ordinally*, that is, analogously to the calendar units. In other words, one would count in each case from 1 to 19, in contrast to the erstwhile scheme whereby units of time smaller than the day are counted starting instead with 0. Thus the first hour of the day, for example, would begin with 1, just as the first day of the month or the first month of the year; the same would hold for the first degree, the first minute and the first second. This arrangement would present no difficulty in reckoning or calculating expressions of duration. It would clearly require some adjustment of thought at first, but the reward would be that the counting conventions of date and time expressions would be reconciled with one another, and that the highly symbolic number nineteen would attain a pervading presence throughout the system of the calibration of time.

8

The Rhythm of Life

So far the discussion concerning the practical introduction of the Badí' calendar has had primarily to do with internal Bahá'í matters. Whether or not 1 Bahá' coincides with some particular day in March will matter just about as little to the non-Bahá'í – who is in all probability not even aware of the existence of this calendar – as the Gregorian equivalent of 1 Tishri does to the non-Jew or that of 1 Muḥarram to the non-Muslim. Even in the event that Bahá'ís employ a different time scale among themselves, the international meridional convention for designating time will nonetheless continue to be used at large. In short, the discussion thus far has to do with decisions which have no immediate consequences for the general society in which the Bahá'í community is embedded.

The prospect of structuring life's routine affairs in compliance with the time divisions derived from the Badí' calendar is another matter altogether. But this objective is, in the end, the whole sense and purpose of introducing the new system of calibrating time. A calendar based on the unit nineteen would be gratuitous if this unit did not in some way form the basis of the rhythm of life for those who adopted this calendar.

This rhythm is indeed already reality, at least when it comes to scheduling internal Bahá'í activities. To what extent it will assume a role in further areas of the lives of Bahá'ís depends on how much the Bahá'í community senses the need for such a development and to what degree Bahá'ís succeed in securing the necessary concessions from the wider community.

As has been mentioned in Chapter 4 and elaborated in 'The week' in Chapter 5, the Badí' calendar also includes the concept of the week. The relationship between these two life rhythms is not self-evident, and the conditions under which they are to co-exist are not made clear in the Writings. The task of explicating this relationship will therefore necessarily devolve to the Universal House of Justice.

The status of the week and the day of rest

The Báb's description of the Badí' calendar, as summarized by Nabíl on the basis of the Kitáb-i Asmá',[1] included the concept of the week. Furthermore, Shoghi Effendi confirmed that the week is a permanent feature of the Badí' calendar:

> The Badi' Calendar will be used generally. The Bahá'í week has seven days.[2]

As we have already seen in 'The week' in Chapter 5, neither the Sabbath nor the seven-day week has any liturgical function in the Bahá'í Faith. Nonetheless, one possible reason for the existence of the week is that it forms the basis for the rhythm of work, or rather, for the rhythm of the day of rest, which the Bahá'í community is to observe and uphold. In this respect the Badí' calendar would be in full conformity with the Semitic tradition of the Sabbath, at least with regard to its practical consequences for the conduct of secular affairs.

There is one text passage which seems at first sight to confirm one day each week (Friday) as a Bahá'í day of rest, to be found in a letter written on behalf of Shoghi Effendi to an individual believer:

> 'Abdu'l-Bahá gives no reason whatever why Friday has been chosen as the day of rest in the Bahá'í calendar. He just affirms it.[3]

Just as interesting as the actual content of this short letter written on Shoghi Effendi's behalf is what is missing: there is no reference to a doctrinal pronouncement either from Bahá'u'lláh or from 'Abdu'l-Bahá, and there is no explanation or exposition on the part of Shoghi Effendi. These omissions invite the supposition that either

- a definitive pronouncement from Bahá'u'lláh or 'Abdu'l-Bahá stipulating Friday as the day of rest does not exist, and/or

- for some reason, Shoghi Effendi did not feel it appropriate or necessary to express himself more extensively on this occasion.

With regard to supposition (a): an unambiguous ruling from the Báb does indeed exist:

> God has created Friday for purity and pleasantness, and the resting of His servants from what they undertake on other days . . .[4]

However, in my searches in the Writings of Bahá'u'lláh and 'Abdu'l-Bahá at my disposal, I have been unable to find any passages which confirm the Báb's ruling or adopt it as Bahá'í orthodoxy, or which shed light on this matter in any manner whatsoever. With the exception of a remark by the editors regarding the Islamic day of congregation, the word 'Friday' (or *Yawmu'l-Jum'at* or *Istiqlál*) does not appear at all in the Kitáb-i Aqdas, that work of Bahá'u'lláh in which all other calendar matters are given detailed attention, whereas the word 'week' (*usbú'*) occurs only once (in connection with personal hygiene).[5] Of course, the absence of an explanatory text passage proves nothing with certainty: it might just as well be that the appropriate literature has not yet been translated from Persian or Arabic, or that it is simply not included in the normally available compilations. This line of argument, however, should not be carried so far that it derogates the content of the Writings which are in fact available.

The most plausible justification for supposition (b) is that Shoghi Effendi did not wish to burden the believers in the West with a commandment which at that time would have been extremely difficult to put into effect. Given the negative nature of this information, the fact that this letter is addressed to an individual believer and not to a National Spiritual Assembly is not overly significant, since Shoghi Effendi was well aware that such communications also achieved wide circulation and that any misunderstanding, once it had come into being, would spread very quickly and be difficult to correct at a later time. On the other hand, it seems to me highly unlikely that Shoghi Effendi would have elected to comment on an official ruling with regard to such a universal matter as this via a letter to an individual believer written by his secretary, and nowhere else in his extensive writings. We should bear in mind that '. . . whenever he [i.e. the Guardian] has something of importance to say, he invariably communicates it to the National Spiritual Assembly or in his general letters. His personal letters to individual friends are only for their personal benefit . . .'[6]

It therefore seems possible that Shoghi Effendi did not consider the utterance from 'Abdu'l-Bahá to have been a statement of doctrine, and also that no other doctrinal statement exists concerning the day of rest. Moreover, to the best of my knowledge there exist neither prayers nor commandments which apply specifically to the day of rest. Naturally, it would help if we knew the circumstances under which 'Abdu'l-Bahá had been asked about the status of Friday, for this context could possibly be of help in evaluating Shoghi Effendi's statement.

Where might the practice of a Bahá'í work-free Friday come from, if not from the teachings? In attempting to answer this question we must take into account conditions which prevailed in the Bahá'í community in former times.

The reminiscences of a believer from the Bahjí period provide an interesting clue to the situation during the early days of the community in Palestine:

> Áqá Muḥammad-i-Tabrízí has recounted how, as a child of four or five, he would go with his family to the Mansion of Bahjí each Friday, as was customary among the believers at that time, to attain the presence of the Blessed Beauty. They would stay all day, using the rooms on the lower floor of the Mansion . . .[7]

Most of the male adults in the Bahá'í community in 'Akká at that time pursued trade and business, and it was incumbent upon them to observe the work rhythm of the predominantly Muslim society in which they were embedded, which included a day of rest on Friday (if at all); otherwise it would have been impossible to maintain normal opening hours and times of work. Furthermore, the fledgling Bahá'í community during Bahá'u'lláh's lifetime consisted almost exclusively of believers who themselves had once been Muslims or who were at most second-generation Bahá'ís, and the Friday rest-day was just as self-evident for them as the work-free Sunday is for Bahá'í communities in the West, whose members stem predominantly from a Christian background. It is worth noting that 'Abdu'l-Bahá encouraged the friends to gather once a week on a regular basis:

> Likewise the public meetings in which one day during the week the believers gather to be engaged in the commemoration of God, to read Communes and deliver effective speeches is acceptable and beloved[8]

and that Sunday, not Friday, was considered an appropriate day for Bahá'í meetings for the Bahá'ís in the West, in compliance with the pattern of life in these cultural areas:

> Regarding arrangements for the Bahai Sunday Meeting for the purpose of worship, this is very suitable. But, in a meeting of worship, first, prayer should be chanted and supplication made until all gather; then, communion should be made. After praying, sacred readings with melodious voices should be read by all together. As this is the commencement of holding meetings, this is sufficient.[9]

Furthermore, although the primary purpose of the following instruction is to circumvent alienation from other religious communities, it makes it clear that 'Abdu'l-Bahá perceived the Sunday meeting as embracing the whole community and that it should include Sunday school for the children:

> Holding your meetings when it is the time of prayer in other churches is not advisable; it would lead to alienation, since the Bahá'í children who have

their own Sunday school would be deprived of it if they tried to attend other Sunday schools.[10]

'Azíz Yazdí, who was a member of the International Teaching Centre in Haifa for fourteen years and who spent several years of his youth in Haifa, recounted during a talk given at the National Centre in Langenhain, Germany on 27 August 1999 (on his 91st birthday) how the community there would assemble once a week in a room on Mount Carmel, near to the Shrine of the Báb. These gatherings, held at the personal invitation of 'Abdu'l-Bahá, took place regularly on Sunday, not on Friday. It was the time of the British protectorate, and the governing authorities had doubtless proclaimed Sunday to be the official day of rest for commerce and public service, just as they were generally inclined to do in British colonies. 'Abdu'l-Bahá's action seems to support the idea that, for Him, observation of Friday as the day of rest was not mandatory, not even in the Orient.

Returning once again to that statement from 'Abdu'l-Bahá mentioned in Shoghi Effendi's letter, it is conceivable that 'Abdu'l-Bahá had on some occasion simply described (perhaps to a Western Bahá'í pilgrim) the predominant practice in the Orient at some particular time, not intending such a remark to be elevated to the status of dogma.

Prompted by the appearance of the first English-language edition of this book, Sen McGlinn[11] searched for and located a probable source of this statement in notes recorded in 1910 by Mason Remey,[12] in which 'Abdu'l-Bahá is reported to have been asked on some unspecified occasion: 'Which day of the week will the Bahá'ís eventually observe as a day of rest?', to which He replied 'Friday.' That fits very well with Shoghi Effendi's statement 'He just affirms it.' The source of this information would thus appear to be a pilgrim's note.

It is important to note that the expression 'day of rest' occurs in the question posed to 'Abdu'l-Bahá, and not in His answer. To Christians, 'the day of rest' is often used as a synonym for 'Sunday,' with no emphasis on abstinence from work or toil; that is, the gist of the question recorded by Remey might well have been 'which day of the week will be to Bahá'ís what Sunday is to Christians?' Furthermore, we don't know the precise wording of the question as it was posed to 'Abdu'l-Bahá in English or Persian – His passive command of English was certainly sufficient. All we know is that, according to a pilgrim's note, 'Abdu'l-Bahá identified Friday as standing out from the other days of the week in some fashion.

In a later revision of his blog article, McGlinn reports having come across a one-line tablet from 'Abdu'l-Bahá to a Persian believer,[13] which he translates:

> The day of rest in this dispensation is Friday. May the glory of the most glorious be with you.

Interestingly, the Persian original reads *yawm-e ráḥat*, which translates literally as 'day of rest.' In this case we can be confident that the expression is being used by 'Abdu'l-Bahá in its literal sense, that is, a day during which the believer is at least not discouraged from abstaining from work. Furthermore, the expression 'in this dispensation' (*dar ín dour*, literally: cycle, era, epoch or 'loop') would appear to imply that the passage from the *Bayán* quoted earlier is applicable throughout the current dispensation, i.e. the Dispensation of Bahá'u'lláh, once circumstances enable its activation. There is nevertheless no way to confirm this assumption in the absence of a Guardian, and the Universal House of Justice will one day have to make a decision which, however obligatory it may then be for the community, apparently cannot ultimately be scripturally substantiated.

Perhaps the only thing one can claim with any certainty at this stage, prior to a ruling from the Universal House of Justice, is that observing the week cycle and the regular weekly day of rest (whether that be a Friday or a Sunday, or for that matter any other day of the week) does not contradict any article of doctrine in the Bahá'í Faith. Thus, for the time being, Bahá'ís in different parts of the world are free to adapt their life rhythms to those which prevail in their respective societies, without fear of being at odds with their own religious practices – with the understanding, of course, that every form of local practice remains valid only up until the time when a world-wide, binding regulation has been enacted.

A further aspect in need of clarification is the relationship between weekday and calendar day. My own experience is that the Bahá'ís in the West treat the weekday exclusively as a feature of the Gregorian calendar, i.e. as a meridional phenomenon. The fact that Gregorian names of the days of the week are used virtually exclusively is certainly a significant factor reinforcing this assumed equivalence, and avoidance of Arabic names is understandable in Western societies, including Bahá'í communities, where acquaintance with the Arabic language is not widespread. Viewed linguistically, however, the inverse causality is generally at work: resistance to language innovation is always strongest where the novel terminology is isomorphic with existing terminology. For example, long after English had otherwise replaced French as his dominant foreign language, Shoghi Effendi consistently reverted to French when reckoning with numbers[14] – the common semiotics in this case being the decimal system. In other words, it is in the first instance the assumed equivalence of the two sets of names for the days of the week which fuels resistance to the introduction of the Badí' names, whether it be the Arabic ones or their English language equivalents (contrast this situation with the community-wide acceptance of the Badí' month names).→[15]

The practice of equating Badí' and Gregorian days of the week is by no means unreasonable. In the normal course of daily life, especially at work, in social interaction with non-Bahá'ís, for the observance of ordinances regarding the sabbath rest and so on, the weekly rhythm of society at large is an all-pervading factor, no less so in Bahá'í circles. The decision whether or not this practice should continue in the future as it has in the past is linked to the question in principle of the status of the week. If the week is to be considered an integral component of Badí' reckoning of time, then the weekday and the calendar day would in my opinion have to be treated as covering the identical period, beginning and ending at sunset. If it be felt instead that the function of the week is to maintain a bridge to the predominant life rhythm of society at large (see 'The week' in Chapter 5) or to provide unbroken continuity for the concept of the

Sabbath as a concession to other monotheistic religions (see 'Semitic calendar systems' in Chapter 2), then the current practice would justifiably continue unaltered, being in total conformity with this understanding. Only the Universal House of Justice can clarify which function the Badí' week is to fulfil in the Bahá'í community.

A further consideration is that, given the cyclic-progressive method, the fifth Ayyám-i Há' does not count as a day of the week: 1 'Alá' is the very next day of the week after the fourth Yawm-i Há' everywhere in the world, also within the region of Há' and in global time. As a result, the days of the week in the Badí' year are invariably 365 in number, and every four years or so one day of the week is lost with respect to the Semitic week. The consequence is that the Badí' day names no longer correspond to their non-Badí' counterparts: whereas in some given year Fiḍál will correspond to Monday (and *Doshanbeh* and *Yom Sheni* and *Yawmu'l-Ithnayn*), at the latest in four years' time it will correspond to Tuesday (and *Sehshanbeh* and *Yom Shlishi* and *Yawmu'th-Thaláthá'*), then Wednesday, and so on in perpetuity.

A possible cyclic-progressive alternative would be to treat intercalary days uniformly, that is, to exclude them collectively from the days of the week, leaving exactly 361 days of the week in every Badí' year. That convention would underpin the special nature of these 'days of giving that precede the season of restraint' and which are not 'bounded by the limits of the year and its months'.[16] Moreover, there would be less danger of people simply 'forgetting' the arrangement during the years in which one would otherwise not be locally affected.

However the concept of the week is defined or conceived, any decision about the role of the week in a future Bahá'í society is automatically also a decision about the role of the nineteen-day Bahá'í month. Neither of these two rhythms can be considered in isolation.

The central role of the Nineteen Day Feast

The nineteen-day rhythm of the Feast is directly associated with that of the Bahá'í month. The Feast was ordained by the Báb in the Arabic

Bayán, confirmed by Bahá'u'lláh in the Most Holy Book,[17] fostered by 'Abdu'l-Bahá both in the Orient and in the West,[18] and given its final form by Shoghi Effendi.[19] 'Abdu'l-Bahá explained that

> The object is concord, that through this fellowship hearts may become perfectly united, and reciprocity and mutual helpfulness established. Because the members of the world of humanity are unable to exist without being bonded together, cooperation and mutual helpfulness is the basis of human society.[20]

The Nineteen Day Feast is 'the very heart of our Bahá'í community life' and the 'foundation of the new World Order'.[21] One must consider that the Bahá'í world community is deeply democratic→[22] in form, in both significant senses of this word: representative and participatory. To be sure, it is the responsibility of the elected representatives, that is, the members of the elected branch at all three administrative levels – local, national and global – to make binding decisions in matters pertinent to their respective levels; but just as important is the participation of every individual member of the community both in the election of the assembly members and in the Nineteen Day Feasts. The monthly Feast has two important functions in addition to that of communal worship, functions which have a direct bearing on the democratic nature of the Bahá'í world community. On the one hand it is a regular opportunity for coming together and for strengthening the bonds of friendship and acquaintance between the individual members of the community, and on the other hand it is a forum for public consultation→[23] over matters concerning the community – both for the announcement, elaboration and discussion of decisions of the assemblies and for the opportunity to offer ideas and suggestions to the assemblies from the community at large:

> The main purpose of the Nineteen Day Feasts is to enable individual believers to offer any suggestion to the local Assembly which in its turn will pass it to the N.S.A. The local Assembly is, therefore, the proper medium through which local Bahá'í communites can communicate with the body of the national representatives.[24]

Every Nineteen Day Feast consists of three phases: a devotional, a consultative and a social. Each and every one is important and indispensable.

The devotional phase differs from a church service in important respects: no ritualized or sacramental acts are performed, i.e. the Nineteen Day Feast is devoid of salvatory function;→25 neither are sermons delivered nor lessons held. Communal prayer is a basic element of Bahá'í community life, and worship is in its own right a central function of the Nineteen Day Feast. At the same time, this sacred act fulfils an additional, equally important function: the reading of prayers revealed by the Báb, by Bahá'u'lláh and by 'Abdu'l-Bahá foster a spiritual atmosphere befitting to the consultation to follow. Without such an atmosphere, proper consultation is impossible. Once the presence of divine assistance is felt by all participants, however, consultation of high quality is guaranteed. 'Abdu'l-Bahá says:

> Every meeting which is organized for the purpose of unity and concord will be conducive to changing strangers into friends, enemies into associates, and 'Abdu'l-Bahá will be present in His heart and soul with that meeting.→26

> Each one of you must think how to make happy and pleased the other members of your Assembly, and each one must consider all those who are present as better and greater than himself, and each one must consider himself less than the rest. Know their station as high, and think of your own station as low. Should you act and live according to these behests, know verily, of a certainty, that that Feast is the Heavenly Food. That Supper is the 'Lord's Supper'! I am the Servant of that gathering.[27]

Apart from the fact that communal worship is a highly rewarding aspect of Bahá'í life in its own right, true consultation is only possible after 'Abdu'l-Bahá has assumed his place among the participants. If the time for worship is kept too short, there will afterwards be much talk but little consultation.

Worship and devotion demands time. Much time. But it's worth it.

Consultation in the Bahá'í sense requires a maximum of humility, selflessness, mutual respect, unity and solidarity:

> The prime requisites for them that take counsel together are purity of motive, radiance of spirit, detachment from all else save God, attraction to His Divine Fragrances, humility and lowliness amongst His loved ones, patience and long-suffering in difficulties and servitude to His exalted Threshold. Should they be graciously aided to acquire these attibutes, victory from the unseen Kingdom of Bahá shall be vouchsafed to them.[28]

The consultative phase of the Nineteen Day Feast is structured. Here is for example no room for pneumatic ecstasy or for emotive bearing of witness; consultation requires a carefully planned business agenda and demands concentration and discipline on the part of those participating. The heart is inclined toward heaven during consultation, but the feet remain firmly on earth.

> It should be borne in mind that all consultation is aimed at arriving at a solution to a problem and is quite different from the sort of group baring of the soul that is popular in some circles these days and which borders on the kind of confession that is forbidden in the Faith.[29]

> Concerning the nature of the Nineteen Day Feast: In the 'Aqdas', Bahá'u'lláh has clearly revealed the spiritual and social character of this institution. Its administrative significance, however, has been stressed by the Guardian in direct response to the growing needs of the Bahá'í community in this formative period of the Bahá'í Era for better training in the principles and practice of Bahá'í administration.[30]

Every contribution to the current topic of consultation, regardless of its initiator, is regarded henceforth as ownerless, one out of an accumulation of gifts from and to all participants. Each individual has the responsibility to express his opinions in as coherent and effective a manner as possible, but he must thereafter detach himself completely from his personal contribution and regard it forthwith as common property. This attitude fosters awareness of group achievement and ensures that consultation is pursued in a positive, objective and solution-oriented fashion.

It is clear that a decision process which is designed to illuminate a topic of discussion from as many sides as possible will generally consume more time than a process whose sole aim is to win over a voting majority for a predetermined point of view. But such a consultative process is capable of producing decisions which are effective, efficient, well thought-out and free of self-interest, decisions which profit from the creativity and experience of the whole community, for the good of the whole community.

Consultation demands time. Much time. But it's worth it.

The third phase of the Nineteen Day Feast should in no way be regarded simply as a refreshment break. The original name of the feast (Arab. *ḍiyáfat*, 'receiving of guests', 'hospitality'; cf. *ḍayf*, 'guest') alone suffices to illustrate the importance of the social aspect. (Contrast this understanding of 'feast' with 'the festival of Naw-Rúz': here festival = arab. *'íd*, 'festival', 'festival day', 'holiday'; cf. *'Ídu'l-Fiṭr*, 'festival of the breaking of the (Islamic) fast'.) Bahá'u'lláh writes:

> Verily, it is enjoined upon you to offer a feast [*ḍiyáfat*], once in every month, though only water be served; for God hath purposed to bind hearts together, albeit through both earthly and heavenly means.[31]

Precisely because of its informality, this phase of the Feast gives each participant the opportunity to come together on an informal basis with fellow believers, many of whom he perhaps seldom sees during the rest of the Bahá'í month, if at all. New Bahá'ís are integrated into the community, existing friendships are strengthened and new friendships forged. This is a good time for discussing themes which have no direct connection with the formal plan of business or which are of immediate interest, relevance or topicality to only a portion of the participants. Recently declared Bahá'ís in particular now find the opportunity to pose questions which they would rather keep to themselves during the more structured phases of the feast. Discussions and deepenings take place *ex tempore* on a wide range of topics, and plans are forged laterally for putting into action the announcements of the Spiritual Assembly or decisions which were reached during consultation. The unity of the community waxes, and individuals get to know one another better. In the course of time each gains clearer ideas of whom he considers suitable for which particular administrative functions and gives expression to these impressions at the various community elections.

Social interaction demands time. Much time. But it's worth it.

In accordance with Shoghi Effendi's instructions, the Nineteen Day Feast occurs whenever possible on the first day of each Bahá'í month:

> Your third question concerns the day on which the Feast should be held every month. The Guardian stated in reply that no special day has been fixed, but it would be preferable and most suitable if the gathering of the friends should be held on the first day of each Bahá'í month.[32]

The timely scheduling of the feast day is indispensable not least out of practical considerations – for the mutual coordination of activities of individual communities and between local, national and global levels. In the meantime, with the continuing increase in believers the world over and the corresponding rise in the number of local and National Spiritual Assemblies, holding the Nineteen Day Feast regularly on the first day of the month has become established practice. This means that, given the seven-day week rhythm, the Nineteen Day Feast can take place on any and every day of the week – that is, predominantly during the evening between two working days, at least in the industrialized world. This circumstance places the Nineteen Day Feast in general under considerable pressure of time and thereby encourages an atmosphere of haste. As a result, the devotional phase often comes to a premature close before 'Abdu'l-Bahá has arrived; the gifts of consultation begin to be unwrapped before all of them have been placed on display; and the social phase is quickly transformed into a parting ritual, since the late hour and the prospect of an early rising the next morning beckons to slumber. For the same reason, many individuals refrain from partaking of the refreshments which are offered in the spirit of hospitality for the delight of the assembled friends and which render the *ḍiyáfat* worthy of its name.

So long as Bahá'í local communities remain relatively small and the dimensions of their activities appropriately modest, this situation, however regrettable, may remain tolerable; but with the growing presence of Bahá'ís in the community at large, a few evening hours will in the long run hardly suffice to cope with the increasing importance of this holy institution. If the effectiveness of the local level of the 'foundation of the new World Order' is to avoid being seriously threatened, the Bahá'í community will in my opinion very soon need a work-free Feast day.

Moreover, Shoghi Effendi – perhaps with just this sort of thing in mind – left clear instructions regarding the preferred time of day for the feast:

> Regarding the time for the holding of the Nineteen Day Feasts and elections: the Guardian would advise your Assembly to urge the friends to hold such gatherings on the prescribed day *before* sunset [my italics]. If impossible, then it is permissible to hold them on the preceding day.[33]

Up to now, at least in the industrialized world, the Bahá'í community has considered it impossible to schedule the Feast before sunset whenever it should fall on a weekday, and it has implemented Shoghi Effendi's instructions accordingly, i.e. it has interpreted 'the preceding day' to mean the preceding meridional day, after sunset. As a result, the Feasts are held during the daylight hours only when they happen to occur on a Sunday, or occasionally also on a Saturday (or in late spring and early summer, in those latitudes where sunset is sufficiently late). But considering the enthusiasm for the Cause of God and the courage to take difficult but consistent decisions for its advancement which the Guardian demonstrates everywhere in his writings, there is another possible reading of this text – a reading which is both justifiable and plausible: in the guise of an 'urgent request' Shoghi Effendi might here be intimating the more distant goal of the realization of a work-free Feast day. Now, with hindsight, the words 'if impossible' can be placed in their historical context. In 1939, as the Guardian made his instructions public, the institutions of the Faith were still in an embryonic form. In his wisdom and foresight, the Guardian left this loophole open for his contemporaries, in the certain knowledge that the time was not ripe for advancing the particular interests of the Bahá'ís in societies which had just gone through the Great Depression and which stood on the brink of a devastating world war. Today there exist many thousands of local Spiritual Assemblies. We must read Shoghi Effendi's words anew, from our current perspective, in order to recognize that they might well harbour a completely different message for us today and in the foreseeable future than they did for the believers eighty or more years ago.

The work-free Feast day

To require that individual Bahá'ís refrain from working on Feast days while otherwise maintaining a 'normal' seven-day work/rest rhythm would present a number of serious problems. If their employer were not prepared to let them take time off for Bahá'í Feast days, either by trading off against week-end work (under traditional employment conditions) or by reckoning against total monthly or yearly credits (in a working time account system), then individual working believers would have no other option but to sacrifice part of their annual holiday – again assuming, of course, that their employer would be willing to cooperate. Considering the nine Holy Days plus 19 – 1 Feast days (the first Feast day of the year coincides with Naw-Rúz), adjusted by the statistical probability of their occurring on a week-end, this solution would force individuals to withdraw an average of 19.2857 days from their annual holiday contingent – a sacrifice which would be totally unrealizable in most countries of the world, and which even in countries with generous holiday arrangements could be shouldered only with difficulty. In the face of these difficulties it would be unrealistic to expect the Nineteen Day Feast to be regularly scheduled during the morning or early afternoon, since doing so would effectively debar any Bahá'í who found it impossible to obtain leave from work on Feast days (or half-days) from participation in the most important community activities. This course of action would be possible only in a select minority of communities – and even then, only until changes in community membership would force them to abandon it again. The fact that there will always be some individuals who are unable to participate in the Feast because of shift work or other complications does not alter the fact that scheduling the Nineteen Day Feast during normal working hours would adversely effect the prospects of participation for the vast majority of working Bahá'ís and in most instances force community life to a standstill.

The work-free Nineteen Day Feast day will remain a practical impossibility until it achieves legal recognition – just like Friday for the Muslim, Saturday for the Jew and Sunday for the Christian in lands where these religious concessions prevail. A privilege of this sort presupposes an act of civil legislation. The climate for an initiative from the Bahá'í community in this respect is particularly encouraging in countries in which the right of unhampered pursuit of religious community activities is coupled with official recognition (or at least with benevolent toleration). In particular in Canada and in the United States of America, but also for example in Germany and the United Kingdom, there are genuine chances for success in the long run. In many countries of the world, of course, the situation is currently less promising. Should the Universal House of Justice ever deem the implementation of a work-free Bahá'í Feast day to be worth pursuing, the responsibility for analysing the legal, social and economic situation and for working out the necessary steps toward achieving this goal would no doubt default in the first instance to the National Spiritual Assemblies of the individual states.

We ought not gloss over the difficulties involved in pursuing such a goal. Even in societies where we may assume an adequately flexible work structure, sufficient good-will and the necessary legal framework, considerable problems in practical realization still remain. In the manufacturing industry, for example, the introduction of profit centres and worker groups presupposes the relatively homogenous availability of the participating co-workers. In the service sector, availability is oriented in the first instance around the demands of the majority – not only in retail and in the professions, but also in civil service, in schools and in universities.

Once overcome, however, these difficulties would quickly transform themselves into advantages. On the one side, the more harmoniously the secular and religious aspects of one's life were to coexist, the easier it would be to 'live the Bahá'í life'. On the other side, commitment to Bahá'í beliefs would be all the more convincingly signalled to the wider community once the individual believer was able to incorporate the Bahá'í rhythm of life into his daily routine, when the practice of his faith could no longer simply be dismissed by colleagues as 'leisure activity'. For those who are hesitant to discuss religious topics openly, the work rhythm of their Bahá'í co-workers would bear mute but unmistakable witness for the Cause of God.

Two negative developments would need to be avoided. One would be the disadvantaging of Bahá'ís on the labour market on account of increased complications in overall personnel planning. (The preference for a Bahá'í solely on account of his willingness to work on days normally free for other workers would be an equally unwelcome development.) The other would be a potential tendency toward the ghettoization of the Bahá'í community, whether through withdrawal (Bahá'í schools, Bahá'í shops, down to Bahá'í neighbourhoods) or through exclusion from society at large. History offers examples of communities for whom ghettoization became characteristic: either perfectionistic communities (such as the Amish in Pennsylvania or the colonies of the German Templars in Haifa and elsewhere), whose adherents consciously distanced themselves from the wider society, or immigrants who never sought full integration (such as the Syrian Knanaya Christians in Kerala in the south of India), or communities which were deliberately isolated on account of their distinctive life style and in response to predominating prejudicial attitudes on the part of the wider community (for example, the Jews in Europe). It would be imprudent for the Bahá'ís to ignore the warnings inherent in these historical precedents. But there are also counter-examples. A fully integrated Jewish majority is to be found alongside the ghettoized Jews in certain urban areas, for example in the United States. Mormons, once outcast, are now respected and represented in all areas of life. The Quakers, a pacifistic community in the United States originally consisting of emigrants chiefly from England, have engendered an American president (Richard M. Nixon 1969–1974), just as the Jews of

Britain have produced a prime minister (Benjamin Disraeli 1874–1881).

The achievement of a work-free Feast day each month would probably be the most far-reaching concession which the Bahá'ís could expect anywhere in the foreseeable future. Although the performance of the Nineteen Day Feast would benefit immensely from the realization of this goal, these considerations also serve to highlight the complexity of the interrelationship between the cycle of the week, which dominates the rhythm of our daily lives, and that of the Bahá'í month. For that reason, we ought now to take a closer look at the cycle of the week with a view to considering ways of reducing or circumventing this complexity.

Seven into nineteen

If we assume that every Friday (or any other invariable day of the week) is work free, plus every day of Bahá' as well (that is, the first day of every Bahá'í month), these preordained days of rest are distributed across a cycle of seven Bahá'í months or nineteen weeks as follows (leaving aside the Ayyám-i Há', which interrupt this rhythm in an irregular manner):

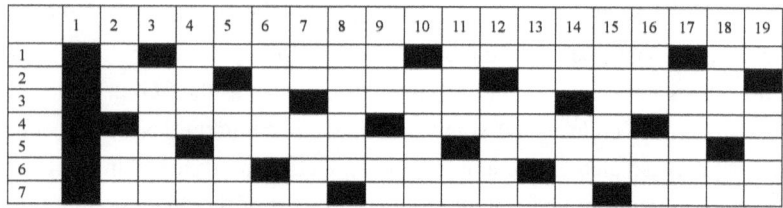

This configuration results in 25 work-free days over a period of 133 days, or roughly 1.32 days per week. The typical number of work-days in succession is six, plus two instances of each of the shorter work periods of one to five days, and there are two instances of a two-day rest period during the whole cycle. This is a rather unfamiliar pattern to say the least. The question is: can additional work-free days be distributed in such a way as to achieve a relatively uniform rhythm of work and rest days and a time-off density roughly comparable to the work situation for society as a whole without disturbing the status of the 25 free days depicted above? For the sake of comparison the following criteria are assumed, based on the currently typical pattern of employment in Germany:

a. an average of no more than seven work-free days per Bahá'í month, which is equivalent to a maximum of 2.58 work-free days per week. This is comparable with the typical German work week with 2.5 work-free days, taking the somewhat different holiday structure into account (see 'The nineteen-day life rhythm' below);
b. not more than five work days in succession; and
c. two-day interruptions between periods of work (maximally three during Nineteen Day Feasts).

In spite of extensive experimentation, I have been unable to find a division which fulfils all the above criteria. The following serves as an example of what might result (the additional rest days are indicated with light shading):

This scheme includes a total of 47 free days, equivalent to a working week with an average of 4.473684211 work days. Other distributions are of course conceivable, for example to achieve parity with working conditions in other countries, but the results look in each case similar.

Facit: in principle, a nineteen-day month rhythm in which the weekly days of rest are retained is possible but complicated. The efficacy of such a scheme is doubtful, however, since the alternation of days of work with days of leisure is not at all constant. Apart from the longer sequences of unbroken rest days in the vicinity of most of the Nineteen Day Feasts, such a scheme doesn't seem to offer much more than the normal week rhythm with substitute work days in lieu of work-free days of Bahá'.

The irreconcilability between the rhythm of the week and that of the month represents nothing new, being a feature common to all calendars which include the Semitic week, with the one exception of the calendar of the Essenes, which included neither the month nor the solar year (see 'The Jewish calendar' in Chapter 2). The difference with the past lies in the fact that the liturgical rhythm of the Bahá'í community is oriented primarily on the (nineteen-day) month, in contrast to most other religious communities, for whom the beginning of the month (however it may be defined) has been reduced for the most part to an interesting but predominantly irrelevant statistic. Thus in modern Islam, the moment of the beginning of the month has significance only for Ramadan and for the start of the year, and in Christianity only for New Year (and, in a sense hardly discernible to the nonspecialist observer, for Easter as well); and the Jewish liturgy has long since done away with its erstwhile orientation on the month. The greatest similarity with regard to the primacy of the monthly rhythm exists between the Bahá'í community and the Zoroastrians. In spite of the pressure of history since the Muslim invasion, this community has never integrated the seven-day rhythm, not least because of the total merging of the regulated month rhythm with the Zoroastrian liturgy.

The nineteen-day life rhythm

Up until now we have been considering the prospect of overlaying the traditional seven-day week with a nineteen-day superstructure, so to speak, whose main purpose is to provide work-free days which coincide with the Nineteen Day Feast. An attempt to provide a scheme in which these two rhythms assumed equal importance was discarded on grounds of impracticability. A logical next step would be to contemplate a scheme in which the nineteen-day cycle functions as the primary, the seven-day cycle as the secondary rhythm. The week would then of course cease entirely to exert an overt influence on the pulse of Bahá'í life, but it would nevertheless continue to fulfil an important function as link with that life rhythm which would undoubtedly continue to hold sway for most of the rest of society at large. Given the assumption that a time will ultimately come in which the Bahá'í calendar will be adopted as the standard calendar for whole populations, the guaranteed unbroken continuity of the week would ensure that communities which still observed the Sabbath or which chose to retain their accustomed seven-day rhythm for other reasons would find their vital interests mirrored in the provisions of the calendar which accompanied their daily lives.

The possibility in principle of introducing such a life rhythm some time in the future is dependent on a pertinent directive from the Universal House of Justice, the supreme legislative authority of the Bahá'í Faith. The vision presented here should therefore be regarded simply as a mental exercise: whether or not it may ever become a reality belongs in the realm of speculation. The time is in any case hardly ripe for pursuing such an objective – but it would nevertheless be imprudent to ignore or underestimate the most recent developments in the world at large. Precisely as a result of increasing flexibility in work conditions, with the breathtaking advances in electronic communication which are providing irresistible momentum to the decentralization of the workplace, and given the ever-increasing transition from a manufacturing to a service-oriented work force, new possibilities for combining employment with individual life styles and rhythms are rapidly emerging. The day is not far away when the traditional motivation behind the resistance to individually tailored time management will have largely dissipated.

My personal conviction is that a nineteen-day life rhythm would lead to improved compatibility between religious activities on the one hand and social and professional activities on the other, and that its effect, once established, would be just as all-pervading for Bahá'ís as the seven-day life rhythm is for Muslims, Jews and Christians. At the same time, however, the conscientious implementation of the nineteen-day rhythm for all aspects of life would inevitably result in additional interface problems with society at large. It would thus be desirable to gain at an early stage a general impression of how this nineteen-day cycle might be structured, rather than to postpone this thought process until social pressure provokes action. As a contribution to this contemplative process, a few embryonic ideas will be presented in the following in the form of a model. This model assumes conditions current in Germany and is not necessarily transferable in detail to other environments. Also, it relies on an analysis of current circumstances: we cannot know how these will change in the future, let alone take such changes into account. This exercise is simply a mental construction which will allow us to make some quantitative comparisons.

Europeans treat matters concerning the terms and conditions of employment with an attention to detail which sets this preoccupation apart from all other aspects of community life, an observation which is borne out by the never-ending negotiations between employer associations and trade unions over fractions of a per cent in workload and remuneration. If a proposed model is to have any prospects of ever reflecting reality, parity must above all be achieved with respect to other members of society in every community in which Bahá'ís live.

The 4½-day, 35-hour working week with 30 days annual holiday is steadily becoming standard in Germany. Furthermore, a total of fourteen legal holidays count as a permanent part of the work-free contingent, being divided into two groups: seven holidays, each of which always occurs on the same day of the week (Good Friday, Easter Sunday, Easter Monday, Whitsunday, Whit-Monday, Ascension of Christ and Corpus Christi, the last two on Thursday), and seven holidays which fall on alternating days of the week (New Year, May Day, Ascension of the Virgin, Day of German Unity, All Saints' Day and Christmas (2 days)) and which do not constitute additional free days when they happen to coincide with the week-end (not identical in every German federal state: the situation presented here is that which obtains in the predominantly Roman Catholic Saarland). After deducting the two holidays which always occur on a week-end and weighting the last-mentioned holidays in accordance with the chance of their falling on a week-day, one arrives at an average of ten additional holidays – a total of 40 work-free days in the year plus weekends (104.3549143 days per solar year). That leaves an average of

220.8872857 work days or 1546.211 working hours in the year. We shall now try to achieve parity with this situation on the basis of a division of the year according to the nineteen-day life rhythm.

For the sake of this comparison we must first imagine how the regular work-free days might be distributed throughout the Bahá'í month. Of all nineteen days, one – the first day of the month – is always reserved for the Feast. The remaining eighteen days can be divided into two portions of nine days each or three portions of six days each. The division by two is very tempting at first glance, since it neatly preserves the symbolically significant number nine in the scheme, but it also poses some problems: either one must tolerate relatively long uninterrupted periods of work, or one must subdivide the portions still further, resulting in relatively few working days at a stretch. By comparison, division by three results in a six-day rhythm which closely resembles the traditional seven-day week. Both alternatives will be taken into consideration in the following discourse.

In the division-by-three model, the first and the last day of every six-day portion is work-free: there remain in total twelve working days in every month. This is equal to a seven-day working week of 4.421052632 days and is roughly comparable to the average German weekly workload. Every Bahá'í month accordingly includes three four-day work periods separated by a 'long week-end' and two 'normal' week-ends. In the division-by-two model, the first, middle and last day of each nine-day portion would be work free, yielding four three-day work periods plus one long and one normal 'week-end' and two 'mini-week-ends'. In the division-by-three model the 1st, 2nd, 7th, 8th, 13th, 14th and 19th days are work free, in the division-by-two model the 1st, 2nd, 6th, 10th, 11th, 15th and 19th. In the latter instance, an alternative apportionment into two six-day working periods plus one three-day and one four-day week-end might also be worth considering.

Common to both schemes are the three consecutive work-free days before, during and after the Nineteen Day Feast, respectively. This arrangement would leave more time for the preparation of the forthcoming Feast as well as for an immediate response to decisions communicated or decided during the Feast. The attendance of Auxiliary Board members and their assistants at the Feasts of dispersed communities would also be facilitated (not everyone likes to travel at night), and the scheduling of Spiritual Assembly meetings immediately before or perhaps after the Nineteen Day Feast would be more practicable than it is at present. A possible alternative would be to displace the work-free days so that the Nineteen Day Feast occurred on either the first or the last day of the 'long week-end' to keep the uncommitted days contingent.

In contrast to the average of ten additional work-free days described above, the Bahá'í religious year includes nine festival days, of which seven are distributed over the days of the month as follows: Naw-Rúz (1); 9 Riḍván (2); 12 Riḍván (5); Declaration of the Báb (8); 1 Riḍván, Ascension of Bahá'u'lláh (13); Martyrdom of the Báb (17) (see 'Bahá'í commemorations' in Chapter 4). Two of these fall on work-days in the division-by-three model and five in the division-by-two model. The remaining two – the Twin Birthdays – can occur on any two consecutive days between 18–19 Mashiyyat and 10–11 Qudrat and must be weighted accordingly, altogether resulting in an average of 3⅓ (in the division-by-three model) or 6⅓ (in the division-by-two model) additional work-free days in the year.

It is here assumed that the four Ayyám-i Há' (five in the region of Há' or during a leap year) are also work free: these are the days reserved for visiting and for receiving guests, for exchanging gifts and for practising neighbourly love, a sort of Bahá'í counterpart to what Christmas has become.→34 That leaves a total of 224⅓ (or 221⅓) Bahá'í work days in comparison with the 220,8872857 working days of non-Bahá'ís in Germany. In the absence of any additional compensation, this means that the Bahá'í works three days, ten hours, forty-two minutes and nineteen seconds more than his non-Bahá'í colleague according to the division-by-three model, or ten hours, forty-two minutes and nineteen seconds more according to the division-by-two model. Given differences of this magnitude, it shouldn't prove difficult to achieve parity to the satisfaction of all parties. In the division-by-three model it would be feasible to retain three of the most important national or religious holidays (e.g. Christmas Day,

Easter Monday, Day of German Unity or Guy Fawkes Day or Independence Day or Bastille Day, etc.), thus respecting the sensitivities of the general public and at the same time ensuring an equitable annual workload.

With respect to child and youth education, the problems are frankly more serious. Administering a school population with divergent learning rhythms presents even greater logistical difficulties than the workplace, and schools will at first certainly prefer to stick with tried-and-true methods. People in Germany are already acquainted with this problem in connection with the Jewish and Muslim communities, although since the discontinuation of Saturday schooling it has become less acute. (Friday is not necessarily a work- or school-free day according to Islam.) If Bahá'í children and youth were to be compelled to comply with the seven-day school rhythm while their parents observed a nineteen-day work rhythm, the result would be heterogeneous life rhythms within Bahá'í family units, with inevitable negative consequences for the cohesion of the family – all the more so in problem cases where both parents are employed full-time. In the case of a marriage between a Bahá'í and a non-Bahá'í, similar difficulties are to be anticipated if both partners are employed full-time. But the situation is not hopeless. Without wishing to reach too deeply into the highly politicized topic of education, I should merely like to point out that the introduction of new pedagogic methods, motivated in particular by advances in information and communication technology, is already now resulting in novel, more flexible learning and teaching environments in which the roles of schoolchildren and students, of teachers and of the classroom are being redefined from within. Wherever the traditional classroom drill is being replaced by individual learning programmes, the possibility emerges for achieving learning goals by combining plenary instruction with more flexible learning strategies which take account of the timetabling exigencies of the individual. The priorities of the Bahá'í community might in the end serve to accelerate this trend toward more flexibility in the school, and in that way, too, exert a positive influence on society at large.

Conclusion

In light of the daunting economical, ecological, social and ethnic problems with which our planet is burdened, the resolution of calendar details is certainly not the Bahá'í community's most urgent priority. On the other hand, the Badí' calendar is a component part of the Divine Manifestation of Bahá'u'lláh, whose statutes must be understood in their *entirety* as medicine for the diseases of our age. Furthermore, introduction of the new calendar is stipulated in the Kitáb-i Aqdas, the Most Holy Book, the observance of whose laws, once in force, is obligatory for the Bahá'í world community. The fact that until recently the calendar law had not been uniformly implemented was nevertheless legitimate and in complete accord with the principle of the 'stepwise enactment of the laws of the Book of Aqdas'[1] which is characteristic of the present period of the Formative Age of the Faith; we may remind ourselves that the law of Ḥuqúqu'lláh first achieved world-wide application as late as 1992 – one hundred years after the Ascension of Bahá'u'lláh. This 'age of stepwise enactment' will not be completed until the calendar legislation has also been fully activated – and that means in my view the consistent employment of the Badí' calendar as the *primary* system for the measurement of time for all Bahá'í announcements and publications the whole world over and as the *sole* system for all internal Bahá'í community matters.

This step requires careful and exhaustive preparation: studies of the logistics of implementation and a great deal of educational and informative material. But in particular it demands a far more stringent definition of the New Year ruling than that which is currently available: one which will not only make possible the development of a perpetual Badí' calendar calculator on a par with those available for other calendars, but also provide the basis of a binding definition of the Bahá'í concept of time, thus enabling the Badí' calendar to fulfil the technical, practical and legal demands which society will place upon it as a calender which, as Shoghi Effendi attested, 'will be used generally'.[2]

When 172 BE / 2015 CE was deemed a propitious time to synchronize the calendrical start of the year throughout the international Bahá'í community, there was really only one sensible course of action, as we have seen at the end of 'The two methods in comparison' in Chapter 6: the elevation of existing Iranian practice to the status of universal standard. In the long term, however, this conservative approach will have serious repercussions for the acceptance of the Badí' calendar, not only worldwide but also within the Bahá'í community itself. As we have already seen in the introductory paragraphs of Chapter 7, the ambiguity which arises from the use of meridional time in combination with an occidental calendar poses an insurmountable impediment to the use of the Badí' calendar in a fashion which lives up to Shoghi Effendi's expectations. Moreover, the peoples and institutions of the world at large will hardly be willing to abandon the status quo in favour of a time calibration system which for them has nothing new to offer beyond legal uncertainty. Within the Bahá'í community, the Badí' calendar will certainly continue to render good service as an insignia for cementing group identity and as an icebreaker for conversations with newcomers; but when getting down to business, the believers will invariably fall back on the Gregorian or Jalálí calendar, as they did in the past and continue to do today – in the West if anything even more tenaciously, ever since the Badí' date forfeited its parity with the Gregorian date. That doesn't exactly signal confidence in the practicability of the Badí' calendar as a universal tool.

The introduction of occidental time would eliminate the most serious pragmatic drawback to the use of the Badí' calendar, but at the cost of enhancing its 'otherness' and introducing an additional psychological barrier to its attractivity to society in general. Widespread acceptance can only be won under the condition that the calendar present something qualitatively superior to that which existing standards already offer. I contend that the principle of cyclic progression satisfies this condition.

In light of these deliberations is indeed opportune that the Will and Testament of 'Abdu'l-Bahá has vested future Houses of Justice with the power to re-evaluate the implementation of the Badí' calendar in light of evolving circumstances:

> Thus for example, the House of Justice enacteth today a certain law and enforceth it, and a hundred years hence, circumstances having profoundly changed and the conditions having altered, another House of Justice will then have power, according to the exigencies of the time, to alter that law.[3]

APPENDIX A

The *Abjad* Number System

The *abjad* number system was the usual form for representing numbers prior to the introduction of Arabic numerals, and its use (*ḥisábu'l-jummal*) is still common today in the Islamic cultural area for literary, poetic and religious works. Named after the first four Arabic letters (*alif, bá', jím, dál*), each of its twenty-eight letters possesses a numerical value. The order of the letters is not that of the modern Arabic alphabet, but rather that of Old Semitic, bearing strong similarity with equivalent number systems in Phoenician, Hebrew and Greek cultural areas (*cf.* alpha, beta, gamma, delta):

alif, hamzaτ	1	*yá'*	10	*qáf*	100	*ghayn*	1000
bá'	2	*káf*	20	*rá'*	200		
jím	3	*lám*	30	*shín*	300		
dál	4	*mím*	40	*tá'*	400		
há'	5	*nún*	50	*thá'*	500		
wáw	6	*sín*	60	*khá'*	600		
záy	7	*'ayn*	70	*dhál*	700		
ḥá'	8	*fá'*	80	*ḍáḍ*	800		
ṭá'	9	*ṣád*	90	*ẓá'*	900		

Remarks

Alif, wáw, yá': When functioning as carriers, normally the *hamzaτ* which they carry counts – even in the event that the *hamzaτ* is not explicitly written – but occasionally instead the carrier itself.→[1]

Wáw, yá' (except as carriers): The numeric value is the same regardless of whether the letter represents a syllabic or non-syllabic vowel or a consonant.

Alif maqṣúraτ (such as the 'á' in *abhá*: see 'Unity in diversity: The numbers nine and nineteen' in Chapter 5), is in fact a variation of *alif*, though in writing it looks like *yá'* without the dots, In Persian, where *yá'* is written in any case without dots and is thus indistinguishable from *alif maqṣúraτ*, it counts as 10, whereas in Arabic it counts as 1.

Tá' marbúṭaτ ('bound t', the feminine singular ending, transcribed 'τ' in the present study) possesses the same numerical value as *há'* (5), with which it possesses an historical affinity. It should be noted that there is no *tá' marbúṭaτ* in Persian orthography, so that the original Arabic ending is sometimes transformed into *té* (= Arab. *tá'*), more often into *hé havaz* (= Arab. *há'*).

Apart from the *hamzaτ*, diacritical signs are ignored, whether or not they are explicitly written (normally they are not). A doubled consonant counts only once, whether or not a *tashdíd* (doubling sign) explicitly occurs.

The *abjad* value of a word is always derived from the Arabic original, even if the available transcription suggests a Persian word form. Letters which do not occur in classical Arabic (such as the Persian *pé, ché, zhé, gáf*) either have no numeric values, or they occasionally assume the value of a closely related Arabic letter (e.g. *gáf* ≡ *káf* [20]).

APPENDIX B
Badí' and Jalálí Leap Years in Comparison

The calculation of start of the year is identical in method for both the Badí' and the Jalálí calendar: Naw-Rúz is the day during which the vernal equinox occurs on or after a given boundary condition: midday in the case of the Jalálí calendar, sunset in the case of the Badí' calendar. In either case, leap years occur at intervals of generally four but occasionally five years, in all approximately 243 times in 1,000 years. The shift of boundary condition from midday to sunset has consequences for the distribution of Badí' leap years in relation to their Jalálí counterparts.

It so happens that the vernal equinox occurs every tropical year 5 hours, 48 minutes and 46 seconds later by the clock→² than it did the previous year. Consequently, in a Jalálí leap year (i.e. in accordance with the midday ruling) the equinox will invariably occur at some moment between midday and 5:48:46 p.m. local solar time at the reference spot. Moreover, since sunset will not occur until 6:03:20 p.m.,→³ the leap year boundary condition for the Badí' calendar obviously cannot be fulfilled in the same tropical year in which a Jalálí leap year takes place.

In the year to follow, however, the time of the equinox will have advanced once again a total of 5 hours, 48 minutes and 46 seconds, so that at this moment the clock will indicate a time of day somewhere between 5:48:46 p.m. and 11:37:32 p.m. solar time at the reference spot. The moment of sunset (i.e. 6:03:20 p.m. solar time) subdivides this time span into two portions, of which the first is 14 minutes and 34 seconds and the second 5 hours, 34 minutes and 12 seconds in length. Since the portion after sunset is far greater in duration than the portion before sunset, there is a correspondingly high statistical probability that the equinox will occur after sunset in that year. In other words, the Badí' leap year is most likely to occur in the very next year after the Jalálí leap year. Occasionally (and irregularly), in just over 0.11 per cent of all cases – about every 274th leap or 1,539th calendar year – the sunset boundary condition will not be fulfilled until the second year following the Jalálí leap year (invariably the nineteenth year of a Jalálí cycle), in which case the equinox occurs some time between 11:37:32 p.m. and 11:52:06 p.m., i.e. well after sunset.[4]

Two minor qualifications

The above description subsumes two assumptions which have marginal consequences for the probability of the Jalálí and Badí' leap years occurring in two successive years:

First, the assertion that the Jalálí ruling is based on solar time undoubtedly holds true for the historical period prior to the partition of the world into time zones near the close of the 19th century (see Chapter 3). However, the possibility cannot be ruled out that midday is nowadays defined in terms of Iran Standard Time (IRST).→[5] I am not in a position to judge among mutually contradicting claims in the internet. On the first day of spring, solar time trails behind mean time by roughly seven minutes and thirty-four seconds (cf. the equation of time), which means that the duration between midday and sunset could potentially be shorter than here assumed. In that event, the probability that the Badí' leap year will trail behind the Jalálí leap year by two years would be reduced by roughly half.

Second, the remarks above are based on the assumption that the sunset and midday criteria are applied with reference to one and the same spot on earth, generally designated 'Teheran' but ostensibly being some specific physical location within the precincts of Golestan Palace, which is located at 51 degrees, 25 minutes and 13 seconds east. Should it transpire that the Jalálí new year is determined nowadays on the basis of mean time, however, then its reference spot will be a purely notional location further east at the standard meridian for IRST (52 degrees and 30 minutes east: IRST is 3½ hours ahead of GMT). What counts is the difference in longitude between the two spots: if they are identical the difference is zero, regardless of location. Should it turn out that these two spots differ – for example, the early community might conceivably have privileged a location such as the birthplace of Bahá'u'lláh[→6] – both reference spots will nevertheless lie somewhere within the historical centre of Teheran and the longitudinal difference will be minimal, resulting in a negligible adjustment to the probability that the Badí' leap year will occur two years after the Jalálí leap year.

APPENDIX C
Date Expressions between the 3rd Yawm-i Há' and 1 'Alá'

Each of the illustrations (see 9a–g) assumes the same perspective: the earth is viewed from a distance of about 50,000 kilometres in space, with the North Pole pointing upward and the two annual thresholds – to the right that of the old year, to the left that of the year approaching – ranged symmetrically on the visual half of the globe. The sun 'circles' clockwise around the 'stationary' earth, and the diurnal threshold advances towards the west and thus from right to left across the face of the globe. The digits 3, 4 and 5 represent the 3rd, 4th and 5th Yawm-i Há', respectively, and the digits 1 and 2 represent 1 and 2 'Alá'; they are in all cases local dates. GT time expressions are given in accordance with the traditional 24-hour system.

3rd Yawm-i Há'   8:54:23 to 20:54:23 GT   [Ill. 9a]

During these twelve hours, the diurnal threshold lies in the here unseen half of the globe. To the east of the date line it is at this moment the 3rd Yawm-i Há', to the west the 4th Yawm-i Há'. A (new) region of Há' does not yet exist.

3rd Yawm-i Há'   24:00 GT = 4th Yawm-i Há' 00:00 GT   [Ill. 9b]

The diurnal threshold crosses the equator exactly at the point of the old year's annual threshold (therefore 24:00 alias 00:00 GT). A new region of Há' has come into being. There are roughly 20.2422 days left until the first day of spring, so that the diurnal threshold runs diagonally from northwest to southeast at an angle of $-7°59'53"$. (Note that the obliquity

Illustration 9

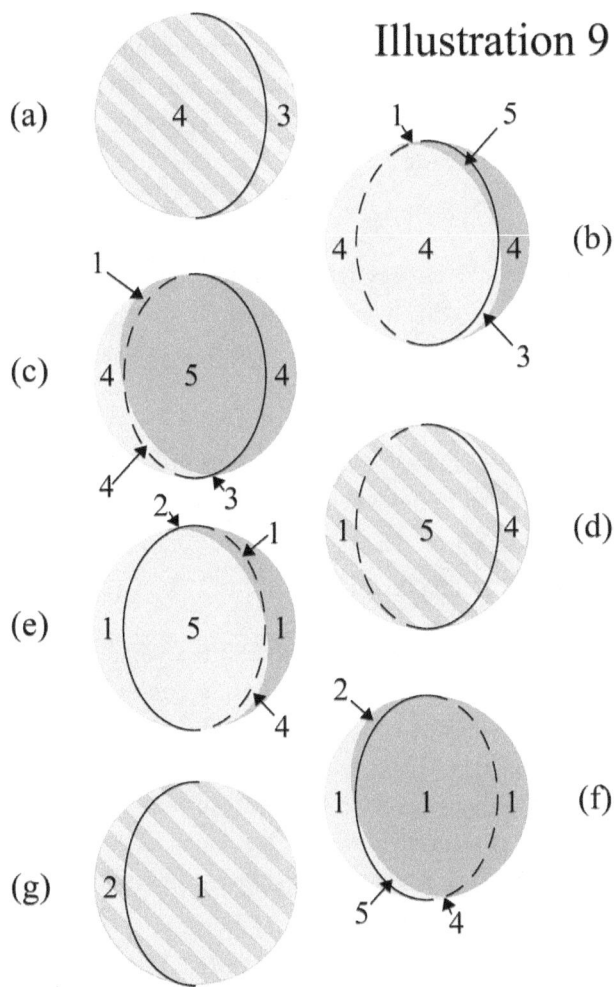

is somewhat exaggerated in the illustrations so that the wedges between the date line and the diurnal threshold are easier to see.) The wedge of the remainder of 3 Yawm-i Há' is retreating southward, and a new wedge has appeared in the north and is advancing correspondingly. Everywhere within this new wedge it is currently the day *after* the 4th Yawm-i Há'. However: within the region of Há' this day is called the 5th Yawm-i Há', otherwise it is called 1 'Alá'.

4th Yawm-i Há'   05:48:46 GT   [Ill. 9c]

The diurnal threshold crosses the equator at the point of the annual threshold of the new year. It is clear to see in this illustration how the areas of the 5th Yawm-i Há' and 1 'Alá' are both expanding.

4th Yawm-i Há'   08:54:23 to 20:54:23 GT   [Ill. 9d]

During these twelve hours, the diurnal threshold lies in that part of the globe which is hidden from view. The GT time of day is still oriented on the old date line.

4th Yawm-i Há'   24:00 GT= 5th Yawm-i Há' 18:11:14 GT   [Ill. 9e]

The diurnal threshold crosses the equator at the point of the old year's annual threshold. The new date line formally comes into force at this moment, together with the new GT orientation. The 5th global Yawm-i Há' begins at 18:11:14 GT instead of the usual 00:00 and lasts about 5h48m46s (with a slight deviation from year to year). At sunset, the final local Yawm-i Há' (the fourth outside of the region of Há', the fifth within it) gives way to 1 'Alá', whereas 1 'Alá' gives way to 2 'Alá'.

5th Yawm-i Há'   24:00 GT = 1 'Alá' 00:00 GT   [Ill. 9f]

The entire region of Há' merges progressively into the date pattern of the area to its east as the diurnal threshold advances across it. The obliquity of the diurnal threshold now amounts to only -7°31'32".

1 'Alá'   03:05:37 to 15:05:37 GT   [Ill. 9g]

The accustomed picture of the rest of the year presents itself. The last vestiges of the old year and of the old annual threshold have disappeared, and there remains only the new date line for (the month of fasting and) the coming year.

APPENDIX D

Annual Thresholds and Leap Years for the Badí' Years 1–250

The following table presents the mean annual thresholds for the first 250 years of the Bahá'í Era. The precision of the astronomical calculations is purely calculatory: the true earth rotation and therewith the annual threshold can in reality vary from the mean by up to several minutes. This variability is due primarily to the movements of the viscous material in the earth's interior, however, so that the anomaly slowly accumulates over a span of many thousands of years. For the relatively short span of 250 years the variability assumes a maximum of ±0,02 seconds of time as a result of fluctuations in the accumulation and melting of the polar ice masses. It may be expected that in the future, if not already, this fluctuation will be influenced by global warming.

The table was generated using the computer program developed originally for the German version of this book, carried over essentially unaltered into the first English edition and extended for the second edition to accommodate the reference spot(s) in Teheran and subsidiary data. Due to computational refinements such as replacing the constants in certain approximations with dynamic variables, some of the carry-over content differs marginally (but not fundamentally) from that of earlier versions of this book.

Two sets of external data have been hard-wired into the program to test the integrity of the results:

- for each year during the period 172-221 BE, the day in March on which

ANNUAL THRESHOLDS AND LEAP YEARS FOR THE BADÍʻ YEARS 1–250

1 Bahá' falls, plus the number of Ayyámi Há', according to the Bahá'í World Centre (BWC) table entitled *Bahá'í Dates 172 to 221 B.E.* appended to the letter of 11 December 2014 from the BWC to all Spiritual Assemblies, data which came into effect on 1 Bahá' 172; and

- for the entire period 1-250 BE, the corresponding Jalálí leap years according to the calendar converter of the Iran Chamber Society (ICS).[7] This online tool has served the worldwide commercial, scientific and cultural community for over twenty years, being of particular interest and value to the Bahá'ís on account of its Islamic perpetual calendar, which follows the same calendar date conventions as those used both currently and historically by the global Bahá'í community.

Each line of the enhanced table presents data relevant to a specific vernal equinox and comprises thirteen fields of data as shown in the following excerpt, in which each white square □ represents a field whose content is either <space> or <plus>:

```
Badi Greg Leap UTC(GMT) Annual  Refspot <-Leap> Length of tropical year
year year G  day-&-time  threshold = BWC = BWC =J (Astronomical Almanac)
-----------------------------------------------------------------------
171  2014 □ 20 16:40:22 18°52'48"E 21  [] □[ ] ⊡ 365.2421917002392888207
172  2015 □ 20 22:29:08 68°18'32"W 21  21 □1-4 ⊡ 365.2421916387027636119

1    2    3  4  5        6         7   8  9A   BC D  (Fields)
```

1. the Badíʻ year which begins on 1 Bahá'.
2. the Gregorian year which began on the 1 January preceding field 1.
3. a plus sign if the Gregorian year is a leap year, otherwise empty.
4. the calculated day in March of the occurrence of the vernal equinox.
5. the calculated time in UT of the occurrence of the vernal equinox.
6. the calculated longitude of the annual threshold (see 'Astronomical Data' in Chapter 6).
7. the calculated day in March on which the Badíʻ year begins.
8. the day in March on which the Badíʻ year begins according to the BWC table (172-221 BE only).
9. a plus sign if the Badíʻ year is a leap year according to the program,[→8] otherwise empty.

A. the Ayyám-i Há' for the given year according to the BWC table (172-221 BE only).
B. a plus sign if the Jalálí year is a leap year according to the program, otherwise empty.
C. a plus sign if the Jalálí year is a leap year according to the ICS data, otherwise empty.
D. the length of the given tropical year.

ANNUAL THRESHOLDS AND LEAP YEARS FOR THE BADÍ' YEARS 1-250

```
Vernal Equinox for the years   1 - 250 Bahá'i Era
Badi`  reference spot 50°38'18"E = 3h 22m 33s time shift
Jalali reference spot 50°38'18"E = 3h 22m 33s time shift
true solar time, sunset offset 91°01'30"

Badi Greg Leap UT (GMT) Annual      Refspot <-Leap>  Length of tropical year
year year G day-&-time  threshold = BWC = BWC =J    (Astronomical Almanac)
-----------------------------------------------------------------------
  1  1844 + 20 12:30:34  81°19'49"E 20 []  + [ ]     365.2422021583560649560
  2  1845    20 18:19:21   5°51'45"W 21 []    [ ]     365.2422020968633091798
  3  1846    21  0:08:07  93°03'18"W 21 []    [ ]     365.2422020353701554995
  4  1847    21  5:56:53 179°45'08"E 21 []    [ ] ++ 365.2422019738766039154
  5  1848 + 20 11:45:39  92°33'34"E 20 []  + [ ]     365.2422019123826544273
  6  1849    20 17:34:26   5°22'00"E 21 []    [ ]     365.2422018508883070353
  7  1850    20 23:23:12  81°49'33"W 21 []    [ ]     365.2422017893936185828
  8  1851    21  5:11:58 169°01'06"W 21 []    [ ] ++ 365.2422017278985322264
  9  1852 + 20 11:00:44 103°47'20"E 20 []  + [ ]     365.2422016664030479660
 10  1853    20 16:49:30  16°35'47"E 21 []    [ ]     365.2422016049072226451
 11  1854    20 22:38:17  70°35'46"W 21 []    [ ]     365.2422015434109994203
 12  1855    21  4:27:03 157°47'19"W 21 []    [ ] ++ 365.2422014819143782915
 13  1856 + 20 10:15:49 115°01'08"E 20 []  + [ ]     365.2422014204174161023
 14  1857    20 16:04:35  27°49'35"E 21 []    [ ]     365.2422013589200560091
 15  1858    20 21:53:21  59°21'58"W 21 []    [ ]     365.2422012974222980120
 16  1859    21  3:42:08 146°33'31"W 21 []    [ ] ++ 365.2422012359241989543
 17  1860 + 20  9:30:54 126°14'56"E 20 []  + [ ]     365.2422011744257588362
 18  1861    20 15:19:40  39°03'23"E 21 []    [ ]     365.2422011129269208141
 19  1862    20 21:08:26  48°08'09"W 21 []    [ ]     365.2422010514277417315
 20  1863    21  2:57:12 135°19'42"W 21 []    [ ] ++ 365.2422009899281647449
 21  1864 + 20  8:45:58 137°28'46"E 20 []  + [ ]     365.2422009284282466979
 22  1865    20 14:34:45  50°17'14"E 21 []    [ ]     365.2422008669279307469
 23  1866    20 20:23:31  36°54'19"W 21 []    [ ]     365.2422008054272737354
 24  1867    21  2:12:17 124°05'51"W 21 []    [ ]     365.2422007439262756634
 25  1868 + 20  8:01:03 148°42'37"E 20 []    [ ] ++ 365.2422006824249365309
 26  1869    20 13:49:49  61°31'05"E 20 []  + [ ]     365.2422006209231994944
 27  1870    20 19:38:35  25°40'27"W 21 []    [ ]     365.2422005594211213975
 28  1871    21  1:27:21 112°51'59"W 21 []    [ ]     365.2422004979187022400
 29  1872 + 20  7:16:08 159°56'30"E 20 []    [ ] ++ 365.2422004364159420220
 30  1873    20 13:04:54  72°44'58"E 20 []  + [ ]     365.2422003749128407435
 31  1874    20 18:53:40  14°26'34"W 21 []    [ ]     365.2422003134093415611
 32  1875    21  0:42:26 101°38'05"W 21 []    [ ]     365.2422002519055013181
 33  1876 + 20  6:31:12 171°10'23"E 20 []    [ ] ++ 365.2422001904013768581
 34  1877    20 12:19:58  83°58'52"E 20 []  + [ ]     365.2422001288968544941
 35  1878    20 18:08:44   3°12'39"W 21 []    [ ]     365.2422000673920479130
 36  1879    20 23:57:30  90°24'10"W 21 []    [ ]     365.2422000058868434280
 37  1880 + 20  5:46:16 177°35'42"W 20 []    [ ] ++ 365.2421999443813547259
 38  1881    20 11:35:02  95°12'47"E 20 []  + [ ]     365.2421998828754681199
 39  1882    20 17:23:48   8°01'16"E 21 []    [ ]     365.2421998213692972968
 40  1883    20 23:12:34  79°10'14"W 21 []    [ ]     365.2421997598627854131
 41  1884 + 20  5:01:21 166°21'45"W 20 []    [ ] ++ 365.2421996983559324690
 42  1885    20 10:50:07 106°26'44"E 20 []  + [ ]     365.2421996368487384643
 43  1886    20 16:38:53  19°15'13"E 21 []    [ ]     365.2421995753412602426
 44  1887    20 22:27:39  67°56'17"W 21 []    [ ]     365.2421995138333841169
 45  1888 + 20  4:16:25 155°07'48"W 20 []    [ ] ++ 365.2421994523252237741
 46  1889    20 10:05:11 117°40'42"E 20 []  + [ ]     365.2421993908167792142
 47  1890    20 15:53:57  30°29'12"E 21 []    [ ]     365.2421993293079367504
 48  1891    20 21:42:43  56°42'19"W 21 []    [ ]     365.2421992677988100695
 49  1892 + 20  3:31:29 143°53'49"W 20 []    [ ] ++ 365.2421992062893991715
 50  1893    20  9:20:15 128°54'41"E 20 []  + [ ]     365.2421991447796472130
```

TIME AND THE BAHÁ'Í ERA

```
Vernal Equinox for the years   1 - 250 Bahá'í Era
Badi`  reference spot 50°38'18"E = 3h 22m 33s time shift
Jalali reference spot 50°38'18"E = 3h 22m 33s time shift
true solar time, sunset offset 91°01'30"

Badi Greg Leap UT (GMT)  Annual      Refspot <-Leap> Length of tropical year
year year G day-&-time   threshold = BWC = BWC =J   (Astronomical Almanac)
-------------------------------------------------------------------------

 51  1894     20 15:09:01   41°43'11"E 21 []      [ ]      365.2421990832695541940
 52  1895     20 20:57:47   45°28'19"W 21 []      [ ]      365.2421990217591769579
 53  1896 +  20  2:46:33  132°39'49"W 20 []      [ ]      365.2421989602484586612
 54  1897     20  8:35:19  140°08'41"E 20 []      [ ] ++   365.2421988987374561475
 55  1898     20 14:24:05   52°57'12"E 20 [] +    [ ]      365.2421988372261125733
 56  1899     20 20:12:51   34°14'18"W 21 []      [ ]      365.2421987757144847819
 57  1900     21  2:01:37  121°25'47"W 21 []      [ ]      365.2421987142025727735
 58  1901     21  7:50:23  151°22'43"E 21 []      [ ] ++   365.2421986526903197046
 59  1902     21 13:39:09   64°11'14"E 21 [] +    [ ]      365.2421985911777824185
 60  1903     21 19:27:55   23°00'16"W 22 []      [ ]      365.2421985296649609154
 61  1904 +  21  1:16:41  110°11'45"W 21 []      [ ]      365.2421984681517983518
 62  1905     21  7:05:26  162°36'46"E 21 []      [ ] ++   365.2421984066383515710
 63  1906     21 12:54:12   75°25'17"E 21 [] +    [ ]      365.2421983451246205732
 64  1907     21 18:42:58   11°46'12"W 22 []      [ ]      365.2421982836106053583
 65  1908 +  21  0:31:44   98°57'41"W 21 []      [ ]      365.2421982220963059262
 66  1909     21  6:20:30  173°50'50"E 21 []      [ ] ++   365.2421981605816654337
 67  1910     21 12:09:16   86°39'22"E 21 [] +    [ ]      365.2421980990667407241
 68  1911     21 17:58:02    0°32'07"W 22 []      [ ]      365.2421980375515886408
 69  1912 +  20 23:46:48   87°43'36"W 21 []      [ ]      365.2421979760360954970
 70  1913     21  5:35:34  174°55'04"W 21 []      [ ] ++   365.2421979145203181361
 71  1914     21 11:24:20   97°53'28"E 21 [] +    [ ]      365.2421978530042565581
 72  1915     21 17:13:06   10°41'59"E 22 []      [ ]      365.2421977914879676064
 73  1916 +  20 23:01:51   76°29'29"W 21 []      [ ]      365.2421977299713375942
 74  1917     21  4:50:37  163°40'57"W 21 []      [ ] ++   365.2421976684544802083
 75  1918     21 10:39:23  109°07'35"E 21 [] +    [ ]      365.2421976069372817619
 76  1919     21 16:28:09   21°56'07"E 22 []      [ ]      365.2421975454198559419
 77  1920 +  20 22:16:55   65°15'21"W 21 []      [ ]      365.2421974839021459047
 78  1921     21  4:05:41  152°26'49"W 21 []      [ ] ++   365.2421974223841516505
 79  1922     21  9:54:27  120°21'43"E 21 [] +    [ ]      365.2421973608658731791
 80  1923     21 15:43:13   33°10'15"E 22 []      [ ]      365.2421972993473673341
 81  1924 +  20 21:31:58   54°01'12"W 21 []      [ ]      365.2421972378285772720
 82  1925     21  3:20:44  141°12'40"W 21 []      [ ] ++   365.2421971763095029928
 83  1926     21  9:09:30  131°35'53"E 21 [] +    [ ]      365.2421971147901444965
 84  1927     21 14:58:16   44°24'25"E 22 []      [ ]      365.2421970532705586265
 85  1928 +  20 20:47:02   42°47'02"W 21 []      [ ]      365.2421969917507453829
 86  1929     21  2:35:47  129°58'29"W 21 []      [ ]      365.2421969302305910787
 87  1930     21  8:24:33  142°50'04"E 21 []      [ ] ++   365.2421968687102662443
 88  1931     21 14:13:19   55°38'37"E 21 [] +    [ ]      365.2421968071896003494
 89  1932 +  20 20:02:05   31°32'50"W 21 []      [ ]      365.2421967456687070808
 90  1933     21  1:50:51  118°44'17"W 21 []      [ ]      365.2421966841475864385
 91  1934     21  7:39:36  154°04'16"E 21 []      [ ] ++   365.2421966226261815791
 92  1935     21 13:28:22   66°52'49"E 21 [] +    [ ]      365.2421965611045493461
 93  1936 +  20 19:17:08   20°18'37"W 21 []      [ ]      365.2421964995826897393
 94  1937     21  1:05:54  107°30'04"W 21 []      [ ]      365.2421964380605459155
 95  1938     21  6:54:40  165°18'29"E 21 []      [ ] ++   365.2421963765381747180
 96  1939     21 12:43:25   78°07'03"E 21 [] +    [ ]      365.2421963150155761468
 97  1940 +  20 18:32:11    9°04'23"W 21 []      [ ]      365.2421962534926933586
 98  1941     21  0:20:57   96°15'50"W 21 []      [ ]      365.2421961919695831966
 99  1942     21  6:09:43  176°32'44"E 21 []      [ ] ++   365.2421961304462456610
100  1943     21 11:58:28   89°21'18"E 21 [] +    [ ]      365.2421960689226239083
```

ANNUAL THRESHOLDS AND LEAP YEARS FOR THE BADÍ' YEARS 1-250

```
Vernal Equinox for the years   1 - 250 Bahá'í Era
Badi`  reference spot 50°38'18"E = 3h 22m 33s time shift
Jalali reference spot 50°38'18"E = 3h 22m 33s time shift
true solar time, sunset offset 91°01'30"

Badi Greg Leap UT (GMT) Annual      Refspot  <-Leap>  Length of tropical year
year year G  day-&-time  threshold = BWC   = BWC =J   (Astronomical Almanac)
-----------------------------------------------------------------------
101 1944 + 20 17:47:14    2°09'52"E 21 []     [ ]      365.2421960073988316253
102 1945   20 23:36:00   85°01'34"W 21 []     [ ]      365.2421959458747551253
103 1946   21  5:24:46  172°13'00"W 21 []     [ ] ++   365.2421958843505080949
104 1947   21 11:13:31  100°35'34"E 21 []   + [ ]      365.2421958228259768475
105 1948 + 20 17:02:17   13°24'09"E 21 []     [ ]      365.2421957613012182264
106 1949   20 22:51:03   73°47'17"W 21 []     [ ]      365.2421956997762322317
107 1950   21  4:39:48  160°58'42"W 21 []     [ ] ++   365.2421956382510757066
108 1951   21 10:28:34  111°49'52"E 21 []   + [ ]      365.2421955767256349645
109 1952 + 20 16:17:20   24°38'27"E 21 []     [ ]      365.2421955151999668487
110 1953   20 22:06:05   62°32'59"W 21 []     [ ]      365.2421954536740713593
111 1954   21  3:54:51  149°44'24"W 21 []     [ ] ++   365.2421953921480053395
112 1955   21  9:43:37  123°04'11"E 21 []   + [ ]      365.2421953306217119462
113 1956 + 20 15:32:22   35°52'46"E 21 []     [ ]      365.2421952690951911791
114 1957   20 21:21:08   51°18'39"W 21 []     [ ]      365.2421952075684430383
115 1958   21  3:09:54  138°30'04"W 21 []     [ ] ++   365.2421951460414675239
116 1959   21  8:58:39  134°18'31"E 21 []   + [ ]      365.2421950845142646358
117 1960 + 20 14:47:25   47°07'07"E 21 []     [ ]      365.2421950229868912174
118 1961   20 20:36:11   40°04'18"W 21 []     [ ]      365.2421949614593472688
119 1962   21  2:24:56  127°15'43"W 21 []     [ ]      365.2421948999315191031
120 1963   21  8:13:42  145°32'53"E 21 []     [ ] ++   365.2421948384035204072
121 1964 + 20 14:02:28   58°21'28"E 20 []   + [ ]      365.2421947768752943375
122 1965   20 19:51:13   28°49'56"W 21 []     [ ]      365.2421947153468977376
123 1966   21  1:39:59  116°01'20"W 21 []     [ ]      365.2421946538182737640
124 1967   21  7:28:45  156°47'15"E 21 []     [ ] ++   365.2421945922894792602
125 1968 + 20 13:17:30   69°35'51"E 20 []   + [ ]      365.2421945307604573827
126 1969   20 19:06:16   17°35'33"W 21 []     [ ]      365.2421944692312649750
127 1970   21  0:55:01  104°46'57"W 21 []     [ ]      365.2421944077018451935
128 1971   21  6:43:47  168°01'40"E 21 []     [ ] ++   365.2421943461722548818
129 1972 + 20 12:32:32   80°50'16"E 20 []   + [ ]      365.2421942846424940399
130 1973   20 18:21:18    6°21'08"W 21 []     [ ]      365.2421942231125058242
131 1974   21  0:10:04   93°32'32"W 21 []     [ ]      365.2421941615823470784
132 1975   21  5:58:49  179°16'05"E 21 []     [ ] ++   365.2421941000519609588
133 1976 + 20 11:47:35   92°04'41"E 21 []   + [ ]      365.2421940385214611524
134 1977   20 17:36:20    4°53'18"E 21 []     [ ]      365.2421939769907339723
135 1978   20 23:25:06   82°18'05"W 21 []     [ ]      365.2421939154598362620
136 1979   21  5:13:51  169°29'29"W 21 []     [ ] ++   365.2421938539287680214
137 1980 + 20 11:02:37  103°19'08"E 20 []   + [ ]      365.2421937923974724072
138 1981   20 16:51:23   16°07'45"E 21 []     [ ]      365.2421937308660631061
139 1982   20 22:40:08   71°03'38"W 21 []     [ ]      365.2421936693344264313
140 1983   21  4:28:54  158°15'01"W 21 []     [ ] ++   365.2421936078026192263
141 1984 + 20 10:17:39  114°33'36"E 20 []   + [ ]      365.2421935462706414910
142 1985   20 16:06:25   27°22'14"E 21 []     [ ]      365.2421934847385500689
143 1986   20 21:55:10   59°49'09"W 21 []     [ ]      365.2421934232062312731
144 1987   21  3:43:56  147°00'32"W 21 []     [ ] ++   365.2421933616737419470
145 1988 + 20  9:32:41  125°48'06"E 20 []   + [ ]      365.2421933001411389341
146 1989   20 15:21:27   38°36'43"E 21 []     [ ]      365.2421932386083085476
147 1990   20 21:10:12   48°34'39"W 21 []     [ ]      365.2421931770753644741
148 1991   21  2:58:58  135°46'01"W 21 []     [ ] ++   365.2421931155421930271
149 1992 + 20  8:47:43  137°02'37"E 20 []   + [ ]      365.2421930540089078931
150 1993   20 14:36:29   49°51'14"E 21 []     [ ]      365.2421929924755090724
```

TIME AND THE BAHÁ'Í ERA

```
Vernal Equinox for the years   1 - 250 Bahá'í Era
Badi`  reference spot 50°38'18"E = 3h 22m 33s time shift
Jalali reference spot 50°38'18"E = 3h 22m 33s time shift
true solar time, sunset offset 91°01'30"

Badi Greg Leap UT (GMT)   Annual     Refspot <-Leap>  Length of tropical year
year year G day-&-time    threshold = BWC = BWC =J   (Astronomical Almanac)
-----------------------------------------------------------------------------

151  1994      20 20:25:14   37°20'08"W  21 []      [ ]     365.2421929309418828780
152  1995      21  2:14:00  124°31'30"W  21 []      [ ]     365.2421928694081429967
153  1996  +   20  8:02:45  148°17'09"E  20 []      [ ]  ++ 365.2421928078742325852
154  1997      20 13:51:30   61°05'47"E  20 [] +    [ ]     365.2421927463401516434
155  1998      20 19:40:16   26°05'35"W  21 []      [ ]     365.2421926848059570148
156  1999      21  1:29:01  113°16'57"W  21 []      [ ]     365.2421926232715918559
157  2000  +   20  7:17:47  159°31'42"E  20 []      [ ]  ++ 365.2421925617370561667
158  2001      20 13:06:32   72°20'20"E  20 [] +    [ ]     365.2421925002024067908
159  2002      20 18:55:18   14°51'01"W  21 []      [ ]     365.2421924386675868845
160  2003      21  0:44:03  102°02'22"W  21 []      [ ]     365.2421923771326532915
161  2004  +   20  6:32:48  170°46'16"E  20 []      [ ]  ++ 365.2421923155975491682
162  2005      20 12:21:34   83°34'55"E  20 [] +    [ ]     365.2421922540623313580
163  2006      20 18:10:19    3°36'26"W  21 []      [ ]     365.2421921925269998610
164  2007      20 23:59:05   90°47'47"W  21 []      [ ]     365.2421921309914978337
165  2008  +   20  5:47:50  177°59'08"W  20 []      [ ]  ++ 365.2421920694558252762
166  2009      20 11:36:35   94°49'31"E  20 [] +    [ ]     365.2421920079200958753
167  2010      20 17:25:21    7°38'11"E  21 []      [ ]     365.2421919463841959441
168  2011      20 23:14:06   79°33'10"W  21 []      [ ]     365.2421918848481823261
169  2012  +   20  5:02:52  166°44'31"W  20 []      [ ]  ++ 365.2421918233119981778
170  2013      20 10:51:37  106°04'09"W  20 [] +    [ ]     365.2421917617757003427
171  2014      20 16:40:22   18°52'48"E  21 []      [ ]     365.2421917002392888207
172  2015      20 22:29:08   68°18'32"W  21  21     1-4     365.2421916387027636119
173  2016  +   20  4:17:53  155°29'52"W  20  20     1-4  ++ 365.2421915771661247163
174  2017      20 10:06:38  117°18'48"E  20  20  +  1-5     365.2421915156293721338
175  2018      20 15:55:24   30°07'27"E  21  21     1-4     365.2421914540924490211
176  2019      20 21:44:09   57°03'53"E  21  21     1-4     365.2421913925554690650
177  2020  +   20  3:32:54  144°15'13"W  20  20     1-4  ++ 365.2421913310183185786
178  2021      20  9:21:40  128°33'28"E  20  20  +  1-5     365.2421912694810544053
179  2022      20 15:10:25   41°22'08"E  21  21     1-4     365.2421912079437333887
180  2023      20 20:59:10   45°49'12"W  21  21     1-4     365.2421911464062418418
181  2024  +   20  2:47:56  133°00'32"W  20  20     1-4     365.2421910848686934514
182  2025      20  8:36:41  139°48'09"E  20  20     1-5  ++ 365.2421910233310313743
183  2026      20 14:25:26   52°36'49"E  20  21  +  1-4     365.2421909617931987668
184  2027      20 20:14:12   34°34'30"W  21  21     1-4     365.2421909002553093160
185  2028  +   20  2:02:57  121°45'49"W  20  20     1-4     365.2421908387173061783
186  2029      20  7:51:42  151°02'51"E  20  20     1-4  ++ 365.2421907771792461972
187  2030      20 13:40:27   63°51'32"E  20  20  +  1-5     365.2421907156410156858
188  2031      20 19:29:13   23°19'47"W  21  21     1-4     365.2421906541027283311
189  2032  +   20  1:17:58  110°31'06"W  20  20     1-4     365.2421905925643272894
190  2033      20  7:06:43  162°17'35"E  20  20     1-4  ++ 365.2421905310258694044
191  2034      20 12:55:28   75°06'16"E  20  20  +  1-5     365.2421904694872978325
192  2035      20 18:44:14   12°05'02"W  21  21     1-4     365.2421904079486125738
193  2036  +   20  0:32:59   99°16'21"W  20  20     1-4     365.2421903464098704717
194  2037      20  6:21:44  173°32'20"E  20  20     1-4  ++ 365.2421902848710146827
195  2038      20 12:10:29   86°21'02"E  20  20  +  1-5     365.2421902233320452069
196  2039      20 17:59:15    0°50'17"W  21  21     1-4     365.2421901617930188877
197  2040  +   19 23:48:00   88°01'35"W  20  20     1-4     365.2421901002539357250
198  2041      20  5:36:45  175°12'53"W  20  20     1-4  ++ 365.2421900387147388756
199  2042      20 11:25:30   97°35'48"E  20  20  +  1-5     365.2421899771754851827
200  2043      20 17:14:16   10°24'30"E  21  21     1-4     365.2421899156361178029
```

ANNUAL THRESHOLDS AND LEAP YEARS FOR THE BADÍʿ YEARS 1–250

```
Vernal Equinox for the years   1 - 250 Bahá'í Era
Badi` reference spot 50°38'18"E = 3h 22m 33s time shift
Jalali reference spot 50°38'18"E = 3h 22m 33s time shift
true solar time, sunset offset 91°01'30"

Badi Greg Leap UT (GMT) Annual    Refspot <-Leap> Length of tropical year
year year G day-&-time  threshold = BWC = BWC =J  (Astronomical Almanac)
-----------------------------------------------------------------------

201 2044 + 19 23:03:01   76°46'48"W 20 20       1-4      365.2421898540966935798
202 2045   20  4:51:46  163°58'06"W 20 20       1-4   ++ 365.2421897925572125132
203 2046   20 10:40:31  108°50'36"E 20 20  +    1-5      365.2421897310176177598
204 2047   20 16:29:16   21°39'19"E 21 21       1-4      365.2421896694779661630
205 2048 + 19 22:18:01   65°31'59"W 20 20       1-4      365.2421896079382577227
206 2049   20  4:06:47  152°43'17"W 20 20       1-4   ++ 365.2421895463984355956
207 2050   20  9:55:32  120°05'26"E 20 20  +    1-5      365.2421894848585566251
208 2051   20 15:44:17   32°54'08"E 21 21       1-4      365.2421894233186776546
209 2052 + 19 21:33:02   54°17'09"W 20 20       1-4      365.2421893617786849973
210 2053   20  3:21:47  141°28'27"W 20 20       1-4   ++ 365.2421893002385786531
211 2054   20  9:10:32  131°20'16"E 20 20  +    1-5      365.2421892386984723089
212 2055   20 14:59:18   44°08'59"E 21 21       1-4      365.2421891771583091213
213 2056 + 19 20:48:03   43°02'18"W 20 20       1-4      365.2421891156180890903
214 2057   20  2:36:48  130°13'35"W 20 20       1-4      365.2421890540777553724
215 2058   20  8:25:33  142°35'08"E 20 20       1-4   ++ 365.2421889925374216546
216 2059   20 14:14:18   55°23'51"E 20 20  +    1-5      365.2421889309970310933
217 2060 + 19 20:03:03   31°47'26"W 20 20       1-4      365.2421888694565836886
218 2061   20  1:51:48  118°58'42"W 20 20       1-4      365.2421888079160794405
219 2062   20  7:40:33  153°50'01"E 20 20       1-4   ++ 365.2421887463755183489
220 2063   20 13:29:19   66°38'44"E 20 20  +    1-5      365.2421886848349004140
221 2064 + 19 19:18:04   20°32'32"W 20 []       [ ]      365.2421886232942824790
222 2065   20  1:06:49  107°43'48"W 20 []       [ ]      365.2421885617535508572
223 2066   20  6:55:34  165°04'55"E 20 []       [ ]   ++ 365.2421885002128192355
224 2067   20 12:44:19   77°53'39"E 20 []  +    [ ]      365.2421884386720307702
225 2068 + 19 18:33:04    9°17'37"W 20 []       [ ]      365.2421883771312423050
226 2069   20  0:21:49   96°28'53"W 20 []       [ ]      365.2421883155903969964
227 2070   20  6:10:34  176°19'51"E 20 []       [ ]   ++ 365.2421882540494948444
228 2071   20 11:59:19   89°08'35"E 20 []  +    [ ]      365.2421881925085358489
229 2072 + 19 17:48:04    1°57'19"E 20 []       [ ]      365.2421881309675768534
230 2073   19 23:36:49   85°13'57"W 20 []       [ ]      365.2421880694266178580
231 2074   20  5:25:34  172°25'12"W 20 []       [ ]   ++ 365.2421880078856020191
232 2075   20 11:14:19  100°23'32"E 20 []  +    [ ]      365.2421879463445293368
233 2076 + 19 17:03:04   13°12'17"E 20 []       [ ]      365.2421878848034566545
234 2077   19 22:51:49   73°58'59"W 20 []       [ ]      365.2421878232623271288
235 2078   20  4:40:34  161°10'14"W 20 []       [ ]   ++ 365.2421877617211976030
236 2079   20 10:29:19  111°38'31"E 20 []  +    [ ]      365.2421877001800680773
237 2080 + 19 16:18:04   24°27'16"E 20 []       [ ]      365.2421876386388817082
238 2081   19 22:06:50   62°44'00"W 20 []       [ ]      365.2421875770976953390
239 2082   20  3:55:35  149°55'15"W 20 []       [ ]   ++ 365.2421875155565089699
240 2083   20  9:44:20  122°53'30"E 20 []  +    [ ]      365.2421874540152657573
241 2084 + 19 15:33:04   35°42'16"E 20 []       [ ]      365.2421873924740225448
242 2085   19 21:21:49   51°28'59"W 20 []       [ ]      365.2421873309327793322
243 2086   20  3:10:34  138°40'14"W 20 []       [ ]   ++ 365.2421872693915361197
244 2087   20  8:59:19  134°08'31"E 20 []  +    [ ]      365.2421872078502929071
245 2088 + 19 14:48:04   46°57'17"E 20 []       [ ]      365.2421871463089928511
246 2089   19 20:36:49   40°13'58"W 20 []       [ ]      365.2421870847676927951
247 2090   20  2:25:34  127°25'12"W 20 []       [ ]      365.2421870232263927392
248 2091   20  8:14:19  145°23'34"E 20 []       [ ]   ++ 365.2421869616851495266
249 2092 + 19 14:03:04   58°12'20"E 19 []  +    [ ]      365.2421869001438494706
250 2093   19 19:51:49   28°58'55"W 20 []       [ ]      365.2421868386025494146
```

Commentary on the table content

The program generates four different solutions, depending on the longitude of the reference spot (or spots):

1. The BWC results can be replicated in full, on condition that the reference longitude is set somewhere between 52°36'49"E and 53°25'20"E inclusive, but at the cost of occasional divergence from the ICS results, notably for our purposes in the years 181–182 BE.
2. The results generated by setting the reference longitude anywhere between 48°25'31"E and 50°38'18"E inclusive are in complete agreement with the ICS data for the entire 250-year period but diverge from those of the BWC for the years 182–183 BE.
3. A relatively good compromise is obtained with the reference spot parameter set somewhere between these two extremes, for example at the location of Golestan Palace in Teheran (51°25'13"E), or alternatively reckoning in mean time in conjunction with the reference longitude of Iran Standard Time (IRST, 52°30'E).[9] In each case, the day of Naw-Rúz 183 is calculated as occuring on 20 (not 21) March.
4. The program was belatedly (November 2022) enhanced to accommodate two reference spots, so that by combining solution 1 for the Badí' and solution 2 for the Jalálí calculations its results are in across-the-board agreement with both the BWC table and the ICS data.

Which solution is appropriate for inclusion in this appendix?

As demonstrated in Appendix B, a distribution which requires that any given year is a leap year in both the Jalálí and the Badí' calendar is at odds with reality; and that is the case for solution 4 with respect to the tropical year which begins on 20 March 2025 (1 Bahá' 182 and 1 Farvardín 1404, respectively), which must therefore be rejected as a candidate.

In the case of solutions 1 and 3 there is a discrepancy with respect to the tropical year which begins on 20 March 1897 (1 Bahá' 54 / 1 Farvardín 1276). Although the calculations themselves are consistent – the program identifies 1896-7 (not 1897-8) CE as the Jalálí leap year – the fact remains that the ICS entry can be confirmed empirically,[10] with the consequence that solutions 1 and 3 are also disqualified.

This leaves as the sole credible result solution 2, which depicts the year 183 (not 182) BE as a Badí' leap year which begins on 20 (not 21) March, but which is otherwise in perfect agreement with both the BWC and the ICS data.

The Bahá'í World Centre was apprised in detail of these findings on 22 August 2021. In its response of 7 September that same year,[11] the Department of the Secretariat explained that it is the policy of the Universal House of Justice that the table released on 10 December 2014 remain the standard until the year 2065.

The computer program is included here for the sake of the interested reader:

```
/* Day of Naw-Ruz for the years 1 to 172 BE, expressed respectively as    */
/* day in March and time of day for U.T., longitude of the annual threshold,   */
/* day in March at the reference spot plus Jaláli and Badí`leap years, in comparison */
/* with the ICS data throughout and with BWC data for the years 172 to 221 BE   */

#include <stdio.h>

#define mean_tropical_year      365.2421925617370561668
                                /* middle value years 1-221 */
#define Julian_century          36525.0
#define Julian_day_2000         2451545.0

#define sec                     * 1.0
#define min                     * 60.0
#define hr                      * 3600.0
#define deg                     * 3600.0
#define time_seconds            ((long)  24 * 3600)
#define degree_seconds          ((long) 360 * 3600)

#define equinox_1995            ((2 hr + 14 min) / time_seconds)

#ifdef SIMPLE_SUNSET
    #define sunset_shift        ((6 hr +  0 min +  0 sec) / time_seconds)
#else
    #define sunset_shift        /* just for the sake of playing with hypotheses */
                                ((6 hr +  4 min +  6 sec) / time_seconds)
                    /* scientific sunset criterion of 6h 3m 20s following midday */
#endif              /* plus 46s for terminator offset for Teheran at 35°39'22"N */

#ifdef IRAN_STANDARD_TIME
    #define equation_of_time    0.0     /* expressions in mean time */
    #define reference_spot              ((52 deg + 30 min +  0 sec) / degree_seconds)
#else
    #define equation_of_time            (-(7 min + 34 sec) / time_seconds)   /* 2015-03-20 */
    #ifdef GOLESTAN_PALACE
```

TIME AND THE BAHÁ'Í ERA

```
    #define reference_spot        ((51 deg + 25 min + 13 sec) / degree_seconds)
  #else
    #ifdef ICS_MIN
    #define reference_spot        ((48 deg + 25 min + 31 sec) / degree_seconds)
    #else
      #ifndef ICS_MAX
        #define reference_spot    ((50 deg + 38 min + 18 sec) / degree_seconds)
      #else
        #ifdef BWC_MIN
          #define reference_spot  ((52 deg + 36 min + 49 sec) / degree_seconds)
        #else
          #ifdef BWC_MAX
            #define reference_spot ((53 deg + 25 min + 20 sec) / degree_seconds)
          #else
            #define reference_spot ((51 deg + 20 min + 52 sec) / degree_seconds)
          #endif    /* longitude of Teheran according to World Geodetic System 1984 */
        #endif
      #endif
    #endif
  #endif
#endif

#ifdef JALALI_SHIFT
  #define jalali_shift (-(2 deg + 6 min + 0 sec) / degree_seconds)
#else                   /* longitudinal difference */
  #define jalali_shift 0.0 /* Badi & Jalali reference spots longitudinally identical */
#endif

#ifdef START_172
  #define start              171       /* before first printable table entry */
#else
  #define start              0         /* start of Baha'i Era */
#endif

#define span                 250       /* number of table entries */
#define columns              1         /* either 1 or 2 */

main()
{   short   pass, Badi_year, extent, halfspan = (span - start + 1) / 2;
    int     tot_days = 0;
    double  total, adjustment_1995 = 0.0,
            leap_min = 18 hr + 3 min + 20 sec, leap_max;

/*fixed values derived from BWC table and perpetual Jalali calender from ICS */

    short   BWC_March_day [] = { 1,0,0,1,1,0,0,1,1,0,0,1,1,0,0,0,1,0,0,0,1,0,0,0,1,
                                 0,0,0,1,0,0,0,1,0,0,0,1,0,0,0,1,0,0,0,0,0,0,0,0,0 };
    short   BWC_Ayyam []     = { 4,4,5,4,4,4,5,4,4,4,5,4,4,4,4,5,4,4,4,5,4,4,  4,5,4,
                                 4,4,5,4,4,4,5,4,4,4,5,4,4,4,4,5,4,4,4,4,5,4,4,4,5,4 };
    short   ICS_leap []      = { 226,230,234,238,242,247,251,255,259,263,267,271,276,
                                 280,284,288,292,296,300,304,309,313,317,321,325,329,
                                 333,337,342,346,350,354,358,362,366,370,375,379,383,
                                 387,391,395,399,404,408,412,416,420,424,428,432,
                                 437,441,445,449,453,457,461,465,470,474,478,9999 };
                    /* www.iranchamber.com/calendar/converter/iranian_calendar_conv */
    short   *j, *jalali_year [2];
```

ANNUAL THRESHOLDS AND LEAP YEARS FOR THE BADÍ' YEARS 1–250

```
struct       RESULT
             { short           UT_March_day, UT_hour, UT_minute, UT_second;
               short           IR_March_day, IR_hour, IR_minute, IR_second;
               short           greg_leap;
               double          tropical_year;
               short           arc_degree, arc_minute, arc_second;
               unsigned char   jalali_leap, badi_leap, East_West;
             };
struct RESULT  result [span], *r = result, *s;
long     seconds;

printf( "%sVernal Equinox for the years %3d - %3d Bahá'í Era\n",
        "            ", start + 1, span);
for( pass = 0; pass < 2; pass++)
{
    seconds = (long) ((reference_spot + (jalali_shift * pass)) * degree_seconds
                                                                 + 0.00001);
    r -> IR_hour = seconds / 3600;
    seconds -= r -> IR_hour * 3600;
    r -> IR_minute = seconds / 60;
    r -> IR_second = seconds - r -> IR_minute * 60;
    printf( "%s%s%s %02d°%02d'%02d\"E",
            "          ", pass ? "Jalali" : "Badi` ", " reference spot",
       (short) r -> IR_hour, (short) r -> IR_minute, (short) r -> IR_second);
    seconds = (long) ((reference_spot + jalali_shift * pass) * time_seconds
                                                                 + 0.00001);
    r -> IR_hour = seconds / 3600;
    seconds -= r -> IR_hour * 3600;
    r -> IR_minute = seconds / 60;
    r -> IR_second = seconds - r -> IR_minute * 60;
    printf( " = %dh %02dm %02ds time shift\n",
         (short) r -> IR_hour, (short) r -> IR_minute, (short) r -> IR_second);
}
seconds = (long) (sunset_shift * degree_seconds);
r -> IR_hour = seconds / 3600;
seconds -= r -> IR_hour * 3600;
r -> IR_minute = seconds / 60;
r -> IR_second = seconds - r -> IR_minute * 60;
printf( "%s%s solar time, sunset offset %2d°%02d'%02d\"\n\n", "          ",
         equation_of_time < 0.0 ? "true" : "mean",
         (short) r -> IR_hour, (short) r -> IR_minute, (short) r -> IR_second);
for( pass = 0; pass < columns; pass++)
{   printf( "Badi Greg Leap UT (GMT) Annual      Refspot <-Leap>");
    if( columns == 1)          printf( "  Length of tropical year");
    if( columns - 1 - pass) printf( "   "); else printf ("\n");
}
for( pass = 0; pass < columns; pass++)
{   printf( "year year G day-&-time   threshold = BWC = BWC =J");
    if( columns == 1)          printf( "  (Astronomical Almanac)");
    if( columns - 1 - pass) printf( "   "); else printf ("\n");
}
for( pass = 0; pass < columns; pass++)
{   printf( "-----------------------------------------");
    if( columns == 1)          printf( "----------------------------");
    if( columns - 1 - pass) printf( "-----------");
                    else printf ("\n");
}
```

TIME AND THE BAHÁ'Í ERA

```
    for( pass = 0; pass < 2; pass++)
    {   total = adjustment_1995;
        for( Badi_year = 1; Badi_year <= span; Badi_year++)
        {   short    Gregorian_year = Badi_year + 1843;
            double   Julian_date = Julian_day_2000
                              + (Gregorian_year - 2000) * mean_tropical_year;
            double   T = (Julian_date - Julian_day_2000) / Julian_century;
            double   tropical_year = mean_tropical_year - 0.615359e-5 * T
                              - 7.29e-10 * T*T + 2.64e-10 * T*T*T;
            long     hour, minute, second;
            long     arc_degree, arc_minute, arc_second;
            double   difference, fraction, tot_sunset;

            total += tropical_year;
            if( !pass)
            {   if( Gregorian_year == 1995)
                {   adjustment_1995 = (long) total - total
                                    + equinox_1995 + 0.0000000001; break;
            }   }
            else
            {   r = result + Badi_year - 1;
                r -> tropical_year = tropical_year;

/* annual threshold */

                fraction = total - (long) total + sunset_shift;
                if( fraction > 1.0) fraction -= 1.0;
                seconds = (long) (fraction * degree_seconds);
                if( seconds > degree_seconds >> 1)
                    { seconds = degree_seconds - seconds; r -> East_West = 'E'; }
                else r-> East_West = 'W';
                arc_degree = seconds / 3600;
                seconds -= arc_degree * 3600;
                arc_minute = seconds / 60;
                arc_second = seconds - arc_minute * 60;
                r -> arc_degree = (short) arc_degree;
                r -> arc_minute = (short) arc_minute;
                r -> arc_second = (short) arc_second;

/* Time at Greenwich (UT) */

                fraction = total - (long) total;
                seconds = (long) (fraction * time_seconds);
                hour = seconds / 3600;
                seconds -= hour * 3600;
                minute = seconds / 60;
                second = seconds - minute * 60;
                tot_days += 365 + (r -> greg_leap = Gregorian_year %    4 ? 0 :
                                Gregorian_year % 100 ? 1 : Gregorian_year % 400 ? 0 : 1);
                r -> UT_March_day = (difference = tot_days - total) > 2.0 ? 19 :
                                difference > 1.0 ? 20 : difference > 0.0 ? 21 : 22;
                while( hour > 23) { hour -= 24; r -> IR_March_day += 1; }
                r -> UT_hour   = (short) hour;
                r -> UT_minute = (short) minute;
                r -> UT_second = (short) second;
```

ANNUAL THRESHOLDS AND LEAP YEARS FOR THE BADÍ' YEARS 1–250

```
/* calculate furthest extent of a possible Jaláli or Badi' leap year */

                s = r - (Badi_year > 1 ? 1 : 0);
                leap_max = (tropical_year - (long) tropical_year
                    + s -> tropical_year - (long) s -> tropical_year) / 2
                    * time_seconds + leap_min;    /* mean value two consecutive years */

/* calculatory time at Badi` reference spot        NB: sunset orientation */

                fraction += reference_spot + sunset_shift;
                seconds = (long) (fraction * time_seconds);
                r -> badi_leap = seconds > leap_max || seconds <= leap_min ? ' ' : '+';
                hour = seconds / 3600;
                seconds -= hour * 3600;
                minute = seconds / 60;
                second = seconds - minute * 60;
                r -> IR_March_day = r -> UT_March_day;
                while( hour > 23) { hour -= 24; r -> IR_March_day += 1; }
                r -> IR_hour      = (short) hour;
                r -> IR_minute    = (short) minute;
                r -> IR_second    = (short) second;

/* Calculate Jalali leap year                      NB: midday orientation */

                fraction += 12 hr / time_seconds + equation_of_time
                                                 - sunset_shift + jalali_shift;
                seconds = (long) (fraction * time_seconds);
                r -> jalali_leap = seconds > leap_max || seconds <= leap_min ? ' ':'+';
    }  }  }
    extent = halfspan * (3 - columns);
    jalali_year [0] = j = ICS_leap; while( *++j < extent + 222); jalali_year [1] = j;
    for( tot_days = 1; tot_days <= extent; tot_days++)
    for( pass = 0; pass < columns; pass++)
    {   Badi_year = tot_days + start + pass * halfspan;
        r = result + Badi_year - 1;
        if( Badi_year > span) printf( "\n");   /* if uneven number of entries */
        else
            {   char plus;

            printf( "%4d %4d %c %2d %2d:%02d:%02d ",
                Badi_year, Badi_year + 1843,
                r -> greg_leap ? '+' : ' ',
                r -> UT_March_day,
                r -> UT_hour, r -> UT_minute, r -> UT_second);
            printf( "%3d°%02d'%02d\"%c %2d ",
                r -> arc_degree, r -> arc_minute, r -> arc_second,
                r -> East_West,
                r -> IR_March_day);
            if( Badi_year < 172 || Badi_year > 220) printf( "[]");
            else printf( "%2d", BWC_March_day [Badi_year - 172] + 20);
            printf( " %c", r -> badi_leap);
            if( Badi_year < 172 || Badi_year > 220) printf( "[ ]");
            else printf( "1-%d", BWC_Ayyam [Badi_year - 172]);
            if( Badi_year < *(jalali_year [pass]) - 222) plus = ' ';
            else { plus = '+'; jalali_year [pass] += 1; }
            printf( " %c%c ", r -> jalali_leap, plus);
```

```
            if( columns == 1) printf( " %3.19f", r -> tropical_year);
            printf( "%s", columns - 1 - pass ? " " : "\n");
      }   }
      printf( "\n");
}
```

Program notes

The background parameters are:

(1) the calculation of the length of the tropical year in days, using formula 12.11-1 of the Supplement to the Astronomical Almanac,[12] i.e.

$$365.24218966698 - 0{,}615359 \times 10^{-6}D - 7{,}29 \times 10^{-10}D^2 + 2{,}64 \times 10^{-10}D^3$$

The result is a decimal value, being the number of days D, whereby D = JD – 2451545.0) / 36525 (see <Julian_Day_2000> below). This formula takes both the rotational deceleration caused by tidal friction and the precession of the earth into account but ignores other periodic fluctuations such as the effect of lunisolar nutation.

(2) the time of day in UTC (Coordinated *Universal Time*, ≈ *GMT*, Greenwich Mean Time) at the moment of the vernal equinox in the year 1995: 02:14 on 21 March (according to the Gregorian calendar), gleaned from *The Astronomical Almanac*.[13]

(3) <equation_of_time>: On the day of the vernal equinox, solar time runs behind mean time by roughly seven minutes and 34 seconds (calculated value for the year 2015. Quelle: https://prlbr.de/2014/uhrzeit-sonne-im-zenit/zeitgleichung-tabelle). In reality, the equation of time varies infinitesimally from year to year as a result of precession. Furthermore, the equation of time is a continuum, whereas the table (along with most sources) assumes mean values for whole days.

(4) <sunset_shift>: the angle of the official sunset relative to midday amounts to 90°50' (in time: $6^h3^m20^s$), taking into account the horizontal

refraction and the angle diameter of the sun. To this must be added a terminator offset (see 'Astronomical data' in Chapter 6) of 0°11'30" ($0^h0^m46^s$) for the latitude of Teheran (35°39'22"N) if the calculation is carried out using true solar time.

(5) <adjustment_1995>: The initial pass through the program with <total> pre-set to 0.0 yields the day fraction for the reference year 1995. The value of <total> is then pre-set to the negative of this day fraction at the start of the second pass so that the day fraction value of 0.0 results for the year 1995.

(6) <length_tropical_year>: This is the mean value ($L_{year1844}$ + $L_{year2064}$) / 2. For the short time span of 250 years, the difference between this value and the length of any specific tropical year is relatively uncritical.

(7) <Julian_day_2000>: The basis of calibration for the formula for calculating the length of the tropical year is the terrestrial dynamic time (TDT), which is in turn based on the Julian day count. 2451545.0 TDT is equivalent to 12:00 on the Julian day (JD) 01.01.2000.

(8) <reference_spot>: the longitude of the location in Iran selected as the basis of calculating the boundary condition for the Badí' new year (see Appendix B).

(9) <jalali_shift>: the difference in time between the Badí' and Jalálí reference spots (0.0 if the two are identical). The sum of the two parameters <reference spot> and <jalali_shift> yields the Jalali equivalent to <reference spot>.

APPENDIX E

Conversion between Time Modes

This appendix provides a detailed description of the strategy behind the exercise introduced in 'Annual celebration' in Chapter 7, subsection 'A concrete example', exploring the relationships between meridional and occidental time and between local, equatorial and global time in a more rigorous fashion than would be appropriate in the main text.

A professional implementation would employ a completely different methodology, using standard formulas and techniques employed in solid geometry. It would probably be more accurate, particularly in the extreme polar regions, but it would be devoid of pedagogical value to the present study. The strategy followed in this appendix employs the same concepts and relationships which have been used throughout this study.

In what follows, the text boxes are intended as an aid to understanding the computations contained in the computer program presented at the end of the appendix. They assume a nodding acquaintance with mathematics in general and trigonometric functions in particular (and if necessary, in the footsteps of the author of this study→[14] the stamina to reactivate technical skills which have lain dormant since secondary school). Readers who feel daunted by mathematical notation may nevertheless skip over boxed text without missing out on the gist of the discussion.

The text as a whole relates to the table which follows it, consisting of twenty-five data modules. The first module sets the framework for the commemoration of a selected event, in this instance the Ascension of 'Abdu'l-Bahá in the year 78 BE (1921 CE); the second module describes the geodetic environment which accompanies the commemoration of this event in a given year (in this case, in the year 183 BE); and the third and subsequent modules place this environment in the spatial context of representative localities throughout the world.

The first data module is devoted to the conversion of the date and time of the Ascension of 'Abdu'l-Bahá from mean time into global time.

Haifa lies at longitude 34°59'30" east. The time expression 1:30 a.m. is zone time, that is, mean (meridional) time for the standard meridian at 30° East. True local time is found by adding the temporal equivalent of the difference between the standard meridian and the longitude of Haifa (= 4°59'30", i.e. $19^m 58^s$), and then augmenting the result by $12^m 4^s$ for the equation of time on 28 November 1921: 'Abdu'l-Bahá departed this world at 2:02:02 a.m. solar time in Haifa. Since meridional time is not influenced by the obliquity of the diurnal threshold, this is also the true meridional local time at the intersection of longitude 34°59'30" east with the equator. Converting this latter expression into equatorial time involves merely adding $5^h 56^m 40^s$ (equivalent to 89°10') to shift the orientation of the day from midnight to sunset. The difference between the longitude of Haifa and the annual threshold for the year 78 (152°26'49" west: see Appendix D) amounts to 187°26'19"; the temporal equivalent of this difference ($12^h 29^m 45^s$) must now be deducted from equatorial time, resulting in the global time expression 19:28:57.

The assumption of mean zone time to indicate the historical moment of an event which took place prior to the introduction in 1884 of Standard Time (see Chapter 3) is arbitrary, since historical details regarding local time conventions crave clarification. We may safely assume, however, that its use is appropriate with respect to both the Ascension of 'Abdu'l-Bahá and the Ascension of Bahá'u'lláh.→[15] And although zone time is irregularly distributed and as a rule cannot be determined algorithmically, the program has been designed to function accurately in this respect at least within the confines of Israel and Iran.

The module displays the following data fields:

```
Global time (GT)     19:28:57        Threshold 1921 CE   152°26'49" W
Haifa solar time      2:02:02        Shift in (deg)      187°26'19"
Mean time             1:30:00        longitude (hms)     12h 29m 45s
Equation of time     0h 12m 4s       Time zone offse     0h 19m 58s
```

The second data module provides information for any given year within the range 1 to 249 BE, based on the values gleaned from the table in Appendix D for the length of the year and the annual thresholds for both the reference year and the year following. As demonstrated by the third and subsequent data modules, the data in this module apply universally for the given year.

The process of converting the global time expression into local time begins with the determination of the obliquity of the diurnal threshold, i.e. the angle at which the diurnal threshold intersects with the equator at the exact moment of occurrence of the commemorative event. The value of the diurnal obliquity lies somewhere within the range of values for the obliquity of the ecliptic (±23°26') and is negative in autumn/winter and positive in spring/summer. Since in the present instance only 24 days remain until the winter solstice, the diurnal obliquity (-21°54'33") will be just slightly greater than its lowest possible value.

> *diurnal obliquity* $R = \sin f(Y, A/L_y) \times Q$, where
>
> f = *a function which delivers the ecliptic longitude (see 'Occidental time' in Chapter 7) for the elapsed portion of a year*
>
> Y = *the current Badí' year (here: 183)*
>
> A = *the age of the year, expressed as the non-integer number of days which have elapsed since the vernal equinox at the start of the reference year (here: 252.812303)*
>
> L_y = *the length of the year y in days (here: L_y = 365.2421909617932 (see table in Appendix D)*
>
> Q = *the obliquity of the ecliptic ($23°26'21''4$ in 2020 CE)*
>
> *The sine curve plots the oscillation $0° \rightarrow +Q \rightarrow 0° \rightarrow -Q \rightarrow 0°$ over the course of the tropical year and reflects the fact that the difference in the lengths of any two successive periods of daylight is most pronounced near the equinoxes and least pronounced near the solstices.*
>
> *The standard (low-precision) formula for calculating the ecliptic longitude[16] based on the Julian day number (see 'Program notes' in Appendix D) and mean time is far too cumbersome for use here. Instead, a method based on the tropical year and true solar time is assumed, whose full functionality, however, awaits the development of an algorithm for determining the proportionate area of a sector of an ellipse with a focus as its origin. Although possible solutions are documented in the Internet, translation into program code presupposes expertise in celestial mechanics and proficiency in numerical integration and is beyond the reach of the present writer. In the meantime we must make do with a surrogate result, tolerating a calculation error of up to $\pm 7°28'28''17$ or just over 2% of the true orbital position of the earth.*

The second task dealt with in the second module is the calculation of the point of intersection of the annual and diurnal thresholds, i.e. the latitude at which the terminator path crosses the date line at the moment of occurrence of the event. This is a two-stage process. The first stage is to derive the product of the longitude of the diurnal threshold and the tangent of the complement of the diurnal obliquity, which represents a theoretically maximum value for the latitude of intersection under the assumption that the earth is cylindrical.

---

maximum latitude of intersection $M = \tan(90 - Q) \times T$, where
  Q = *diurnal obliquity*
  T = *diurnal threshold*

The second stage is to determine the true latitude of intersection by projecting this cylinder onto a sphere. This is accomplished on the basis of two relationships. The first of these is the effect of meridional constriction, i.e. the amount by which the diurnal threshold curves inwards towards the date line proportionate to the distance from the equator.

---

meridional constriction $C = (T / \cos I) - T$, where
  T = *diurnal threshold*
  I = *putative latitude of intersection*

The second relationship is the width of the diurnal threshold at a given latitude of intersection within the range 0 to B, where $B \leq M$.

> *base B = (M − I) / M × T*, where
> *M = maximum absolute latitude of intersection*
> *I = putative absolute latitude of intersection*
> *T = diurnal threshold*
> B decreases in inverse proportion to an increase in I, while at the same time C (previous box) increases as a function of the cosine of I. The value of I which best satisfies the condition $B \approx C$ can accordingly be identified using a technique known as iterative approximation.

A calculated latitude of intersection within the range ±89°10' indicates that the diurnal threshold and the date line intersect at this latitude (within an arbitrarily designated tolerance, in the present case ca. 0.1 arc seconds). A value outwith this range means that intersection does not take place.

The latitude of intersection remains virtually constant year after year for any given global time expression. Minute differences accumulate over the millennia, however, primarily on account of drift in the equation of time due to precession.

The data fields of the second module are as follows:

```
Length 2026 CE      365.24219096179      Threshold 2026 CE     52°36'49" E
elapsed so far        0.69217569603      Threshold 2027 CE     34°34'30" W
Diurnal obliquity -  21°54'33"           Diurnal threshold     67°45'49" W
Intersection         53°31'42" S         Threshold of Ha'      87°11'19" W
```

The annual thresholds for the current and the coming year shown to the right are meridional earth coordinates gleaned from the table in Appendix D; the arc distance between the two is the threshold of Há', which for the short period of 250 years is always 87°11'19", give or take a fraction of an arc second. The diurnal threshold is the occidental re-expression of global time in the context of the annual threshold for the current year (183 BE / 2026 CE). To the left is displayed the length of the current year (gleaned from the table in Appendix D), followed by that portion of the current year which has elapsed so far: a key factor in calculating the diurnal obliquity, which in turn is used among other things for identifying the point of intersection of the date line and the diurnal threshold. The bottommost entry on the left is the point of intersection of the annual and diurnal thresholds, i.e. the point at which the terminator which delineates two consecutive Badí' days crosses the occidental date line precisely at 19:28:57 GT (cf. module 1) on 6 Qawl in the year 183 BE.

Each of the third and subsequent modules in the table combines the data from the first two modules with individual meridional coordinates to translate the global time expression into equatorial and local time for a specific location on earth. As places of special interest, the sites of the various Bahá'í commemorative events themselves have also been included in this list, the remaining localities being selected from around the globe. The coordinates for the commemorative events are the precise locations of the sites with which they are associated: for the Declaration of the Báb, the Shi'i shrine built on the site of the Báb's house in Shiraz; for the Martyrdom of the Báb, the Barracks in Tabríz; for the Ascension of Bahá'u'lláh, the Mansion House in Bahjí; and for the Ascension of 'Abdu'l-Bahá, the Master's house at Haparsim Street 7 in Haifa. The remaining coordinates are larger-scale approximations.[17]

The first step is to determine the terminator offset (explained in detail in the boxed text in 'Astronomical data' in Chapter 6), i.e. the longitudinal displacement of the terminator relative to the latitude of the locality in question. Here is the formula once again:

Longitudinal terminator displacement at latitude $L = (1 / \cos L - 1) \times 0°50'$

The second step is to calculate the diurnal offset for the locality. This is the amount by which the time expression must be increased (if positive) or decreased (if negative) to accommodate the obliquity of the diurnal threshhold at the latitude of the reference location and thus to derive local time (LT) from equatorial time (ET).

CONVERSION BETWEEN TIME MODES

> *local time = equatorial time – diurnal offset, where*
> *diurnal offset = tan R × L / cos L, where*
> *R = the obliquity of the diurnal threshold (positive in spring/ summer, negative in autumn/winter)*
> *L = the local latitude (positive for the northern, negative for the southern hemisphere)*
> *The product of the tangent of R yields the arc distance between the longitude of the diurnal threshold at the equator and that at latitude L; and division by the cosine of L accounts for the constriction of the longitudes at latitude L.*

For each locality, the longitude is converted into that locality's so-called grid longitude (see 'Program notes' below, paragraph 2), which is by definition the arc equivalent of the equatorial time (ET) for that locality.

There remains merely the task of determining the local date in accordance with the description in 'The occidental day and the calendar date' in Chapter 7.

The data fields are, for instance, as follows:

```
6 Qawl            183   13:50:52      Latitude              61°13'09" N
Equatorial time         10:26:19      Longitude (merid)    149°54'37" W
Terminator offset  0h    3m  35s      Longitude (occid)    156°34'43" E
Diurnal offset    - 3h  24m  33s      In region of Ha'?         FALSE
```

The left-hand columns display the LT and ET for the selected locality (here: Anchorage, Alaska, being the first in the program's list of localities: see table below), followed by the two offset values which participate in the derivation of LT from ET. The right-hand side displays the latitude and the longitude of the locality – in the latter case in both the standard coordinate system and in the occidental grid.

The final field is a truth value indicating whether or not the reference locality is situated within the region of Há', i.e. whether its grid longitude lies between the date line and approximately 87°11'19"W, i.e. between the grid-adjusted values of the current and coming thresholds.

TIME AND THE BAHÁ'Í ERA

Here is the table in full:

```
OCCIDENTAL TIME OF THE ASCENSION OF `ABDU'L-BAHÁ AND OF ITS COMMEMORATION

Convert meridional to occidental time
   Global time (GT)     19:28:57           Threshold 1921 CE   152°26'49" W
   Haifa solar time      2:02:02           Shift in    (deg)   187°26'19"
   Mean time             1:30:00           Longitude (hms)     12h 29m 45s
   Equation of time     0h 12m  4s         Time zone offset    0h 19m 58s

Commemoration in year 183 BE
   Length 2026 CE      365.24219096179
   elapsed so far        0.69217569603     Threshold 2026 CE    52°36'49" E
   Diurnal obliquity -  21°54'33"          Threshold 2027 CE    34°34'30" W
   Intersection         53°31'42" S        Diurnal threshold    67°45'49" W
                                           Threshold of Ha'     87°11'19" W

Anchorage
   LT  6 Qawl    183   13:50:52            Latitude             61°13'09" N
   Equatorial time     10:26:19            Longitude (merid)   149°54'37" W
   Terminator offset   0h  3m 35s          Longitude (occid)   156°34'43" E
   Diurnal offset    - 3h 24m 33s          In region of Há'?        FALSE

Vancouver
   LT  6 Qawl    183   14:16:51            Latitude             49°17'02" N
   Equatorial time     12:15:18            Longitude (merid)   123°07'00" W
   Terminator offset   0h  1m 47s          Longitude (occid)   176°10'28" W
   Diurnal offset    - 2h  1m 33s          In region of Há'?        FALSE

Denver
   LT  6 Qawl    183   14:51:45            Latitude             39°48'17" N
   Equatorial time     13:28:24            Longitude (merid)   105°02'13" W
   Terminator offset   0h  1m  0s          Longitude (occid)   157°54'07" W
   Diurnal offset    - 1h 23m 21s          In region of Há'?        FALSE

Chicago
   LT  6 Qawl    183   16:08:11            Latitude             41°52'56" N
   Equatorial time     14:37:41            Longitude (merid)    87°40'43" W
   Terminator offset   0h  1m  9s          Longitude (occid)   140°34'41" W
   Diurnal offset    - 1h 30m 30s          In region of Há'?        FALSE

Montreal
   LT  6 Qawl    183   17:18:13            Latitude             45°30'31" N
   Equatorial time     15:33:45            Longitude (merid)    73°35'34" W
   Terminator offset   0h  1m 25s          Longitude (occid)   126°33'44" W
   Diurnal offset    - 1h 44m 28s          In region of Há'?        FALSE

Halifax
   LT  6 Qawl    183   17:54:50            Latitude             44°38'51" N
   Equatorial time     16:13:53            Longitude (merid)    63°34'46" W
   Terminator offset   0h  1m 21s          Longitude (occid)   116°31'52" W
   Diurnal offset    - 1h 40m 57s          In region of Há'?        FALSE

Nuuk
   LT  7 Qawl    183   20:55:55            Latitude             64°11'04" N
   Equatorial time     16:58:49            Longitude (merid)    51°36'14" W
   Terminator offset   0h  4m 19s          Longitude (occid)   105°17'52" W
   Diurnal offset    - 3h 57m  7s          In region of Há'?        FALSE

Reykjavík
   LT  7 Qawl    183   22:53:59            Latitude             64°08'48" N
   Equatorial time     18:57:20            Longitude (merid)    21°58'25" W
   Terminator offset   0h  4m 19s          Longitude (occid)    75°39'54" W
   Diurnal offset    - 3h 56m 39s          In region of Há'?         TRUE
```

CONVERSION BETWEEN TIME MODES

```
London
  LT   7 Qawl    183   22:39:48          Latitude                  51°31'15" N
  Equatorial time      20:26:36          Longitude (merid)          0°13'52" W
  Terminator offset   0h  2m  1s         Longitude (occid)         53°21'02" W
  Diurnal offset    - 2h 13m 12s         In region of Há'?          TRUE

Frankfurt
  LT   7 Qawl    183   23:08:15          Latitude                  50°06'45" N
  Equatorial time      21:02:32          Longitude (merid)          8°42'52" E
  Terminator offset   0h  1m 52s         Longitude (occid)         44°21'55" W
  Diurnal offset    - 2h  5m 43s         In region of Há'?          TRUE

Capetown
  LT   7 Qawl    183   20:36:47          Latitude                  33°56'21" S
  Equatorial time      21:42:36          Longitude (merid)         18°26'00" E
  Terminator offset   0h  0m 41s         Longitude (occid)         34°21'05" W
  Diurnal offset      1h  5m 49s         In region of Há'?          TRUE

Tromsø
  LT   7 Qawl    183    3:01:18          Latitude                  69°39'08" N
  Equatorial time      21:39:03          Longitude (merid)         18°56'25" E
  Terminator offset   0h  6m 15s         Longitude (occid)         35°14'12" W
  Diurnal offset    - 5h 22m 15s         In region of Há'?          TRUE

Kisumu
  LT   7 Qawl    183   22:46:21          Latitude                   0°00'00" N
  Equatorial time      22:46:21          Longitude (merid)         34°12'09" E
  Terminator offset   0h  0m  0s         Longitude (occid)         18°24'40" W
  Diurnal offset      0h  0m  0s         In region of Há'?          TRUE

Haifa
  LT   7 Qawl    183   23:51:42          Latitude                  32°49'05" N
  Equatorial time      22:48:53          Longitude (merid)         34°59'30" E
  Terminator offset   0h  0m 38s         Longitude (occid)         17°46'49" W
  Diurnal offset    - 1h  2m 49s         In region of Há'?          TRUE

Bahji
  LT   7 Qawl    183   23:52:26          Latitude                  32°56'36" N
  Equatorial time      22:49:16          Longitude (merid)         35°05'31" E
  Terminator offset   0h  0m 38s         Longitude (occid)         17°40'53" W
  Diurnal offset    - 1h  3m  9s         In region of Há'?          TRUE

Tabriz
  LT   7 Qawl    183    0:51:36          Latitude                  38°04'21" N
  Equatorial time      23:33:48          Longitude (merid)         46°17'20" E
  Terminator offset   0h  0m 54s         Longitude (occid)          6°33'60" W
  Diurnal offset    - 1h 17m 48s         In region of Há'?          TRUE

Teheran
  LT   7 Qawl    183    1:04:26          Latitude                  35°39'22" N
  Equatorial time      23:53:50          Longitude (merid)         51°15'57" E
  Terminator offset   0h  0m 46s         Longitude (occid)          1°32'24" W
  Diurnal offset    - 1h 10m 36s         In region of Há'?          TRUE

Shiraz
  LT   7 Qawl    183    0:54:00          Latitude                  29°36'47" N
  Equatorial time      23:59:12          Longitude (merid)         52°32'26" E
  Terminator offset   0h  0m 30s         Longitude (occid)          0°11'54" W
  Diurnal offset    - 0h 54m 48s         In region of Há'?          TRUE

Trawler
  LT   5 Qawl    183   21:26:48          Latitude                  55°00'00" S
  Equatorial time       0:01:04          Longitude (merid)         53°30'00" E
  Terminator offset   0h  2m 29s         Longitude (occid)          0°16'01" E
  Diurnal offset      2h 34m 16s         In region of Há'?          FALSE

Rawalpindi
  LT   6 Qawl    183    2:13:18          Latitude                  32°56'25" N
```

279

TIME AND THE BAHÁ'Í ERA

```
                 Equatorial time        1:10:10          Longitude (merid)       70°18'48" E
                 Terminator offset   0h  0m 38s          Longitude (occid)       17°32'24" E
                 Diurnal offset    - 1h  3m  9s          In region of Há'?           FALSE

            Hong Kong
                 LT  6 Qawl    183      4:43:60          Latitude                21°53'30" N
                 Equatorial time        4:05:03          Longitude (merid)      113°56'21" E
                 Terminator offset   0h  0m 16s          Longitude (occid)       61°15'39" E
                 Diurnal offset    - 0h 37m 57s          In region of Há'?           FALSE

            Melbourne
                 LT  6 Qawl    183      4:51:35          Latitude                37°49'08" S
                 Equatorial time        6:08:36          Longitude (merid)      144°59'06" E
                 Terminator offset   0h  0m 53s          Longitude (occid)       92°08'59" E
                 Diurnal offset      1h 17m  1s          In region of Há'?           FALSE

            Auckland
                 LT  6 Qawl    183      6:53:41          Latitude                36°50'59" S
                 Equatorial time        8:07:46          Longitude (merid)      174°45'49" E
                 Terminator offset   0h  0m 50s          Longitude (occid)      121°56'31" E
                 Diurnal offset      1h 14m  5s          In region of Há'?           FALSE
```

As an aid to recognizing the geographical orientation of this table it is helpful first to scan through the whole list and take note of those localities where the field <Region of Há'> is TRUE. The last-encountered (here: Shiraz) lies just west of the date line (i.e. the annual threshold), and the very next locality (here: a trawler in the Indian Ocean) lies just east of the date line.

Cross-comparison of the individual locality modules brings some interesting properties to light, such as the correlation between the latitude and the terminator offset. The greater the distance from the equator, the higher the offset value: compare the northernmost example Tromsø in Norway, at 69°39'08" just over 3° north of the arctic circle with a terminator offset of 6¼ minutes, with Hong Kong at 21°53'30" and a terminator offset of only 16 seconds, or indeed with Kisumu, which lies directly on the equator and whose terminator offset is therefore zero.

The effect of the latitude on the diurnal offset is even more dramatic. Note that, when travelling steadily eastwards around the globe from Anchorage to Auckland, equatorial time (which is influenced by neither offset) increases in direct proportion to the shift in longitude. By contrast, the irregular progression of local time (the first data item in each locality module) is primarily the consequence of the obliquity of the diurnal threshold, which runs diagonally from north-west to south-east at an angle just slightly less extreme than that of mid-winter, so that its offset is positive in the southern and negative in the northern hemisphere and its absolute value increases proportionally to the absolute value of the latitude of a given locality. As a result, the daylight period is longer than the night hours on 6 Qawl in the southern hemisphere and vice versa in the northern hemisphere.

Note that with meridional time this difference is equally distributed between the two halves of the natural day: sunrise over- or undershoots 5:56:40 a.m. to the same extent as sunset under- or overshoots 6:03:20 p.m. By contrast, sunset in occidental time is always exactly 0:00 whatever the age of the year, so that sunrise takes the full brunt of this seasonal variation: sunrise will deviate from the middle value (11.53:20) by *twice* the value of the diurnal offset. In our example, sunrise in Cape Town is $2^h11^m38^s$ earlier than the middle value, that in Tromsø is $10^h44^m30^s$ later: while the people in Cape Town can count on over two additional early morning hours of sunlight on 5 Qawl, those in Tromsø – which lies just north of the arctic circle, but whose longitude is nearly identical to that of Cape Town, so that the equatorial times of the two localities differ by a mere 3½ minutes – experience just under eleven extra morning hours of winterly darkness on 6 Qawl.

Four of the 23 selected localities lie in the area of 7 Qawl, i.e. north of the point of intersection and west of the date line (cf. 'The occidental day and the calendar date' in Chapter 7, but note that Illustration 8 must be mentally adjusted to reflect the converse seasonal orientation). Because of the advanced hour (19:29:43 GT) the cutting edge of the shadow (i.e. the diurnal threshold) has made considerable inroads into the area west of the date line, especially in the north. The area of 7 Qawl stretches accordingly from Tabríz all the way across to Tromsø.

One entry (a trawler, in the Indian Ocean about 1,000 kilometres southwest of the Kerguelen Islands) bears the current date of 5 Qawl because its circumstances are the exact reverse of those in the area of 7 Qawl, i.e. it lies south of the point of intersection and just east of the date line, and it is still bathed in sunlight: compare this with Shiraz, which, although its longitude is less than a half a degree further west, is separated from the trawler by over 90° of latitude and lies in darkness. Thus Shiraz is at this moment (though not for long) 2 calendar days ahead of the trawler.

The remaining localities lie in area 3 of Illustration 8 in 'The occidental day and the calendar date' in Chapter 7, i.e. they do not satisfy the criteria for inclusion in one of the wedges and therefore carry the date 6 Qawl.

Comparison of the table results over a succession of years highlights further interesting properties. Unfortunately, that is a privilege reserved for individuals in possession of a running version of the the program, which can step forwards and backwards through the years in quick succession. It is fascinating to observe, for example, how equatorial and local time progresses in concert with the grid longitude; how some data elements remain nearly constant, whilst others change radically from year to year; and how the region of Há' progresses in a wave-like motion through the individual localities, each making an appearance in the region of Há' for one year before disappearing again, only to reappear four or five years later.

Program notes

These notes are a recapitulation in plain language of the structure and content of the program with which the above table was generated. They appear here (in advance of the program listing) primarily out of concern for readers who may prefer to forego the challenge of perusing formal program code. But they also provide insights into the strategy which would otherwise require intensive study of the program, so that the technically experienced reader may also find them useful as preliminary orientation. But first, a word or two regarding methodology:

Whereas the base reference for longitudinal coordinates and meridional time is the prime meridian through Greenwich,→18 occidental time, and in particular global time, is an expression of temporal distance from the date line. It is quite possible to base all calculations on the internationally standard earth coordinate system, converting each occidental time expression into its meridional equivalent whenever it participates in a calculation, but the resulting program code is unwieldy and opaque. The task is far more elegantly resolved by regarding occidental expressions in a mathematically more natural environment, i.e. by introducing an alternative grid of coordinates (here called an *occidental grid*), comparable to the accustomed Greenwich-based grid but with longitude 0° – and therewith the reference longitude of the occidental date line – set equal to the reference year's annual threshold. Because of the cyclic progression of the annual threshold, each year has its own grid. The longitudinal equivalent of the global time expression is accordingly identical by definition to the reference longitude of the current diurnal threshold, i.e. the longitude at which the advancing edge of the earth's shadow intersects with the equator at the precise moment of the recurrence of the commemorative event in that year. Subsequently, once the input longitudes for the individual localities have been converted from the meridional to the occidental grid, computation proceeds in blissful ignorance of the relationship between standard and grid longitude.

A second unique property of the occidental grid is that its 'longitudes' represent equinoctial terminator paths instead of meridians (see 'Astronomical data' in Chapter 6).→[19] As a result, once the initial longitude of the reference locality has been adjusted in accordance with the terminator offset (see boxed text above), this complication can simply be ignored in all subsequent computations.

It must be emphasized that the occidental grid is not a feature of cyclic-progressive occidental time; its sole purpose is to facilitate computation in the program accompanying this appendix.

A further feature of program design which considerably eases the handling of the numerous data categories is that all internal spatial and temporal data are handled indiscriminately as degrees of arc. Calculations can accordingly be carried out with complete disregard for the origin of the participating terms, and results may be displayed in whatever format is appropriate to the context. For example, in the first data module, <Longitude shift> is displayed twice: once as an ARC expression (to illustrate how it came about) and once as a TIME expression (to highlight its calculatory function). Similarly, <Equatorial time> and <Grid longitude> in the second data module are two perspectives of one and the same data item. But the most significant advantage lies in the compactness and transparency of the program code which it makes possible.

The individual components of the program are as follows:

(1) Function <wrap> returns an arc value (assumed to be longitudinal) guaranteed to be in the range 0° to 360°. A calculation involving longitudes which returned a value beyond this range in either direction would otherwise 'fall off the edge' of the occidental grid – as if the earth were flat – with undefinable consequences.

(2) Function <dms2dd> is used to process input data prior to calculation. It accepts any entity expressed as degrees (or hours), minutes and seconds and returns its value as a floating-point decimal expression. If the entity's input format is temporal (TIME), the result is automatically rescaled from 24 hours to 360 degrees. If the input format is latitudinal (NORTH or SOUTH), it returns a value in the range 0.0 to 90.0 for the northern, 0.0 to -90.0 for the southern hemisphere. If the format is WEST, it converts longitude W to 360.0 – W, with the result that all longitudes are identical to their arc equivalents in the full range 0° to 360°.

(3) Function <str2dd> interprets a string of characters representing a numerical expression and returns its floating-point decimal equivalent. It is used for processing input data in lieu of the C function <sscanf>.

(4) Function <dd2dms> converts a floating-point decimal value into a string containing degrees (or hours, as appropriate), minutes and seconds, which it passes back, appropriately formatted, to the calling routine for the purpose of display. A value whose display format is WEST will be output as an expression of degrees, minutes and seconds in the range 0° to 180°, followed by either E or W. The same value marked as EAST will result in an expression in the range 0° to 360° E. Similarly, NORTH will display a positive value followed by N or S, whereas SOUTH will display a signed but otherwise unmarked latitude. All other formatting is self-explanatory.

(5) Function <fetch_longitude> interprets a string of characters representing a longitudinal expression and returns its arc equivalent. It is used to input the annual threshold from the corresponding field in the file <appendix_d_table>.

(6) Function <proportion_of_year> determines how much of the current year has transpired up to a specified Badí' calendar date and time. The Ayyám-i Há' are passed to the function as days 1-4 (or 1-5) of month 0, whereas program-internally they are tacked onto the end of the month of Mulk (18) for the purpose of calculation. If the date lies within the month of 'Alá (19), the age of the year is determined by deducting from the year length the number of days remaining until the end of the year; otherwise it is determined by reckoning upwards from 1 Bahá' to maximally the beginning of the fifth Yawm-i Há'. This strategy ensures that that portion of the year in excess of 365 days is automatically assigned to the fifth Yawm-i Há': in local and equatorial time expressions this portion is either 24 or 0 hours, depending on whether or not the reference longitude lies within the region of Há'; and for global time expressions it is a non-integer value derived from the precise length of the tropical year, for example 0.24219071564 days or 5 hours, 48 minutes and 45.27648 seconds in the year 2030. In addition, the function generates a date-and-time character string expression, for example <1 'Aẓamat 187 21:24:43 GT>, which it holds in readiness for display.

(7) Function <sector> is designed to calculate the area of a sector P_1CP_2 relative to the area of an ellipse which models the orbit of the earth around the sun, whereby P_1 and P_2 are points on the circumference of the ellipse and origin C is that focus of the ellipse which corresponds to the sun-earth barycentre. The epoch is the ecliptic longitude relative to the perihelion at 00:00 on 1 Bahá' of the year 1 BE. P_1 = epoch - <precession>, $P_2 = P_1$ + <coord>. Pending proper implementation the function returns a surrogate value.

(8) Function <ecliptic_longitude> transforms the age of the year from an expression of duration to one of position in conformity with Kepler's second law of planetary motion. Pending the enhancement of <sector>) it behaves as if the earth orbit were a perfect circle.

(9) Function <crosspoint> establishes the latitude at which the diurnal threshold crosses the annual threshold (i.e. the date line), delivering a value beyond the range ±89°10' if they do not in fact intersect.

(10) Functions <increment_date> and <decrement_date> determine the next/previous date according to the Badí' calendar, taking due account of the Ayyám-i Há' and the region of Há'.

(11) Routine <display> uses the data submitted by successive invocations to produce a two-column table, complete with data module titles and field labels. The output is self-formatting.

(12) Routine <profile> ascertains the equatorial and local time (ET and LT) of a given locality on the basis of its meridional earth coordinates [generates data modules ≥ 3].

(13) Routine <header> employs the global date and time given for the event in question, together with geodetic information from external sources, to establish a set of parameters which serve as the fundament for all subsequent calculations [generates data module 2].

(14) Routine <mean2global> converts a Badí' date and meridional time expression into its global (occidental) date and time equivalent (GT) [generates data module 1].→[20]

(15) Routine <main> is the driver program which first invokes <mean2global> for one of four selected commemorative events, then <header> with respect to the selected year of commemoration, and finally <profile> once each for any number of selected localities, each specified by name, longitude and latitude. It supplies the arbitrarily extendable data sets both for the commemorative events and for the localities.

CONVERSION BETWEEN TIME MODES

```c
/* conversion between meridional, global, equatorial and local time */

#include <stdio.h>
#include <math.h>

#define         OBLIQUITY_OF_THE_ECLIPTIC  23.439291112     /* as at 3.1.2020 */
#ifdef OWN_PI
#define PI      3.1415926535897932384626433832795
#else
#define PI      M_PI
#endif
#define rad(D)          D*PI/180
#define sine(D)         sin(rad(D))
#define cosine(D)       cos(rad(D))
#define tangent(D)      tan(rad(D))
                                /* ======= APPLICATION-SPECIFIC DATA FORMATS ======== */
#define EAST    'E'     /* assign    0° to 180°   display    0° to 360°           */
#define WEST    'W'     /* assign  360° to 180°   display    0° to 180° E / W     */
#define NORTH   'N'     /* assign    0° to  90°   display  -90° to  90°           */
#define SOUTH   'S'     /* assign  -90° to  90°   display    0° to  90° N / S     */
#define ARC     'A'     /* assign -360° to 360°   display -360° to 360°           */
#define TIME    'T'     /* assign  ±hms * 15      display up to 23h 59m 59s       */
#define CLOCK   'C'     /* (not used for input)   display up to 23:59:59          */
#define FLOAT   'F'     /* (not used for input)   display fixed-point decimal     */
#define LABEL   'L'     /* (not used for input)   display header text only        */
#define TEXT    'X'     /* (not used for input)   display text, ignore value      */
#define TRUTH   'R'     /* (not used for input)   display TRUE or FALSE           */

#define SPREAD  1       /* 0 = compact display, 1 = spaced out for legibility */

static int      fd;                     /* file descriptor for link to external file */
static short    badi_day, badi_month, badi_year;        /* basic badi calendar data */

static double diurnal_threshold,  /* grid equivalent of the time of the event in GT  */
              annual_threshold,   /* longitude of diurnal threshold at vernal point  */
              threshold_of_ha,    /* occidental coming_threshold - quasi constant    */
              diurnal_obliquity,  /* obliquity of diurnal threshold acc age of year  */
              intersection;       /* intersection of diurnal and annual thresholds   */

double wrap( expr) double expr;
{       return( expr > 360 ? expr - 360 : expr < 0 ? expr + 360: expr);
}       /* wrap */


double dms2dd( deg, min, sec, format)   /* convert time or arc expressions to float */
        short   deg, min, sec;
        char    format;
{
        double dd = ((deg * 3600 + min * 60 + sec) / 3600.0);

             if( format == WEST)  dd = 360.0 - dd;
        else if( format == SOUTH) dd = -dd;
        else if( format == TIME)  dd *= 15;
        return( dd);
}       /* dms2dd */

void dd2dms( dms, dd, format)   /* convert float to string of appropriate type format */
        double dd;
        char   *dms, format;
{
        short  deg, min, sec, rem;
        char   sign = ' ';

        if( dd < 0) { sign = '-'; dd = -dd; }                   /* time or latitude south or error */
        else if( format == WEST)  { if( dd > 180) dd = 360 - dd; else format = EAST;  }
        else if( format == SOUTH) { if( dd <   0) dd =   0 - dd; else format = NORTH; }
        if( format == TIME || format == CLOCK) { dd /= 15; if( dd > 24) dd = 24 - dd; }
        deg = (short) dd; dd -= deg; dd *= 60;
        min = (short) dd; dd -= min; dd *= 60;
        sec = (short) dd; dd -= sec;
        if( dd > 0.5)                   /* round up if more than half a second left */
           if( ++sec == 60)
              if( ++min == 60)
                 if( ++deg > (format == TIME || format == CLOCK ? 24 : 360)) deg = 0;
        switch( format)
        {   case CLOCK:
                        sprintf(dms, "%c%3d:%02d:%02d        ", sign, deg, min, sec); break;
            case TIME:
                        sprintf(dms, "%c%2dh %2dm %2ds       ", sign, deg, min, sec); break;
```

TIME AND THE BAHÁ'Í ERA

```
                case ARC:
                        sprintf(dms, "%c%3d°%02d'%02d\"   ",   sign, deg, min, sec); break;
                case WEST:
                case SOUTH:
                        sprintf(dms, " %3d°%02d'%02d\" %c  ",  deg, min, sec, format); break;
                default:
                        sprintf(dms, "%c%3d°%02d'%02d\" %c  ", sign, deg, min, sec, format);
        }   }   /* dd2dms */


    double str2dd( p )                               /* convert string expression to float */
        char *p;
    {
        char   ch;
        short  sign = 0;
        double dd = 0, power = 0;

        while( *p == ' ') ++p;                       /* skip leading spaces */
        while( ch = *(p++))
        {       if( ch == '-')                       { if( sign ) break; else sign = -1; }
                else if( ch == '.')                  { if( power) break; else power = 1; }
                else if( ch >= '0' && ch <= '9' )    { dd = dd * 10 + ch - '0'; power *= 10; }
                else break;
        }
        return( ++sign * dd / (power ? power : 1));
    }   /* str2dd */


    double fetch_longitude( p )                      /* get arc value from input file */
        char *p;
    {
        char   sdg[4], smn[3], ssc[3], EW;

        (void) sscanf( p + 24, "%3s", sdg);
        (void) sscanf( p + 29, "%2s", smn);
        (void) sscanf( p + 32, "%2s", ssc);
        (void) sscanf( p + 35, "%c",  &EW);
        return (dms2dd( (short) str2dd( sdg),
                        (short) str2dd( smn),
                        (short) str2dd( ssc), EW));
    }   /* fetch_longitude */


    double proportion_of_year( p, day, month, year, day_so_far, length_of_year)
        char  *p;                                    /* calculate year-to-date */
        short day, month, year;
        double day_so_far, length_of_year;
    {
        static char *badi [] =
            { "AyyámiHá'", "Bahá'   ", "Jalál   ", "Jamál   ", "`Azamat ",
              "Núr     ", "Rahmat  ", "Kalimát ", "Kamál   ", "Asmá'   ",
              "`Izzat  ", "Mashiyyat", "`Ilm    ", "Qudrat  ", "Qawl    ",
              "Masá'il ", "Sharaf  ", "Sultán  ", "Mulk    ", "`Alá    " };

        static char text [75];          /* static, so that the content remains after exiting */
        char        time [ 9], *q = text;
        double      proportion = 0.0;   /* to guarantee returning a defined string */

        if( day)           /* 0 when called simply to retrieve the stored date/time string */
        {   dd2dms( time, day_so_far, CLOCK);
            sprintf( text, "LT %2d %-9s%3d%8s", day, badi [month], year, time);
            day_so_far /= 360;
            if( month == 0) { month = 18; day += 19; }  /* 1-5 Ayyám-i-Há' -> 20-24 Mulk */
            if( month == 19)
                  proportion = ( length_of_year - 20 + day + day_so_far) / length_of_year;
            else  proportion = ((month - 1) * 19 + day - 1 + day_so_far) / length_of_year;
        }
        while( *(p++) = *(q++));              /* copy static buffer into external string */
        return( proportion);                  /* value between 0 and 1, being proportion of whole year */
    }                                         /* proportion_of_year */


    double sector( precession, coord)
        double precession, coord;             /* returns a value between 0 and 1, being the area */
    {                                         /* of a sector expressed as a proportion of the    */
        return( coord / 360);                 /* area of an ellipse which models the earth orbit */
    }   /* surrogate sector */                /* with the sun-earth barycentre as sector origin  */


    double ecliptic_longitude( year, proportion)
        short  year;
        double proportion;
```

CONVERSION BETWEEN TIME MODES

```
{
    double precession, area, longitude, lower, upper;

    precession = --year * 360 / 25850.0;            /* to be deducted from epoch */
    longitude = proportion * 360;                   /* convert to arc degrees */
    upper = dms2dd( 7, 28, 29, ARC); lower = longitude - upper; upper += longitude;
                                    /* minimum and maximum theoretical deviation from the mean */
    do                              /* calculate longitudinal distance since start of current year */
    {       if( area = sector( precession, longitude) > proportion) upper = longitude;
        else if( area < proportion) lower = longitude; else  upper = lower = longitude;
        longitude = (lower + upper) / 2;            /* mean value */
    }  while( (upper - lower) > 0.000027777778);    /* accurate to ca 0.1 arc second */
    return( longitude);
}                                                   /* ecliptic_longitude */


double crosspoint( threshold, obliquity)
    double threshold,                 /* distance east or west of occidental grid longitude 0 */
           obliquity;                 /* right or left tilt of shadow edge at moment of event */
{
    double top, dot, upper, lower;
    short  count = 0, sign = -1;

    if( obliquity < 0) obliquity = -obliquity; else sign = -sign;
    if( threshold < 180) sign = -sign;          else threshold = 360 -threshold;
    if( obliquity < 0.35808) top = 160 * threshold;    /* avoid gargantuan tangent */
    else { obliquity = 90 - obliquity; top = tangent( obliquity) * threshold; }

    upper = top; lower = 0;                     /* prime iteration */
    while( (upper - lower) > 0.000027777778)    /* accurate to ca 0.1 arc second */
    {   dot = (upper + lower) / 2;              /* middle value */
        if( (threshold / cosine( dot)) - threshold > (top - dot) / top * threshold)
             upper = dot; else lower = dot;     /* home in from both ends */
    }   /* typically between 22-24 iterations, more if tolerance value is decreased */
    return( dot * sign);
}   /* crosspoint */


void increment_date( day, month, year, leap)
    short *day, *month, *year, leap;
{
    if( *month == 0 && *day >= 4)
    {   if( leap && *day == 4) *day = 5;
        else { *month = 19; *day = 1; }
    }
    else if( *day < 19) ++*day;
    else
    {   *day = 1;
        if( *month == 18) *month = 0;
        else if( ++*month == 20) { *month = 1; ++*year; }
}   }                           /* increment_date will be confused by invalid data */


void decrement_date( day, month, year, leap)
    short *day, *month, *year, leap;
{
    if( ! --*day)
    if( *month == 19) { *month = 0; *day = 4 + leap; }
    else
    {   *day = 19;
        if( *month == 0) *month = 18;
        else if( --*month == 0) { *month = 19; --*year; }
}   }                           /* decrement_date will be confused by invalid data */


void display( label, value, format)         /* send results to standard output */
    char   *label, format;
    double  value;
{
    static short tabs = -1;                 /* failsafe */

    if( format == LABEL) { if( SPREAD) printf( "\n"); printf( "\n"); tabs = 1; }
    else if( tabs < 1)  printf( "\n\t"); else printf( "\t");        /* block title */
    tabs = -tabs;                                    /* left/right column flip-flop */
         if( format == TEXT || format == LABEL) printf( "%-32s", label);
    else if( format == FLOAT) printf( "%-17s %4.11f ", label, value);
    else if( format == TRUTH) printf( "%-17s %10s       ", label,
                                  (short) value ? "TRUE" : "FALSE");
    else
    {   char   text [75];
```

TIME AND THE BAHÁ'Í ERA

```
                dd2dms( &text, value, format);
                printf( "%-17s %s", label, text);
    }   }   /* display */


void profile( locality, latitude, longitude)
    char    *locality;
    double  latitude, longitude;
{
    double  meridional_longitude,       /* longitude relative to the prime meridian */
            terminator_offset,          /* bias due to longitudinal taper: see Chapter 6 */
            local_time,                 /* time of day at the given locality */
            diurnal_offset;             /* longitudinal extent of wedge at given latitude */
    short   north, east, temp;          /* used to adjust daycount */
    short   region_of_ha;               /* TRUE if given locality lies within region of Há' */
    short   day = badi_day, month = badi_month, year = badi_year;   /* working copies */
    char    text [75];                  /* storage buffer for display */

/* determine locality-specific values */

    meridional_longitude = longitude;   /* preserve for display */
    terminator_offset   = (1 / cosine( latitude) - 1) * dms2dd( 0, 50, 0, ARC);
    longitude           = wrap( meridional_longitude - annual_threshold
                                - terminator_offset);
    diurnal_offset      = tangent( diurnal_obliquity) * latitude / cosine( latitude);
    local_time          = wrap( longitude - diurnal_offset);
    region_of_ha        = (longitude >= threshold_of_ha);

/* test for day shift */

    north = intersection < latitude;    /* north of wedge intersection */
    east  = longitude < wrap( diurnal_threshold + diurnal_offset);   /* east of DL */
    if( temp = diurnal_obliquity > 0 ? north ? east ? -1 :  0 : east ?  0 :  1
                                     : north ? east ?  0 :  1 : east ? -1 :  0)
        if( temp > 0) increment_date( &day, &month, &year, region_of_ha);
        else          decrement_date( &day, &month, &year, region_of_ha);

/* display results */

    display( locality,              0.0,                        LABEL);

    (void) proportion_of_year( text, day, month, year, local_time,
                               region_of_ha ? 366.0 : 365.0);
    display( text,                  0.0,                        TEXT);
    display( "Latitude",            latitude,                   SOUTH);

    display( "Equatorial time",     longitude,                  CLOCK);
    display( "Longitude (merid)",   meridional_longitude,       WEST);

    display( "Terminator offset",   terminator_offset,          TIME);
    display( "Longitude (occid)",   longitude,                  WEST);

    display( "Diurnal offset",      diurnal_offset,             TIME);
    display( "In region of Há'?",   (double) region_of_ha,      TRUTH);
}   /* profile */


void header( label)
    char    *label;
{
    double  length_of_year,             /* tropical year beginning midday on 1. 1. <year> BE */
            coming_threshold,           /* longitude of annual threshold in coming year */
            proportion;                 /* portion of Badi` year elapsed so far */
    char    string [50], text [76], buff [50];
                                lseek( fd, (long) (badi_year * 76 + 380), 0);
/* input file parameters */     (void) read( fd, text, 75);     text [75] = 0;
                                (void) sscanf( text + 1, "%3s",         string);
    if( (short) str2dd( string) != badi_year)
        fprintf( stderr, "\n\t%d vs %d\n", (short) str2dd( string), badi_year);
                                (void) sscanf( text + 51, "%s",         string);
    length_of_year   = str2dd( string);
    annual_threshold = fetch_longitude( text);
                                lseek( fd, 1L, 1);
                                (void) read( fd, text, 75);     text [75] = 0;
    coming_threshold = fetch_longitude( text);

/* determine locality-neutral values */

    threshold_of_ha   = wrap( coming_threshold - annual_threshold);
    proportion        = proportion_of_year( text, badi_day, badi_month, badi_year,
                                            diurnal_threshold, length_of_year);
    diurnal_obliquity = sine( ecliptic_longitude( badi_year, proportion))
```

CONVERSION BETWEEN TIME MODES

```
                                              * OBLIQUITY_OF_THE_ECLIPTIC;
    intersection    = crosspoint( diurnal_threshold, diurnal_obliquity);

/* display results */

    sprintf( buff, label, badi_year);
    display( buff,                0.0,                  LABEL);

    sprintf( text, "Length %4d CE",   badi_year + 1843);
     display( text,                   length_of_year,       FLOAT);
    sprintf( text, "Threshold %4d CE", badi_year + 1843);
     display( text,                   annual_threshold,     WEST);

    display( "elapsed so far      ",  proportion,           FLOAT);
    sprintf( text, "Threshold %4d CE", badi_year + 1844);
     display( text,                   coming_threshold,     WEST);

    display( "Diurnal obliquity",     diurnal_obliquity,    ARC);
    display( "Diurnal threshold",     diurnal_threshold,    WEST);

    display( "Intersection",          intersection,         SOUTH);
    display( "Threshold of Ha'",      threshold_of_ha,      WEST);
}   /* header */


void mean2global( event, day, month, year, time, equation_of_time,
                                          locality, latitude, longitude)
    short   day, month, year;
    double  time, equation_of_time, latitude, longitude;
    char    *event, *locality;
{
    double solar_time, longitude_shift, zone_factor, length_of_year;
    char   string [50], text [76];
                                      lseek( fd, (long) (year * 76 + 380),  0);
/* input file parameters */           (void) read( fd, text, 75); text [75] = 0;
                                      (void) sscanf( text + 1, "%3s", string);
    if( (short) str2dd( string) != year)
        fprintf( stderr, "\n\t%d vs %d\n", (short) str2dd( string), year);
                                             (void) sscanf( text + 50, "%s", string);
    length_of_year    = str2dd( string);
    annual_threshold  = fetch_longitude( text);

/* prime constants */

    badi_day    = day;
    badi_month  = month;
    badi_year   = year;

/* calculate time zone offset, solar and global time (works for Israel and Iran */

    if( longitude >= dms2dd( 44, 3, 2, EAST) && longitude <= dms2dd( 63, 19, 15, EAST))
        zone_factor = dms2dd( 3, 30, 0, TIME);            /* Iran Standard Time */
    else
    {   short hour  = (short) dms2dd( 1, 0, 0, TIME);

        zone_factor = ((short) longitude / hour ) * hour;
        if( longitude - zone_factor > dms2dd( 0, 30, 0, TIME)) zone_factor += hour;
    }
    zone_factor      = longitude - zone_factor;        /* pos if east, neg if west */
    solar_time       = wrap( time + zone_factor + equation_of_time);
    longitude_shift  = wrap( longitude - annual_threshold);     /* grid alignment */
    diurnal_threshold = wrap( solar_time + dms2dd( 89, 10, 0, ARC) - longitude_shift);

/* display results */

    printf( "OCCIDENTAL TIME OF THE %s AND OF ITS COMMEMORATION", event);

    display( "Convert meridional to occidental time",  0.0,      LABEL);

    display( "Global time (GT)",      diurnal_threshold,     CLOCK);
    sprintf( string, "Threshold %4d CE", badi_year + 1843);
    display( string,                  annual_threshold,      WEST);

    sprintf( string, "%s solar time", locality);
    display( string,                  solar_time,            CLOCK);
    display( "Shift in    (deg)",     longitude_shift,       ARC);

    display( "Mean time",             time,                  CLOCK);
    display( "  longitude (hms)",     longitude_shift,       TIME);

    display( "Equation of time",      equation_of_time,      TIME);
    display( "Time zone offset",      zone_factor,           TIME);
```

TIME AND THE BAHÁ'Í ERA

```c
}   /* mean2global */


main()
{
    char    ch, event;

    if( (fd = open( "appendix_d_table", 0)) == EOF)             /* symbolic link */
        { fprintf( stderr, "\nInput file not found\n"); /* exit( 1); */ }
        /* exit and exit() both generate tiresome warning message in C compiler */

    event = 'A';                    /* either 'D', 'M', 'B' or 'A' depending on event */
    switch( event)
    {
        case 'D':
            mean2global( "DECLARATION OF THE BÁB",          8,   4,   1,
                            dms2dd( 21, 27,  0, TIME),  dms2dd(  0,  3, 28, TIME),
                    /* 2 hours and 11 minutes after sunset mean time on 22 May 1844 */
                "Shiráz",   dms2dd( 29, 36, 47, NORTH), dms2dd( 52, 32, 26, EAST));
            break;
        case 'M':
            mean2global( "MARTYRDOM OF THE BÁB",            17,  6,   7,
                            dms2dd( 12,  0,  0, TIME), -dms2dd(  0,  4, 57, TIME),
                "Tabriz",   dms2dd( 38, 04, 21, NORTH), dms2dd( 46, 17, 20, EAST));
            break;
        case 'B':
            mean2global( "ASCENSION OF BAHÁ'U'LLÁH",        13,  4,  49,
                            dms2dd(  3,  0,  0, TIME),  dms2dd(  0,  2, 46, TIME),
                "Bahji",    dms2dd( 32, 56, 36, NORTH), dms2dd( 35,  5, 31, EAST));
            break;
        case 'A':
            mean2global( "ASCENSION OF `ABDU'L-BAHÁ",        6, 14,  78,
                            dms2dd(  1, 30,  0, TIME),  dms2dd(  0, 12,  4, TIME),
                "Haifa",    dms2dd( 32, 49, 05, NORTH), dms2dd( 34, 59, 30, EAST));
            break;
        default: fprintf( stderr, "\n\tChoose one of 'D','M', 'B' or 'A'");
    }
    badi_year = 183;                        /* adjustable starting point */
    while( badi_year && badi_year < 250)    /* so long as year is in valid range */
    {
        header( "Commemoration in year %d BE");
        profile( "Anchorage",   dms2dd( 61, 13,  9, NORTH), dms2dd( 149, 54, 37, WEST));
        profile( "Vancouver",   dms2dd( 49, 17,  2, NORTH), dms2dd( 123,  7,  0, WEST));
        profile( "Denver",      dms2dd( 39, 48, 17, NORTH), dms2dd( 105, 02, 13, WEST));
        profile( "Chicago",     dms2dd( 41, 52, 56, NORTH), dms2dd(  87, 40, 43, WEST));
        profile( "Montreal",    dms2dd( 45, 30, 31, NORTH), dms2dd(  73, 35, 34, WEST));
        profile( "Halifax",     dms2dd( 44, 38, 51, NORTH), dms2dd(  63, 34, 46, WEST));
        profile( "Nuuk",        dms2dd( 64, 11, 04, NORTH), dms2dd(  51, 36, 14, WEST));
        profile( "Reykjavík",   dms2dd( 64,  8, 48, NORTH), dms2dd(  21, 58, 25, WEST));
        profile( "London",      dms2dd( 51, 31, 15, NORTH), dms2dd(   0, 13, 52, WEST));
        profile( "Frankfurt",   dms2dd( 50,  6, 45, NORTH), dms2dd(   8, 42, 52, EAST));
        profile( "Capetown",    dms2dd( 33, 56, 21, SOUTH), dms2dd(  18, 26,  0, EAST));
        profile( "Tromsø",      dms2dd( 69, 39,  8, NORTH), dms2dd(  18, 56, 25, EAST));
        profile( "Kisumu",      dms2dd(  0,  0,  0, NORTH), dms2dd(  34, 12,  9, EAST));
        profile( "Haifa",       dms2dd( 32, 49, 05, NORTH), dms2dd(  34, 59, 30, EAST));
        profile( "Bahji",       dms2dd( 32, 56, 36, NORTH), dms2dd(  35,  5, 31, EAST));
        profile( "Tabriz",      dms2dd( 38, 04, 21, NORTH), dms2dd(  46, 17, 20, EAST));
        profile( "Teheran",     dms2dd( 35, 39, 22, NORTH), dms2dd(  51, 15, 57, EAST));
        profile( "Shiráz",      dms2dd( 29, 36, 47, NORTH), dms2dd(  52, 32, 26, EAST));
        profile( "Trawler",     dms2dd( 55,  0,  0, SOUTH), dms2dd(  53, 30,  0, EAST));
        profile( "Rawalpindi",  dms2dd( 32, 56, 25, NORTH), dms2dd(  70, 18, 48, EAST));
        profile( "Hong Kong",   dms2dd( 21, 53, 30, NORTH), dms2dd( 113, 56, 21, EAST));
        profile( "Melbourne",   dms2dd( 37, 49,  8, SOUTH), dms2dd( 144, 59,  6, EAST));
        profile( "Auckland",    dms2dd( 36, 50, 59, SOUTH), dms2dd( 174, 45, 49, EAST));
        printf( "\n");

        write( 2, "\n\tincrement (+) decrement (-) exit (0) year (n) --> ", 52);
        (void) read( 0, &ch, 1); ch &= 0377;    /* mask out sign extension bits */
            if( ch == '-') badi_year -= 1;
        else if( ch == '+') badi_year += 1;
        else badi_year = 0;             /* actually, any char other than '+' or '-' */
        (void) read( 0, &ch, 1);        /* remove <return> byte from buffer */
    }
    close( fd);
}   /* main */
```

Bibliography

'Abdu'l-Bahá. *Abdul Baha on Divine Philosophy*. Comp. Isabel Fraser Chamberlain. Boston: The Tudor Press, 1916.
— *Faith for Every Man: Extracts for the Works of 'Abdu'l-Bahá*. London: Baha'í Publishing Trust, 1972.
— *Paris Talks*. London: Bahá'í Publishing Trust, 12th ed. 1995.
— *The Promulgation of Universal Peace*. Wilmette, IL: Bahá'í Publishing Trust, 2nd ed. 1982.
— *The Secret of Divine Civilization*. Trans. Marzieh Gail. Wilmette, IL: Bahá'í Publishing Trust, 1957.
— *Selections from the Writings of 'Abdu'l-Bahá*. Haifa: Bahá'í World Centre, 1978.
— *Some Answered Questions*. Wilmette, IL: Bahá'í Publishing Trust, 4th ed. 1981.
— *Tablets of Abdul-Baha Abbas*. Vols. I-III. New York: Bahá'í Publishing Society, 1909-1919.
— *The Will and Testament of 'Abdu'l-Bahá*. Manchester, Bahá'í Publishing Trust, 1950; Wilmette, IL: Bahá'í Publishing Trust, 1971.

Abu'l-Faḍl Gulpáygání, Mírzá. *The Bahá'í Proofs (Hujaja'l-Bahíyyih) and A Short Sketch of the History of the Lives of the Leaders of This Religion* (1914). Trans. Ali-Kuli Khan. Facsimile of the 1929 edition. Wilmette, IL: Bahá'í Publishing Trust, 1983.

Adam, Karl. *Urformen des Kalenders*. Modautal-Brandau: Hagenberg-Verlag, 1996.

Amanat, Abbas. *Resurrection and Renewal: The Making of the Bábí Movement in Iran, 1844–1850*. Ithaca, New York and London: Cornell University Press, 1989.

The Báb. *Selections from the Writings of the Báb*. Haifa: Bahá'í World Centre, 1976.

Bagherzadeh Rafsanjani, H. *Introduction to Khayam*. http://www.payvand.com/calendar/intro.html.

BAHÁ'Í-Information 7, Umwelt und Wertordnung. Autorenkollektiv N.N.. Hofheim-Langenhain: Bahá'í-Verlag, 2nd ed. 1978.

Bahá'í Prayers, London: Bahá'í Publishing Trust, 4th ed. 1975.

Bahá'í World, The. Vols III–XX: vol. III (1928–1930), New York: Bahá'í Publishing Committee, 1930; vol. VI (1934–1936), New York, Bahá'í Publishing Committee, 1937; vol. VIII (1938–1940), Wilmette, IL: Bahá'í Publishing Committee, 1942; vol. XIII (1954–1963), Haifa: The Universal House of Justice, 1970; vol. XIV (1963–1968), Haifa: The Universal House of Justice, 1974. Vol. XX (1987–1992), Haifa: Bahá'í World Centre, 2000.

The Bahá'í World: 1993–1994. Haifa: World Centre Publications 1994.

The Bahá'í World: 1994–1995. Haifa: World Centre Publications 1996.

The Bahá'í World: 1995–1996. Haifa: World Centre Publications 1997.

Bahá'í World Faith. Wilmette, IL: Bahá'í Publishing Trust, 2nd ed. 1976.

Bahá'u'lláh. *Epistle to the Son of the Wolf.* Wilmette, IL: Bahá'í Publishing Trust, 3rd ed. 1979.

— *Gleanings from the Writings of Bahá'u'lláh.* London: Bahá'í Publishing Trust, 2nd ed. 1978.

— *The Hidden Words of Bahá'u'lláh.* Bundoora: Century Press, 1994; Wilmette, IL: Bahá'í Publishing Trust, 1985.

— *Kitáb-i Aqdas* (Arabic/Persian). Haifa: Bahá'í World Centre, 1995.

— *Kitáb-i Aqdas: Das Heiligste Buch.* Hofheim-Langenhain: Bahá'í-Verlag, 2000.

— *The Kitáb-i-Aqdas: The Most Holy Book.* Haifa: Bahá'í World Centre, 1992.

—*Kitáb-i-Íqán: The Book of Certitude.* Wilmette, IL: Bahá'í Publishing Trust, 6th ed. 1974.

— *Prayers and Meditations by Bahá'u'lláh.* Wilmette: Bahá'í Publishing Trust, 1987.

— *The Seven Valleys and the Four Valleys.* Wilmette, IL: Bahá'í Publishing Trust, 3rd ed. 1975.

— *The Summons of the Lord of Hosts: Tablets of Bahá'u'lláh.* Haifa: Bahá'í World Centre, 2002.

— *Tablets of Bahá'u'lláh Revealed after the Kitáb-i-Aqdas.* Haifa: Bahá'í World Centre, 1978.

Balyuzi, H. M. *Bahá'u'lláh: The King of Glory.* Oxford: George Ronald, 2nd ed. 1991.

Bamji, Soli. *Zoroastrian Calendar.* http://132.246.176.35/bamji/cal.html.

BIBLIOGRAPHY

Bible: *The Holy Bible.* Authorized King James Version. Oxford: Oxford University Press, various dates.

Blaise, Clark. *Time Lord: Sir Sandford Fleming and the Creation of Standard Time.* New York: Vintage, 2002.

Boyce, Mary. *The Zoroastrians.* London: Routledge and Kegan Paul, 1979.

Brockhaus Enzyklopädie. Leipzig/Mannheim, 19th ed. 1996.

Brunner, Linus. *Die gemeinsamen Wurzeln des semitischen und indogermanischen Wortschatzes. Versuch einer Etymologie.* Bern/München: Francke Verlag, 1969.

Bürgel, Christoph. 'Die Bahá'í-Religion und der Friedensdanke', in Bürgel and Shayani, p. 20.

Bürgel, Christoph; Shayani, Isabel. *Iran im 19. Jahrhundert und die Entstehung der Bahá'í-Religion.* Hildesheim: Georg Olms Verlag, 1998.

Consultation: A Compilation. Comp. Research Department of the Universal House of Justice. Wilmette, IL: Bahá'í Publishing Trust, 1980.

Daniel, Glyn; Rehork, Joachim. *Enzyklopädie der Archäologie.* Augsburg: Weltbild Verlag, 1990.

Developing Distinctive Baha'i Communities: Guidelines for Spiritual Assemblies. National Spiritual Assembly of the Bahá'ís of the United States. Wilmette, IL: Bahá'í Publishing Trust, rev.ed. 1998.

Ekbal, Kamran. 'Der Messianismus des frühen 19. Jahrhunderts und die Entstehung der Bahá'í-Religion', in Bürgel and Shayani, pp. 159–86.

Eliade, Mircea. *Cosmos and History: The Myth of the Eternal Return.* Trans. Willard Trask. New York: Harper, 1954.

Encyclopaedia Britannica. London, Chicago: University of Chicago Press 1997.

Encyclopaedia Judaica. Jerusalem: Keter Publishing House 1971.

Eschragi, Armin. 'Undermining the Foundations of Orthodoxy: Some Notes on the Báb's Sharí'a (Sacred Law)', in Lawson and Gaemmaghami.

Esslemont, J. E. *Bahá'u'lláh and the New Era.* Wilmette, IL: Bahá'í Publishing Trust, 4th ed. 1980.

Fazel, S.; Fananapazir, K. 'A Bahá'í Approach to the Claim of Finality in Islam', in *Journal of Bahá'í Studies*, vol.5, no.3 (1993).

Ferraby, John. *All Things Made New: A Comprehensive Outline of the Bahá'í Faith.* London: Bahá'í Publishing Trust, 2nd ed. 1975.

Furútan, 'Alí-Akbar. *Stories of Bahá'u'lláh*. Oxford: George Ronald, 1997.

Gesellschaft für Bahá'í-Studien. *Aspekte des Kitáb-i Aqdas*. Hofheim-Langenhain: Bahá'í-Verlag 1995.

Grossmann, Hermann. *Das Bündnis Gottes in der Offenbarungsreligion*. Hofheim-Langenhain: Bahá'í-Verlag, 1981.

von Grunebaum, C. E. *Muhammadan Festivals*. London: Curzon Press, 1976.

Hamid, Idris Samawi. *The Metaphysics and Cosmology of Process according to Shaykh 'Aḥmad al-'Ahsá'í: Critical Edition, Translation, and Analysis of Observations in Wisdom*. Ph.D. Dissertation, State University of New York at Buffalo, 1998.

Hatcher, John S.; Hatcher, William S. *The Law of Love Enshrined*. Oxford: George Ronald, 1996.

Hatcher, William S. 'The Kitáb-i Aqdas: The Causality Principle in the World of Being', in Hatcher and Hatcher, pp. 149–150; also in *The Bahá'í World 1993–1994*, p. 228.

Hermann, Joachim. *Wörterbuch zur Astronomie*. München: DTV-Verlag, 1996.

Isḥráq-Khavárí, Abu'l-Hamid (ed.). *Ganjineh-ye Hudud va Ahkam* (Treasury of Laws and Ordinances).

Keil, Gerald. *Die Zeit im Bahá'í-Zeitalter: eine Studie über den Badí'-Kalender*. Schriftreihe der Gesellschaft für Bahá'í-Studien. Hofheim-Langenhain: Bahá'í-Verlag, 2005.

Keil, Gerald. 'Text Context and Literary Criticism: a Case Study based on a Letter from Shoghi Effendi', in *Lights of 'Irfán*, vol. 11, Evanston: Bahá'í National Center, 2010 , pp. 55–98.

Khoury, A.-Th.. *Einführung in die Grundlagen des Islams*. Graz: Styria Verlag, 1978.

Kirste, Reinhard; Schultze, Herbert; Tworuschka, Udo. *Die Feste der Religionen*. Gütersloh: Gütersloher Verlagshaus, 1995.

Der Koran. Trans.Max Henning (German). Stuttgart: Reclam, 1984.

Koran: Der Heilige Qur-án. Rabwah, Pakistan: Ahmadiyya Muslim Jamaat, 1996.

The Koran Interpreted. Trans. A.J.Arberry. London: George Allen and Unwin, 1980.

Kreiser, K.; Wielandt, R. *Lexikon der Islamischen Welt*. Stuttgart: Kohlhammer Verlag, 1992.

Lambden, Stephen. 'The Background and Centrality of Apophatic Theology in Bábí and Bahá'í Scripture', in McLean, J. (ed.), pp. 57–58.
— 'Prophecy in the Johannine Farewell Discourse: The Advents of the Paraclete, Aḥmad and the Comforter', in Momen, M (ed.), *Scripture and Revelation*, p. 77.
— 'The Word *Bahá*': Quintessence of the Greatest Name', in *Bahá'í Studies Review*, vol 3, no.1. London: Association for Bahá'í Studies for English-Speaking Europe, 1993.

Lawson, Todd. 'Seeing Double: The Covenant and the Tablet of Ahmad', in Momen, M. (ed.), *The Bahá'í Faith and the World's Religions*, pp. 39–88.
— 'The Role of Wonder in Creating Identity', in *Religions*, vol. 14, no. 6 (2023), 762, https://www.mdpi.com/2077-1444/14/6/762.

Lawson, Todd; Ghaemmaghami, Omid (eds). *A Most Noble Pattern: Collected Essays on the Writings of the Báb*. Oxford: George Ronald, 2012.

Lights of Guidance: A Bahá'í Reference File. Comp. Helen Hornby. New Delhi: Bahá'í Publishing Trust, 3rd ed. 1994.

Löwith, Karl. *Meaning in History: The Theological Implications of the Philosophy of History*. Chicago: University of Chicago Press, 1949.

MacEoin, Denis. 'Hierarchy, Authority, and Eschatology', in Smith, Peter (ed.), *In Írán*.

Martin, Hans-Peter; Schumann, Harald. *Die Globalisierungsfalle: Der Angriff auf Demokratie und Wohlstand*. Reinbeck: Rowohlt Verlag, 1996.

Mattig, Wolfgang. *Die Sonne*. München: Beck, 1995.

McGlinn, Sen. 'Changes in the Bahá'í Calendar: What, how and especially, why?'. https://senmcglinn.wordpress.com/2014/09/22/changes-in-bahai-calendar-what-how-why/
— 'It's Friday: thank God'. https://senmcglinn.wordpress.com/2009/04/11/its-friday-thank-god/

McLean, J. (ed.). *Revisioning the Sacred: New Perspectives on a Bahá'í Theology*. Studies in the Bábí and Bahá'í Religions, vol. 8. Los Angeles: Kalimát Press, 1997.

Mihrshahi, Robin. *Our Days Are Numbered*. Bundoora: Bahá'í Publications Australia, 1996.
— 'Symbolism in the Badí` Calendar', in *Bahá'í Studies Review*, vol. 12, pp. 15-31. London: Association for Bahá'í Studies for English-Speaking Europe, 1994. (Chapters 1-5.1 of *Our Days are Numbered*).

Momen, Moojan. 'The Bahá'í Community in Iran during the 19th Century', in Bürgel and Shayani.

— (ed.). *The Bahá'í Faith and the World's Religions.* Oxford: George Ronald, 1993.

— *Islam and the Bahá'í Faith.* Oxford: George Ronald, 2000.

— (ed.). *Scripture and Revelation.* Bahá'í Studies, vol.3. Oxford: George Ronald, 1997.

— (ed.). *Selections from the Writings of E. G. Browne on the Bábí and Bahá'í Religions.* Oxford: George Ronald, 1987.

Momen, Wendi (ed.). *A Basic Bahá'í Dictionary.* Oxford: George Ronald, 1996.

Nabíl-i-A'ẓam (Muḥammad-i-Zarandí). *The Dawn-Breakers: Nabíl's Narrative of the Early Days of the Bahá'í Revelation.* Trans. and edited by Shoghi Effendi. Wilmette, IL: Bahá'í Publishing Trust, 2nd ed. 1996.

Panáhí, Badí'u'lláh. 'Der Kitáb-i Aqdas und die Bahá'í-Religion', in Gesellschaft für Bahá'í-Studien, *Aspekte des Kitáb-i Aqdas.*

Piff, David M. *Bahá'í Lore.* Oxford: George Ronald, 2000.

Principles of Bahá'í Administration. London: Bahá'í Publishing Trust, 4th edn 1976

The Prosperity of Humankind. A statement prepared by the Office of Public Information, Bahá'í World Centre. Haifa: Bahá'í World Centre, 1995.

Pschyrembel. *Klinisches Wörterbuch.* http://www.jiftc.de/ganz2/rhythmen; http://abt4pc.bio.virginia.edu/tutorial/HUMANCLOCK.html;).

Rabbani, Rúḥíyyih. *The Priceless Pearl.* London: Bahá'í Publishing Trust, 1969.

Rudgley, Richard. *Lost Civilizations of the Stone Age.* London: Century, 1998.

Saiedi, Nader. *Logos and Civilization.* Bethesda: University of Maryland Press, 2000.

Savi, Julio. *Towards the Summit of Reality: An Introduction to the Study of Bahá'u'lláh's Seven Valley and Four Valleys.* Oxford: George Ronald, 2008.

Schaefer, Udo. *Bahá'í Ethics in Light of Scripture.* Vol. 1: *Doctrinal Fundamentals.* Oxford: George Ronald, 2007. Vol. 2.....
— *Heilsgeschichte und Paradigmenwechsel.* Prague: Zero Palm Press, 1992.
— *The Imperishable Dominion.* Oxford: George Ronald, 2nd ed. 1983.
— *In a Blue Haze: Smoking and Bahá'í Ethics.* Hofheim-Langenhain: Bahá'í-Verlag, 1996.

Schaefer, U.; Towfigh, N.; Gollmer, U. *Making the Crooked Straight: A Contribution to Bahá'í Apologetics.* Oxford: George Ronald, 2000.

BIBLIOGRAPHY

Science and Engineering Research Council. *The Astronomical Almanac for the Year 1995.* London: HMSO, 1994.

Sears, William. *Thief in the Night: The Case of the Missing Millenium.* Oxford: George Ronald 1992 (18th reprint).

Seidelmann, P. Kenneth (ed.). *Explanatory Supplement to the Astronomical Almanac.* Mill Valley: University Science Books, 1992.

Shoghi Effendi. *The Advent of Divine Justice.* Wilmette, IL: Bahá'í Publishing Trust, rev ed. 1984.

— *The Bahá'í Faith – The World Religion: A Summary of Its Aims, Teachings and History. US Bahá'í News,* no. 85 (July 1934). Available in Ocean Research Library.

— *Bahá'í Procedure.* Comp. National Spiritual Assembly of the Bahá'ís of the United States and Canada. Wilmette, IL: Bahá'í Publishing Committee, 2nd ed. 1942.

— *Directives from the Guardian.* Comp. G. Garrida. New Delhi: Bahá'í Publishing Trust for the National Spiritual Assembly of the Bahá'ís of the Hawaiian Islands, 1973.

— *God Passes By.* Wilmette, IL: Bahá'í Publishing Trust, 3rd ed. 1974.

— *The Light of Divine Guidance.* 2 vols. Hofheim-Langenhain: Bahá'í-Verlag, 1985.

— *The Promised Day is Come.* Wilmette, IL: Bahá'í Publishing Trust, rev. ed. 1980.

— *The World Order of Bahá'u'lláh: Selected Letters.* Wilmette, IL: Bahá'í Publishing Trust, 2nd rev.ed. 1980.

Simpson, D. P. *Cassell's New Latin Dictionary.* New York: Funk and Wagnalls, 1959.

Smith, Peter. *The Babi and Baha'i Religions: From Messianic Shi'ism to a World Religion.* Cambridge: Cambridge University Press, 1987.

— (ed.). *In Írán.* Studies in Bábí and Bahá'í History, vol. 3. Los Angeles: Kalimát Press, 1986.

Star of the West, vol. 4, no. 7 (13 July 1913); vol. 5, no. 1 (21 March 1914). Chicago: Bahá'í News Service. RP George Ronald, 1978.

Stegemann, Hartmut. *Die Essener, Qumran, Johannes der Täufer und Jesus.* Freiburg im Breisgau: Herder, 1998.

Stemberger, Günter. *Jüdische Religion.* München: Beck, 1996.

Stockman, Robert. *The Bahá'í Faith in America,* vol. 2. Oxford: George Ronald, 1995.

Sturm-Berger, M. *Sonne, Spiegel, Lebensbaum: Beiträge zur Religionsforschung.* Berlin-Tempelhof, 1999.

Taherzadeh, Adib. *The Covenant of Bahá'u'lláh.* Oxford: George Ronald, 1992.

— *The Revelation of Bahá'u'lláh* (4 volumes). Oxford: George Ronald, 1974–1987.

Taqizadeh, Siyyid Hasan. *Old Iranian Calendars.* http://www.avesta.org/taqizad.htm.

Topper, Uwe. *Erfundene Geschichte.* München: Herbig Verlag, 3rd ed. 1999.

Towfigh, Nicola. *Schöpfung und Offenbarung aus der Sicht der Bahá'í-Religion.* Hildesheim: Georg Olms Verlag, 1989.

The Universal House of Justice. *The Compilation of Compilations: Prepared by the Universal House of Justice 1963-1990.* Maryborough: Bahá'í Publications Australia, 1991.

— *Messages from the Universal House of Justice 1963-1986: The Third Epoch of the Formative Age.* Comp. Geoffry W. Marks. Wilmette, IL.: Bahá'í Publishing Trust, 1996

— *The Promise of World Peace.* Haifa: Bahá'í World Centre, 1985.

— *A Synopsis and Codification of the Kitáb-i Aqdas, the Most Holy Book of Bahá'u'lláh.* Haifa: Bahá'í World Centre, 1973.

Varqá, 'Alí-Muḥammad. 'Huququ'lláh, the socio-economic and spiritual law of the Book of Aqdas', Address in June 1997 at various gatherings in the United States.

Walbridge, John. *Sacred Acts, Sacred Space, Sacred Time.* Oxford: George Ronald, 1996.

Wehr, Hans. *Arabisches Wörterbuch für die Schriftsprache der Gegenwart.* Leipzig: VEB Otto Harrassowitz, 2nd ed. 1956.

Westrheim, Margo. *Calendars of the World.* Oxford: Oneworld Publications, 1994.

Wishnitzer, Avner. 'Our Time: On the Durability of the Alaturka Hour System in the Late Ottoman Empire', Journal of Turkish Studies, vol. 16 (2010), nos. 1–2, pp. 47–69. https://www.researchgate.net/publication/328554827_Our_Time_On_the_Durability_of_the_Alaturka_Hour_System_in_the_Late_Ottoman_Empire.

Wübbenhorst. *5000 Jahre Gießen von Metallen.* Düsseldorf: Giesserei-Verlag, 1984.

Notes and References

Foreword to the 2008 Edition

1. Hugo v. Hoffmannsthal, libretto of the opera *Der Rosenkavalier*, Act 1, Marschallin.
2. Goethe, *Faust*, Part 2, Act 5.
3. Löwith, Meaning in History, provides an excellent overview of historical-philosophical models.
4. The striking parallelism between the Jewish-Christian belief in salvation and political messianism has been discussed in Schaefer, *The Imperishable Dominion*, pp. 12f. The whole process of history as outlined in the *Communist Manifesto* corresponds to the general scheme of the Jewish-Christian interpretation of history as a providential advance toward a final goal. The communist philosophy of history has been called 'a pseudo-morphosis of Jewish-Christian messianism' (Löwith, Meaning in History, pp. 44ff.).
5. According to the Qur'án and the Bahá'í teachings, Adam was a prophet.
6. 33:40.
7. Qur'án 78:17.
8. See Bahá'u'lláh, Kitáb-i Íqán, paras. 121–128, 153, 182 for an allegorical interpretation of this term.
9. Wáhid 5, Chapter 3.
10. paras. 16, 127.
11. Bahá'u'lláh, *Gleanings* 4:2; see also 143:3.
12. Mark 8:30; 9:9; see also Matt. 16:20; 17:9; Luke 9:21. On the theme of 'messianic secret' see also Gollmer, in Schaefer et al., *Making the Crooked Straight*, pp. 571ff.
13. The self-description of the Báb as *dhikr* und *nuqa* in his Qayyúmu'l-Asma' already prove this assertion (cf. Amanat, Resurrection and Renewal, pp. 201ff.; Gollmer, in Schaefer et al., *Making the Crooked Straight*, p. 588, note 61). See also 'Unity in diversity: The number nineteen' in Chapter 5 of the present study.
14. In place of the phrase 'In the name of God, the Merciful, the Compassionate', which introduces every Súrah in the Qur'án except the 9th, the

Bayán opens with 'In the name of God, the Most Inaccessible, the Most Holy' (see also Persian Bayán 3:6 and 'A brief history' in Chapter 4 of the present study).

15 The logic of the Roman sentence '*Lex posterior derogate legi priori*' (A later law cancels an earlier: Dig. 1,4,4 (Modestin)) holds for salvation history as well.

16 The reader is referred to Dr Armin Eschraghi's illuminating article, 'Undermining the Foundations of Orthodoxy. Some Notes on the Báb's Sharí'a (Sacred law)', forthcoming.

17 Armin Eschraghi offers many details in his informative paper.

18 Shoghi Effendi, quoted from Bahá'u'lláh, Kitáb-i Aqdas, note 109.

19 Shoghi Effendi, *God Passes By*, p. 25.

20 Schaefer et al., *Making the Crooked Straight*, pp. 180f.

21 As if by inspiration, animated by the Holy Spirit.

22 The Universal House of Justice, letter dated 22 August 1977, available in Ocean Research Library.

23 Shoghi Effendi, *The Bahá'í Faith – The World Religion: A Summary of Its Aims, Teachings and History*; also printed in US *Bahá'í News*, No. 85 (July 1934), p. 1. Available in Ocean Research Library.

24 'Abdu'l-Bahá, talk given 16 August 1912, in *Promulgation*, p. 253.

25 Shoghi Effendi, 'The Dispensation of Bahá'u'lláh', in *World Order of Bahá'u'lláh*, p. 100.

26 Bahá'u'lláh, *Gleanings* 95:1.

27 Cf. Bahá'u'lláh, *Hidden Words*, Arabic 2; Tablets 17:24; *Gleanings* 75:1; Kitáb-i Íqán 176. On the whole subject of the independent search for truth see Schaefer, *Bahá'í Ethics*, vol. 1, pp. 50ff., 68ff., 301ff.; 341ff; vol. 2, § 43, section 4.

28 Bahá'u'lláh, *Tablets* 10:23, p. 157.

29 ibid.

30 ibid. 4:36, p. 43.

31 Bahá'u'lláh, *Gleanings* 75:1.

32 'Abdu'l-Bahá, talk given 10 October 1912, in *Promulgation*, p. 355.

33 *Principles of Bahá'í Administration*, pp. 24f.

1 The Prehistoric Concept of Time

1 See Pschyrembel, *Klinisches Wörterbuch*.

2 Eliade, *Cosmos and History*, p. 4.

3 Rudgley, *Lost Civilizations*, Chapter VI 'Paläowissenschaft', especially pp. 158–64.

NOTES AND REFERENCES

4 Eliade, *Cosmos and History*, pp. 86, 88.
5 Old Norse *hundrað* designated the 'long hundred' of six score. In pre-conquest England, assessment of land tax was based everywhere on multiples of one hundred hides (or sulungs or ploughlands), representing six score in the Danelaw and five score elsewhere. The existence of the word *femsynnontywffwe* ('five times twenty') in Old Danish suggests that the earlier denotation of the Modern Danish word *hundrede* extended at least into the 12th century ce, in all probability obtaining its modern meaning through the influence of the (Low German speaking) Hansa, which from the middle of that century dominated trade and commerce in the North Sea and Baltic area. The long hundred continued in use in Great Britain and colonies well into the 18th century ce as a unit of measure for certain commodities.
6 In the present study 'solar year' means either *synodic year* or *tropical year*, i.e. either the time the earth takes to complete exactly one orbit around the sun or the period of time between two successive vernal equinoxes, depending on the context.
7 Adam, *Urformen des Kalenders*, pp. 14–16.
8 Brunner, *Die gemeinsamen Wurzeln*, Chapter 1, no. 7, p. 19, keyword 'med'.
9 In Geneva, there is a special chestnut tree whose flowering marks the beginning of spring, and there is a local official who verifies it: see http://en.wikipedia.org/wiki/Geneva, 'Traditions and Customs'. I am indebted to May Hofman for bringing this item to my attention.
10 But note that the obliquity of the ecliptic is variable, whereby the distance between the outer markings varies by about 22.56% over a period of 40,000 years or about 0.009% over the nutation period of 18.61 tropical years. In addition, the orientation of the earth's pole (and therefore the apparent path of the sun) is not constant; it wanders around a middle value in a period of 428 days on the average (the so-called *Chandler period*). However, this amounts only to circa 30m (0.1 arc seconds) and is therefore detectable only with refined techniques of measurement.
11 More precisely, 0.8% or 2°52'48". Due to precession this discrepancy will be even smaller in the year 2100: 0.5% or 1°48'. Five thousand years ago the North Star was Thuban, the principal star of Draconis.
12 Strictly speaking, a star is only then circumpolar for a given spot on earth when at its lowest culmination it is still above the horizon relative to that spot.
13 Examining a star map on which the individual constellations are not highlighted with, say, image outlines or lines connecting the constituent fixed dtars, a non-specialist would be hard put to identify the individual constellations and their boundaries. The division is in itself aritrary, and one might marel over the degree of similarity between the constellation schemes of the different cultures of the world, especially with respect to the stars of the zodiac (albeit with varying nomenclature). That this agreement is not

dictated by the positions of the individual stars themselves is demonstrated by the fact that division into twelfths is by no means universal.

14 The Metonic Cycle of 19 years or (almost exactly) 235 synodic months is the only example of a fit which is anywhere near ideal. It is significant that this cycle played an important role in the historical development of the calendar, even though it is of limited practical value for the affairs of daily life.

15 The earliest bronze castings (in the Near and Middle East and in India) have been dated to roughly 3000 bce (Wubbenhorst, *5000 Jahre*, p. 3). The development of metal casting is taken to be the real beginning of the age of metal, though it is known that wrought metallic objects have existed at least since about 9500 bce (Daniel, *Enzyklopädie der Archäologie*, p. 323, Keyword 'Metallgewinnung und -verarbeitung').

16 Rudgley, *Lost Civilizations*, p. 50.

17 See also Sears, *Thief in the Night*, pp. 14–16.

18 Num.14:34.

19 Ezek.4:4-6.

2 The Calendar in History

1 Kirste et al., *Feste der Religionen*, pp. 81–2.

2 Sturm-Berger, *Sonne, Spiegel, Lebensbaum*, pp. 11ff. (from a copy kindly made available to me by the author).

3 Eliade, M., *Cosmos and History*, p. 125.

4 Boyce, *Zoroastrians*, pp. 32–4.

5 ibid. p. 73.

6 Bürgel, J.C., 'Die Bahá'í-Religion', p. 20.

7 Bamji, *Zoroastrian Calendar.*

8 Boyce, *Zoroastrians*, pp. 104–6.

9 ibid. pp. 128–9.

10 ibid. pp. 159–60.

11 Bamji, *Zoroastrian Calendar.*

12 Boyce, *Zoroastrians*, pp. 189–90.

13 ibid. pp. 212–13.

14 Bamji, *Zoroastrian Calendar.*

15 See Boyce, *Zoroastrians*, p. 212; Taherzadeh, *Revelation of Bahá'u'lláh*, vol. 3, pp. 268–73; Shoghi Effendi, *God Passes By*, pp. 195, 302–3; Momen, 'The Bahá'í Community in Iran during the 19th Century' in Burgel and Shayani, *Iran im 19. Jahrhundert*, pp. 44–5; Ekbal, 'Der Messianismus des frühen 19. Jahrhunderts und die Entstehung der Bahá'í-Religion', ibid. pp. 184–5; Smith, *Babi and Baha'i Religions*, pp. 93–7.

16 See Taqizadeh, *Old Iranian Calendars* for further details, including hypotheses which deviate in part significantly from the present version.
17 Bagherzadeh, *Introduction to Khayam*.
18 Hermann, *Wörterbuch zur Astronomie*, keyword 'Kalender'.
19 ibid., keyword 'Metonischer Zyklus'.
20 *Encyclopaedia Britannica*, keyword 'calendar'.
21 Simpson, *New Latin Dictionary*, p. iv.
22 Luke 2:1.
23 Topper, *Erfundene Geschichte*, pp. 19ff.
24 *Brockhaus Enzyklopädie*, keyword 'Kalender'.
25 Kirste et al., *Feste der Religionen*, p. 34.
26 Mattig, *Sonne*, pp. 19–20.
27 See Topper, *Erfundene Geschichte*.
28 See Ps. 104:19.
29 Lunar calendars of the more northern regions are typically oriented around the full moon, since in summer and autumn the new moon crescent is not visible during the first several days of its existence (in the extreme polar regions the crescent remains completely hidden from view for a considerable part of the year). In temperate and tropical regions the crescent is visible during all seasons on the western horizon for a short while following sunset. This condition is one of the explanations for the fact that lunar calendars of more southerly climes prefer to conceive of the day as beginning at sunset.

It is interesting to note that the lunation has never been reckoned starting with the half moon, although this practice would have definite practical advantages: on account of the perfectly straight line dividing light from shadow, the moment of occurrence is discernible with a precision exact almost to the hour; and the half moon is always visible at convenient times of day (descending half moon in the morning, ascending half moon in the afternoon). The fact that preference has instead always been given to either the full or the new moon – the first being at best approximately determinable, the second being only indirectly perceivable – indicates the symbolic importance which has always been associated with these two 'perfected' moon conditions. Moreover, the half moon stands at right angles to the sun – a state ('the quadrature') which astrologers have always considered 'disharmonic'.
30 Adam, *Urformen des Kalenders*, p. 9.
31 Exod. 20:8-11 (see also Gen. 2:3, Exod. 16:23-30, Exod. 31:12-17, Lev. 23:3, Deut. 5:12-15).
32 Qur'án 41:13, 65:13.
33 Qur'án 25:60. Actually, in six ages; after that, God ascended the throne. The number seven first becomes clear through comparison with Gen. 2:3. Note

that Shaykh Aḥmad al-Ahsá'í (founder of the Shaykhí School, which exerted considerable influence on the development of the Bábí movement in general and on the Báb in particular) interprets the word *ayyám* here as 'modalities' of creation, i.e. the subsistence factors (*muqawwimát*) of essence: quantity, quality, durational mode, space, orientation and rank (Hamid, *Metaphysics*, p. 248).

34 Gen. 41:1-4.
35 Job 5:19.
36 Isa. 30:26.
37 Kirste et al., *Feste der Religionen*, p. 13.
38 *Encyclopaedia Judaica*, keyword 'calendar'.
39 The attribution of the discovery of the Metonic Cycle (also called lunar cycle) to the Greek Meton in 432 bce is not undisputed. The names of the Jewish months are derived from those of the Babylonian calendar (there: *Nisanu, Ayaru, Simanu, Du'uzu, Abu, Ululu, Tashritu, Arakh-Samma, Kislimu, Tebetu, Shabatu, Adaru*). It is easy to suppose that the Jewish calendar, along with its lunisolar cycle, evolved in connection with the Babylonian Exile in 587 bce – a good 50 years before Meton's discovery – if not indeed earlier: after all, Israel was part of the Babylonian and later the Persian empire.
40 Kirste et al., *Feste der Religionen*, p. 13.
41 Stemberger, *Jüdische Religion*, p. 78.
42 ibid. p. 79.
43 Lev. 23:5.
44 Zach. 1:7.
45 Exod. 23:16.
46 Eliade, *Cosmos and History*, p. 55.
47 Stemberger, *Jüdische Religion*, p. 80.
48 ibid. p. 17.
49 Lev. 25:2-4.
50 – that is, the forty-ninth; in classical antiquity, ordinal numbers were often interpreted inclusively (cf. German. '*heute in acht/fünfzehn Tagen*', seven/fourteen [German: eight/fifteen] days from today). Modern Judaism has settled for an exclusive interpretation.
51 Lev. 25:8-13.
52 Gen. 1:3-5.
53 Lev. 23:32.
54 Stegemann, *Essener*, pp. 231–41.
55 ibid. p. 211.
56 *dhú* + *al* = *dhu'l* (written long, pronounced short).

57 Kreiser and Wieland (eds), *Lexikon der Islamischen Welt*, keyword 'Monat'.
58 Khoury, *Einführung in die Grundlagen des Islams*, pp. 22–3.
59 'The Pilgrimage is in months well-known; . . .' (Qur'án 2:198).
60 Qur'án 9:36. References to the holy months are found in Qur'án 2:218, 9:1-3, 9:37.
61 Kirste et al., *Feste der Religionen*, p. 63.
62 Qur'án 10:5.
63 Kreiser and Wielandt (eds), *Lexikon der Islamischen Welt*, keyword 'Kalendersysteme'.

3 The Time of Day

1 Westrheim, *Calendars of the World*, p. 12.
2 Sources tend to be vague about this point. Those that mention night-hours at all either omit any comparison with day-hours or assume – anachronistically – that there had always been twelve night-hours. In fact, prior to the introduction of the mechanical clock the only universally available way of keeping track of the passage of time at night was to monitor the progression of the celestial sphere.
3 Wishnitzer, 'Our Time: On the Durability of the Alaturka Hour System in the Late Ottoman Empire', p. 48.
4 ibid. p. 51.
5 ibid. p. 58.
6 https://en.wikipedia.org/wiki/Muwaqqit.
7 https://de.wikipedia.org/wiki/Alaturka-Uhrzeit.
8 https://www.chabad.org/calendar/zmanim_cdo/jewish/Halachic-Times.htm.

4 An Overview

1 The Arabic equivalent of 'Badí' calendar' is *al-yawmiyyatu'l-badí'at*, the Persian *taqvím-e badí'*; those who have not mastered the articulation of the Arabic *'ayn* can replace it with a glottal stop (as Persians do) or simply drop it altogether (i.e. /bæ'diyʔ/ or /bæ'diy/). With respect to the terms 'Badí' calendar' and 'Bahá'í calendar', there currently exists a relative freedom of usage. In a contrastive context the semantic differentiation is clear: the former refers to the calendar as revealed in the writings of the Báb and as employed, with variations, by the Bábís themselves and later by the Azalís, whereas the latter includes the clarifications and extensions introduced by Bahá'u'lláh. In addition, 'Badí' calendar' is a hyponym (roughly 'Bábí-Bahá'í calendar') and is used in the present study mainly in this sense. The term 'Bahá'í calendar' seems to be a popular description which is also more suitable when addressing a non-Bahá'í audience.

2 The Báb, *Selections*, p. 41.
3 Lambden, available at http://www.hurqalya.pwp.blueyonder.co.uk/03-THE%20BAB/QAYYUM%20AL-ASMA'/Q-ASMA. 001.htm.
4 For a detailed disquisition on the use of the term *badí'* in the writings of the Báb see Lawson, 'The Role of Wonder in Creating Identity'
5 Also referred to by Bahá'u'lláh as *al-ayyámu'z-zá'idat* (*'an ash-shuhúr*), 'the excess days [days in excess of the months]' (see Kitáb-i Aqdas, para. 16, which adds: 'We have ordained that these . . . be the manifestations of the letter Há'.').
6 Momen (ed.), *Selections from the Writings of E. G. Browne*, 'A Summary of the Persian Bayan', Wáḥid V, Chapter 3.
7 ibid. Wáḥid VIII, Chapter 18.
8 See Wáḥid IX, Chapter 10.
9 Quoted in *Bahá'í World*, vol. XIII; see also *Directives from the Guardian*, no. 75, p. 30.
10 'Abdu'l-Bahá was the son of Bahá'u'lláh and head of the Faith following the Ascension of His father on 28 May 1892.
11 Letter of 5 July 1950 on behalf of Shoghi Effendi to the National Spiritual Assembly of the United States, in *Lights of Guidance*, no. 1026, pp. 301–2; *Directives from the Guardian*, no. 75, p. 46. Shoghi Effendi was the great-grandson of Bahá'u'lláh and Guardian of the Faith of God following the Ascension of his grandfather, 'Abdu'l-Bahá, from 21 November 1921 until his own death in November 1957.
12 'The first number of every volume of the Star of the West from 1910 to 1922 is dated 1 Baha and March 21st. From 1923 the Star of the West switched to appearing 12 times per year rather than 19, but a number of articles in the Star of the West in 1925 and 1928 show that Naw Ruz continued to be celebrated on March 21' (McGlinn, 'Changes in the Bahá'í Calendar: What, how and especially, why?')
13 Esslemont, *Bahá'u'lláh and the New Era*, p. 178.
14 Quoted in Towfigh, *Schöpfung und Offenbarung*, pp. 161–2.
15 Nabíl, *The Dawn-Breakers*, p. 12.
16 'Abdu'l-Bahá, in *Bahá'í World Faith*, p. 358, quoted by Lawson, 'Seeing Double', in Momen, M. (ed.), *The Bahá'í Faith and the World's Religions*.
17 The garden of Najíb Páshá, called Najíbiyyih, renamed by Bahá'u'lláh the Garden of Riḍván (Arab. *riḍwán*, from *raḍiya*, 'to be content/pleased'; literally 'Garden of [God's] good pleasure').
18 Some individual believers had already inwardly recognized Bahá'u'lláh's station before this announcement, or at least suspected it, in some cases very early during the Bábí Dispensation (in particular Majdhúb [lit. 'the obsessed one', a typical epithet for a dervish]: see Nabil, *The Dawn-Breakers*, Part II,

p. 118), along with Ṭáhirih and Shaykh Ḥasan-i Zunúzí, in the latter case in fulfilment of a promise from the Báb (Taherzadeh, *Revelation of Bahá'u'lláh*, vol. 1, p. 207). 'Abdu'l-Bahá had recognized the station of His father since the time of His imprisonment in the Síyáh-Chál, others during the banishment in Baghdad, not least through the Writings He completed at this time: Kitáb-i Íqán, Seven Valleys, Gems of Divine Mysteries and Hidden Words. The general announcement of His Dispensation occurred little by little from his later posts of exile, Istanbul and Edirne, in full publicity at the latest in 1867 by virtue of his Tablets to the kings and rulers of the world. For further details see Schaefer et al., *Making the Crooked Straight*, p. 371, note 285.

19 'Abdu'l-Bahá, in *Bahá'í World Faith*, p. 359, quoted by Lawson, 'Seeing Double', op.cit.

20 In a letter dated 5 October 2018 to the present writer, the Secretariat of the Bahá'í World Centre explained that this date is based on a statement from 'Abdu'l-Bahá in one of His Tablets (source not disclosed), in which he refers to the date of the Ascension of Bahá'u'lláh as 'the seventieth day of Naw-Rúz,' i.e. the seventieth day of the year.

21 Stockman, *The Bahá'í Faith in America*, vol. 2, p. 56.

22 Kitáb-i Aqdas, Questions and Answers 2.

23 Quoted in the memorandum of 10 July 2014 from the Universal House of Justice to the Bahá'ís of the World (source not given).

24 This calculation bears some resemblance to the calculation of Easter in Western Christianity (the first Sunday after the first full moon after 21 March, i.e. the first day of spring). In other words, the timing of Easter encapsulates elements from all three Semitic time cycles: the solar year, the lunar year and the week.

25 Technically, this is not an epact (see 'The Jewish calendar' and 'The Islamic calendar' in Chapter 2), since the Badí' ruling invokes the age of the moon after (completion of) the day of Naw-Rúz, i.e. up to one complete day following the vernal equinox.

26 Letter of 5 October 2018 to the present writer from the Secretariat of the Bahá'í World Centre, written on behalf of the Universal House of Justice.

5 Symbolic Implications

1 The Báb, *Selections* 4:10:6, p. 126 (from the Dalá'il-i Sab'ih, 'The Seven Proofs').

2 Bahá'u'lláh, *Gleanings* 22:3, p. 52.

3 ibid. 24:1, pp. 59–60.

4 ibid. 34:3, pp. 78–9.

5 ibid. 34:6, p. 80.

6 ibid. 38:1, p. 87.

7 Qur'án 33:41: _khátamu'n-nabiyyín_. The Qur'ánic context of this expression invites a wide variety of interpretations. Bahá'u'lláh explains that expressions such as 'first' and 'last', 'beginning' and 'seal' refer to divine attributes which in light of the essential unity (*jawhar-e tafríd*) of the Messengers of God are equally applicable to all the Manifestations (Kitáb-i Íqán 171–4, 182, 196). On another level of interpretation is His explanation that Muḥammad is the final prophet of the Age of Prophecy, which came to an end with the Advent of the Báb (*Gleanings* 25, p. 60). A complementary but purely personal understanding of my own is derived from the fact that the word _khátam_ actually means 'signet ring' or 'seal' (i.e. a device) rather than '(wax) seal' or 'impression' (= _khatm_). According to this understanding, Muḥammad, in his capacity as seal *ring* of the prophets, guaranteed the continued validity of the former divine Messengers (see Qur'án 3:4) and at the same time the conservation both of their missions and that of his own ('. . . he [Muḥammad] brought the truth, and confirmed the Envoys [*al-mursalín*]' – Qur'án 37:36) until the appearance of the next prophet (which he himself predicted: see Qur'án 10:48; 16:90; 43:64; 99:2-6). The actual function of the signet ring is only then fulfilled when the (wax) seal has subsequently been legally removed, whereby the signet ring itself is by no means destroyed (cf. Bahá'u'lláh, Kitáb-i Aqdas K5: '. . . We have unsealed the choice Wine . . . [*fataḥná khatma'r-raḥíqi'l-khutúm*]'; Súratu'l-Haykal 249: '. . . For the present, however, since the season is not ripe, the tongue of My utterance hath been stilled and the wine of exposition sealed up until such time as God, through the power of His might, shall please to unseal it' (*Summons of the Lord of Hosts*, p. 126); the Báb, Bayán, Wáḥid II, Chapter 19: 'The Writings of the Manifestation of the Truth in each Theophany are a gift from God to Him in His next Manifestation.' In para. 118 of the Kitáb-i Íqán, which begins 'We seal our theme with that which was formerly revealed unto Muḥammad that the seal thereof may shed the fragrance of that holy musk . . .', the root kh-t-m occurs twice: once in *akhtimu*, 'we conclude' (lit. 'secure with a seal'), and again in _khitámuhu_ (literally 'the sealing-wax thereof': the metaphor of this Arabic verse would not have been evident in Persian, in which _khitám_ merely means 'conclusion, end'). Mírzá Abu'l-Faḍl-i Gulpaygání wrote in *The Bahá'í Proofs*: '. . . the Divine prophecies recorded in the Holy Scriptures, as is clearly testified by their very texts, are no other than symbolical and sealed words, and the essential purpose thereof is closed up and unknown. But the opening of these seals and the elucidation of these allegories have been apportioned to the coming of the time of the end, and to the advent of the great Hour' (p. 201) . . . He hath broken the seal of the "Sealed Wine" with His Generous Fingers' (p. 129). See Daniel 12:9: 'And he said, Go thy way, Daniel: for the words are closed up and sealed till the time of the end'.

Regarding the development of the Islamic exclusivist interpretation of the expression 'Seal of the Prophets' and the Bahá'í response thereto see

Fazel and Fananapazir, 'A Bahá'í Approach to the Claim of Finality in Islam',; Momen, M., *Islam and the Bahá'í Faith*, pp. 34–59; Gollmer, in Schaefer, Towfigh and Gollmer, *Making the Crooked Straight*, p. 582, note 40: a translation of the ḥadíth which is mentioned in this last reference can be found in Lambden, 'Prophecy in the Johannine Farewell Discourse', p. 77.

8 The Báb, *Selections* 6:11:5, p. 161.
9 The Báb, Persian Bayán 5:8, in *Selections* 3:32:1, p. 104.
10 The Báb, Kitáb-i-Asmá' 17:1, in *Selections* 5:9:2, p. 138.
11 Shoghi Effendi, 'The Unfoldment of World Civilization', in *World Order of Bahá'u'lláh*, p. 202.
12 For more to this theme see Schaefer, Heilsgeschichte und Paradigmenwechsel.
13 Esslemont, *Bahá'u'lláh and the New Era*, p. 179.
14 Bahá'u'lláh, *Seven Valleys*, p. 21.
15 ibid. p. 38.
16 The Báb, Persian Bayán 4:12, in *Selections* 3:34:1, p. 105.
17 Bahá'u'lláh, *Seven Valleys*, p. 39.
18 'Abdu'l-Bahá, *Some Answered Questions* 38:5, p. 152.
19 The Báb, *Selections* 4:10:6, p. 126 (from the Dalá'il-i Sab'ih).
20 The Báb, Persian Bayán 8:1, in *Selections* 3:26:1, p. 97.
21 Quoted in Shoghi Effendi, *Promised Day Is Come*, pp. 110–11.
22 Bahá'u'lláh, Kitáb-i Íqán 15, p. 15.
23 'Abdu'l-Bahá, *Some Answered Questions* 14:9, p. 76.
24 Eric Hadley-Ives' useful compilation of springtime metaphors in the writings of Bahá'u'lláh, 'Abdu'l-Bahá and Shoghi Effendi was, at the time of writing, available online under http://bahai-library.com/?file=compilation_springtime_metaphors and as an illustrated Internet publication under http://www.blurb.com/bookstore/detail/53927metaphors. The author is contemplating an eventual 'real' publication (personal correspondence, 21 May 2007).
25 'Abdu'l-Bahá, *Some Answered Questions* 14:6, p. 74.
26 Bahá'u'lláh, *Gleanings* 85:1, p. 167.
27 ibid. 150, p. 319.
28 'Abdu'l-Bahá, quoted in Shoghi Effendi, 'The Dispensation of Bahá'u'lláh', in *World Order of Bahá'u'lláh*, p. 110.
29 From *The Prosperity of Humankind*, quoted in *Bahá'í World 1994–95*, p. 295.
30 See Shoghi Effendi, *The Faith of Bahá'u'lláh*, quoted in *Bahá'í World 1993–94*, p. 9.

31 Shoghi Effendi, 'The Unfoldment of World Civilization', in *World Order of Bahá'u'lláh*, p. 202.
32 The Universal House of Justice, *Promise of World Peace*, para. 9.
33 Bahá'u'lláh, quoted in Shoghi Effendi, *Advent of Divine Justice*, p. 68.
34 See for example Martin and Schumann, *Die Globalisierungsfalle*.
35 Schaefer, *Imperishable Dominion*, pp. 25ff.
36 Bahá'u'lláh, quoted in Shoghi Effendi, *Advent of Divine Justice*, p. 63.
37 The Báb, Persian Bayán 6:14, in Momen (ed.), *Selections from the Writings of E.G. Browne*, 'A Summary of the Persian Bayan', Wáhid VI, Chapter 14.
38 In many Bahá'í prayer books, e.g. *Bahá'í Prayers*, p. 30.
39 Gen. 9:13.
40 Gen. 17:7-14.
41 Grossmann, *Das Bündnis Gottes*, pp. 12–14; Shoghi Effendi, *God Passes By*, pp. 30–31: Towfigh, *Schöpfung und Offenbarung*, pp. 36–43; Ferraby, *All Things Made New*, p. 241–55.
42 'Abdu'l-Bahá, *Paris Talks* 7:7, p. 22.
43 Bahá'u'lláh, *Gleanings* 14:1, p. 27.
44 The Báb, Persian Bayán 6:16, in Selections 3:12:2, p. 87.
45 See Shoghi Effendi, 'The Unfoldment of World Civilization', in *World Order of Bahá'u'lláh*, pp. 162–3.
46 'Abdu'l-Bahá, *Promulgation of Universal Peace*, p. 55.
47 Bahá'u'lláh, Kitáb-i Aqdas, para. 99.
48 'Abdu'l-Bahá, talk given on 21 March 1913, in Star of the West, vol. 5, no. 1 (quoted in Mihrshahi, Our Days are Numbered, p. 27).
49 'Abdu'l-Bahá, quoted in Shoghi Effendi, *World Order of Bahá'u'lláh*, p. 36.
50 According to the definition cited here, the first prime number is the number 1. In the view of some mathematicians, however, 1 is technically a square ($1^2 = 1$) and therefore not a prime number.
51 The *abjad* value of the word *bahá'* and therefore also the number of entrances to the Mashriqu'l-Adhkár is nine, as is the number of historically documented world religions including the Bábí Faith and the Bahá'í Faith. Nine years lie between the proclamation of the Mission of the Báb and the divine summoning of Bahá'u'lláh in the dungeon of the Síyáh-Chál. The number of members of the elected Bahá'í bodies (i.e. spiritual assemblies or the Universal House of Justice) is at least nine. The number 2,520 (the smallest number which is integrally divisible by all values from 1 to 9 inclusive) is a veiled reference to the year of the Revelation of the Báb (Nabíl, *The Dawn-Breakers*, p. 49) and for example the basic unit used in the apportionment of inheritance (Kitáb-i Aqdas, para. 20, Q5).

52 'Abdu'l-Bahá, *Paris Talks* 15:6, p. 45.
53 Bahá'u'lláh, *Gleanings* 112.
54 For what it is worth, note that the cross sum of 19 is also 1: $19 \rightarrow 1 + 9 = 10 \rightarrow 1 + 0 = 1$. Since this is the case for one sixth of all prime numbers, however, the probability of a pure coincidence is too high to warrant speculation of the sort occasionally encountered in the literature on numerology. The cross sum of 361 is likewise 1. However, note that this is the case for two ninths of the squares of all natural numbers, a third of the squares of all prime numbers and the squares of all natural numbers themselves having a cross sum of 1. The high degree of structure in cross-sum distributions detracts substantially from the persuasiveness of any hermeneutics in which they participate.
55 Qur'án 57:2-3.
56 Bahá'u'lláh, *Seven Valleys*, p. 37.
57 Bahá'u'lláh, Kitáb-i Aqdas, para. 66.
58 Momen (ed.), *Selections from the Writings of E. G. Browne*, 'A Summary of the Persian Bayan', pp. 316–406.
59 ibid., Exordium, p. 322.
60 ibid., Wáhid VI, Chapter 8, p. 379.
61 ibid., Wáhid VI, Chapter 3, p. 376.
62 See Lambden, S., 'Background and Centrality of Apophatic Theology in Bábí and Bahá'í Scripture', pp. 57–58, including his footnote 94, for a discussion of this poem in relation to the ḥadíth of 'Amá', an Islamic tradition concerning the absolute ipseity and unknowability of God.
63 Taherzadeh, *Revelation of Bahá'u'lláh*, vol. 1, pp. 44–46.
64 Bahá'u'lláh, Kitáb-i Aqdas, para. 18: literally "God is more glorious [than all other things]," Arab. Alláhu abhá'.
65 The word *ḥuqúq* (plural of *ḥaqq*, 'truth'; also 'rightful possession') means i.a. 'entitlement', 'legal claim'. *Ḥuqúqu'lláh* are literally 'God's due rights', that is, the amounts payable in accordance with the law of Ḥuqúqu'lláh as explicated in the Kitáb-i Aqdas.
66 *Kitáb-i-Aqdas*, para. 49 and Glossary, keyword 'Mithqál'.
67 Bahá'u'lláh, Kitáb-i Aqdas, para. 97, Q23, and note 78; Momen (ed.), *Selections from the Writings of E. G. Browne*, 'A Summary of the Persian Bayan', Wáhid V, Chapter 19, pp. 373–4.
68 Nabíl, *Dawn-Breakers*, p. 63.
69 ibid. p. 123.
70 In Badí'u'lláh Panáhí's article 'Der Kitáb-i Aqdas und die Bahá'í-Religion' the editor states in note 17: 'The names of the months correspond to the attributes of God listed in the fasting prayer [*du'á'u's-sahar*, 'awakening (i.e. dawn) prayer' – GK] of Imám Ja'far aṣ-Ṣádiq (734–765 ce). Bahá'u'lláh

TIME AND THE BAHÁ'Í ERA

makes reference to this, and in particular to the Most Great Name *Bahá'* which occurs as the first in the list, in a Tablet to be found in *Má'idiy-i Asmání* IV, p. 23' [my translation from the German]. Some sources assign the authorship of this prayer instead to Ja'far's predecessor, Imám Muḥammadu'l-Báqir. The prayer begins: 'O my God! I beseech Thee by thy Bahá' in its supreme splendour (bi-Abhá'hu), for all thy *Bahá'* is truly luminous (*al-Bahiyy*). I verily, O my God, beseech Thee by the fullness of Thy Splendour (*Bahá'ika*).' This supplication is then repeated eighteen times, each time substituting the word bahá' and its derivatives with another of the divine attributes used by the Báb as the names of the months (Lambden, 'The Word *Bahá'*'). A complete English-language translation of this prayer appears in Mihrshahi, *Our Days Are Numbered*, Appendix II.

With two exceptions, the names of the months as they generally appear in Bahá'í literature differ from the conventions used in the present study only in the use of Persian *-at* for Arabic *-aτ*. The assumption made here that the names were originally Arabic and that the present usage resulted from the orthographic habits of Persian copyists (of whom many were perhaps unaccustomed to copying Arabic) is not devoid of justification. *Asmá'* is an exclusively Arabic word form (in Persian the name of the month would have to be *Asámí*), as are several of the names of the days of the week and of the *wuḥdán*. Furthermore, the prayer from the sixth (or fifth) Imám from which the month names are derived is in Arabic.

The two exceptions mentioned above: (a) the commonly used form *Bahá* is a transcriptional anomaly – in the original script the *hamzaτ* is always written out, regardless of whether the text is Persian or Arabic (compare *Asmá'*, *'Alá'*); and (b) the *-íyy-* in the commonly used variation *Mashíyyaτ* would, if taken literally, stand for the highly unconventional combination (long) vocalic *yá'* followed by consonantal *yá'* with *tashdíd* (doubling), whereas the original, whether Persian or Arabic, has a (written or implied) *kasraτ* (short *i* diacritic) before the double consonant *yá'*, transcribed *-iyy-*. Note in this connection that the conventional word form in Arabic is *mashí'aτ*, from *shá'a*, 'to will', but the form presented here (i.e. without *hamzaτ*) occurs as a technical term in Shí'ite metaphysics (cf. Hamid, The Metaphysics and Cosmology of Process).

71 The word-form *bahí* (*bahiyy*) is derived from the morphologically similar and semantically related root bhw.
72 Mihrshahi, *Our Days are Numbered*, especially Chapter VI and Appendix I.
73 Walbridge, *Sacred Acts, Sacred Space, Sacred Time*, pp. 189–205.
74 Bahá'u'lláh, Kitáb-i Aqdas, para. 16.
75 Bahá'u'lláh, *Prayers and Meditations*, no. CLVII, p. 250.
76 See Bahá'u'lláh, Kitáb-i-Aqdas, note 28.
77 See for example Saiedi, *Logos and Civilization*, pp. 53–61; Savi, *Towards the Summit of Reality*, pp. 31–6, 270–80.

78 Lambden,'The Background and Centrality of Apophatic Theology in Bábí and Bahá'í Scripture', pp. 49–50.
79 Provisional translation by Lambden, ibid. p. 61.
80 See Momen (ed.), *Selections from the Writings of E. G. Browne* 'A Summary of the Persian Bayan', Wáhid V, Chapter 6, footnote.
81 See Walbridge, loc.cit.
82 Shoghi Effendi, *God Passes By*, pp. 54, 100.
83 Schaefer, *Bahá'í Ethics in Light of Scripture*, vol. 2, pp. 443–5.
84 Bahá'u'lláh, *Gleanings* 88, p. 175.
85 Bahá'u'lláh, Kitáb-i Aqdas, para. 45.
86 ibid. para. 125.
87 Schaefer, loc.cit.
88 Bahá'u'lláh, Hidden Words, Arabic 2.
89 See Shoghi Effendi, *Promised Day is Come*, p. 123.
90 'Abdu'l-Bahá, *Some Answered Questions* 59:8, p. 222.
91 Bahá'u'lláh, *Seven Valleys*, pp. 11–12.
92 Momen, (ed.), *Selections from the Writings of E. G. Browne*, 'A Summary of the Persian Bayan', Wáhid II, Chapter 17.
93 Bahá'u'lláh, Kitáb-i Aqdas, para. 1.
94 According to Walbridge, this is a neologism from the Báb and implies something like 'the quality of being bounteous' (*Sacred Acts, Sacred Space, Sacred Time*, p. 194), and should perhaps be transcribed *Faḍál*.
95 Walbridge (op.cit. p. 195) suggests that this should perhaps be transcribed *'Adál*.
96 Letter on behalf of Shoghi Effendi to an individual believer, 28 October 1949, quoted in Hornby, *Lights of Guidance*, no. 1658, p. 494.
97 See 'Abdu'l-Bahá, *Faith for Every Man*, p. 43 (quoted in Hatcher, W., 'The Concept of Spirituality', in Hatcher, J. and W., *The Law of Love Enshrined*, p. 236). Regarding the status of matrimony as 'divine creation' see 'Abdu'l-Bahá, *Tablets*, vol. 2, p. 474. That the week of the Jewish tradition is not an eternal truth – that is, one which has no beginning and no end – is confirmed by the testimony of the Pentateuch, in which keeping the sabbath is a law which was not explicated prior to the exodus from Egypt (for a discussion of the sabbath see *Semitic calendar systems* in Chapter 2). Shoghi Effendi's words 'As to where the idea of a seven-day week originated, it is certainly very ancient' confirm the fact that the week was at some time introduced into human society, however far back this event may lie.
98 Bahá'u'lláh, Bishárát, The twelfth Glad-Tidings, in *Tablets* 3:22, p. 26.
99 Mihrshahi, *Our Days are Numbered*, p. 17.

100 ibid. pp. 44–50; see also Saiedi, *Logos and Civilization*, pp. 53–61.
101 ibid. p. 21.
102 ibid. pp. 22–3.
103 Qur'án 2:183.
104 With the exception of the significance of the lunar conjunction for determining the start of 'eid-e moulúd (see 'Bahá'í commemorations' in Chapter 4).
105 Bahá'u'lláh, Kitáb-i Aqdas, Q76.
106 Bahá'u'lláh, *Hidden Words*, Arabic 32.
107 ibid. Arabic 33.
108 Bahá'u'lláh, *Gleanings* 81, p. 157.
109 Qur'án 10:7.
110 John 3:3-6; see Bahá'u'lláh, Kitáb-i Íqán 125, p. 118.
111 Bahá'u'lláh, Kitáb-i Íqán 120, p. 114.
112 Luke 9:59-61.
113 Qur'án 35:20-23; see Bahá'u'llah, Kitáb-i Íqán 129, p. 121.
114 ibid. 6:123.
115 Bahá'u'lláh, *Gleanings* 106:3, p. 213 (from Lawḥ-i Mánik<u>ch</u>í- Ṣáḥib).
116 Bahá'u'lláh, Kitáb-i Íqán 216, pp. 195–6.
117 Bahá'u'lláh, Hidden Words, Arabic 59.
118 ibid. Persian 7.
119 ibid. Arabic 5.
120 ibid. Persian 30.
121 Bahá'u'lláh, *Gleanings* 164:2, p. 345.
122 'Abdu'l-Bahá, *Promulgation of Universal Peace*, p. 226.
123 Bahá'u'lláh, Hidden Words, Arabic 62.
124 Bahá'u'lláh, *Gleanings* 34:8, p. 81.
125 Bahá'u'lláh, *Gleanings* 77, p. 149.
126 Bahá'u'lláh, Kitáb-i Íqán 214, p. 194.
127 Bahá'u'lláh, Kitáb-i Aqdas, para. 33; see also Bishárát, The twelfth Glad-Tidings, in *Tablets* 3:22, p. 26.

6 Determining the Day of Naw-Rúz

1 In previous editions of this study the terminator offset and the diurnal offset (introduced in Appendix E) were designated *longitudinal* and *latitudinal* offset (*Längenausgleich* and *Breitenausgleich*), respectively. The nomenclature was rather arbitrary, however, inasmuch as each involves both longitude and latitude. The terms used in this edition are easier to distinguish, the first

NOTES AND REFERENCES

having meaning only in conjunction with equinoctial terminator paths and the latter only with diurnal thresholds (see above, *Astronomical data*).

2 Note that L = 89°10' should theoretically yield 90°, but my computer produces this result for L = 89°28'27"38. The inaccuracy is almost certainly a rounding error due to the finite number of bits used for storing floating-point decimals: The above result, which has been obtained using double precision variables, is closer to 90° than the same calculation using single precision, and both results are more accurate than that obtained with a scientific pocket calculator.

3 Bahá'u'lláh, Kitáb-i Aqdas, Q35.

4 The Báb, Persian Bayán 6:14, in Momen (ed.), *Selections from the Writings of E. G. Browne*, 'A Summary of the Persian Bayán', Wáḥid VI, Chapter 14.

5 From a letter written on behalf of Shoghi Effendi, quoted in *The Kitáb-i-Aqdas*, Introduction, p. 8.

6 For a description of Baha'u'lláh's ability to access information on demand see *Epistle to the Son of the Wolf*, p. 165; Lawḥ-i-Ḥikmat 34, in *Tablets*, p. 149; Kitáb-i Aqdas, paras. 175, 176.

7 'Abdu'l-Bahá, *Divine Philosophy*, p. 74.

8 Kirste et.al., *Die Feste der Religionen*, pp. 70–74.

9 Bahá'u'lláh, Kitáb-i Aqdas, Q1.

10 ibid. para. 111.

11 ibid. para. 16.

12 Rumours circulating in the Bahá'í community would have it that, in the future, the prime meridian will be adjusted to pass through some symbolic Bahá'í location (Bahjí, Teheran, Baghdad or the obelisk on Mount Carmel marking the site of the future Mashriqu'l-Adhkár, depending on the version: see Piff, *Bahá'í Lore*, p. 371, entries E9-006a through e). These rumours have no basis in the authoritative teachings. Notwithstanding an endnote (1372) in which he linked these rumours with unresolved calendar issues, David Piff confirmed in a private communication (19 June 2007) that they reflect nothing more than triumphalistic sentiments and are to the best of his knowledge not associated with the reference spot in the minds of his informants. Nevertheless, assuming (1) congruency between prime meridian and reference spot and (2) a corresponding realignment of the date line at the (new) 180th meridian, this adjustment would provide optimal physical conditions for the implementation of the reference spot method.

13 The Universal House of Justice, letter to a National Spiritual Assembly, 30 October 1974, quoted in *Developing Distinctive Bahá'í Communities*.

14 The Universal House of Justice, letter of 27 November 1973, in *Ausgewählte Botschaften des Universalen Hauses der Gerechtigkeit 1963–1988*.

15 Quoted in Bahá'u'lláh, The Kitáb-i Aqdas, note 26.
16 *Directives from the Guardian*, no. 76, p. 30; also Hornby, *Lights of Guidance*, Part I, No. 1027, p. 302, but without the final sentence.
17 For a thoroughgoing literary-critical analysis of the potential meaning of this passage see Keil, 'Text Context and Literary Criticism: a Case Study based on a Letter from Shoghi Effendi', in *Lights of 'Irfán* Vol.11, pp. 55–98, url: https://bahai-library.com/keil_literary_criticism.
18 Communicated in a private correspondence from the Research Department of the Bahá'í World Centre on 31 July 2006.
19 Quoted in Hornby, *Lights of Guidance*, Part I, No. 1026, pp. 301–2.
20 The original German-language edition of this study, which was published before I could examine this enquiry from the National Spiritual Assembly of the United States and Canada, draws a somewhat different conclusion regarding the interpretation of Shoghi Effendi's response (see Keil, *Die Zeit im Bahá'í-Zeitalter: eine Studie über den Badí'-Kalender*).
21 I am indebted to the Research Department of the Bahá'í World Centre for providing me with this excerpt.
22 Shoghi Effendi, *God Passes By*, pp. 366–7.
23 *Bahá'í World*, vol. VI (1934–1936), pp. 363–79.
24 *Bahá'í World*, vol. VIII (1938–1940), pp. 493–9, as well as in the two subsequent volumes.
25 The Lesser Covenant comprises matters regarding the successorship of guidance and leadership of the Bahá'í community as stipulated by Bahá'u'lláh and 'Abdu'l-Bahá: see Momen, W. (ed.), *A Basic Bahá'í Dictionary*, keyword 'Covenant, Greater and Lesser'; Towfigh, *Schöpfung und Offenbarung aus der Sicht der Bahá'í-Religion*, pp. 40–42.
26 'Abdu'l-Bahá, Will and Testament 2:8, pp. 17–18; see also Taherzadeh, *Covenant*, p. 425.
27 Shoghi Effendi, 'The Dispensation of Bahá'u'lláh', in *World Order of Bahá'u'lláh*, p. 150.
28 The Universal House of Justice, letter of 27 November 1973, in *Ausgewählte Botschaften des Universalen Hauses der Gerechtigkeit 1963–1988*.
29 Shoghi Effendi, quoted in Hornby, *Lights of Guidance*, no. 1437.
30 *Report from the Early Days of the Bahá'í Revelation* (page number not available), original Persian-language text kindly made available to me by the Research Department of the Bahá'í World Centre at my request.
31 Bahá'u'lláh, Kitáb-i Aqdas, Q35.
32 Westrheim, *Calendars of the World*, p. 87.
33 The Universal House of Justice, letter to a National Spiritual Assembly, 30 October 1974, quoted in Developing Distinctive Bahá'í Communities; letter

of 27 November 1973, in *Ausgewählte Botschaften des Universalen Hauses der Gerechtigkeit 1963–1988*.

34 See Balyuzi, Bahá'u'lláh: *The King of Glory*, pp. 441–4 for the recounting of an episode which speaks for a positive change of attitude at the highest political level.

35 *Bahá'í World*, vol. XIII (1954–1963), p. 854.

36 ibid. pp. 119–21.

37 Bahá'í World Centre, Memorandum of 18 April 2001.

38 Bahá'u'lláh, Kitáb-i Aqdas, para. 99.

39 ibid. Q35.

40 ibid. para. 16.

41 ibid. para. 17.

42 For example, a perspective must be found which accounts for the fact that the Kitáb-i Aqdas was completed some nine years before a date line convention was ratified internationally (see Chapter 3).

43 Whatever else it might imply, the one-minute clause would certainly have provided the flexibility required in the nineteenth and early twentieth century to compensate for measuring errors. Nowadays such measurements are carried out to an accuracy of a fraction of a second and projected almost indefinitely into the future.

7 The Badí' Calendar and the Time of Day

1 Bahá'u'lláh, Kitáb-i Aqdas, para. 10.

2 Esslemont, *Bahá'u'lláh and the New Era*, p. 179.

3 Note that this oscillation is several orders of magnitude greater than that indicated by the equation of time.

4 The obliquity of the ecliptic is not constant, but instead wanders between 21°55' and 28°18' over a period of 40,000 years. In the year 2000 it amounted to 23°26'21"45 and by 2008 it will have shrunk to 23°26'17"7. Nutation results in a secondary displacement of the obliquity of the ecliptic by a maximum of ±9.21" spread over the nutation period of 18.6 years.

5 Nabíl's Narrative, vol. II, quoted in *Bahá'í World*, vols. III to XX, various pages; e.g. vol. XIV (1963–1968), p. 549.

6 https://www.weather.gov/media/ind/seasons.pdf. For the equation of time see also *program notes* in Appendices D and E.

7 Bahá'u'lláh, Kitáb-i Aqdas, para. 10.

8 ibid. Q64.

9 ibid. para. 10.

10 ibid. Q103.

11 Bahá'u'lláh, *Kitáb-i-Aqdas*, note 17.
12 The Universal House of Justice, letter of 8 August 1969 to the National Spiritual Assembly of the British Isles, quoted in *Lights of Guidance*, Part I, no. 781, p. 235.
13 The Universal House of Justice, letter of 27 July 1976 to a National Spiritual Assembly, quoted in *Lights of Guidance*, Part II, no. 1531, p. 466.
14 Astrology is an example of the separation of symbols from the astronomical objects to which they refer: the astrological positions of the stars, which are supposed to exert great influence on life and destiny, are in disaccord with the astronomical facts – because of the precession of the earth, even more so today than several millennia ago (for the Bahá'í view of astrology see Shoghi Effendi, *Lights of Guidance*, Part I, nos. 1746–1750).
15 Roland Philipp, private letter from ca. 1998 [my translation from the German].
16 The Universal House of Justice, letter to all National Spiritual Assemblies, 15 March 1992.
17 Letter written on behalf of Shoghi Effendi, 27 November 1938.

8 The Rhythm of Life

1 'Additional Material Gleaned from Nabíl's Narrative, Regarding the Bahá'í Calendar', in *Bahá'í World*. This subsection appears for the first time in vol. III (1928–1930) and in every volume thereafter to vol. XX (1987–1992, the last in the series) in the section on the Bahá'í calendar.
2 31 March 1949, in *The Light of Divine Guidance*, vol. II, p. 82.
3 Letter on behalf of Shoghi Effendi to an individual believer, 10 July 1939, quoted in Hornby, *Lights of Guidance*, no. 372, p. 169.
4 Momen (ed.), *Selections from the Writings of E. G. Browne*, 'A Summary of the Persian Bayan', Wáḥid VII, Chapter 17.
5 Bahá'u'lláh, Kitáb-i Aqdas, para. 106.
6 Letter on behalf of Shoghi Effendi to the National Spiritual Assembly of the United States and Canada, 16 November 1932.
7 Furútan, *Stories of Bahá'u'lláh*, p. 69.
8 'Abdu'l-Bahá, in *Bahá'í World Faith*, p. 411.
9 *Tablets of Abdul Baha Abbas*, vol. I, pp. 15–16.
10 'Abdu'l-Bahá, *Selections* no. 125, p. 144.
11 McGlinn, 'It's Friday: thank God.'
12 *Star of the West*, vol. 1, no. 12, p. 2.
13 *Ishráq-Khávarí (ed.), Ganjineh-ye Hudud va Ahkam* (Treasury of Laws and Ordinances).

14 Rabbani, *Priceless Pearl*, p. 15.
15 In the event of the adoption of occidental time, the concept of the seven-day week would no longer hold for the Badí' calendar in the same manner which applies to all other calendars – which effectively means that the two conceptions would be irreconcilable with each other. Whatever other consequences this situation would imply, it would definitely necessitate the use of different sets of name conventions.
16 Bahá'u'lláh, Kitáb-i Aqdas, para. 16.
17 Bahá'u'lláh, Kitáb-i Aqdas, para. 57.
18 See *Compilation of Compilations*, vol. 1, nos. 918–934.
19 ibid. no. 936.
20 ibid. no. 934.
21 From a statement of the National Spiritual Assembly of the United States, quoted in Bahá'í Procedure, Part 1, Leaf 6 (1933), and on p. 11 of the 2nd edition (1942). This statement was described as 'comprehensive and faithful' by Shoghi Effendi (*Compilation of Compilations* vol. 1, no. 936).
22 In the sense that the members of the Spiritual Assemblies and of the Universal House of Justice are not appointed, but rather elected through secret ballot. Once elected, however, a member is in no sense the bearer of a constituency mandate, his participation in the decisions of the body being guided alone by his own conscience, in the spirit of prayer and with the assurance of divine assistance (see Shoghi Effendi, 'The Dispensation of Bahá'u'lláh', in *The World Order of Bahá'u'lláh*, pp. 152–4), in particular: 'The Administrative Order of the Faith of Bahá'ú'lláh must in no wise be regarded as purely democratic in character inasmuch as the basic assumption which requires all democracies to depend fundamentally upon getting their mandate from the people is altogether lacking in this Dispensation' (p. 153).
23 'Public' in the sense of community-wide: non-Bahá'ís are excluded from the consultations. This has less to do with secrecy or – at least in the West – with security than it does with the fact that the kind of consultation which takes place among Bahá'ís must first be learned, and it would be unreasonable to expect informed participation from a non-Bahá'í. Furthermore, the topics are restricted to internal community matters. In recent years there has been a tendency to impose this restriction less stringently.
24 Letter on behalf of Shoghi Effendi to the National Spiritual Assembly of the United States and Canada, 18 November 1933, quoted in *Bahá'í Procedure*, pp. 11–12.
25 That participation in Nineteen Day Feasts is non-obligatory (Kitáb-i Aqdas Q48) is in my view to be understood in this context. The statement of the National Spiritual Assembly of the United States cited above (note 17) clarifies: 'The National Spiritual Assembly understands that it is incumbent upon every believer, unless ill or absent from the city, to attend each of these

Feasts.' Shoghi Effendi further commented that the Feast has 'both a social and an administrative significance and as such should be regularly attended by all confirmed believers' (12 April 1935, in *Compilation of Compilations*, vol. 1, no. 938).

26 *Tablets of Abdul-Baha Abbas*, p. 553, in *Consultation: A Compilation*, no. 21. The reference to 'enemies' among the believers or between Bahá'ís and non-Bahá'ís (this passage holds for all circumstances of consultation, not only during Nineteen Day Feasts) is not to be understood literally. It is apparently an allusion to the well-known Qur'ánic *jihád* verse (60:1): 'O believers, take not My enemy and your enemy for friends, offering them love, though they have disbelieved in the truth that has come to you . . .'. By transforming it into its opposite, 'Abdu'l-Bahá makes it clear that consultation is *not* concerned with questions of belief and doctrine. But his central objective here is another: 'Abdu'l-Bahá is warning each of us in a very vivid manner not to consider his own opinions to be divinely ordained and opinions to the contrary to be erroneous in principle.

27 'Abdu'l-Bahá, from *Star of the West*, vol. IV, no. 7 (13 July 1913), p. 120, in *Compilation of Compilations*, vol. 1, no. 932, p. 429.

28 'Abdu'l-Bahá, *Selections* 43, p. 87.

29 The Universal House of Justice, letter to the National Spiritual Assembly of Canada, 19 March 1973, in Consultation: A Compilation, no. 47.

30 From a letter on behalf of Shoghi Effendi to the National Spiritual Assembly of the Bahá'ís of the United States and Canada, 29 July 1935, in *Compilation of Compilations*, vol. 1, no. 939, p. 433.

31 Bahá'u'lláh, Kitáb-i Aqdas, para.57.

32 From a letter of 1 December 1936 on behalf of Shoghi Effendi to an individual believer, translated from the Persian, in *Compilation of Compilations*, vol. I, no. 945, p. 435.

33 From a letter on behalf of Shoghi Effendi to the National Spiritual Assembly of the United States and Canada, 24 December 1939, ibid. no. 946, p. 435.

34 See Shoghi Effendi, *Directives from the Guardian*, no. 98: '. . . it is surely preferable and even highly advisable that the friends should in their relation to each other discontinue observing such holidays as Christmas and New Years, and to have their festival gatherings of this nature instead during the Intercalary Days and Naw-Rúz . . .'

Conclusion

1 'Alí-Muḥammad Varqá, 'Huqúqu'lláh, the socio-economic and spiritual law of the Book of Aqdas', Address in June 1997 at various gatherings in the United States.

2 Shoghi Effendi, *The Light of Divine Guidance*, vol. II, p. 82.

3 'Abdu'l-Bahá, *Will and Testament* 2:9, p. 18.

APPENDIXES

1 Cf. MacEoin, 'Hierarchy, Authority, and Eschatology', p. 135, where the word *qá'im* may assume the value of either 142 or 151, implying either QA'M (i.e. the *hamzaτ* is counted) or QAYM (i.e. the dotless *yá'*-carrier is counted). I suspect this represents an intrinsic degree of freedom which may be exercised or not, depending on opportunity, necessity and individual preference.

2 All chronometric expressions in this appendix imply solar time except where otherwise indicated. References to "clocks" accordingly imply notional timepieces which indicate solar time rather than mean time.

3 Sunset occurs at 90 degrees and 50 minutes relative to the zenith distance of the centre of the solar disc (see '*Astronomical data*' in Chapter 6), i.e. 6 hours, 3 minutes and 20 seconds after true solar midday.

4 During the first millennium of the Bahá'í Era there are no natural occurrences of such 'tardy' leap years, albeit instances can be generated artificially by adjusting the UT specification of the equinox in 1995 CE in the program in Appendix D. A 1000-pass analysis with successive UT specifications at seven-second intervals produces for example the following results:

Total number of calculatory leap years: 1 million tropical year units)	242996 (24.30% of
Total numcer of instances of 'tardy' leap years: calculatory leap years)	268 (0.11% of
Distribution of instances over 1000 passes:	
Passes in which no instances occur: instances	767 (76,7%), 0
Passes in which one instance occurs: 198 instances (73.881%)	198 (19,8%),
Passes in which two instances occur: instances (26.119%)	35 (3.5%), 70
Passes in which three or more instances occur: instances	0 (0.0%), 0

Altering the time slice and/or the intervals for the UT specifications has no appreciable effect on the results.

5 . . . but see Appendix D, which sheds doubt upon this hypothesis.

6 Bahá'u'lláh was born in the house of his father, Mirza Buzurg, which before its destruction in June 2004 in an act of 'cultural cleansing' (see http://news.bahai.org/story/323) was located in the district called Darvazil Shimran (Shimran Gate) to the north and within the confines of old Teheran: see Balyuzi, *Bahá'u'lláh:The King of Glory* (Oxford: George Ronald, 2nd edn. 1991) p. 19.

7 https://www.iranchamber.com/calendar/converter/iranian_calendar_converter.php.

8 Note that the results for the period 1–171 BE are purely calculatory, those for 221–250 be provisional.

9 In a letter of 5 October 2018, the Secretariat of the Bahá'í World Centre informed me that the ad-hoc committee responsible for working out details of the BWC table had obtained its coordinates for 'Teheran, Iran' from the World Geodetic System 1984, which as at the date of writing was ostensibly no longer accessible. It seems in the meantime to function again, since I was able to obtain from it a longitudinal coordinate for Teheran (51°20'51"558 E), whose results are identical to those generated with the longitude set to Golestan Palace.

10 I am endebted to Iskandar Hai for drawing my attention to a tabular calendar converter published in Iran by Ahmad Najmabadí in 1955, which covers the period 1851 to 1954 CE. Najmabadí states in the introduction that, for the years 1860 to 1927 CE, his work is based on official calendars published in Iran for contemporary use. The data confirm that the last day of the Jalálí year 1276 (54 BE) was indeed Yekshambeh (Sunday), 30 Esfand.

11 I am greatly endebted to the Secretariat of the Universal House of Justice for complying with my request for urgency, so that its response could be taken into account prior to the (then envisaged) date of publication.

12 Seidelmann, *Explanatory Supplement to the Astronomical Almanac*, p. 577.

13 Science and Engineering Research Council, *The Astronomical Almanac for the Year 1995*, p. A1.

14 The author makes no claims to expertise in astronomy, geodetics or related areas of astrophysics and mathematics, and until such time as they have been scrutinized by individuals with the necessary professional qualifications, the calculations presented in this book, and particularly in this appendix, are to be regarded at best as examples.

15 Summer time (daylight saving(s) time in the United States and Canada) plays a role neither in the case of the Ascension of 'Abdu'l-Bahá (which occurred in winter) nor in the case of the Ascension of Bahá'u'lláh (which pre-dated its introduction in the twentieth century).

16 Seidelmann, *Explanatory Supplement to the Astroomical Almanac*, pp. 311–12.

17 Coordinates in this study have been obtained with the aid of Google Maps (url: https://www.google.com/maps).

18 ... in reality, about 102 metres to the east of the original null meridian, a consequence of tectonic shift.

19 A reader who – like the author – habitually seeks ways to visualize mathematical configurations is invited to imagine a parallel universe in which the equinoctial terminator paths and the meridians switch roles: the former are

straight lines (as if they were great circles), whereas the latter are warped so that they appear as reverse terminator paths, i.e. they resemble elongated closing round brackets. In this projection, the poles are not points at the north and south extremities, but instead circles at what would be latitude ±89°10' in our accustomed universe.

There is nothing uncanny about cartographic deformation: in fact, any flat projection of the earth's surface is necessarily distorted. The only difference is that the Mercator projection for example is familiar to us, whereas the occidental grid is a novelty which upon initial encounter quite literally challenges our 'world view'.

20 The values for the equation of time are obtained from an online calculator (url: https://planetcalc.com/9235/).

Index

'Abdu'l-Bahá xvii, 37, 77, 79-80, 108, 113, 140, 160, 162, 166, 215, 217, 219-22, 226, 229, 244
   Ascension of 80, 122, 210-12, 270, 271, 276
Aberdeen 203
abjad xvi, 102-5, 109, 112, 177, 245-6, 312
   ḥisábu'l-jummal 245
Abraham 86, 99
abstinence 98, 101, 110, 125-6, 179, 203
ab urbe condita 49
Achaemenids 38, 42-3, 49
Adam 86, 87, 112, 121
ad calendas graecas 47
*adh-dh*átu'l-iláhí 111
adolescence 95
Afghanistan 46, 176
Africa 148, 176
Age of Bahá 92
Age of Prophecy 310
Ahura Mazda 38
'Akká 219
al-Ahsá'í, Shaykh Aḥmad 121, 306
'álamu'l-amr 142
'álamu'l-khalq 142
Al-Azhar University 62
Alaska 277
Albania 52
alcohol 125
Aleutian Islands 207
alignment 50, 62 *see also* date boundary, date line, moon, (re)alignment
All Things 75, 104 *see also kullu shay'*
Alrukaba 17
altitude 13
America 148, 150
   North 176
   South 176

Amesha Spentas 38
Amish 233
Anglo-Saxon 189
animal husbandry 3
annual holiday 231, 238
Antarctica 203
apex 199
Arabic xiii, xvi, xviii, 109, 111, 112, 117, 138, 140, 141, 157, 218, 223, 246, 314
Ardashir 39
Aristotelian 115
artificial memory systems 7
Asia 148, 150, 176
   Central 36, 46, 92
Assyria 38, 43
astrology 320
Astronomical Almanac 146
astronomy, astronomical x, xii, xiv, xix, 15, 21, 23, 46, 61-2, 77, 92, 131, 133, 135, 141, 145-6, 150, 152, 157-8, 172, 179, 188, 196, 208-9, 210
   archeo-astronomical 15
   unit 133
Atlantic 176
atmosphere 16, 96, 134
Augustus, Emperor (Octavian) 48, 49, 52
Australia 148, 186
Avesta 36-7
ayyám (age) 54, 306
Azalí 307
azimuth 112

ba'd akmálihá 144
báb 112
Báb, the xi, 73-6, 78-9, 85, 87-9, 102, 104-9, 112, 118-19, 121, 138-40, 151, 162, 164, 195, 210, 218, 224, 226, 307
   Birth of the Báb 78, 210

Declaration of the Báb 79, 210, 212, 240
Martyrdom of the Báb 79, 185, 212, 240
revelation of 73, 75, 94, 312
Shrine 221
Bábí Faith, history, writings 77, 89, 104, 109, 183, 210, 307
Bábí community 164, 165
Babylon, Babylonian 38, 43, 56, 60, 65, 215
Babylonian Exile 306
badí' 73
  al-amru'l-badí' 73
  Al-Badí' 73
Badí' calendar *see* calendar
Baghdad 79
Bahá, Age of 92 *see also* Bahá'í Era
bahá' 105, 109, 312
Bahá', month of *see* month
Bahá'í belief, Faith, teachings, writings xvi, 87, 89, 91-3, 97, 102-5, 108-9, 113, 115, 117-20, 125-6, 137, 142, 166-7, 182-3, 189, 207, 209-10, 216, 220, 222-3, 228, 230-31, 233, 237, 240, 241-3
Bahá'í clusters 182
Bahá'í commemorations 270 *see also* 'Abdu'l-Bahá; the Báb; Bahá'u'lláh; covenant: Day of the Covenant; festival: Riḍván
Bahá'í community ix, 75, 79, 99, 101, 164, 166, 182, 189, 216, 219-20, 224, 226-7, 230, 232-3, 236, 241-2
  local 230
  world 75, 185, 225, 242
Bahá'í Era xi, 74, 147, 188, 254
Bahá'í World, The 157, 167-70
Bahá'í World Centre xiii, 157, 168, 180, 255, 263, 293-4, 300
Bahá'u'lláh xi, 73, 75-7, 79-80, 85, 87-8, 91-2, 95-8, 101, 105-6, 108, 110-12, 114-15, 121-2, 126, 130, 137, 139-42, 148, 151, 159, 161-4, 166-7, 178, 182, 187-8, 198-9, 201-2, 210, 217-18, 220, 225-6, 228, 242, 307
  Ascension of Bahá'u'lláh 79, 80, 210, 212, 240, 242
  Birth of Bahá'u'lláh 78, 210, 249
  Blessed Beauty 79, 219

Dispensation of Bahá'u'lláh 78, 139
  revelation of 88, 94
Bahjí 79, 148, 150, 202, 276
  Mansion 219
Bahman Yasht 37
Baltic countries 52
barter and trade 29
Bayán xiii, 75, 76, 86, 104, 139, 140-41
  Arabic 224
  Persian xiii, 75
Baytu'l-'Adl 114 *see also* Universal House of Justice
Belgium 52
Bering Strait 147
Bible, biblical 53-7, 59, 87, 121
bid'at 78
birth 126
  second birth 127, 129
Bombay 41
Brazil 176
British
  currency 27
  dependencies 147
  Parliament 33
  protectorate 211, 221
  time 197
Bronze Age 29-30
Bulgaria 52

Cairo 62
calendae 47, 145
calendar 32, 47, 176, 188-9, 242
  Achaemenid 38, 42-3, 49
  alignment *see* (re)alignment: calendar
  al-yawmiyyatu'l-badí'at 307
  astronomical 22
  Bábí 307
  Babylonian 306
  Badí' xi, 73, 152-3, 164-5, 188-90, 196, 209-10, 214, 242, 247-9, 254-5, 285-6, 307
    structural principle of 107
  Bahá'í xi, xiv, 73, 156, 167, 217, 307
  Bastání 42
  Christian 38, 74 *see also* calendar: Gregorian
  Egyptian 39, 53, 58
  Essene 59
  Greek 46
  Gregorian 42, 44, 50-52, 56, 63, 75,

INDEX

77-8, 147, 156, 159, 165, 169, 186, 188-91, 208, 210, 215, 223 *see also* (re)alignment: Gregorian reform
hijrī 63
Hindu 37
historical 78, 208
Iranian national *see* calendar: Jalālī
Islamic 44, 59-63, 74, 78, 80, 165, 188, 208, 209
Jalālī (Iranian national) 74, 156, 169
Jewish 55-60, 63, 74, 188, 208
Julian 49, 51, 52
lunar 26, 30, 35-6, 42, 46, 52-3, 55, 59, 78, 305 *see also* cycle: lunar
lunisolar 46-7 *see also* cycle: lunisolar
Mesopotamian 38, 49
natural 25, 35
Neolithic 28, 209
notch 35
pocket 155
printed 35
Qadīmī 42
realignment *see* (re)alignment: calendar
regulated 34-6, 43, 208
Republican 47
Romulus 47
Semitic 53-63
Sháhensháhí 42
solar 58-9, 78, 82
staff 35
taqvīm-e hijrī-ye qamarī 45
week-based 59
Zoroastrian 37-44
calendar reform 39, 48, 61
    Gregorian 36, 51 *see also* (re)alignment: Gregorian reform
    Islamic 60
    Julian 48-9, 51
    Zoroastrian 39-40
calendar systems xi, 4, 35, 36, 53-63, 59, 121
calendrical observatory (*Visurenkalender*) 14, 16, 21-2
calibration xi, 23-4, 28, 32, 34, 37, 64, 69, 188, 191-2, 196, 215, 243, 269 *see also* time: calibration of
Canada 157, 232
celebration(s) 39, 44, 56, 75, 92, 98, 101, 133, 141-2, 211-12 *see also* festival

Chandler period 303
China 37, 52
Christian(s) 49, 56, 59, 75, 119-20, 189, 209, 220, 232, 236-7
    Christian Era 49
    Knanaya Christians 233
chronology 32
chronometer 68
church service 226
circumcision 99
classroom 241
clock(s) 1, 66, 68, 122-3, 125, 183, 187-8, 190, 192, 194, 197, 201-2
    atomic 195
    hour-glass 66
    inner 5, 125
    mechanical 66, 185, 213
    meridional 188
    occidental 194
    watch 183
    water 66
colour 5, 123
commemoration(s) 63, 100, 133, 183, 208, 211-12 *see also* Bahá'í commemorations
commerce and management 30, 221
compass 64, 122
confession 227
Constantine, Emperor 49
constellation(s) 9, 17, 19-21, 33, 135 *see also* zodiac
    Aquarius 19, 21, 135
    Aries (ram)19, 21, 75, 98, 135, 137-8, 140, 157, 163
    Camelopardalis 19
    Cancer 19, 21
    Canes Venatici 19
    Capricorn 19
    Cassiopeia 19
    Cepheus 19
    Draconis 19, 303
    Gemini 19, 21
    Lacerta 19
    Leo 19, 21
    Libra 19
    Lynx 19
    Ophiuchus 19
    Perseus 19
    Pisces (fish) 19, 21, 75, 98, 138
    Sagittarius 19

Taurus 19
Ursa Major 19
Ursa Minor 17, 19
Virgo 19, 21
consultation 183, 225-9
Council of Nicaea 51
covenant 99, 116, 119
   Centre of the Covenant 79
   Day of the Covenant 99, 100, 101
   Eternal Covenant 100, 101
   Greater Covenant 79, 99
   Lesser Covenant 160, 161
creation myth 118
cross sum 313
culmination of the sun 13, 122
cult 11, 29, 59
culture(s) xxi, 11, 30, 32, 36, 38, 77, 93,
   113, 118, 120, 189, 207-8, 303
cuneiform 31, 43
cycle(s) *see also* rhythm
   temporal
   annual 133
   backward 60
   lunar, moon 7-9, 23, 25, 35-6, 46, 52,
      56, 306
   lunisolar 46, 102, 306
   market *see nundina*
   Metonic Cycle 55, 304, 306
   natural 30
   seasonal 8
   solar 11, 52
   wáḥid 76, 83, 102, 105, 108
   week, 7-day 222, 234
   year 207, 215
   12-month 60
   18.61-year 15-16 *see* dragon points
   19-day 102, 119-20, 213, 224, 235-41
      see also cycle: *wáḥid*
   19-week 239-40
   19-year 56, 99, 114
   33-year 45 *see also* calendar: Jalálí
   7-year 55
   revelatory
   Bahá'í 78 *see also* Bahá'í Era
   divine 93
   prophetic xxi, 87, 112, 121
   spiritual 92-3
cyclic progression 136, 173, 243, 283
cyclic-progressive 136, 147, 174, 178-81,
   183, 195, 204, 207, 209, 210

   see also date line: cyclic-progressive
cylinder 178

Dalá'il-i Sab'ih 78
Dark Ages 52
darkness 124, 126, 128, 193
date(s) 31, 32, 57, 146-50, 155, 173, 176,
   183, 187, 190, 204, 206, 210, 250
   Bahá'í 152, 255
   boundary date 190, 269
   calendar date 25, 32, 121, 148, 174,
      176, 179, 181, 206, 209, 211
   conversion 58
   display 183
   global 197, 207
   Gregorian 57, 197
   local 207
   shift 179
   zones 148, 151
   see also day: change of; Naw-Rúz
date line 147-8, 151-2, 165, 171, 173-4,
   176, 179, 181-3, 205-7, 209, 250, 252
   cyclic-progressive 147, 181, 183-4,
      195, 204, 207
   international 69, 147-8, 178, 189, 207
dawn 17-18, 20, 89, 123, 130
   see also sunrise
Dawn-Breakers, The 168
dawreh-ye badí' 78
day(s) 4, 16, 23-6, 32-6, 38, 47, 49, 53, 58-
   9, 61-6, 68, 74, 76, 98, 109, 118, 122,
   124-7, 134, 137-50, 155, 163, 171-3,
   176-7, 185, 188, 190-92, 196, 202-4,
   208-10, 213-15
   age of the 172, 210
   Bahá'í 125
   boundary 68, 194-5, 198-9
   calendar day 46, 98, 121, 144-5, 147-8,
      150, 152-3, 157, 187, 189-90,
      206, 223
   canonical 146, 178
   change of 121-2, 124, 190, 193, 198,
      199, 203-4
   count 32, 148, 173
   Feast *see* Nineteen Day Feast
   of festivity 76 *see* festivals
   global 183, 195-6, 209
   of Há' *see* Há'; intercalary days
   intercalary *see* intercalary days
   leap day 81, 177-8

INDEX

length 24, 65-6, 68, 187, 191-2
of the Letters 76, 98
local 171, 179, 183, 196
meridional 188, 191-2
nahár 138-9
name day 38
natural 138, 146-7, 172
of Naw-Rúz *see* Naw-Rúz
nominal 121, 209
occidental 124, 191-2
religious 190
of remembrance 119
of the Lord *see* Sabbath
rúz 138, 141, 178
shift 40, 148 *see also* date: shift
solar 18, 19, 23, 66, 199, 213
start of the 121, 187-8
stellar 19
synodic 213
week-day 223, 230, 238
work-free 125-6, 219-20, 230, 232, 234-6, 238-40
working 192 *see also* work
yawm 138-9, 142-3, 178
day one 11
days of the week 54, 56, 59, 62-3
  Chahar*shanbeh* 45
  Do*shanbeh* 45
  Fiḍál 118
  Friday 45, 58, 62, 118, 119, 217-22, 232, 234, 241
  'Idál 118
  Istijlál 118
  Istiqlál 118, 218
  Jalál 118
  Jamál 118
  Jom'eh 45
  Kamál 118
  Monday 62, 111
  Panj*shanbeh* 45
  Saturday 45, 50, 58, 62, 118, 119, 232, 241
  Seh*shanbeh* 45
  Shanbeh 45
  Sunday 45, 56, 58-9, 62, 118, 119, 220-22, 232
  Thursday 45, 58, 62, 118
  Tuesday 45, 58, 62
  Wednesday 45, 58, 62, 118
  Yawmu'l-Aḥad 62

Yawmu'l-Arbi'á' 62
Yawmu'l-Ithnayn 62
Yawmu'l-Jum'aτ 62, 119, 218
Yawmu'l-Khamís 62
Yawmu's-Sabt 62
Yawmu'th-Thaláthá' 62
Yek*shanbeh* 45
Yom Chamishi 58
Yom Revi'i 58
Yom Rishon 58
Yom Shabbat 58
Yom Sheni 58
Yom Shevi'i 58
Yom Shishi 58
Yom Shlishi 58
daylight 18, 124, 138, 187, 201, 230
  saving 193, 212 *see also* time: summer time
daytime 4, 64-6, 125-6, 134-5, 190, 192, 198, 201-2
dead, the 127-8
death 8, 116, 126-7, 129-30
Decalogue 54
decimal system 8, 223
deepening 228
Denmark 52
dhawí'l-qurbá 110
diaspora 63
dispensation 87, 92-3, 103, 106, 119, 183-4
  Bábí 107
  Bahá'í 99
Disraeli, Benjamin 234
divine
  assistance 99, 226
  attribute 107
  grace 88, 101
  law 100, 114, 145-6, 152-3, 157-8, 171-3, 179, 183
doctrine 162-3, 217, 219, 222
dogma 221
Dover 194
dragon points 15
drugs 125
du'á'u's-sahar 313
Dublin 202
dusk 17-18, 123
dynasty 33

earth 4, 6, 10, 12, 15, 18-19, 23, 66, 69, 76, 96, 121, 133-4, 136-7, 144, 154, 171-2,

174, 183, 191, 196, 198, 204, 206, 214, 250, 254
Easter *see* festival
ecliptic 12, 15, 19, 195, 196
   ecliptic longitude 196, 210, 212
   obliquity of the ecliptic 194, 272-3, 303
economic 97, 232
education 241
egotism 93
Egypt 52, 58, 157
Egyptian statement 157
Eichung see muʻáyarat
Elam 38
electronic data communication 194
Eliphaz 54
elliptical orbit of the earth 21, 44, 65, 68
employment 233, 237, 238
England 69, 232
English ix, x, xiii, xviii, xix, 10, 108, 137-9, 141, 143, 153, 167, 168, 223
epact 56, 62
epagomenae 52
equator 12, 134-6, 150-51, 176, 185, 191-3, 195, 201, 203, 205, 250, 252, 271
   celestial 12
equinoctial terminator path 135-6, 147, 181, 195
equinox xiii, 14-16, 39-40, 56, 93, 101, 117, 134-5, 140-41, 146, 148, 150, 154, 156-7, 173, 177, 179, 196, 198, 204-6, 247-8, 255, 268, 273
   autumnal 14, 16, 52, 57, 192, 196, 198, 206
   day of the 17, 146
   moment of the 17, 45, 93, 134-5, 140-41, 146-8, 150-52, 158, 173-4, 177, 180, 195, 198-9, 201, 205, 268
   vernal (spring) 14, 16, 38, 42, 45, 46-7, 101, 134-5, 137, 140-41, 145-8, 150-52, 154-5, 158-9, 167, 169, 171-4, 179, 191-2, 195-6, 198-9, 201, 203, 247, 255, 268, 273
era
   Era of Fulfilment 112
   Prophetic 112
Essenes 58-9, 236
essential unity 310
Etruscan 48

Europe 148, 167, 176, 233
   Eastern 194
   Western 189
exegesis 57, 85, 91, 182

family 7, 118, 124-5, 241
Fasli 42
Fast, the 82, 110, 142, 156, 176, 201
fasting 61, 62, 75-6, 98, 101, 110, 123, 125-6, 130, 144, 176, 179, 187, 192, 198-9, 201-3
fátihat 121
festival(s) ix, 38-41, 44, 46, 79, 98-101, 137-8, 140-42, 144, 176, 182, 208, 210-12, 228, 240
   All Saints' Day 238
   Ascension of Christ 238
   Ascension of the Virgin 238
   Christmas 117, 238, 240
   Corpus Christi 238
   Day of German Unity 238
   Day of the Covenant 79, 209
   Easter 56, 209, 236, 309
   Easter Monday 238
   Easter Sunday 238
   ʻeid 137-8, 140-42, 144, 178-9 *see also* festivals: *ʻíd*
   ʻeid-e moulúd 80
   Februum 47
   Fravashi 38-40, 43
   Gahambar (Spenta) 38, 40
   Garden of Riḍván 210
   Gatha 39, 43
   Good Friday 238
   ʻíd 140-41, 144, 228 *see also* festivals: *ʻeid*
   ʻÍduʼl-Aḍḥá 141
   ʻÍduʼl-Aʻẓam 79, 141
   ʻÍduʼl-Fiṭr 141, 228
   May Day 238
   Most Great Festival (*ʻÍduʼl-Aʻẓam*) 79, 1415 *see also* festivals: Riḍván
   Naw-Rúz Feast 156 *see also* Naw-Rúz
   Pesach 56
   Puja 37
   of purification 48
   Riḍván 79, 141, 212, 240
   Spenta 38 *see* festivals: Gahambar
   Twin Birthdays 80-83
   Whit-Monday 238

INDEX

Whitsunday 238
  see also Abdu'l-Bahá; the Báb;
  Bahá'u'lláh; Naw-Rúz
festivity 117, 141-2
fetish of national sovereignty 88
folk legend 32
France, French 10, 52, 229
Frankfurt am Main 136, 192, 201, 279, 292
free will 120
friendship 228
fuqará' 110

Garden of Riḍván 210, 308
Genesis 118
geodetic 141, 145
geoid 136
Germany, German 10, 11, 52, 64, 123, 143, 153, 155-6, 221, 232, 238-9, 241
  mini-states 52
German Templars 233
ghettoization 233
globalization 97
global positioning 183, 198
global time *see* time: global
globe 39, 136, 147-8, 151, 172, 174, 197, 205, 207, 250, 252 *see also* earth
gnomon 12-16 20, 65
God 73, 75-6, 89-94, 98-101, 103, 110-12, 116-17, 119, 128-30, 143
  attributes of 107, 109, 112, 116, 310, 313-14
  Plan of 98
  Spirit of 119
Great Britain 52
great circle 135-6, 147
Greece, Greek 10, 46, 52
  antiquity 102
Greenland 176
Greenwich 69, 189, 266, 268, 282-3
Gregory XIII, Pope 50
grid 277, 282, 283-4, 284, 325
Guardian *see* Shoghi Effendi
Gujarat 41

há' 76, 111-12, 177
  Ayyám-i Há' 74, 76, 111-13, 117-18, 177, 214, 234, 240
  Ayyámu'l-Há' 74
  region of Há' 177, 180, 183, 209-10, 240, 250, 252 *see also* leap area

Yawm-i Há' 146, 180, 195-6, 207, 250, 252
  see also intercalary days
ḥadíth 89, 311, 313
ḥafala 141
Háhút 112
Haifa 221, 233, 271, 276
ḥajj 61, 83, 102, 104-6, 109
hamán 138
Hamburg 194
ḥaqq 313 *see* Ḥuqúqu'lláh
hemisphere 13, 134-5, 140, 193, 197, 199, 202, 205
hermeneutic 85, 102
hierocracy 253
hijraτ 63, 119
Hinduism 36
historical 94, 106, 150, 152, 183, 211, 230
holiday 59, 141, 165, 228, 231, 238, 240
Holley, Horace 168
Holy Day(s) 231
holy scripture, writings 89, 100, 108, 125, 133, 142, 215
Hong Kong 280, 292
horizon 5, 12, 13, 16, 19, 20, 64, 90, 123, 134
hour *see* time: hour
House of Worship 99-100
human race, humankind 95-7, 103 *see also* mankind
Hungary 52
Ḥuqúqu'lláh 105, 242, 313
Ḥusayn-i Bushrú'í, Mullá 106
huwa 112
huwa 'lláh 111
huwiyyaτ 112
hypothalamus 5

'ibádaτ 116-17
Iceland 176, 202
iḥtifál 141
imám 78, 314
imsák 110
India, Indian 36, 37, 39, 208, 233
Indian circle 13
Indian Ocean 176
Indo-European 36
Indo-Iranian 36
Indonesia 150
intercalary days (*Ayyám-i Há'*) 58, 59, 74,

75, 77, 110, 112, 176, 177, 195
   fifth 77, 176, 177
   see also há'
intercalation 25, 47, 48, 51, 60, 61, 176
international date line (IDL) see date line:
   international
International Teaching Centre 221
interpretation 55, 85, 89-91, 145, 160, 179,
   182, 187
Iran, Iranian 10, 36-8, 40-44, 46, 92, 106,
   117, 147, 163-5, 176, 186 see also
   Persia
Iran Chamber Society 255
Iraq 46
Ireland 202
'irfán 116-17
Isaiah 54
Islam, Islamic 36, 54, 61, 109, 236, 241
   Sufi Islam 116
Istanbul 79
Italy 52
i'tidál 117

Jabarút 112
Ja'far aṣ-Ṣádiq, Imám 313
jáhiliyyat 60
Jalálu'd-Din Malek-Sháh-i Saljuqí 46
Japan 52
jawhar-e tafríd 310
Jerusalem 58
Jesus 49, 86, 106, 119, 127, 189
Jew, Jewish 57-9, 61, 119-20, 189, 208,
   232-3, 236-7, 241
Job 54
Julius Caesar 48-9
Juno 47
Jupiter 47
justice 88, 96, 113-17
   'adl 113-18
   inṣáf 113-16, 118
   iustitia communativa 114
   iustitia distributiva 113
   iustitia legalis 113

Ka'bat 61
Kadmí 41
Kassel 194
Kerala 233
Kerguelan Islands 281
khalífat 78

khátamu'n-nabiyín 310
Khayyam, Omar 46
Kisumu 279, 280, 292
Kitáb-i 'Ahd 80
Kitáb-i Aqdas 76, 80, 116-17, 139-43, 153-
   4, 156-7, 178, 218, 227, 242, 319 see
   also Most Holy Book
Kitáb-i Asmá' 76,
kullu shay', kull-i shay 83, 98, 102, 104,
   106, 107, 109, 214 see also All Things
Kurdish 92

labour 29, 54, 125 see also work
Láhút 112
Langenhain 221
language 84
Latin 8, 10
latitude 14, 16, 68, 136, 172, 186, 192,
   199, 202
latitudinal offset 316
Lawḥ-i Ittiḥád xiii
leap area 177 see also há': region of Há'
legislation, legal xi, 139, 143, 145, 166,
   179, 232, 242
Leipzig 194
leisure 125
Lesser Peace 115
letters 76, 97, 105, 109, 245-6
   days of the 76, 98
   of the Living 107
   of the Unity 75-6
light 124-6
liturgical 37, 56, 58, 60, 119, 141, 209
London 151, 213
longitude 68, 135-6, 147, 151, 174, 177,
   186, 192, 194, 199, 271
   ecliptic longitude 83
   longitudinal offset 316
   reference longitude 135-6, 262, 283,
      285
love 110, 128, 130
Low Countries 52
Luxembourg 52

mah 10
Malakút 112
Man yuẓhiruhu'lláh 88, 105, 107, 112
Manifestation (of God) 75, 85-6, 90, 93,
   101, 103, 105, 114, 116, 139, 180, 183,
   242 see also Messenger

INDEX

mankind 87-8, 94-7, 99-100, 103, 114-15, 119-20 *see also* human race
marriage 7, 119, 241
Mars 47
Mashriqu'l-Adhkár 99
materialism 93
measurement 4, 6, 9, 13ff, 20ff, 28, 35-6, 45, 50, 65-6, 68, 100, 139-40, 144, 186, 192, 194, 220-21, 249
Medeans 38, 43
Medina 63
meditation 125, 196
Mecca 63
Melanesia 150
melatonin 5
memory 1
men 10
mensis 10
mensor 10
menstruation 7
Mercator projection 135
meridian 16, 19, 66, 192, 203
    180th 69
    of solar transit 17, 191, 199
    prime 69, 136, 151, 189, 317
    standard 186, 248, 262
    Standard Meridian Convention 69
meridies 66
meridional 66, 122, 124, 147, 185-92, 194-5, 198, 204, 210, 216, 271
mes 10
Mesopotamian
    civilizations 43
    cultural area 106
Messenger (of God) 93-4, 101 *see also* Manifestation
metal casting 304
metaphor 74, 89, 92, 180, 183
Micronesia 150
Middle Ages 190
Middle East 176
mirror 89-90
Mirror of divine Names and Attributes 112
mis 10
misákín 110
Mishnah 57
mithqál 105-6, 213
model 238
mois 10
Monat 10

month(s) 9-10, 23-6, 28, 34-6, 38-44, 46-9, 51, 53-62, 74-6, 98, 102, 108-9, 112-13, 120, 143-4, 179, 195, 214-15, 229, 236, 239, 314
    Ábán 44
    Abu 306
    Adar 55
    Adaru 306
    'Alá' 108, 110, 112, 179, 192, 250, 252
    April 79
    Aprilis mensis 47
    Arakh-Samma 306
    Asmá' 107
    Augustus mensis 48
    Aw 55
    Ayaru 306
    'Aẓamat 79, 107
    Ázar 44
    Bahá' 76, 83, 107, 112, 142, 144, 146-8, 172-3, 176, 178-80, 185, 195-6, 216, 234, 236
    Bahá'í 224, 228-9, 234, 239
    Bahman 44
    calendar 53
    Cheshvan 55
    December mensis 47, 48
    Déi 44
    Dhu'l-Ḥijjat 60-62
    Dhu'l-Qa'dat 60-61
    Du'uzu 306
    Elul 55
    Esfand 44
    Farvardín 40, 44, 46
    Februarius mensis 47-9
    February 186
    Februum 47
    Ianuarius mensis 47-8
    Ijar 55
    'Ilm 80, 108, 223
    Intercalaris mensis 47
    intercalary 40, 46, 47-8, 53, 55, 56, 60
    Iunius mensis 47
    'Izzat 107, 196, 206
    Jalál 79, 107
    Jamál 79, 107
    July 79, 185-6
    Jumádá'l-Ákhirat 60
    Jumádá'l-Úlá 60, 82
    Kalimát 107
    Kamál 107

Khordád 44
Kislev 55
Kislimu 306
lunar 9, 11, 23-6, 46, 57, 59, 77
Maius mensis 47
March 185, 216
Martius mensis 47
Masá'il 108, 196, 206
Mashiyyat 82, 107
May 79, 212
Mehr 44
Mercedonius mensis 47
Mordád 44
Muḥarram 81, 82
Mulk 108, 110
natural 61
Nisan 55, 56
Nisanu 306
November 78, 80, 81, 186
November mensis 47
Núr 107, 196, 205, 206
October 78, 81
October mensis 47
Ordí behesht 44, 55
Qawl 79, 80, 108, 209
Qudrat 80, 82, 108
Quinctilis mensis 47
Rabí' I 60
Rabí' II 60
Rabí'u'l-Awwál 60
Rabí'u'th-Thání 60
Raḥmat 79, 107, 185, 187, 189
Rajab 60
Ramaḍán 60-62, 236
regulated 61
round 39, 52
Ṣafar 60
September mensis 47
Sextilis mensis 47, 48
Sha'bán 60
Shahrívar 44
Sharaf 108
Shawwál 60
Shebat 56
sidereal 9, 23
Simanu 306
Siwan 55
stellar 9
Sulṭán 108

synodic 9-10, 23, 46-7, 53, 304
Tammus 55
Tashritu 56, 306,
Tebetu 306
Tewet 55
Tír 44
Tishri 55-6, 57
Ululu 306
moon 7-10, 15, 18, 20, 22-3, 25-7, 53, 56, 61, 64, 89-92, 102, 174, 208
   dark 83
   full 8-9, 25, 37, 305, 309
   half 9, 25-6, 174
   houses of the 9
   interlunium 53, 59, 124
   lunar phase 37
   lunation 9-10, 20, 43, 47, 53, 55
   Metonic cycle 46, 56, 102
   moon circle 102
   moon phase 9-10, 23, 25-8, 32, 92, 213
   new 8-9, 26, 47, 53, 56, 61-2, 82, 124, 305
Mormon 233
Mosaic laws 54
Moses 86, 119
Most Great Peace 97, 100, 115
Most Holy Book 137, 160, 225, 242 *see also* Kitáb-i Aqdas
Mount Carmel 221
mu'áyarat (*Eichung*) 10 *see also* (re)alignment: phase, phasal
Muḥammad 45, 61, 63, 79, 86-7, 119, 123
   Emigration of 45, 63, 119
Muḥammadu'l-Báqir, Imám 314
Muqawwimát 306
musical scale 24, 28
Muslim 40-41, 43, 60-61, 63, 78, 119, 120, 216, 220, 232, 236-7, 241
mystical 104-5, 107, 121, 125

Nabíl-i A'ẓam 76, 163-5, 167-8, 195
Nabíl's Narrative 167
Najíbiyyih 308 *see also* Garden of Riḍván
nakhud 105, 213
Násút 112
natural number 102-4, 107
navigation system 68
Naw-Rúz 38-41, 46, 75-6, 98-101, 137, 140-42, 144, 148, 150, 154-5, 157-8,

163-5, 169, 176, 192, 195, 204, 208, 228, 231, 240, 247
  day of 45, 82, 98, 101, 140, 143, 15-8, 150-51, 156, 159, 163, 169, 171-2, 179
Near East 176
Nebuchadnezzar 58
Neolithic 3, 8, 15-16, 21, 25, 27, 30-31, 34, 36, 38, 42, 146, 196
New Zealand 141, 150, 207
night 4, 16-18, 22, 64-5, 98, 127, 129, 135, 138-9, 163, 202, 204
  leyl 139
  laylaτ 138
nine 57, 100, 103-5, 109, 239, 240, 312
nineteen 46, 74, 76, 98, 101-9, 120-21, 201, 213-16, 232, 234, 237, 239 *see also* cycle
Nineteen Day Feast 75, 108, 120, 225-31, 234-6, 239-40, 321
  consultative part 226-7
  devotional part 226, 229
  social part 226, 229
Nixon, Richard M. 233
Noah 86, 99
nomad 176
non-Bahá'ís 75, 100, 117, 169, 189, 216, 223, 240-41
  and Bahá'í events 75, 100
Norway 52
nundina 47
nutation 15-16, 69, 195, 268, 303, 319

obligatory prayer 204
  long (*aṣ-ṣalátu'l-kabír*) 204
  medium (*aṣ-ṣalátu'l-wasṭá*) 204
  short (*aṣ-ṣalátu'ṣ-ṣaghír*) 115, 117, 204
obliquity 250, 252
  diurnal 272-5, 278, 287, 290-91
  see also ecliptic: obliquity of the ecliptic
Occident 66
Octavian *see* Augustus, Emperor
ontology 163
oral teachings 162
oral tradition 32
oral transmission 162
orbit 6, 16, 18, 21, 45, 66, 68, 128, 165, 192, 210, 212, 214, 259
Orient 167, 221

Pacific, South 147, 207
pagan symbol system 49
Pahlavi, Reza Shah 46
Pakistan 147-8, 176
Palestine 219
parallax 134
Pars, Parsí 38, 41 *see also* Iran, Persian
peace 96, 118, 120, 126
pebbles 13
Pennsylvania 233
Persian 8, 38, 43, 78, 104, 112, 137-41, 157, 169, 170, 218, 246, 314 *see also* Iran
phase, phasal alignment, realignment *see* (re)alignment: phase, phasal
pineal organ 5
place of reference 62, 145, 150, 151, 164, 166, 170 *see also* reference spot
pneumatic 227
pole, polar 199, 203
  circle 12, 201, 203, 206
  ice masses 254
  North Pole 171, 176, 250
  region 69, 198, 199, 201, 206
  South Pole 171, 176
political boundaries 193
Polynesia 148
Portugal 52
prayer 62-3, 98-9, 105, 125, 130, 182, 187, 196, 201-2, 204, 219, 314
  communal 226
preaching 127
precession 15, 21, 44, 195-6, 268, 275
pregnancy 7
priesthood xiii, 92
Primal Will 86
prime number 103, 312, 313
primus 103
proclamation 182
prophet, prophethood 33, 37, 40, 63, 86-8, 90, 93, 99, 100, 183
prophetic day 33

Qayyúmu'l-Asmá' 73, 106
Qiblih 166
Quaker 233

Qur'án, qur'ánic 61, 78, 87, 121

railway 69
rainbow 99
Rashḥ-i 'Amá' 105
Rawalpindi 279, 292
(re)alignment 24, 27, 28, 51, 56, 57, 60
   calendar 48, 51, 54, 56, 58, 60
   Gregorian reform 36, 51
   phase, phasal 10-11, 24, 27-8 *see also*
      mu'áyaraτ
reference spot 144-8, 150-58, 162-3, 166-7,
   170, 178-9 *see also* place of reference
   method 146, 152, 170-71, 178-80, 204
refraction 134
   horizontal 16, 134, 199, 201
religio 99
religion 37-9, 75, 91, 99, 103-4, 113, 115,
   142, 209
   Bábí 36, 85, 93, 140 *see also* Bábí
   Bahá'í 36-7, 42, 73, 85, 92-3, 100, 103,
      113, 115-16, 119, 120, 140-41,
      151, 155, 162, 165-7, 180, 222,
      237 *see also* Bahá'í
   Buddhism 36-7
   Christianity 36
   Hinduism 36
   Islám *see* Islám
   Judaism 36, 57 *see also* Jew, Jewish
   Mormon 233
   Quaker 233
   Shaykhí School 306
   state 40
   Zoroastrian 36, 38-9
Rennes 194
Resurrection 50
revelation 73-4, 78, 86, 88-91, 93-4, 99,
   103, 106-7, 119, 121, 124, 128, 139-40,
   142, 180
   Bábí 73, 75, 94, 312
   Bahá'í 94, 101
   divine 87, 139, 189
   of God 89
   progressive 106
   Self-Revelation 89
   see also the Báb: revelation of;
      Bahá'u'lláh: revelation of
Reykjavik 176, 202
rhythm 3-4, 5-7, 18, 23-4, 27, 29-30, 37,
   47, 75, 194, 208, 212, 234, 237 *see
   also* cycle
   biological 5-6
   of the body 124
   celestial 20
   of the day 6
   day-night 6
   of the hour 213
   of labour 119
   learning 241
   of life, 3, 8, 28, 74-5, 120, 209, 216,
      222-3, 233, 237, 239, 241
   liturgical 236
   lunar 8, 35, 78, 208
   monthly 236
   of moon 20, 23
   nineteen-day 119-20, 224, 237
   nineteen-day month 235
   rhythmic alteration 5
   of the seasons 30
   school 241
   septadian 54
   seven-day 119-20
   six-day 239
   solar 35, 208
   unit of 36
   of the week 54, 58-9, 119, 223, 229, 236
   of work 234
   of the year 6, 208
rite 91
   of passage 7
Rome, Roman 49, 145
   Empire 49
   forum 47
Romania 52
Rúḥiyyih Khánum, Amatu'l-Bahá 168
rumour 317

Saarland 238
sabbath 50, 54, 57-8, 119-20, 223, 315
   day 57
   of rest 57 *see also* day: of rest
   of the land 57
   of years 57
   year 57
   shabbat 119
sacrament 226
sacred 6, 61, 140, 161, 166, 226
Sasanid dynasty 39

INDEX

schoolchildren 241
science 113, 118, 142-3, 209
sea 96, 151
seafaring 68
sea level 134
Seal of the Prophets 87, 310
season (s) 6, 8, 11-12, 21, 23, 36, 44, 53, 57, 60, 100, 101, 129, 191, 195, 197
   autumn 56, 197
      first day of 21, 39, 55, 192 *see also* equinox: autumnal
      first point of 197
      first point of Aries 52, 135, 171-3, 179, 195-6, 204, 211 *see also* equinox: vernal (spring)
   spring 11, 27, 43, 56, 60, 93-5, 99, 100, 197, 208
      advent of 11, 77, 92-3, 97
      first day of 20-22, 27-8, 40-42, 53, 74, 92-3, 98, 148, 150, 172, 194, 206, 250 *see also* equinox: vernal (spring)
      herald of 21
      vernal point 15, 134-5, 145, 152, 171 *see also* equinox: vernal (spring)
   summer 12, 18, 40, 44, 129, 187, 192-3, 197, 199
      first day of 13-14, 192, 194, 202, 205 *see also* solstice: summer (aestival)
   winter 12, 18, 40, 45, 66, 88, 93, 122, 183, 188-9, 192, 194-5, 199
      first day of 13-14, 192, 194, 202, 206 *see also* solstice: winter (hibernal)
semiotics 85, 109, 223
Semitic cultural area 106
sermon 108, 226
seven 9, 37-8, 53-5, 57, 59, 106, 118, 120-21, 189, 217, 234, 237, 241, 305, 315
shadow 12-14, 16, 171, 174, 199, 201
shahádaτ 112
Sháhensháhí 41, 42
shahr 61
shara'a 56
Shí'ite 46, 78, 121, 165-6, 314
ships 68
Shiraz 78-9

Shoghi Effendi, Guardian of the Bahá'í Faith 37, 77, 112, 118, 151, 153-7, 160, 162, 166-8, 170, 188, 195, 212, 217-19, 221, 223, 225, 227, 229, 230, 231
shurri 56
sidereal 6, 145, 146, 151, 194
sighting 18, 47, 61-2, 124, 151
signet ring 310
Síyáh-Chál 105, 312
social 2, 7, 11, 28-31, 75, 88, 95, 103, 110, 115, 118, 121, 141, 165, 223, 227-8, 232, 237, 238, 242
solstice 13, 194, 196, 198, 206, 272, 273
   summer (aestival) 196, 205
   winter (hibernal) 192, 196
soul 127-30
Spain, Spanish 10, 52
special-case area, ruling 198-9, 201-4
spirit 91, 126-8, 130
   Holy Spirit 129
spirituality, spiritual 96
   condition 123
   qualities 126
   values 93
Spirit of God 119
Spiritual Assembly
   local 181. 228-9
   National 154-9, 162, 218-19, 229, 232
square root 104
Stand 64
star(s) 12, 17, 19-21, 33, 64, 89, 90, 91
   ar-rukbaτ 17
   celestial sphere 16-20, 22, 64, 122
   circumpolar 18-20, 303
   heliacal rising, setting 20
   North Star 303
   Pole Star 17-19
   starlight 18
   Thuban 303
   zodiacal 20
   see also sun: Day Star
Stone Age 3, 12, 30, 38
   Late Paleolithic period 7
   New Stone Age 3, 28
   Old Stone Age 3, 19, 21, 28, 197
Stonehenge 15, 28
student 241
study class 182
Stunde 64

Sturm-und-Drang 97
subtropical regions 6
Sudan 157
Sufi 112, 116
sun 5-7, 10, 12-22, 44, 53, 61, 64-6, 69, 89-93, 101-2, 122-3, 129, 133-9, 155, 157, 163, 169, 171-2, 190-91, 196, 202, 208, 212, 150
   aphelion 44
   Day Star 87, 93
   perihelion 44
   sunlight 5, 65, 133-4, 193
   see also sunrise; sunset
sundial 65
Sunnite 78
Sun of Truth 89-92, 101
sunrise 5, 16, 20-21, 38, 66, 121, 123-5, 127-8, 130, 134, 179, 190, 198, 201-4, 281
sunset 5, 16, 19, 20-21, 38, 58-9, 66, 74, 76, 98, 121-30, 134, 137-8, 140, 142-59, 163-4, 167, 169, 171-4, 179, 185-99, 203-4, 206, 212, 230, 247-8, 252, 268, 271, 281
   conceptual 199
   ghorúb 137-8, 142, 178, 182
   local 155, 179
   natural 198-9
suprachiasmic nucleus 5
Súratu'l-Haykal 310
Súratu'l-Mulk 73
Súraτu Yúsuf 106
Sweden 52
Switzerland 52
syllogism 158-61
symbolism, symbolic 43, 54, 73-4, 84-5, 92-3, 101-3, 121, 124, 151-2, 166, 180-81, 184, 208-9, 215, 239
   Abrahamic 55
   meanings 109
synchronization 25, 54, 101, 112, 147, 180, 194-5
   phase synchronization 23

Tablet of Visitation 212
Tabríz 79
Tafsír-i Hú 112
talisman 184
Talmud 56
teachers, teaching 182, 241 *see also* education
technology 143, 197-8, 241
Teheran 82, 148, 150, 180
   Golestan Palace 150, 248, 262, 263, 324
temporality 1-2, 209
terminator 134, 136, 199
Terra del Fuego 203
threshold
   annual 135-6, 147-8, 150-51, 153, 171, 173-4, 176, 181-3, 195-6, 201, 205-7, 250, 252, 254, 271 *see also* date line: cyclic-progressive
   criterion 146, 177
   diurnal 134-5, 147-8, 171-3, 177, 194, 199, 201-7, 250, 252, 271-5, 277, 280, 283, 286
throne succession 33
time 1, 66
   afternoon 231
   Badí' 213-14
   calibration of 23, 28, 37, 69, 112, 191-2, 196, 243
   Coordinated Universal Time 268
   of day 65-6, 123, 134, 188-9, 191, 194-6, 211-12, 214, 252
   daylight saving 193, 212
   daytime 4, 64-6, 125-6, 134-5, 190, 192, 198, 201-2
   degree 213-15
   difference 150, 152, 193-4, 201, 213-14
   dynamic 195
   ephemeral 316
   equation of 68-9, 122, 186, 192, 195, 248, 268, 271, 275
   equatorial 194-5, 197, 270, 276-7, 280-83, 285-6
   equinoctial hour 66
   evening, eventide 7, 13, 19-20, 58, 125, 130, 148, 229
   expression 28, 143, 185-7, 190, 195, 210-11, 214, 250
   free 125
   gloaming 134
   global 195-7, 210-12, 252, 254, 270-72, 275-6, 282-3, 285-6
   Greenwich Mean Time 69, 189, 266, 268, 282-3
   hora 64

hour 64-5, 190, 213-15
  temporal 190
  intersubjective 2
  legal 212
  local 68, 190, 197, 209-11, 247, 250, 252, 270-72, 276, 280, 282, 285-6
  mean 68-9, 186, 210, 248, 262, 268, 323
measurement of 4, 6, 14, 17, 22, 28, 35, 49, 64, 92, 196, 215, 242
meridional 191, 198, 212, 271
midday 13-14, 16, 20-21, 38, 45-6, 64-6, 79, 121-2, 124, 163-4, 172, 190, 192, 199, 203-4, 212
mid-morning 38
midnight 18, 21, 38, 46, 64-6, 121-4, 147, 153, 172, 190-92, 195, 198-9, 203, 271
minute 65, 213-15
  one 137-8, 140, 142-3, 153, 163, 182 *see also yek daqíqeh*
morning 58, 231
night-time 64, 66, 134-5, 190, 192, 201-2
normal 69, 212
occidental 66, 124, 147, 188, 190-95, 198, 210, 212-13, 215, 243, 270, 281-3, 286
second 65, 69, 213-15
solar 68-9, 122, 150, 186, 191, 193, 195, 247-8, 268, 271, 323
standard 212
summer 185, 193, 212
time zone 69, 185-6, 192-4, 197
twilight 123, 193
unit of 28, 36, 60, 214
yek daqíqeh 137-8, 142-3, 153, 178, 182
zone time 122, 186, 193, 197, 210, 271
time of preparation 125
time of reparation 125
tobacco 125
toil 126 *see also* work
tokens 30
trade 11
transcription xvi, xviii, 140, 246, 314
translation ii, ix, xiv, xix, 108, 117, 123, 138, 141, 143-4, 153, 155, 157, 163, 168
transliteration xvi, xviii

Tropic of Cancer 12
Turkey, Turkish 52, 92
twelve 65

Ulm 194
unerring balance 101, 178
United Nations 189
United States 52, 154, 156, 157, 167, 232, 233
unity 75, 86, 89, 96-7, 100, 102-4, 113, 226, 229
  in diversity 103
  principle of 102
Universal House of Justice 77, 114, 121, 131, 137, 152, 154-5, 159-62, 166-7, 180, 211-12, 222, 224, 232, 237, 244
Ural Mountains 176
USSR 52

Vedas 36

wáḥid 76, 102-9
  wuḥdán 104, 109, 314
war 30, 32, 47, 61, 88, 96, 100, 231
  of spoils 30
Warsaw 213
wedge 206, 252
week 9-10, 20, 22-6, 28, 35-6, 38, 49, 53-5, 59, 62, 76, 118-21, 189, 217-18, 221, 223-4, 239, 314-15
  Badí' 224
  lunar 9-11, 23-6, 28
  Semitic 49, 118, 236
  seven-day 58
  solar 9, 55
  usbú' 218
  Wechsel 10
week-end 120, 231, 238-40
Welsh 10
Weltanschauung 101
West Gothic 49
Will and Testament (of 'Abdu'l-Bahá) 244
work 54, 56, 120, 125, 220, 223, 231-3, 235, 239, 241
work-free days *see* days: work-free
World Order of Bahá'u'lláh 74, 115, 225, 230
worship 38, 98, 100, 108, 116, 120, 125, 182, 225-6

wujúd 103
Yathrib 63
Yazdí 42
Yazdí, 'Azíz, 221
year 4, 9, 11-15, 18, 20-22, 24-7, 32-4, 36, 38-9, 42-57, 60-61, 65-6, 74-7, 93, 98, 101-2, 104-5, 108-9, 112, 122, 137, 144, 150, 177, 179, 181, 189, 191-2, 197, 199, 208-9, 214 *see also* cycle(s): temporal
  Ab 108
  Abad 108
  Abhá 108
  aera 49
  age of the 14, 21
  Aḥad 109
  Alif 108, 109
  Anno Domini 49
  år 49
  astronomical 196
  Bá' 108, 109
  Báb 108
  Badí' 109, 145
  Bahá' 109
  Bahá'í 78, 93, 98, 102, 117, 133, 174
  Bahháj 109
  Bahí 109
  beginning of the 10, 26, 27, 47-8, 56, 62, 133, 137, 176, 236
  birth of the 21
  calendar 25, 36, 38-40, 46, 48, 50-51, 53, 58, 76-7, 98, 101, 137, 143, 165, 196, 208, 214
  common 48, 50, 55, 80-81, 110
  Dál 108, 109
  era (Julian, Spanish) 49
  gap 45
  global 207
  Ḥubb 109
  Islamic 60
  Jád 108
  Jawáb 109
  jēra 49
  Jewish 57
  of jubilee 57, 208
  Julian 51
  leap 36, 42, 44-5, 48-51, 55, 59, 77, 80-81, 110, 177, 209-10, 240, 247-9, 255
  leap year formula 101
  length of the 273
  lunar 10, 45, 80
  lunisolar 102
  new 43, 46, 53, 56, 98, 164, 173
  New Year 25-7, 39, 62, 75-7, 93, 100, 135, 142, 152-3, 155-8, 164-7, 170, 172-3, 179, 236, 238
  Platonic 15
  religious 209, 240
  round 38, 52-3
  scientific definition of 93
  sabbath *see* sabbath: year
  Semitic 56
  solar 8, 10-11, 13, 19, 21-6, 28, 34, 39-40, 45-8, 50-51, 53-5, 58, 60, 74, 76-8, 92, 102, 195, 214, 238, 303
  start of the 11, 14, 55-6, 142, 145, 153, 155, 165, 176
  synodic 303
  tropical xiii, 15, 45, 50, 68, 112-13, 136-7, 165, 172-3, 196, 247, 255-6, 268-9, 273, 285, 303
  Wáḥid 108
  Wahháb 109
  Wáw 108, 109
  Widád 109
  world 15
  year one 33, 49
yuhallilanna 111
yukabbiranna 111
yumajjidanna 111
yusabbiḥanna 111

zenith distance 134
zodiac 19-21
  constellation 9, 19, 64 *see also* constellation(s)
  signs of 20-21
Zoroaster, Zoroastrian(s) 37, 39, 43, 46, 49, 54, 59, 208-9, 236

www.ingramcontent.com/pod-product-compliance
Lightning Source LLC
Chambersburg PA
CBHW030105010526
44116CB00005B/101